Lives of Donne and Herbert

Various

Table of Contents

Lives of Donne and Herbert..1

    Various..1

    INTRODUCTORY NOTE..2

    THAT WE SHOULD NOT JUDGE OF OUR HAPPINESSE UNTILL AFTER OUR

    DEATH...4

    THAT TO PHILOSOPHISE IS TO LEARNE HOW TO DIE...6

    OF THE INSTITUTION AND EDUCATION OF CHILDREN; TO THE LADIE

    DIANA OF FOIX, COUNTESSE OF GURSON...20

    OF FRIENDSHIP...45

    OF BOOKS...55

MONTAIGNE. WHAT IS A CLASSIC?..63

    INTRODUCTORY NOTE...63

    MONTAIGNE...64

    WHAT IS A CLASSIC?..73

THE POETRY OF THE CELTIC RACES...80

    INTRODUCTORY NOTE...80

    THE POETRY OF THE CELTIC RACES..81

THE EDUCATION OF THE HUMAN RACE..109

    INTRODUCTORY NOTE...109

    THE EDUCATION OF THE HUMAN RACE..109

LETTERS UPON THE AESTHETIC EDUCATION OF MAN...125

    INTRODUCTORY NOTE...125

    LETTER I..125

    LETTER II...126

    LETTER III..127

    LETTER IV..129

    LETTER V...131

    LETTER VI..132

    LETTER VII...136

    LETTER VIII..137

    LETTER IX..138

    LETTER X...141

    LETTER XI..143

    LETTER XII...145

    LETTER XIII..146

    LETTER XIV..148

    LETTER XV...149

    LETTER XVI..152

    LETTER XVII...154

    LETTER XVIII..155

    LETTER XIX..156

    LETTER XX...159

    LETTER XXI..160

    LETTER XXII...161

Table of Contents

Lives of Donne and Herbert

  LETTER XXIII..163

  LETTER XXIV..165

  LETTER XXV...168

  LETTER XXVI..170

  LETTER XXVII..173

FUNDAMENTAL PRINCIPLES OF THE METAPHYSIC OF MORALS....................178

  INTRODUCTORY NOTE...178

  PREFACE..178

  FIRST SECTION. TRANSITION FROM THE COMMON RATIONAL

  KNOWLEDGE OF MORALITY TO THE PHILOSOPHICAL.................................182

  SECOND SECTION. TRANSITION FROM POPULAR MORAL PHILOSOPHY TO

  THE METAPHYSIC OF MORALS..189

  THIRD SECTION. TRANSITION FROM THE METAPHYSIC OF MORALS TO

  THE CRITIQUE OF PURE PRACTICAL REASOH..213

BYRON AND GOETHE...224

  INTRODUCTORY NOTE...224

Lives of Donne and Herbert

Various

Kessinger Publishing reprints thousands of hard—to—find books!

Visit us at http://www.kessinger.net

- INTRODUCTORY NOTE
- THAT WE SHOULD NOT JUDGE OF OUR HAPPINESSE UNTILL AFTER OUR DEATH
- THAT TO PHILOSOPHISE IS TO LEARNE HOW TO DIE
- OF THE INSTITUTION AND EDUCATION OF CHILDREN; TO THE LADIE DIANA OF FOIX, COUNTESSE OF GURSON
- OF FRIENDSHIP
- OF BOOKS
- MONTAIGNE. WHAT IS A CLASSIC?

  - INTRODUCTORY NOTE
  - MONTAIGNE
  - WHAT IS A CLASSIC?

- THE POETRY OF THE CELTIC RACES

  - INTRODUCTORY NOTE
  - THE POETRY OF THE CELTIC RACES

- THE EDUCATION OF THE HUMAN RACE

  - INTRODUCTORY NOTE
  - THE EDUCATION OF THE HUMAN RACE

- LETTERS UPON THE AESTHETIC EDUCATION OF MAN

  - INTRODUCTORY NOTE
  - LETTER I.
  - LETTER II.
  - LETTER III.
  - LETTER IV.
  - LETTER V.
  - LETTER VI.
  - LETTER VII.
  - LETTER VIII.
  - LETTER IX.
  - LETTER X.

- LETTER XI.
- LETTER XII.
- LETTER XIII.
- LETTER XIV.
- LETTER XV.
- LETTER XVI.
- LETTER XVII.
- LETTER XVIII.
- LETTER XIX.
- LETTER XX.
- LETTER XXI.
- LETTER XXII.
- LETTER XXIII.
- LETTER XXIV.
- LETTER XXV.
- LETTER XXVI.
- LETTER XXVII.

- FUNDAMENTAL PRINCIPLES OF THE METAPHYSIC OF MORALS

  - INTRODUCTORY NOTE
  - PREFACE
  - FIRST SECTION. TRANSITION FROM THE COMMON RATIONAL KNOWLEDGE OF MORALITY TO THE PHILOSOPHICAL
  - SECOND SECTION. TRANSITION FROM POPULAR MORAL PHILOSOPHY TO THE METAPHYSIC OF MORALS
  - THIRD SECTION. TRANSITION FROM THE METAPHYSIC OF MORALS TO THE CRITIQUE OF PURE PRACTICAL REASOH

- BYRON AND GOETHE

  - INTRODUCTORY NOTE

INTRODUCTORY NOTE

Michel Eyquem De Montaigne, the founder of the modern Essay, was born February 28, 1533, at the chateau of Montaigne in Pirigord. He came of a family of wealthy merchants of Bordeaux, and was educated at the College de Guyenne, where he had among his teachers the great Scottish Latinist, George Buchanan. Later he studied law, and held various public offices; but at the age of thirty-eight he retired to his estates, where he lived apart from the civil wars of the time, and devoted himself to study and thought. While he was traveling in Germany and Italy, in 1580–81, he was elected mayor of Bordeaux, and this office he filled for four years. He married in 1565, and had six daughters, only one of whom grew up. The first two books of his "Essays" appeared in 1580; the third in 1588; and four years later he died.

These are the main external facts of Montaigne's life: of the man himself the portrait is to be found in his book. "It is myself I portray," he declares; and there is nowhere in literature a volume of self−revelation surpassing his in charm and candor. He is frankly egotistical, yet modest and unpretentious; profoundly wise, yet constantly protesting his ignorance; learned, yet careless, forgetful, and inconsistent. His themes are as wide and varied as his observation of human life, and he has written the finest eulogy of friendship the world has known. Bacon, who knew his book and borrowed from it, wrote on the same subject; and the contrast of the essays is the true reflection of the contrast between the personalities of their authors.

Shortly after Montaigne's death the "Essays" were translated into English by John Florio, with less than exact accuracy, but in a style so full of the flavor of the age that we still read Montaigne in the version which Shakespeare knew. The group of examples here printed exhibits the author in a variety of moods, easy, serious, and, in the essay on "Friendship," as nearly impassioned as his philosophy ever allowed him to become.

Reader, be here a well−meaning Booke. It doth at the firth entrance forewarne thee, that in contriving the same I have proposed unto my selfe no other than a familiar and private end: I have no respect or consideration at all, either to thy service, or to my glory: my forces are not capable of any such desseigne. I have vowed the same to the particular commodity of my kinsfolks and friends: to the end, that losing me (which they are likely to doe ere long), they may therein find some lineaments of my conditions and humours, and by that meanes reserve more whole, and more lively foster the knowledge and acquaintance they have had of me. Had my intention beene to forestal and purchase the world's opinion and favour, I would surely have adorned myselfe more quaintly, or kept a more grave and solemne march. I desire therein to be delineated in mine owne genuine, simple and ordinarie fashion, without contention, art or study; for it is myself e I pourtray. My imperfections shall therein be read to the life, and my naturall forme discerned, so farre−forth as publike reverence hath permitted me. For if my fortune had beene to have lived among those nations which yet are said to live under the sweet liberty of Nature's first and uncorrupted lawes, I assure thee, I would most willingly have pourtrayed my selfe fully and naked. Thus, gentle Reader, myself I am the groundworke of my booke: it is then no reason thou shouldest employ thy time about so frivolous and vaine a subject.

Therefore farewell.

From MONTAIGNE,
  The First of March, 1580.

THAT WE SHOULD NOT JUDGE OF OUR HAPPINESSE UNTILL AFTER OUR DEATH

scilicet ultima semper
Expectanda dies homini est, dicique beatus
Ante obitum nemo, supremaque funera debat.
[Footnote: Ovid. Met. 1, iii. 135.]

We must expect of man the latest day,
Nor ere he die, he's happie, can we say.

The very children are acquainted with the storie of Croesus to this purpose: who being taken by Cyrus, and by him condemned to die, upon the point of his execution, cried out aloud: "Oh Solon, Solon!" which words of his, being reported to Cyrus, who inquiring what he meant by them, told him, hee now at his owne cost verified the advertisement Solon had before times given him; which was, that no man, what cheerefull and blandishing countenance soever fortune shewed them, may rightly deeme himselfe happie, till such time as he have passed the last day of his life, by reason of the uncertaintie and vicissitude of humane things, which by a very light motive, and slight occasion, are often changed from one to another cleane contrary state and degree. And therefore Agesilaus answered one that counted the King of Persia happy, because being very young, he had gotten the garland of so mightie and great a dominion: "yea but said he, Priam at the same age was not unhappy." Of the Kings of Macedon that succeeded Alexander the Great, some were afterward seene to become Joyners and Scriveners at Rome: and of Tyrants of Sicilie, Schoolemasters at Corinth. One that had conquered halfe the world, and been Emperour over so many, Armies, became an humble and miserable suter to the raskally officers of a king of AEgypte: At so high a rate did that great Pompey purchase the irkesome prolonging of his life but for five or six moneths. And in our fathers daies, Lodowicke Sforze, tenth Duke of Millane, under whom the State of Italic had so long beene turmoiled and shaken, was seene to die a wretched prisoner at Loches in France, but not till he had lived and lingered ten yeares in thraldom, which was the worst of his bargaine. The fairest Queene, wife to the greatest King of Christendome, was she not lately scene to die by the hands of an executioner? Oh unworthie and barbarous cruelties And a thousand such examples. For, it seemeth that as the sea−billowes and surging waves, rage and storme against the surly pride and stubborne height of our buildings, so are there above, certaine spirits that envie the rising prosperities and greatnesse heere below.

Vsque adeb res humanas vis abdita quadam
Obterit, et pulchros fasces savsecures
Proculcare, ac ludibrio sibi habere videtur.
[Footnote: LUCRET. I. v. 1243.]

A hidden power so mens states hath out−worne
Faire swords, fierce scepters, signes of honours borne,
It seemes to trample and deride in scorne.

And it seemeth Fortune doth sometimes narrowly watch the last day of our life, thereby to shew her power, and in one moment to overthrow what for many yeares together she had been erecting, and makes us cry after Laberius, Nimirum hoc die una plus vixi, mihi quam vivendum fuit. [Footnote: MACHOB, 1, ii. 7.] Thus it is, "I have lived longer by this one day than I should." So may that good advice of Solon be taken with reason. But forsomuch as he is a Philosopher, with whom the favours or disfavours of fortune, and good or ill lucke have no place, and are not regarded by him; and puissances and greatnesses, and accidents of qualitie, are well–nigh indifferent: I deeme it very likely he had a further reach, and meant that the same good fortune of our life, which dependeth of the tranquillitie and contentment of a welborne minde, and of the resolution and assurance of a well ordered soule, should never be ascribed unto man, untill he have beene scene play the last act of his comedie, and without doubt the hardest. In all the rest there may be some maske: either these sophisticall discourses of Philosophie are not in us but by countenance, or accidents that never touch us to the quick, give us alwaies leasure to keep our countenance setled. But when that last part of death, and of our selves comes to be acted, then no dissembling will availe, then is it high time to speake plaine English, and put off all vizards: then whatsoever the pot containeth must be shewne, be it good or bad, foule or cleane, wine or water.

Nam vera voces tum demum pectore ab imo
Ejiciuntur, et eripitur persona, manet res.
[Footnote: LUCEET. 1. iii. 57.]

For then are sent true speeches from the heart,
We are ourselves, we leave to play a part.

Loe heere, why at this last cast, all our lives other actions must be tride and touched. It is the master–day, the day that judgeth all others: it is the day, saith an auncient Writer, that must judge of all my forepassed yeares. To death doe I referre the essay [Footnote: Assay, exact weighing.] of my studies fruit. There shall wee see whether my discourse proceed from my heart, or from my mouth. I have scene divers, by their death, either in good or evill, give reputation to all their forepassed life. Scipio, father–in–law to Pompey, in well dying, repaired the ill opinion which untill that houre men had ever held of him. Epaminondas being demanded which of the three he esteemed most, either Chabrias, or Iphicrates, or himselfe: "It is necessary," said he, "that we be scene to die, before your question may well be resolved." [Footnote: Answered.] Verily, we should steale much from him, if he should be weighed without the honour and greatnesse of his end. God hath willed it, as he pleased: but in my time three of the most execrable persons that ever I knew in all abomination of life, and the most infamous, have beene seen to die very orderly and quietly, and in every circumstance composed even unto perfection. There are some brave and fortunate deaths. I have seene her cut the twine of some man's life, with a progresse of wonderful advancement, and with so worthie an end, even in the flowre of his growth and spring of his youth, that in mine opinion, his ambitious and haughtie couragious signes, thought nothing so high as might interrupt them who without going to the place where he pretended, arived there more gloriously and worthily than either his desire or hope aimed at, and by his fall fore–went the power and name, whither by his course he aspired. When I judge of other men's lives, I ever respect how they have behaved themselves in their end; and my chiefest study is, I may well demeane my selfe at my last gaspe, that is to say, quietly and constantly.

THAT TO PHILOSOPHISE IS TO LEARNE HOW TO DIE

Cicero saith, that to Philosophise is no other thing than for a man to prepare himselfe to death: which is the reason that studie and contemplation doth in some sort withdraw our soule from us, and severally employ it from the body, which is a kind of apprentisage and resemblance of death; or else it is, that all the wisdome and discourse of the world, doth in the end resolve upon this point, to teach us not to feare to die. Truly either reason mockes us, or it only aimeth at our contentment, and in fine, bends all her travell to make us live well, and as the holy Scripture saith, "at our ease." All the opinions of the world conclude, that pleasure is our end, howbeit they take divers meanes unto and for it, else would men reject them at their first comming. For, who would give eare unto him, that for it's end would establish our paine and disturbance? The dissentions of philosophicall sects in this case are verbal: Transcurramus solertissimas Hugos [Footnote: Travails, labours.] "Let us run over such over-fine fooleries and subtill trifles." There is more wilfulnesse and wrangling among them, than pertains to a sacred profession. But what person a man undertakes to act, he doth ever therewithal! personate his owne. Allthough they say, that in vertue it selfe, the last scope of our aime is voluptuousnes. It pleaseth me to importune their eares still with this word, which so much offends their hearing. And if it imply any chief pleasure or exceeding contentments, it is rather due to the assistance of vertue, than to any other supply, voluptuousnes being more strong, sinnowie, sturdie, and manly, is but more seriously voluptuous. And we should give it the name of pleasure, more favorable, sweeter, and more naturall; and not terme it vigor, from which it hath his denomination. Should this baser sensuality deserve this faire name, it should be by competencie, and not by privilege. I finde it lesse void of incommodities and crosses than vertue. And besides that> her taste is more fleeting, momentarie, and fading, she hath her fasts, her eyes, and her travels, and both sweat and blood. Furthermore she hath particularly so many wounding passions, and of so severall sorts, and so filthie and loathsome a societie waiting upon her, that shee is equivalent to penitencie. Wee are in the wrong, to thinke her incommodities serve her as a provocation and seasoning to her sweetnes, as in nature one contrarie is vivified by another contrarie: and to say, when we come to vertue, that like successes and difficulties overwhelme it, and yeeld it austere and inaccessible. Whereas much more properly then unto voluptuousnes, they ennobled, sharpen, animate, and raise that divine and perfect pleasure, which it meditates and procureth us. Truly he is verie unworthie her acquaintance, that counter-ballanceth her cost to his fruit, and knowes neither the graces nor use of it. Those who go about to instruct us, how her pursuit is very hard and laborious, and her jovisance [Footnote: Enjoyment] well-pleasing and delightfull: what else tell they us, but that shee is ever unpleasant and irksome? For what humane meane [Footnote: Human meana. man's life is subject, it is not with an equall care: as well because accidents are not of such a necessitie, for most men passe their whole life without feeling any want or povertie, and othersome without feeling any griefe or sicknes, as Xenophilus the Musitian, who lived an hundred and six yeares in perfect and continuall health: as also if the worst happen, death may at all times, and whensoever it shall please us, cut off all other inconveniences and crosses. But as for death, it is inevitable.] did ever attaine unto an absolute enjoying of it? The perfectest have beene content but to aspire and approach her, without ever possessing her. But they are deceived; seeing that of all the pleasures we know, the pursute of them is pleasant. The enterprise is perceived by the qualitie of the thing, which it hath regard unto: for it is a good portion of the effect, and consubstantiall. That happines and felicitie, which shineth in vertue, replenisheth her approaches and appurtenances, even unto, the first entrance and utmost barre. Now of all the benefits of vertue, the contempt of death is the chiefest, a meane that furnisheth our life with an ease-full tranquillitie, and gives us a pure and amiable taste of it: without which every other voluptuousnes is extinguished. Loe, here the reasons why all rules encounter and agree with this article. And albeit they all leade us with a common accord to despise povertie, and other accidental! crosses, to which

Omnes eodem cogimur, omnium
Versatur urna, serius, ocius
Sors exitura, et nos in aeternum
Exilium impositura cymbae,
[Footnote: Hor. I. iii. Od. iii. 25.]

All to one place are driv'n, of all
Shak't is the lot-pot, where-hence shall
Sooner or later drawne lots fall,
And to deaths boat for aye enthrall.

And by consequence, if she makes us affeard, it is a continual subject of torment, and which can no way be eased. There is no starting-hole will hide us from her, she will finde us wheresoever we are, we may as in a suspected countrie start and turne here and there: quae quasi saxum Tantalo semper impendet.[Footnote: Cic. De Fin. I. i.] "Which evermore hangs like the stone over the head of Tantalus:" Our lawes doe often condemne and send malefactors to be executed in the same place where the crime was committed: to which whilest they are going, leade them along the fairest houses, or entertaine them with the best cheere you can,

non Siculae dapes Dulcem elaborabunt saporem:
Non avium, citharaeque cantus
Somnum reducent.
[Footnote: Hor. I. iii. Od. i, 12.]

Not all King Denys daintie fare,
Can pleasing taste for them prepare:
No song of birds, no musikes sound
Can lullabie to sleepe profound.

Doe you thinke they can take any pleasure in it? or be any thing delighted? and that the finall intent of their voiage being still before their eies, hath not altered and altogether distracted their taste from all these commodities and allurements?

Audit iter, numeratque dies, spatioque viarum
Metitur vitam, torquetur peste futura.
[Footnote: Claud, in Ruff. 1. ii. 137]

He heares his journey, counts his daies, so measures he
His life by his waies length, vext with the ill shall be.

The end of our cariere is death, it is the necessarie object of our aime: if it affright us, how is it possible we should step one foot further without an ague? The remedie of the vulgar sort is, not to think on it. But from what brutall stupiditie may so grosse a blindnesse come upon him? he must be made to bridle his Asse by the taile,

> Qiti capite ipse suo instituit vestigia retro.
> [Footnote: Lucret. l. iv. 474]

> Who doth a course contrarie runne
> With his head to his course begunne.

It is no marvell if he be so often taken tripping; some doe no sooner heare the name of death spoken of, but they are afraid, yea the most part will crosse themselves, as if they heard the Devill named. And because mention is made of it in mens wils and testaments, I warrant you there is none will set his hand to them, til the physitian hath given his last doome, and utterly forsaken him. And God knowes, being then betweene such paine and feare, with what sound judgment they endure him. For so much as this syllable sounded so unpleasantly in their eares, and this voice seemed so ill boding and unluckie, the Romans had learned to allay and dilate the same by a Periphrasis. In liew of saying, he is dead, or he hath ended his daies, they would say, he hath lived. So it be life, be it past or no, they are comforted: from whom we have borrowed our phrases quondam, alias, or late such a one. It may haply be, as the common saying is, the time we live is worth the mony we pay for it. I was borne betweene eleven of the clocke and noone, the last of Februarie 1533, according to our computation, the yeare beginning the first of Januarie. It is but a fortnight since I was 39 yeares old. I want at least as much more. If in the meane time I should trouble my thoughts with a matter so farre from me, it were but folly. But what? we see both young and old to leave their life after one selfe-same condition. No man departs otherwise from it, than if he but now came to it, seeing there is no man so crazed,[Footnote: Infirm] bedrell, [Footnote: Bedridden.] or decrepit, so long as he remembers Methusalem, but thinkes he may yet live twentie yeares. Moreover, seely [Footnote: Simple, weak.] creature as thou art, who hath limited the end of thy daies? Happily thou presumest upon physitians reports. Rather consider the effect and experience. By the common course of things long since thou livest by extraordinarie favour. Thou hast alreadie over-past the ordinarie tearmes of common life: And to prove it, remember but thy acquaintances, and tell me how many more of them have died before they came to thy age, than have either attained or outgone the same: yea, and of those that through renoune have ennobled their life, if thou but register them, I will lay a wager, I will finde more that have died before they came to five and thirty years, than after. It is consonant with reason and pietie, to take example by the humanity of Jesus Christ, who ended his humane life at three and thirtie yeares. The greatest man that ever was, being no more than a man, I meane Alexander the Great, ended his dayes, and died also of that age. How many severall meanes and waies hath death to surprise us!

> Quid quisque vitet, nunquam homini satis
> Cautum est in horas
> [Footnote: Hor. l. ii. Od. xiii. 13.]

> A man can never take good heed,

Hourely what he may shun and speed.

I omit to speak of agues and pleurisies; who would ever have imagined that a Duke of Brittanie should have beene stifled to death in a throng of people, as whilome was a neighbour of mine at Lyons, when Pope Clement made his entrance there? Hast thou not seene one of our late Kings slaine in the middest of his sports? and one of his ancestors die miserably by the chocke [Footnote: Shock.] of an hog? Eschilus fore threatned by the fall of an house, when he stood most upon his guard, strucken dead by the fall of a tortoise shell, which fell out of the tallants of an eagle flying in the air? and another choaked with the kernell of a grape? And an Emperour die by the scratch of a combe, whilest he was combing his head? And Aemylius Lepidus with hitting his foot against a doore–seele? And Aufidius with stumbling against the Consull–chamber doore as he was going in thereat? And Cornelius Gallus, the Praetor, Tigillinus, Captaine of the Romane watch, Lodowike, sonne of Guido Gonzaga, Marquis of Mantua, end their daies betweene womens thighs? And of a farre worse example Speusippus, the Platonian philosopher, and one of our Popes? Poore Bebius a Judge, whilest he demurreth the sute of a plaintife but for eight daies, be hold, his last expired: And Caius Iulius a Physitian, whilest he was annointing the eies of one of his patients, to have his owne sight closed for ever by death. And if amongst these examples, I may adde one of a brother of mine, called Captain Saint Martin, a man of three and twentie yeares of age, who had alreadie given good testimonie of his worth and forward valour, playing at tennis, received a blow with a ball, that hit him a little above the right eare, without apparance of any contusion, bruse, or hurt, and never sitting or resting upon it, died within six houres after of an apoplexie, which the blow of the ball caused in him. These so frequent and ordinary examples, hapning, and being still before our eies, how is it possible for man to forgo or for get the remembrance of death? and why should it not continually seeme unto us, that shee is still ready at hand to take us by the throat? What matter is it, will you say unto me, how and in what manner it is, so long as a man doe not trouble and vex himselfe therewith? I am of this opinion, that howsoever a man may shrowd or hide himselfe from her dart, yea, were it under an oxe–hide, I am not the man would shrinke backe: it sufficeth me to live at my ease; and the best recreation I can have, that doe I ever take; in other matters, as little vain glorious, and exemplare as you list.

   —praetulerim delirus inersque videri,
    Dum mea delectent mala me, vel denique fallant,
    Quam sapere et ringi
    [Footnote: Hor. 1. ii. Episi. ii 126]

   A dotard I had rather seeme, and dull,
    Sooner my faults may please make me a gull,
    Than to be wise, and beat my vexed scull.

But it is folly to thinke that way to come unto it. They come, they goe, they trot, they daunce: but no speech of death. All that is good sport. But if she be once come, and on a sudden and openly surprise, either them, their wives, their children, or their friends, what torments, what out cries, what rage, and what despaire doth then overwhelme them? saw you ever anything so drooping, so changed, and so distracted? A man must looke to it, and in better times fore–see it. And might that brutish carelessenesse lodge in the minde of a man of understanding (which I find altogether impossible) she sels us her ware at an overdeere rate: were she an enemie by mans wit to be avoided, I would advise men to borrow the weapons of cowardlinesse: but since it may not be, and that be you either a coward or a runaway, an honest or valiant man, she overtakes you,

> Nempe et fugacem persequitur virum,
> Nec parcit imbellis juventae
> Poplitibus, timidoque tergo.
> [Footnote: Hor. 1. iii. Od. ii. 14.]

> Shee persecutes the man that flies,
> Shee spares not weake youth to surprise,
> But on their hammes and backe turn'd plies.

And that no temper of cuirace [Footnote: Cuirass.] may shield or defend you,

> Ille licet ferro cauius se condat et aere,
> Mors tamen inclusum protraket inde caput.
> [Footnote: Propert. 1. iii. et xvii. 5]

> Though he with yron and brasse his head empale,
> Yet death his head enclosed thence will hale.

Let us learne to stand, and combat her with a resolute minde. And being to take the greatest advantage she hath upon us from her, let us take a cleane contrary way from the common, let us remove her strangenesse from her, let us converse, frequent, and acquaint our selves with her, let us have nothing so much in minde as death, let us at all times and seasons, and in the ugliest manner that may be, yea with all faces shapen and represent the same unto our imagination. At the stumbling of a horse, at the fall of a stone, at the least prick with a pinne, let us presently ruminate and say with our selves, what if it were death it selfe? and thereupon let us take heart of grace, and call our wits together to confront her. Amiddest our bankets, feasts, and pleasures, let us ever have this restraint or object before us, that is, the remembrance of our condition, and let not pleasure so much mislead or transport us, that we altogether neglect or forget, how many waies, our joyes, or our feastings, be subject unto death, and by how many hold-fasts shee threatens us and them. So did the AEgyptians, who in the middest of their banquetings, and in the full of their greatest cheere, caused the anatomie [Footnote: Skeleton] of a dead man to be brought before them, as a memorandum and warning to their guests.

> Omnem crede diem tibi diluxisse supremum,
> Grata superveniet; quae non sperabitur, hora?
> [Footnote: Hor. 1. i. Epist. iv. 13.]

> Thinke every day shines on thee as thy last,
> Welcome it will come, whereof hope was past.

It is uncertaine where death looks for us; let us expect her everie where: the premeditation of death, is a forethinking of libertie. He who hath learned to die, hath unlearned to serve. There is no evill in life, for him that hath well conceived, how the privation of life is no evill. To know how to die, doth free us from all subjection and constraint. Paulus AEmilius answered one, whom that miserable king of Macedon his prisoner sent to entreat him he would not lead him in triumph, "Let him make that request unto himselfe." Verily, if Nature afford not some helpe in all things, it is very hard that art and industrie should goe farre before. Of my selfe, I am not much given to melancholy, but rather to dreaming and sluggishness. There is nothing wherewith I have ever more entertained my selfe, than with the imaginations of death, yea in the most licentious times of my age.

Iucundum, cum atas florida ver ageret
[Footnote: Catul. Eleg. iv. 16.]

When my age flourishing
Did spend its pleasant spring.

Being amongst faire Ladies, and in earnest play, some have thought me busied, or musing with my selfe, how to digest some jealousie, or meditating on the uncertaintie of some conceived hope, when God he knowes, I was entertaining my selfe with the remembrance of some one or other, that but few daies before was taken with a burning fever, and of his sodaine end, comming from such a feast or meeting where I was my selfe, and with his head full of idle conceits, of lore, and merry glee; supposing the same, either sickness or end, to be as neere me as him.

Iam fuerit, nec post, unquam revocare licebit.
[Footnote: Lucr. I. iii. 947.]

Now time would be, no more You can this time restore.

I did no more trouble my selfe or frowne at such conceit, [Idea.] than at any other. It is impossible we should not apprehend or feele some motions or startings at such imaginations at the first, and comming sodainely upon us; but doubtlesse, he that shall manage and meditate upon them with an impartiall eye, they will assuredly, in tract [Course.] of time, become familiar to him: Otherwise, for my part, I should be in continuall feare and agonie; for no man did ever more distrust his life, nor make lesse account of his continuance: Neither can health, which hitherto I have so long enjoied, and which so seldome hath beene crazed, [Enfeebled.] lengthen my hopes, nor any sicknesse shorten them of it. At every minute me thinkes I make an escape. And I uncessantly record unto my selfe, that whatsoever may be done another day, may be effected this day. Truly hazards and dangers doe little or nothing approach us at our end: And if we consider, how many more there remaine, besides this accident, which in number more than millions seeme to threaten us, and hang over us; we shall find, that be we sound or sicke, lustie or weake, at sea or at land, abroad or at home, fighting or at rest, in the middest of a battell or, in our beds, she is ever alike neere unto us. Nemo altero fragilior est, nemo in crastinum sui certior: "No man is weaker then other; none surer of himselfe (to live) till to morrow." Whatsoever I have to doe before death, all leasure to end the same seemeth short unto me, yea were it but of one houre. Some body, not long since turning over my writing tables, found by chance a memoriall of something I would have done after my death: I told him (as indeed it was true), that being but a mile from my house, and in perfect health and lustie, I had made haste to write it, because I could not assure my self I should ever come home in safety: As one that am ever hatching of mine owne thoughts, and place them in my selfe: I am ever prepared about that which I may be:

nor can death (come when she please) put me in mind of any new thing. A man should ever, as much as in him lieth, be ready booted to take his journey, and above all things, looke he have then nothing to doe but with himselfe.

Quid brevi fortes jaculamur aevo
Multa:
[Footnote: Hor. 1. ii. Od. Xiv]

To aime why are we ever bold,
At many things in so short hold?

For then we shall have worke sufficient, without any more accrease. Some man complaineth more that death doth hinder him from the assured course of an hoped for victorie, than of death it selfe; another cries out, he should give place to her, before he have married his daughter, or directed the course of his childrens bringing up; another bewaileth he must forgoe his wives company; another moaneth the losse of his children, the chiefest commodities of his being. I am now by meanes of the mercy of God in such a taking, that without regret or grieving at any worldly matter, I am prepared to dislodge, whensoever he shall please to call me: I am every where free: my farewell is soone taken of all my friends, except of my selfe. No man did ever pre pare himselfe to quit the world more simply and fully, or more generally spake of all thoughts of it, than I am assured I shall doe. The deadest deaths are the best.

—Miser, de miser (aiunt) omnia ademit.
Vna dies infesta mihi tot praemia vitae:
[Footnote: Luce. 1. iii. 941.]

O wretch, O wretch (friends cry), one day,
All joyes of life hath tane away:

And the builder,

—manent (saith he) opera interrupta,
minaeque Murorum ingentes.
[Footnote: Virg. Aen. 1. iv. 88.]

The workes unfinisht lie,
And walls that threatned hie.

A man should designe nothing so long afore-hand, or at least with such an intent, as to passionate[Footnote: Long passionately.] himselfe to see the end of it; we are all borne to be doing.

Cum moriar, medium solvar et inter opus
[Footnote: Ovid. Am. 1. ii. El. x. 36]

When dying I my selfe shall spend,

Ere halfe my businesse come to end.

I would have a man to be doing, and to prolong his lives offices as much as lieth in him, and let death seize upon me whilest I am setting my cabiges, carelesse of her dart, but more of my unperfect garden. I saw one die, who being at his last gaspe, uncessantly complained against his destinie, and that death should so unkindly cut him off in the middest of an historie which he had in hand, and was now come to the fifteenth or sixteenth of our Kings.

Illud in his rebus non addunt, nec tibi earum,
Iam desiderium rerum super insidet uno.
[Footnote: Luce. 1. iii. 44.]

Friends adde not that in this case, now no more
Shalt thou desire, or want things wisht before.

A man should rid himselfe of these vulgar and hurtful humours. Even as Churchyards were first place adjoyning unto churches, and in the most frequented places of the City, to enure (as Lycurgus said) the common people, women and children, not to be skared at the sight of a dead man, and to the end that continuall spectacle of bones, sculs, tombes, graves and burials, should forewarne us of our condition, and fatall end.

Quin etiam exhilarare viris convivia caede
Mos olim, et miscere epulis spectacula dira
Certantum ferro, saepe et super ipsa cadentum
Pocula, respersis non parco sanguine mensis.
[Footnote: Syl. 1. xi. 51]

Nay more, the manner was to welcome guests,
And with dire shewes of slaughter to mix feasts.
Of them that fought at sharpe, and with bords tainted
Of them with much bloud, who o'er full cups fainted.

And even as the AEgyptians after their feastings and carousings caused a great image of death to be brought in and shewed to the guests and bytanders, by one that cried aloud, "Drinke and be merry, for such shalt thou be when thou art dead: "So have I learned this custome or lesson, to have alwaies death, not only in my imagination, but continually in my mouth. And there is nothing I desire more to be informed of than of the death of men; that is to say, what words, what countenance, and what face they shew at their death; and in reading of histories, which I so attentively observe. It appeareth by the shuffling and hudling up[Footnote: Collecting] of my examples, I affect[Footnote: Like] no subject so particularly as this. Were I a composer of books, I would keepe a register, commented of the divers deaths, which in teaching men to die, should after teach them to live. Dicearcus made one of that title, but of another and lesse profitable end. Some man will say to mee, the effect exceeds the thought so farre, that there is no fence so sure, or cunning so certaine, but a man shall either lose or forget if he come once to that point; let them say what they list: to premeditate on it, giveth no doubt a great advantage: and it is nothing, at the least, to goe so farre without dismay or alteration, or without an ague? There belongs more to it: Nature her selfe lends her hand, and gives us courage. If it be a short and violent death, wee have no leisure to feare it; if otherwise, I perceive that according as I engage my selfe in sicknesse, I doe naturally fall into some disdaine and contempt of life. I finde that I have more adoe to digest this resolution, that I shall die when I am in health, than I have when I am troubled with a fever: forsomuch as I have no more such fast hold on the commodities of life, whereof I begin to lose the use and pleasure, and view death in the face with a lesse undanted looke, which makes me hope, that the further I goe from that, and the nearer I approach to this, so much more easily doe I enter in composition for their exchange. Even as I have tried in many other occurrences, which Caesar affirmed, that often some things seeme greater, being farre from us, than if they bee neere at hand: I have found that being in perfect health, I have much more beene frighted with sicknesse, than when I have felt it. The jollitie wherein I live, the pleasure and the strength make the other seeme so disproportionable from that, that by imagination I amplifie these commodities by one moitie, and apprehended them much more heavie and burthensome, than I feele them when I have them upon my shoulders. The same I hope will happen to me of death. Consider we by the ordinary mutations, and daily declinations which we suffer, how Nature deprives us of the sight of our losse and empairing; what hath an aged man left him of his youths vigor, and of his forepast life?

Heu senibus vita portio quanta manet
[Footnote: Com. Gal. 1. i. 16.]

Alas to men in yeares how small
A part of life is left in all?

Caesar, to a tired and crazed [Footnote: diseased] Souldier of his guard, who in the open street came to him, to beg leave he might cause himselfe to be put to death; viewing his decrepit behaviour, answered pleasantly: "Doest thou thinke to be alive then?" Were man all at once to fall into it, I doe not thinke we should be able to beare such a change, but being faire and gently led on by her hand, in a slow, and as it were unperceived descent, by little and little, and step by step, she roules us into that miserable state, and day by day seekes to acquaint us with it. So that when youth failes in us, we feele, nay we perceive no shaking or transchange at all in our selves: which in essence and veritie is a harder death, than that of a languishing and irkesome life, or that of age. Forsomuch as the leape from an ill being unto a not being, is not so dangerous or steepie; as it is from a delightfull and flourishing being unto a painfull and sorrowfull condition. A weake bending, and faint stopping bodie hath lesse strength to beare and under goe a heavie burden: So hath our soule. She must bee rouzed and raised against the violence and force of this adversarie. For as it is impossible she should take any rest whilest she feareth: whereof if she be assured (which is a thing exceeding humane [Footnote: human] condition) she may boast that it is impossible unquietnesse, torment, and feare, much lesse the least displeasure should lodge in her.

Non vultus instantis tyranni
Mente quatit solida, neque Auster,
Dux inquieti turbidus Adria,
Nec fulminantis magna Jovis manus.
[Footnote: Hor. I. iii. Od. iii.]

No urging tyrants threatning face,
Where minde is found can it displace,
No troublous wind the rough seas Master,
Nor Joves great hand, the thunder–caster.

She is made Mistris of her passions and concupiscence, Lady of indulgence, of shame, of povertie, and of all for tunes injuries. Let him that can, attaine to this advantage: Herein consists the true and soveraigne liberty, that affords us meanes wherewith to jeast and make a scorne of force and injustice, and to deride imprisonment, gives [Footnote: Gyves, shackles] or fetters.

—in manicis, et
Compedibus, savo te sub custode tenebo.
Ipse Deus simui atque volam, me solvet: opinor
Hoc sentit, moriar. Mors ultima linea rerum est.
[Footnote: Hor. I. i. Ep. xvi. 76.]

In gyves and fetters I will hamper thee,
Under a Jayler that shall cruell be:
Yet, when I will, God me deliver shall,
He thinkes, I shall die: death is end of all.

Our religion hath had no surer humane foundation than the contempt of life. Discourse of reason doth not only call and summon us unto it. For why should we feare to lose a thing, which being lost, cannot be moaned? but also, since we are threatened by so many kinds of death, there is no more inconvenience to feare them all, than to endure one: what matter is it when it commeth, since it is unavoidable? Socrates answered one that told him, "The thirty tyrants have condemned thee to death." "And Nature them," said he. What fondnesse is it to carke and care so much, at that instant and passage from all exemption of paine and care? As our birth brought us the birth of all things, so shall our death the end of all things. Therefore is it as great follie to weepe, we shall not live a hundred yeeres hence, as to waile we lived not a hundred yeeres agoe. "Death is the beginning of another life." So wept we, and so much did it cost us to enter into this life; and so did we spoile us of our ancient vaile in entring into it. Nothing can be grievous that is but once. Is it reason so long to fear a thing of so short time? Long life or short life is made all one by death. For long or short is not in things that are no more. Aristotle saith, there are certaine little beasts alongst the river Hyspanis, that live but one day; she which dies at 8 o'clocke in the morning, dies in her youth, and she that dies at 5 in the afternoon, dies in her decrepitude, who of us doth not laugh, when we shall see this short moment of continuance to be had in consideration of good or ill fortune? The most and the least is ours, if we compare it with eternitie, or equall it to the lasting of mountains, rivers, stars, and trees, or any other living creature, is not lesse ridiculous. But nature compels us to it. Depart (saith she) out of this world, even as you came into it. The same way you came from death to life, returne without passion or amazement, from life to death: your death is but a peece of the worlds order, and but a parcell of the worlds life.

—inter se mortales mutua vivunt,
Et quasi cursores vitae lampada tradunt.

[Footnote: Lucret. ii. 74. 77.]

Mortall men live by mutuall entercourse:
And yeeld their life–torch, as men in a course.

Shal I not change this goodly contexture of things for you? It is the condition of your creation: death is a part of yourselves: you flie from yourselves. The being you enjoy is equally shared betweene life and death. The first day of your birth doth as wel addresse you to die, as to live.

Prima quae vitam dedit, hora, carpsit.
[Footnote: Sen. Her. Sw. ckor. Iii.]

The first houre, that to men
Gave life, strait, cropt it then.

Nascentes morimur, finisque ab origine pendet:
[Footnote: Manil. At. l. iv]

As we are borne we die; the end
Doth of th' originall depend.

All the time you live, you steale it from death: it is at her charge. The continuall worke of your life, is to contrive death: you are in death, during the time you continue in life: for, you are after death, when you are no longer living. Or if you had rather have it so, you are dead after life: but during life, you are still dying: and death doth more rudely touch the dying than the dead, and more lively and essentially. If you have profited by life, you have also beene fed thereby, depart then satisfied.

Cur non ut plenus vitae conviva recedis?
[Footnote: Lucret. 1. iii. 982.]

Why like a full–fed guest,
Depart you not to rest?

If you have not knowne how to make use of it: if it were unprofitable to you, what need you care to have lost it to what end would you enjoy it longer?

—cur amplius addere quaeris
Rursum quod pereat male,
et ingratum occidat omne?
[Footnote: Lucret. 1. iii. 989.]

Why seeke you more to gaine, what must againe
All perish ill, and passe with griefe or paine?

Life in itselfe is neither good nor evill: it is the place of good or evill, according as you prepare it for them. And if you have lived one day, you have seene all: one day is equal to all other daies. There is no other light, there is no other night. This Sunne, this Moone, these Starres, and this disposition, is the very same which your forefathers enjoyed, and which shall also entertaine your posteritie.

> Non alium videre patres, aliumve nepotes
> Aspicient.
> [Footnote: Manil. i. 523.]

> No other saw our Sires of old,
> No other shall their sonnes behold.

And if the worst happen, the distribution and varietie of all the acts of my comedie, is performed in one yeare. If you have observed the course of my foure seasons; they containe the infancie, the youth, the viriltie, and the old age of the world. He hath plaied his part: he knowes no other wilinesse belonging to it, but to begin againe, it will ever be the same, and no other.

> Versamur ibidem, atque insumus usque,
> [Footnote: Lucret. 1. iii. 123.]

> We still in one place turne about,
> Still there we are, now in, now out.

> Atque in se sua per vestigia volvitur annus.
> [Footnote: Virg. Georg. 1. ii. 403.]

> The yeare into it selfe is cast
> By those same steps, that it hath past.

I am not purposed to devise you other new sports.

> Nam tibi praterea quod machiner, inveniamque
> Quod placeat nihil est; eadem suni omnia semper.
> [Footnote: Lucret. 1. ii. 978.]

> Else nothing, that I can devise or frame,
> Can please thee, for all things are still the same.

Make roome for others, as others have done for you. Equalitie is the chiefe ground-worke of equitie, who can complaine to be comprehended where all are contained? So may you live long enough, you shall never diminish anything from the time you have to die: it is bootlesse; so long shall you continue in that state which you feare, as if you had died, being in your swathing-clothes, and when you were sucking.

> —licet, quot vis, vivendo vincere secla.
> Mors sterna tamen, nihilominus ilia manebit.

17

[Footnote: Ib. 1126.]

Though yeares you live, as many as you will,
Death is eternall, death remaineth still.

And I will so please you, that you shall have no discontent.

In vera nescis nullum fore morte alium te,
Qui possit vivus tibi te lugere peremptum,
Stansque jacentem.
[Footnote: Idt. 1. Iii. 9.]

Thou know'st not there shall be not other thou,
When thou art dead indeed, that can tell how
Alive to waile thee dying, Standing to waile thee lying.

Nor shall you wish for life, which you so much desire

Nec sibi enim quisquam tum se vitamque requirit,
[Footnote: ib. 963.]
Nec desiderium nostri nos afficit ullum.
[Footnote: Ib. 966.]

For then none for himselfe or life requires:
Nor are we of our selves affected with desires.

Death is lesse to be feared than nothing, if there were anything lesse than nothing.

—multo mortem minus ad nos esse putandum,
Si minus esse potest quam quod nihil esse videmus.
[Footnote: Ib. 970.]

Death is much less to us, we ought esteeme,
If lesse may be, than what doth nothing seeme.

Nor alive, nor dead, it doth concern you nothing. Alive because you are: Dead, because you are no more. Moreover, no man dies before his houre. The time you leave behinde was no more yours than that which was before your birth, and concerneth you no more.

Respice enim quam nil ad nos anteacta vetustas
Temporis aeterni fuerit.
[Footnote: Ib. 1016.]

For marke, how all antiquitie foregone
Of all time ere we were, to us was none.

Wheresoever your life ended, there is it all. The profit of life consists not in the space, but rather in the use. Some man hath lived long, that hath a short life, Follow it whilst you have time. It consists not in number of yeeres, but in your will, that you have lived long enough. Did you thinke you should never come to the place, where you were still going? There is no way but hath an end. And if company may solace you, doth not the whole world walke the same path?

—Omnia te, vita perfuncta, sequentur.
[Footnote: Ib. 1012.]

Life past, all things at last
Shall follow thee as thou hast past.

Doe not all things move as you doe, or keepe your course? Is there any thing grows not old together with yourselfe? A thousand men, a thousand beasts, and a thousand other creatures die in the very instant that you die.

Nam nox nulla diem, neque noctem aurora sequuta est,
Que non audierit mistus vagitibus aegris
Ploratus, mortis comites et funeris atri.
[Footnote: Id. i. ii. 587.]

No night ensued day light; no morning followed night,
Which heard not moaning mixt with sick–mens groaning,
With deaths and funerals joyned was that moaning.

To what end recoile you from it, if you cannot goe backe. You have seene many who have found good in death, ending thereby many many miseries. But have you seene any that hath received hurt thereby? Therefore it is meere simplicitie to condemne a thing you never approve, neither by yourselfe nor any other. Why doest thou complaine of me and of destinie? Doe we offer thee any wrong? is it for thee to direct us, or for us to governe thee? Although thy age be not come to her period, thy life is. A little man is a whole man as well as a great man. Neither men nor their lives are measured by the Ell. Chiron refused immortalitie, being informed of the conditions thereof, even by the God of time and of continuance, Saturne his father. Imagine truly how much an ever–during life would be lesse tolerable and more painfull to a man, than is the life which I have given him. Had you not death you would then uncessantly curse, and cry out against me, that I had deprived you of it. I have of purpose and unwittingly blended some bitternesse amongst it, that so seeing the commoditie of its use, I might hinder you from over– greedily embracing, or indiscreetly calling for it. To continue in this moderation that is, neither to fly from life nor to run to death (which I require of you) I have tempered both the one and other betweene sweetnes and sowrenes. I first taught Thales, the chiefest of your Sages and Wisemen, that to live and die were indifferent, which made him answer one very wisely, who asked him wherefore he died not: "Because," said he, "it is indifferent. The water, the earth, the aire, the fire, and other members of this my universe, are no more the instruments of thy life than of thy death. Why fearest thou thy last day? He is no more guiltie, and conferreth no more to thy death, than any of the others. It is not the last step that causeth weariness: it only declares it. All daies march towards death, only the last comes to it." Behold heere the good precepts of our universall mother Nature. I have oftentimes bethought my self whence it proceedeth, that in times of warre, the visage of death (whether wee see it in us or in others) seemeth without all comparison much lesse dreadful and terrible unto us, than in our houses, or in our beds, otherwise it should be an armie of Physitians and whiners, and she ever being one, there must needs bee much more assurance amongst countrie–people and of base condition, than in others. I verily believe, these fearefull lookes, and astonishing countenances wherewith we encompass it, are those that more amaze and terrifie us than death: a new forme of life; the out cries of mothers; the wailing of women and children; the visitation of dismaid and swouning friends; the assistance of a number of pale–looking, distracted, and whining servants; a darke chamber; tapers burning round about; our couch beset round with Physitians and Preachers; and to conclude, nothing but horror and astonishment on every side of us: are wee not already dead and buried? The very children are afraid of their friends, when they see them masked; and so are we. The maske must as well be taken from things as from men, which being removed, we shall find nothing hid under it, but the very same death, that a seely[Footnote: weak, simple] varlet, or a simple maid–servant, did latterly suffer without amazement or feare. Happie is that death which takes all leasure from the preparations of such an equipage.

OF THE INSTITUTION AND EDUCATION OF CHILDREN; TO THE LADIE DIANA OF FOIX, COUNTESSE OF GURSON

I never knew father, how crooked and deformed soever his sonne were, that would either altogether cast him off, or not acknowledge him for his owne: and yet (unlesse he be meerely besotted or blinded in his affection) it may not be said, but he plainly perceiveth his defects, and hath a feeling of his imperfections. But so it is, he is his owne. So it is in my selfe. I see better than any man else, that what I have set downe is nought but the fond imaginations of him who in his youth hath tasted nothing but the paring, and seen but the superficies of true learning: whereof he hath retained but a generall and shapelesse forme: a smacke of every thing in generall, but nothing to the purpose in particular: After the French manner. To be short, I know there is an art of Phisicke; a course of lawes; foure parts of the Mathematikes; and I am not altogether ignorant what they tend unto. And perhaps I also know the scope and drift of Sciences in generall to be for the service of our life. But to wade further, or that ever I tired my selfe with plodding upon Aristotle (the Monarch of our moderne doctrine 1) or obstinately continued in search of any one science: I confesse I never did it. Nor is there any one art whereof I am able so much as to draw the first lineaments. And there is no scholler (be he of the lowest forme) that may not repute himselfe wiser than I, who am not able to oppose him in his first lesson: and if I be forced to it, I am constrained verie impertinently to draw in matter from some generall discourse, whereby I examine, and give a guesse at his naturall judgement: a lesson as much unknowne to them as theirs is to me. I have not dealt or had commerce with any excellent booke, except Plutarke or Seneca, from whom (as the Danaides) I draw my water, uncessantly filling, and as fast emptying: some thing whereof I fasten to this paper, but to my selfe nothing at all. And touching bookes: Historie is my chiefe studie, Poesie my only delight, to which I am particularly affected: for as Cleanthes said, that as the voice being forciblie pent in the narrow gullet of a trumpet, at last issueth forth more strong and shriller, so me seemes, that a sentence cunningly and closely couched in measure keeping Posie, darts it selfe forth more furiously, and wounds me even to the quicke. And concerning the naturall faculties that are in me (whereof behold here an essay), I perceive them to faint under their owne burthen; my conceits, [Footnote: Ideas.] and my judgement march but uncertaine, and as it were groping, staggering, and stumbling at every rush: And when I have gone as far as I can, I have no whit pleased my selfe: for the further I saile the more land I descrie, and that so dimmed with fogges, and overcast with clouds, that my sight is so weakned, I cannot distinguish the same. And then undertaking to speake indifferently of all that presents it selfe unto my fantasie, and having nothing but mine owne naturall meanes to imploy therein, if it be my hap (as commonly it is) among good Authors, to light upon those verie places which I have undertaken to treat off, as even now I did in Plutarke reading his discourse of the power of imagination, wherein in regard of those wise men, I acknowledge my selfe so weake and so poore, so dull and grose–headed, as I am forced both to pittie and disdaine my selfe, yet am I pleased with this, that my opinions have often the grace to jump with theirs, and that I follow them a loofe–off, [Footnote: At a distance.] and thereby possesse at least, that which all other men have not; which is, that I know the utmost difference betweene them and my selfe: all which notwithstanding, I suffer my inventions to run abroad, as weake and faint as I have produced them, without bungling and botching the faults which this comparison hath discovered to me in them. A man had need have a strong backe, to undertake to march foot to foot with these kind of men. The indiscreet writers of our age, amidst their triviall [Footnote: Commonplace.] compositions, intermingle and wrest in whole sentences taken from ancient Authors, supposing by such filching–theft to purchase honour and reputation to themselves, doe cleane contrarie. For, this infinite varietie and dissemblance of lustres, makes a face so wan, so il–favored, and so uglie, in respect of theirs, that they lose much more than gaine thereby. These were two contrarie humours: The Philosopher Chrisippus was wont to foist–in amongst his bookes, not only whole sentences and other long–long discourses, but whole bookes of other Authors, as in one, he brought in Euripides his Medea. And Apollodorus was wont to say of him, that if one should draw from out his bookes what he had stolne from others, his paper would remaine blanke. Whereas Epicurus cleane contrarie to him in three hundred volumes he left behind him, had not made use of one allegation. [Footnote: Citation.] It was my fortune not long since to light upon such a place: I had languishingly traced after some French words, so naked and shallow, and so void either of sense or matter, that at last I found them to be nought but meere French words; and after a tedious and wearisome travell, I chanced to stumble upon an high, rich, and even to the clouds–raised piece, the descent whereof had it been somewhat more pleasant or easie, or the ascent reaching a little further, it had been excusable, and to be borne with–all; but it was such a steepie downe–fall, and by meere strength hewen out of the maine rocke, that by reading of the first six words, me thought I was carried into another world: whereby I perceive the bottome whence I came to be so low and deep, as I durst never more adventure to go through it; for, if I did stuffe any one of my discourses with those rich spoiles, it would manifestly cause the sottishnesse [Footnote: Foolishness.] of others to appeare. To reprove mine owne faults in others, seemes to me no more unsufferable than to reprehend (as I doe often) those of others in my selfe. They ought to be accused every where, and have all places of Sanctuarie taken from them: yet do I know how over boldly, at all times I adventure to equall my selfe unto my filchings, and to march hand in hand with them; not without a fond hardie hope, that I may perhaps be able to bleare the eyes of the Judges from discerning them. But it is as much for the benefit of my application, as for the good of mine invention and force. And I doe not furiously front, and bodie to bodie wrestle with those old champions: it is but by flights, advantages, and false offers I seek to come within them, and if I can, to give them a fall. I do not rashly take them about the necke, I doe but touch them, nor doe I go so far as by my bargaine I would seeme to doe; could I but keepe even with them, I should then be an honest man; for I seeke not to venture on them, but where they are strongest. To doe as I have seen some, that is, to shroud themselves under other armes, not daring so much as to show their fingers ends unarmed, and to botch up all their works (as it is an easie matter in a common subject, namely for the wiser sort) with ancient inventions, here and there hudled up together. And in those who endeavoured to hide what they have filched from others, and make it their owne, it is first a manifest note of injustice, then a plaine argument of cowardlinesse; who having nothing of any worth in themselves to make show of, will yet under the countenance of others sufficiencie goe about to make a faire offer: Moreover (oh great foolishnesse) to seek by such cosening [Footnote: Cheating.] tricks to forestall the ignorant approbation of the common sort, nothing fearing to discover their ignorance to men of understanding (whose praise only is of value) who will soone trace out such borrowed ware. As for me, there is nothing I will doe lesse. I never speake of others, but that I may the more speake of my selfe. This concerneth not those mingle-mangles of many kinds of stuffe, or as the Grecians call them Rapsodies, that for such are published, of which kind I have (since I came to yeares of discretion) seen divers most ingenious and wittie; amongst others, one under the name of Capilupus; besides many of the ancient stampe. These are wits of such excellence, as both here and elsewhere they will soone be perceived, as our late famous writer Lipsius, in his learned and laborious work of the Politikes: yet whatsoever come of it, for so much as they are but follies, my intent is not to smother them, no more than a bald and hoarie picture of mine, where a Painter hath drawne not a perfect visage, but mine owne. For, howsoever, these are but my humors and opinions, and I deliver them but to show what my conceit [Footnote: notion] is, and not what ought to be beleeved. Wherein I ayme at nothing but to display my selfe, who peradventure (if a new prentiship change me) shall be another to morrow. I have no authoritie to purchase beliefe, neither do I desire it; knowing well that I am not sufficiently taught to instruct others. Some having read my precedent Chapter [Footnote: "Of Pedantism"], told me not long since in mine owne house, I should somewhat more have extended my selfe in the discourse concerning the institution of children. Now (Madam) if there were any sufficiencie in me touching that subject, I could not better employ the same than to bestow it as a present upon that little lad, which ere long threatneth to make a happie issue from out your honorable woombe; for (Madame) you are too generous to begin with other than a man childe. And having had so great a part in the conduct of your successeful marriage, I may challenge some right and interest in the greatnesse and prosperitie of all that shall proceed from it: moreover, the ancient and rightfull possession, which you from time to time have ever had, and still have over my service, urgeth me with more than ordinarie respects, to wish all honour, well-fare and advantage to whatsoever may in any sort concerne you and yours. And truly, my meaning is but to show that the greatest difficultie, and importing all humane knowledge, seemeth to be in this point, where the nurture and institution of young children is in question. For, as in matters of husbandrie, the labor that must be used before sowing, setting, and planting, yea in planting itselfe, is most certaine and easie. But when that which was sowen, set and planted, commeth to take life; before it come to ripenesse, much adoe, and great varietie of proceeding belongeth to it. So in men, it is no great matter to get them, but being borne, what continuall cares, what diligent attendance, what doubts and feares, doe daily wait to their parents and tutors, before they can be nurtured and brought to any good? The fore-shew of their inclination whilest they are young is so uncertaine, their humours so variable, their promises so changing, their hopes so false, and their proceedings so doubtful, that it is very hard (yea for the wisest) to ground any certaine judgment, or assured successe upon them. Behold Cymon, view Themistocles, and a thousand others, how they have differed, and fallen to better from themselves, and deceive the expectation of such as knowe them. The young whelps both of Dogges and Beares at first sight shew their naturall disposition, but men headlong embracing this custome or fashion, following that humor or opinion, admitting this or that passion, allowing of that or this law, are easily changed, and soone disguised; yet it is hard to force the naturall propension or readinesse of the mind, whereby it followeth, that for want of heedie fore–sight in those that could not guide their course well, they often employ much time in vaine, to addresse young children in those matters whereunto they are not naturally addicted. All which difficulties notwithstanding, mine opinion is, to bring them up in the best and profitablest studies, and that a man should slightly passe over those fond presages, and deceiving prognostikes, which we over precisely gather in their infancie. And (without offence be it said) me thinks that Plato in his "Commonwealth" allowed them too– too much authoritie.

Madame, Learning joyned with true knowledge is an especiall and gracefull ornament, and an implement of wonderful use and consequence, namely, in persons raised to that degree of fortune wherein you are. And in good truth, learning hath not her owne true forme, nor can she make shew of her beauteous lineaments, if she fall into the hands of base and vile persons. [For, as famous Torquato Tasso saith: "Philosophie being a rich and noble Queene, and knowing her owne worth, graciously smileth upon and lovingly embraceth Princes and noble men, if they become suiters to her, admitting them as her minions, and gently affoording them all the favours she can; whereas upon the contrarie, if she be wooed, and sued unto by clownes, mechanicall fellowes, and such base kind of people, she holds herselfe disparaged and disgraced, as holding no proportion with them. And therefore see we by experience, that if a true Gentleman or nobleman follow her with any attention, and woo her with importunitie, he shall learne and know more of her, and prove a better scholler in one yeare, than an ungentle or base fellow shall in seven, though he pursue her never so attentively."] She is much more readie and fierce to lend her furtherance and direction in the conduct of a warre, to attempt honourable actions, to command a people, to treat a peace with a prince of forraine nation, than she is to forme an argument in Logick, to devise a Syllogisme, to canvase a case at the barre, or to prescribe a receit of pills. So (noble Ladie) forsomuch as I cannot perswade myselfe, that you will either forget or neglect this point, concerning the institution of yours, especially having tasted the sweetnesse thereof, and being descended of so noble and learned a race. For we yet possesse the learned compositions of the ancient and noble Earles of Foix, from out whose heroicke loynes your husband and you take your of–spring. And Francis Lord of Candale, your worthie uncle, doth daily bring forth such fruits thereof, as the knowledge of the matchlesse qualitie of your house shall hereafter extend itselfe to many ages; I will therefore make you acquainted with one conceit of mine, which contrarie to the common use I hold, and that is all I am able to affoord you concerning that matter. The charge of the Tutor, which you shall appoint your sonne, in the choice of whom consisteth the whole substance of his education and bringing up; on which are many branches depending, which (forasmuch as I can adde nothing of any moment to it) I will not touch at all. And for that point, wherein I presume to advise him, he may so far forth give credit unto it, as he shall see just cause. To a gentleman borne of noble parentage, and heire of a house that aymeth at true learning, and in it would be disciplined, not so much for gane or commoditie to himselfe (because so abject an end is far unworthie the grace and favour of the Muses, and besides, hath a regard or dependencie of others) nor for externall shew and ornament, but to adorne and enrich his inward minde, desiring rather to shape and institute an able and sufficient man, than a bare learned man; my desire is therefore, that the parents or overseers of such a gentleman be very circumspect, and careful in chusing his director, whom I would rather commend for having a well composed and temperate braine, than a full stuft head, yet both will doe well. And I would rather prefer wisdome, judgement, civill customes, and modest behaviour, than bare and meere literall learning; and that in his charge he hold a new course. Some never cease brawling in their schollers eares (as if they were still pouring in a tonell) to follow their booke, yet is their charge nothing else but to repeat what hath beene told them before. I would have a tutor to correct this part, and that at first entrance, according to the capacitie of the wit he hath in hand, he should begin to make shew of it, making him to have a smacke of all things, and how to choose and distinguish them, without helpe of others, sometimes opening him the way, other times leaving him to open it by himselfe. I would not have him to invent and speake alone, but suffer his disciple to speake when his turne commeth. Socrates, and after him Arcesilaus, made their schollers to speake first, and then would speake themselves. Obest plerumque iis qui discere volunt, auctoritas eorum qui docent: [Footnote: CIC. De Nat. 1. i] "Most commonly the authoritie of them that teach, hinders them that would learne."

It is therefore meet that he make him first trot-on before him, whereby he may the better judge of his pace, and so guesse how long he will hold out, that accordingly he may fit his strength; for want of which proportion we often marre all. And to know how to make a good choice, and how far forth one may proceed (still keeping a due measure), is one of the hardest labours I know. It is a signe of a noble, and effect of an undanted spirit, to know how to second, and how far forth he shall condescend to his childish proceedings, and how to guide them. As for myselfe, I can better and with more strength walke up than downe a hill. Those which, according to our common fashion, undertake with one selfe-same lesson, and like maner of education, to direct many spirits of divers formes and different humours, it is no marvell if among a multitude of children, they scarce meet with two or three that reap any good fruit by their discipline, or that come to any perfection. I would not only have him to demand an accompt of the words contained in his lesson, but of the sense and substance thereof, and judge of the profit he hath made of it, not by the testimonie of his memorie, but by the witnesse of his life. That what he lately learned, he cause him to set forth and pourtray the same into sundrie shapes, and then to accommodate it to as many different and severall subjects, whereby he shal perceive, whether he have yet apprehended the same, and therein enfeoffed himselfe, [Footnote: Taken possession.] at due times taking his instruction from the institution given by Plato. It is a signe of cruditie and indigestion for a man to yeeld up his meat, even as he swallowed the same; the stomacke hath not wrought his full operation, unlesse it have changed forme, and altered fashion of that which was given him to boyle and concoct.

[Wee see men gape after no reputation but learning, and when they say, such a one is a learned man, they thinke they have said enough;] Our minde doth move at others pleasure, and tyed and forced to serve the fantasies of others, being brought under by authoritie, and forced to stoope to the lure of their bare lesson; wee have beene so subjected to harpe upon one string, that we have no way left us to descant upon voluntarie; our vigor and libertie is cleane extinct. Nunquam tutelae suae fiunt: "They never come to their owne tuition." It was my hap to bee familiarlie acquainted with an honest man at Pisa, but such an Aristotelian, as he held this infallible position; that a conformitie to Aristotles doctrine was the true touchstone and squire [Footnote: Square.] of all solid imaginations and perfect veritie; for, whatsoever had no coherencie with it, was but fond Chimeraes and idle humors; inasmuch as he had knowne all, seene all, and said all. This proposition of his being somewhat over amply and injuriously interpreted by some, made him a long time after to be troubled in the inquisition of Rome. I would have him make his scholler narrowly to sift all things with discretion, and harbour nothing in his head by mere authoritie, or upon trust. Aristotles principles shall be no more axiomes unto him, than the Stoikes or Epicurians. Let this diversitie of judgements be proposed unto him, if he can, he shall be able to distinguish the truth from falsehood, if not, he will remaine doubtful.

Che non men che saper dubbiar m'aggrata.
[Footnote: DANTE, Inferno, cant. xi. 93.]

No lesse it pleaseth me,
To doubt, than wise to be.

For if by his owne discourse he embrace the opinions of Xenophon or of Plato, they shall be no longer theirs, but his. He that meerely followeth another, traceth nothing, and seeketh nothing: Non sumus sub Rege, sibi quisque se vindicet: [Footnote: SEN. Epist. xxxiii.] "We are not under a Kings command, every one may challenge himselfe, for let him at least know that he knoweth." It is requisite he endevour as much to feed himselfe with their conceits, as labour to learne their precepts; which, so he know how to applie, let him hardily forget, where or whence he had them. Truth and reason are common to all, and are no more proper unto him that spake them heretofore, then unto him that shall speake them hereafter. And it is no more according to Platoes opinion than to mine, since both he and I understand and see alike. The Bees do here and there sucke this and cull that flower, but afterward they produce the hony, which is peculiarly their owne, then is it no more Thyme or Majoram. So of peeces borrowed of others, he may lawfully alter, transforme, and confound them, to shape out of them a perfect peece of worke, altogether his owne; alwaies provided his judgement, his travell, [Footnote: Travail, labor.] studie, and institution tend to nothing, but to frame the same perfect. Let him hardily conceale where or whence he hath had any helpe, and make no shew of anything, but of that which he hath made himselfe. Pirates, pilchers, and borrowers, make a shew of their purchases and buildings, but not of that which they have taken from others: you see not the secret fees or bribes Lawyers take of their Clients, but you shall manifestly discover the alliances they make, the honours they get for their children, and the goodly houses they build. No man makes open shew of his receits, but every one of his gettings. The good that comes of studie (or at least should come) is to prove better, wiser and honester. It is the understanding power (said Epicharmus) that seeth and heareth, it is it that profiteth all and disposeth all, that moveth, swayeth, and ruleth all: all things else are but blind, senselesse, and without spirit. And truly in barring him of libertie to doe any thing of himselfe, we make him thereby more servile and more coward. Who would ever enquire of his scholler what he thinketh of Rhetorike, of Grammar, of this or of that sentence of Cicero? Which things thoroughly fethered (as if they were oracles) are let flie into our memorie; in which both letters and syllables are substantiall parts of the subject. To know by roat is no perfect knowledge, but to keep what one hath committed to his memories charge, is commendable: what a man directly knoweth, that will he dispose of, without turning still to his booke or looking to his pattern. A meere bookish sufficiencie is unpleasant. All I expect of it is an imbellishing of my actions, and not a foundation of them, according to Platoes mind, who saith, constancie, faith, and sinceritie are true Philosophie; as for other Sciences, and tending elsewhere, they are but garish paintings. I would faine have Paluel or Pompey, those two excellent dauncers of our time, with all their nimblenesse, teach any man to doe their loftie tricks and high capers, only with seeing them done, and without stirring out of his place, as some Pedanticall fellowes would instruct our minds without moving or putting it in practice. And glad would I be to find one that would teach us how to manage a horse, to tosse a pike, to shoot−off a peece, to play upon the lute, or to warble with the voice, without any exercise, as these kind of men would teach us to judge, and how to speake well, without any exercise of speaking

25

or judging. In which kind of life, or as I may terme it, Prentiship, what action or object soever presents itselfe into our eies, may serve us in stead of a sufficient booke. A prettie pranke of a boy, a knavish tricke of a page, a foolish part of a lackey, an idle tale or any discourse else, spoken either in jest or earnest, at the table or in companie, are even as new subjects for us to worke upon: for furtherance whereof, commerce or common societie among men, visiting of forraine countries, and observing of strange fashions, are verie necessary, not only to be able (after the manner of our yong gallants of France) to report how many paces the Church of Santa Rotonda is in length or breadth, or what rich garments the curtezan Signora Livia weareth, and the worth of her hosen; or as some do, nicely to dispute how much longer or broader the face of Nero is, which they have seene in some old ruines of Italie, than that which is made for him in other old monuments else—where. But they should principally observe, and be able to make certaine relation of the humours and fashions of those countries they have seene, that they may the better know how to correct and prepare their wits by those of others. I would therefore have him begin even from his infancie to travell abroad; and first, that at one shoot he may hit two markes he should see neighbour— countries, namely where languages are most different from ours; for, unlesse a mans tongue be fashioned unto them in his youth, he shall never attaine to the true pronunciation of them if he once grow in yeares. Moreover, we see it received as a common opinion of the wiser sort, that it agreeth not with reason, that a childe be alwaies nuzzled, cockered, dandled, and brought up in his parents lap or sight; forsomuch as their naturall kindnesse, or (as I may call it) tender fondnesse, causeth often, even the wisest to prove so idle, so over—nice, and so base—minded. For parents are not capable, neither can they find in their hearts to see them checkt, corrected, or chastised, nor indure to see them brought up so meanly, and so far from daintinesse, and many times so dangerously, as they must needs be. And it would grieve them to see their children come home from those exercises, that a Gentleman must necessarily acquaint himselfe with, sometimes all wet and bemyred, other times sweatie and full of dust, and to drinke being either extreme hot or exceeding cold; and it would trouble them to see him ride a rough—untamed horse, or with his weapon furiously incounter a skilful Fencer, or to handle or shoot—off a musket; against which there is no remedy, if he will make him prove a sufficient, compleat, or honest man: he must not be spared in his youth; and it will come to passe, that he shall many times have occasion and be forced to shocke the rules of Physicke.

> Vitamque sub dio et trepidis agat
> In rebus.
> [Footnote: Hor. I. i. Od. ii. 4.]

> Leade he his life in open aire,
> And in affaires full of despaire.

It is not sufficient to make his minde strong, his muskles must also be strengthened: the mind is over—borne if it be not seconded: and it is too much for her alone to discharge two offices. I have a feeling how mine panteth, being joyned to so tender and sensible [Footnote: Sensitive.] a bodie, and that lieth so heavie upon it And in my lecture, I often perceive how my Authors in their writings sometimes commend examples for magnanimitie and force, that rather proceed from a thicke skin and hardnes of the bones. I have knowne men, women and children borne of so hard a constitution, that a blow with a cudgell would lesse hurt them, than a filip would doe me, and so dull and blockish, that they will neither stir tongue nor eyebrowes, beat them never so much. When wrestlers goe about to counterfeit the Philosophers patience, they rather shew the vigor of their sinnewes than of their heart. For the custome to beare travell, is to tolerate griefe: Labor callum obducit dolori. [Footnote: Cic. Tusc. Qu. I. ii.] "Labour worketh a hardnesse upon sorrow." Hee must be enured to suffer the paine and hardnesse of exercises, that so he may be induced to endure the paine of the colicke, of cauterie, of fals, of sprains, and other diseases incident to mans bodie: yea, if need require, patiently to beare imprisonment and other tortures, by which sufferance he shall come to be had in more esteeme and accompt: for according to time and place, the good as well as the bad man may haply fall into them; we have seen it by experience. Whosoever striveth against the lawes, threats good men with mischiefe and extortion. Moreover, the authoritie of the Tutor (who should be soveraigne over him) is by the cockering and presence of the parents, hindred and interrupted: besides the awe and respect which the houshold beares him, and the knowledge of the meane, possibilities, and greatnesse of his house, are in my judgement no small lets [Footnote: Hindrances.]in a young Gentleman. In this schoole of commerce, and societie among men, I have often noted this vice, that in lieu of taking acquaintance of others, we only endevour to make our selves knowne to them: and we are more ready to utter such merchandize as we have, than to ingrosse and purchase new commodities. Silence and modestie are qualities very convenient to civil conversation. It is also necessary that a young man be rather taught to be discreetly–sparing and close–handed, than prodigally–wastfull and lavish in his expences, and moderate in husbanding his wealth when he shall come to possesse it. And not to take pepper in the nose for every foolish tale that shall be spoken in his presence, because it is an uncivil importunity to contradict whatsoever is not agreeing to our humour: let him be pleased to correct himselfe. And let him not seeme to blame that in others which he refuseth to doe himselfe, nor goe about to withstand common fashions, Licet sapere sine pompa, sine invidia: [Footnote: SEN. Epist. ciii. f.] "A man may bee wise without ostentation, without envie." Let him avoid those imperious images of the world, those uncivil behaviours and childish ambition wherewith, God wot, too–too many are possest: that is, to make a faire shew of that which is not in him: endevouring to be reputed other than indeed he is; and as if reprehension and new devices were hard to come by, he would by that meane acquire into himselfe the name of some peculiar vertue. As it pertaineth but to great Poets to use the libertie of arts; so is it tolerable but in noble minds and great spirits to have a preheminence above ordinarie fashions. Si quid Socrates et Aristippus contra morem et consuetudinem fecerunt, idem sibi ne arbitretur licere: Magis enim illi et divinis bonis hanc licentiam assequebantur: [Footnote: CIC. Off. 1. i.] "If Socrates and Aristippus have done ought against custome or good manner, let not a man thinke he may doe the same: for they obtained this licence by their great and excellent good parts:" He shall be taught not to enter rashly into discourse or contesting, but when he shall encounter with a Champion worthie his strength; And then would I not have him imploy all the tricks that may fit his turne, but only such as may stand him in most stead. That he be taught to be curious in making choice of his reasons, loving pertinency, and by consequence brevitie. That above all, he be instructed to yeeld, yea to quit his weapons unto truth, as soone as he shall discerne the same, whether it proceed from his adversarie, or upon better advice from himselfe; for he shall not be preferred to any place of eminencie above others, for repeating of a prescript [Footnote: Fixed beforehand.] part; and he is not engaged to defend any cause, further than he may approove it; nor shall he bee of that trade where the libertie for a man to repent and re–advise himselfe is sold for readie money, Neque, ut omnia, que praescripta et imperata sint, defendat, necessitate ulla cogitur: [Footnote: CIC. Acad. Qu. I. iv.] "Nor is he inforced by any necessitie to defend and make good all that is prescribed and commanded him." If his tutor agree with my humour, he shall frame his affection to be a most loyall and true subject to his Prince, and a most affectionate and couragious Gentleman in al that may concerne the honor of his

Soveraigne or the good of his countrie, and endevour to suppresse in him all manner of affection to undertake any action Otherwise than for a publike good and dutie. Besides many inconveniences, which greatly prejudice our libertie by reason of these particular bonds, the judgment of a man that is waged and bought, either it is lesse free and honest, or else it is blemisht with oversight and ingratitude. A meere and precise Courtier can neither have law nor will to speake or thinke otherwise than favourablie of his Master, who among so many thousands of his subjects hath made choice of him alone, to institute and bring him up with his owne hand. These favours, with the commodities that follow minion [Footnote: Favorite.] Courtiers, corrupt (not without some colour of reason) his libertie, and dazle his judgement. It is therefore commonly scene that the Courtiers– language differs from other mens, in the same state, and to be of no great credit in such matters. Let therefore his conscience and vertue shine in his speech, and reason be his chiefe direction, Let him be taught to confesse such faults as he shall discover in his owne discourses, albeit none other perceive them but himselfe; for it is an evident shew of judgement, and effect of sinceritie, which are the chiefest qualities he aymeth at. That wilfully to strive, and obstinately to contest in words, are common qualities, most apparent in basest mindes: That to readvise and correct himselfe, and when one is most earnest, to leave an ill opinion, are rare, noble, and Philosophicall conditions. Being in companie, he shall be put in minde, to cast his eyes round about, and every where: For I note, that the chiefe places are usually seezed upon by the most unworthie and lesse capable; and that height of fortune is seldome joyned with sufficiencie. I have scene that whilst they at the upper end of a board were busie entertaining themselves with talking of the beautie of the hangings about a chamber, or of the taste of some good cup of wine, many good discourses at the lower end have utterly been lost. He shall weigh the carriage of every man in his calling, a Heardsman, a Mason, a Stranger, or a Traveller; all must be imployed; every one according to his worth; for all helps to make up houshold; yea, the follie and the simplicitie of others shall be as instructions to him. By controlling the graces and manners of others, he shall acquire unto himselfe envie of the good and contempt of the bad. Let him hardly be possest with an honest curiositie to search out the nature and causes of all things: let him survay whatsoever is rare and singular about him; a building, a fountaine, a man, a place where any battell hath been fought, or the passages of Caesar or Charlemaine.

Quae tellus sit lenta gelu, qua putris ab aestu,
Ventus in Italiam quis bene vela ferat.
[Footnote: Prop. 1. iv. El. iii. 39.]

What land is parcht with heat, what clog'd with frost.
What wind drives kindly to th' Italian coast.

He shall endevour to be familiarly acquainted with the customes, with the meanes, with the state, with the dependances and alliances of all Princes; they are things soone and pleasant to be learned, and most profitable to be knowne. In this acquaintance of men, my intending is, that hee chiefely comprehend them, that live but by the memorie of bookes. He shall, by the help of Histories, in forme himselfe of the worthiest minds that were in the best ages. It is a frivolous studie, if a man list, but of unvaluable worth to such as can make use of it, and as Plato saith, the only studie the Lacedemonians reserved for themselves. What profit shall he not reap, touching this point, reading the lives of our Plutark? Always conditioned, the master bethinke himselfe whereto his charge tendeth, and that he imprint not so much in his schollers mind the date of the ruine of Carthage, as the manners of

Hanniball and Scipio, nor so much where Marcellus died, as because he was unworthy of his devoire [Footnote: Task.] he died there: that he teach him not so much to know Histories as to judge of them. It is amongst things that best agree with my humour, the subject to which our spirits doe most diversly applie themselves. I have read in Titus Livius a number of things, which peradventure others never read, in whom Plutarke haply read a hundred more than ever I could read, and which perhaps the author himselfe did never intend to set downe. To some kind of men it is a meere gramaticali studie, but to others a perfect anatomie [Footnote: Dissection, analytical exposition.] of Philosophie; by meanes whereof the secretest part of our nature is searched into. There are in Plutarke many ample discourses most worthy to be knowne: for in my judgement, he is the chiefe work– master of such works, whereof there are a thousand, whereat he hath but slightly glanced; for with his finger he doth but point us out a way to walke in, if we list; and is sometimes pleased to give but a touch at the quickest and maine point of a discourse, from whence they are by diligent studie to be drawne, and so brought into open market. As that saying of his, That the inhabitants of Asia served but one alone, because they could not pronounce one onely syllable, which is Non, gave perhaps both subject and occasion to my friend Boetie to compose his booke of voluntarie servitude. If it were no more but to see Plutarke wrest a slight action to mans life, or a word that seemeth to beare no such sence, it will serve for a whole discourse. It is pittie men of understanding should so much love brevitie; without doubt their reputation is thereby better, but we the worse. Plutarke had rather we should commend him for his judgement than for his knowledge, he loveth better to leave a kind of longing–desire in us of him, than a satietie. He knew verie well that even in good things too much may be said: and that Alexandridas did justly reprove him who spake verie good sentences to the Ephores, but they were over tedious. Oh stranger, quoth he, thou speakest what thou oughtest, otherwise then [Footnote: Than.] thou shouldest. Those that have leane and thin bodies stuffe them up with bumbasting. [Footnote: Padding.] And such as have but poore matter, will puffe it up with loftie words. There is a marvelous cleerenesse, or as I may terme it an enlightning of mans judgement drawne from the commerce of men, and by frequenting abroad in the world; we are all so contrived and compact in our selves, that our sight is made shorter by the length of our nose. When Socrates was demaunded whence he was, he answered, not of Athens, but of the world; for he, who had his imagination more full and farther stretching, embraced all the world for his native Citie, and extended his acquaintance, his societie, and affections to all man– kind: and not as we do, that looke no further than our feet. If the frost chance to nip the vines about my village, my Priest doth presently argue that the wrath of God hangs over our head, and threatneth all mankind: and judgeth that the Pippe [Footnote: A disease.] is alreadie falne upon the Canibals.

In viewing these intestine and civill broiles of ours, who doth not exclaime, that this worlds vast frame is neere unto a dissolution, and that the day of judgement is readie to fall on us? never remembering that many worse revolutions have been seene, and that whilest we are plunged in griefe, and overwhelmed in sorrow, a thousand other parts of the world besides are blessed with happinesse, and wallow in pleasures, and never thinke on us? whereas, when I behold our lives, our licence, and impunitie, I wonder to see them so milde and easie. He on whose head it haileth, thinks all the Hemispheare besides to be in a storme and tempest. And as that dull–pated Savoyard said, that if the seelie [Footnote 31: Simple.] King of France could cunningly have managed his fortune, he might verie well have made himselfe chiefe Steward of his Lords household, whose imagination conceived no other greatnesse than his Masters; we are all insensible of this kind of errour: an errour of great consequence and prejudice. But whosoever shall present unto his inward eyes, as it were in a Table,

29

the Idea of the great image of our universall mother Nature, attired in her richest robes, sitting in the throne of her Majestic, and in her visage shall read so generall and so constant a varietie; he that therein shall view himselfe, not himselfe alone, but a whole Kingdome, to be in respect of a great circle but the smallest point that can be imagined, he onely can value things according to their essentiall greatnesse and proportion. This great universe (which some multiplie as Species under one Genus) is the true looking–glasse wherein we must looke, if we will know whether we be of a good stamp or in the right byase. To conclude, I would have this worlds–frame to be my Schollers choise–booke. [Footnote: Book of examples] So many strange humours, sundrie sects, varying judgements, diverse opinions, different lawes, and fantasticall customes teach us to judge rightly of ours, and instruct our judgement to acknowledge his imperfections and naturall weaknesse, which is no easie an apprentiship: So many innovations of estates, so many fals of Princes, and changes of publike fortune, may and ought to teach us, not to make so great accompt of ours: So many names, so many victories, and so many conquests buried in darke oblivion, makes the hope to perpetuate our names but ridiculous, by the surprising of ten Argo–lettiers, [Footnote: Mounted Bowmen.] or of a small cottage, which is knowne but by his fall. The pride and fiercenesse of so many strange and gorgeous shewes: the pride–puft majestie of so many courts, and of their greatnesse, ought to confirme and assure our sight, undauntedly to beare the affronts and thunder–claps of ours, without feeling our eyes: So many thousands of men, lowlaide in their graves afore us, may encourage us not to feare, or be dismaied to go meet so good companie in the other world, and so of all things else. Our life (said Pithagoras) drawes neare unto the great and populous assemblies of the Olympike games, wherein some, to get the glorie and to win the goale of the games, exercise their bodies with all industrie; others, for greedinesse of gaine, bring thither marchandise to sell: others there are (and those be not the worst) that seek after no other good, but to marke how wherefore, and to what end, all things are done: and to be spectators or observers of other mens lives and actions, that so they may the better judge and direct their owne. Unto examples may all the most profitable Discourses of Philosophic be sorted, which ought to be the touch– stone of human actions, and a rule to square them by, to whom may be said,

——quid fas optare, quid asper
Vtile nummus habet, patriae charisque propinquis
Quantum elargiri deceat, quem te Deus esse
Iussit, et humana qua parte locaius es in re.
[Footnote: Pers. Sat. iii. 69.]
Quid sumus, aut quidnam victuri gignimur.
[Footnote: Ib. 67.]

What thou maiest wish, what profit may come cleare,
From new–stampt coyne, to friends and countrie deare
What thou ought'st give: whom God would have thee bee,
And in what part mongst men he placed thee.
What we are, and wherefore,
To live heer we were bore.

What it is to know, and not to know (which ought to be the scope of studie), what valour, what temperance, and what justice is: what difference there is betweene ambition and avarice, bondage and freedome, subjection and libertie, by which markes a man may distinguish true and perfect contentment, and how far–forth one ought to feare or apprehend death, griefe, or shame.

> Et quo quemque modo fugiatque. feratque laborem.
> [Footnote: Virg. Aen. 1. iii. 853.]

> How ev'ry labour he may plie,
> And beare, or ev'ry labour flie.

What wards or springs move us, and the causes of so many motions in us: For me seemeth, that the first discourses, wherewith his conceit should be sprinkled, ought to be those that rule his manners and direct his sense; which will both teach him to know himselfe, and how to live and how to die well. Among the liberall Sciences, let us begin with that which makes us free: Indeed, they may all, in some sort stead us, as an instruction to our life, and use of it, as all other things else serve the same to some purpose or other. But let us make especiall choice of that which may directly and pertinently serve the same. If we could restraine and adapt the appurtenances of our life to their right byase and naturall limits, we should find the best part of the Sciences that now are in use, cleane out of fashion with us: yea, and in those that are most in use, there are certaine by–wayes and deep–flows most profitable, which we should do well to leave, and according to the institution of Socrates, limit the course of our studies in those where profit is wanting.

> ——sapere aude,
> Incipe: vivendi qui recte prorogat horam,
> Rusticus expectat dum defluat amnis, at ille
> Labitur, et labetur in omne volubilis avum.
> [Footnote: Hor. I. i. Epist. ii. 40.]

> Be bold to be wise: to begin, be strong,
> He that to live well doth the time prolong,
> Clowne–like expects, till downe the streame be run,
> That runs, and will run, till the world be done.

It is mere simplicitie to teach our children,

> Quid moveant Pisces, animosaque signa Leonis,
> Lotus et Hesperia quid Capricornus aqua.
> [Footnote: Prop. I. El. i. 85.]
> What Pisces move, or hot breath'd Leos beames,
> Or Capricornus bath'd in western streames,

the knowledge of the starres, and the motion of the eighth spheare, before their owne;
> [Greek text quote omited]
> [Footnote: Anacr. Od. xvii. 10, 12.]

> What longs it to the seaven stars, and me,

31

Or those about Bootes be.

Anaximenes writing to Pythagoras, saith, "With what sense can I amuse my selfe in the secrets of the Starres, having continually death or bondage before mine eyes?" For at that time the Kings of Persia were making preparations to war against his Countrie. All men ought to say so: Being beaten with ambition, with avarice, with rashnesse, and with superstition, and having such other enemies unto life within him. Wherefore shall I study and take care about the mobility and variation of the world? When hee is once taught what is fit to make him better and wiser, he shall be entertained with Logicke, naturall Philosophy, Geometry, and Rhetoricke, then having setled his judgement, looke what science he doth most addict himselfe unto, he shall in short time attaine to the perfection of it. His lecture shall be somtimes by way of talke and sometimes by booke: his tutor may now and then supply him with the same Author, as an end and motive of his institution: sometimes giving him the pith and substance of it ready chewed. And if of himselfe he be not so throughly acquainted with bookes, that hee may readily find so many notable discourses as are in them to effect his purpose, it shall not be amisse that some learned man bee appointed to keepe him, company, who at any time of need may furnish him with such munition as hee shall stand in need of; that hee may afterward distribute and dispense them to his best use. And that this kind of lesson be more easie and naturall than that of Gaza, who will make question? Those are but harsh, thornie, and unpleasant precepts; vaine, idle and immaterial words, on which small hold may be taken; wherein is nothing to quicken the minde. In this the spirit findeth substance to bide and feed upon. A fruit without all comparison much better, and that will soone be ripe. It is a thing worthy consideration, to see what state things are brought unto in this our age; and how Philosophie, even to the wisest, and men of best understanding, is but an idle, vaine and fantasticall name, of small use and lesse worth, both in opinion and effect. I thinke these Sophistries are the cause of it, which have forestalled the wayes to come unto it: They doe very ill that goe about to make it seeme as it were inaccessible for children to come unto, setting it foorth with a wrimpled [Footnote: wrinkled.] gastlie, and frowning visage; who hath masked her with so counterfet, pale, and hideous a countenance? There is nothing more beauteous, nothing more delightful, nothing more gamesome; and as I may say, nothing more fondly wanton: for she presenteth nothing to our eyes, and preacheth nothing to our eares, but sport and pastime. A sad and lowring looke plainly declareth that that is not her haunt. Demetrius the Gramarian, finding a companie of Philosophers sitting close together in the Temple of Delphos, said unto them, "Either I am deceived, or by your plausible and pleasant lookes, you are not in any serious and earnest discourse amongst your selves;" to whom one of them, named Heracleon the Megarian, answered, "That belongeth to them, who busie themselves in seeking whether the future tense of the verbe , hath a double, or that labour to find the derivation of the comparatives, [omitted] and of the superlatives [omitted], it is they that must chafe in intertaining themselves with their science: as for discourses of Philosophie they are wont to glad, rejoyce, and not to vex and molest those that use them."

Deprendas animi tormenta latentis in agro
Corpore, deprendas et gaudia; sumit utrumque
Inde habitum facies.
[Footnote: Juven, SAT. ix, 18]

You may perceive the torments of the mind,
Hid in sicke bodie, you the joyes may find;

The face such habit takes in either kind.

That mind which harboureth Philosophie, ought by reason of her sound health, make that bodie also sound and healthie: it ought to make her contentment to through-shine in all exteriour parts: it ought to shapen and modell all outward demeanours to the modell of it: and by consequence arme him that doth possesse it, with a gracious stoutnesse and lively audacite, with an active and pleasing gesture, and with a setled and cheerefull countenance. The most evident token and apparant signe of true wisdome is a constant and unconstrained rejoycing, whose estate is like unto all things above the Moone, that is ever cleare, alwaies bright. It is Baroco [Footnote: Mnemonic words invented by the scholastic logicians] and Baralipton [Footnote: Mnemonic words invented by the scholastic logicians], that makes their followers prove so base and idle, and not Philosophie; they know her not but by heare-say; what? Is it not shee that cleereth all stormes of the mind? And teacheth miserie, famine, and sicknesse to laugh? Not by reason of some imaginarie Epicicles [Footnote: A term of the old astronomy.], but by naturall and palpable reasons. Shee aymeth at nothing but vertue; it is vertue shee seekes after; which as the schoole saith, is not pitcht on the top of an high, steepie, or inaccessible hill; for they that have come unto her, affirme that cleane-contrarie shee keeps her stand, and holds her mansion in a faire, flourishing, and pleasant plaine, whence as from an high watch tower, she survaieth all things, to be subject unto her, to whom any man may with great facilitie come, if he but know the way or entrance to her palace: for, the pathes that lead unto her are certaine fresh and shadie greene allies, sweet and flowrie waies, whose ascent is even, easie, and nothing wearisome, like unto that of heavens vaults. Forsomuch as they have not frequented this vertue, who gloriously, as in a throne of Majestie sits soveraigne, goodly, triumphant, lovely, equally delicious, and couragious, protesting her selfe to be a professed and irreconcileable enemie to all sharpnesse, austeritie, feare, and compulsion; having nature for her guide, fortune and voluptuousnesse for her companions; they according to their weaknesse have imaginarily fained her, to have a foolish, sad, grim, quarelous, spitefull, threatning, and disdainfull visage, with an horride and unpleasant looke; and have placed her upon a craggie, sharpe, and unfrequented rocke, amidst desert cliffes and uncouth crags, as a scar-crow, or bugbeare, to affright the common people with. Now the tutour, which ought to know that he should rather seek to fill the mind and store the will of his disciple, as much, or rather more, with love and affection, than with awe, and reverence unto vertue, may shew and tell him, that Poets follow common humours, making him plainly to perceive, and as it were palpably to feele, that the Gods have rather placed labour and sweat at the entrances which lead to Venus chambers, than at the doores that direct to Pallas cabinets.

And when he shall perceive his scholler to have a sensible feeling of himselfe, presenting Bradamant [Footnote: A warlike heroine in Boiardo's "Orlando Innamorato" and Ariosto's "Orlando Furioso."] or Angelica [Footnote: The faithless princess, on account of whom Orlando goes mad, in the same poems.] before him, as a Mistresse to enjoy, embelished with a naturall, active, generous, and unspotted beautie not uglie or Giant-like, but blithe and livelie, in respect of a wanton, soft, affected, and artificiall-flaring beautie; the one attired like unto a young man, coyfed with a bright-shining helmet, the other disguised and drest about the head like unto an impudent harlot, with embroyderies, frizelings, and carcanets of pearles: he will no doubt deeme his owne love to be a man and no woman, if in his choice he differ from that effeminate shepheard of Phrygia. In this new kind of lesson he shall declare unto him, that the prize, the glorie, and height of true vertue, consisted in the facilitie, profit, and pleasure of his exercises: so far from difficultie and incumbrances, that children as well as men, the simple as soone as the wise, may come unto her. Discretion and temperance, not force or way–wardnesse are the instruments to bring him unto her. Socrates (vertues chiefe favorite) that he might the better walke in the pleasant, naturall, and open path of her progresses, doth voluntarily and in good, earnest, quit all compulsion. Shee is the nurse and foster–mother of all humane [Footnote: Human.] pleasures, who in making them just and upright, she also makes them sure and sincere. By moderating them, she keepeth them in ure [Footnote: Practice.] and breath. In limiting and cutting them off, whom she refuseth; she whets us on toward those she leaveth unto us; and plenteously leaves us them, which Nature pleaseth, and like a kind mother giveth us over unto satietie, if not unto wearisomnesse, unlesse we will peradventure say that the rule and bridle, which stayeth the drunkard before drunkennesse, the glutton before surfetting, and the letcher before the losing of his haire, be the enemies of our pleasures. If common fortune faile her, it cleerely scapes her; or she cares not for her, or she frames another unto herselfe, altogether her owne, not so fleeting nor so rowling. She knoweth the way how to be rich, mightie and wise, and how to lie in sweet–perfumed beds. She loveth life; she delights in beautie, in glorie, and in health. But her proper and particular office is, first to know how to use such goods temperately, and how to lose them constantly. An office much more noble than severe, without which all course of life is unnaturall, turbulent, and deformed, to which one may lawfully joyne those rocks, those incumbrances, and those hideous monsters. If so it happen, that his Disciple prove of so different a condition, that he rather love to give eare to an idle fable than to the report of some noble voiage, or other notable and wise discourse, when he shall heare it; that at the sound of a Drum or clang of a Trumpet, which are wont to rowse and arme the youthly heat of his companions, turneth to another that calleth him to see a play, tumbling, jugling tricks, or other idle lose–time sports; and who for pleasures sake doth not deeme it more delightsome to returne all sweatie and wearie from a victorious combat, from wrestling, or riding of a horse, than from a Tennis–court or dancing schoole, with the prize or honour of such exercises; The best remedy I know for such a one is, to put him prentice to some base occupation, in some good towne or other, yea, were he the sonne of a Duke; according to Platoes rule, who saith "That children must be placed, not according to their fathers conditions, but the faculties of their mind." Since it is Philosophie that teacheth us to live, and that infancie as well as other ages, may plainly read her lessons in the same, why should it not be imparted unto young Schollers?

> Vdum et molle lutum est, nunc nunc properandus, et acri
> Fingendus sine fine rota.
> [Footnote: PES. Sat. iii. 23.]

> He's moist and soft mould, and must by and by
> Be cast, made up, while wheele whirls readily.

We are taught to live when our life is well–nigh spent. Many schollers have been infected with that loathsome and marrow–wasting disease before ever they came to read Aristotles treatise of Temperance. Cicero was wont to say, "That could he out–live the lives of two men, he should never find leasure to study the Lyrike Poets." And I find these Sophisters both worse and more unprofitable. Our childe is engaged in greater matters; And but the first fifteene or sixteene yeares of his life are due unto Pedantisme, the rest unto action: let us therefore imploy so short time as we have to live in more necessarie instructions. It is an abuse; remove these thornie quiddities of Logike, whereby our life can no whit be amended, and betake our selves to the simple discourses of Philosophy; know how to chuse and fitly to make use of them: they are much more easie to be conceived than one of Bocace his tales. A childe comming from nurse is more capable of them, than he is to learne to read or write. Philosophy hath discourses, whereof infancie as well as decaying old–age may make good use. I am of Plutarkes mind, which is, that Aristotle did not so much ammuse his great Disciple about the arts how to frame Syllogismes, or the principles of Geometric, as he endevoured to instruct him with good precepts concerning valour, prowesse, magnanimitie, and temperance, and an undanted assurance not to feare any thing; and with such munition he sent him, being yet verie young, to subdue the Empire of the world, only with 30000 footmen, 4000 horsemen, and 42000 Crownes in monie. As for other arts and sciences; he saith Alexander honoured them, and commended their excellencie and comlinesse; but for any pleasure he tooke in them, his affection could not easily be drawne to exercise them.

—petite hinc juvenesque senesque
Finem animo certum, miserisque viatica canis.
[Footnote: Sat. v. 64]

Young men and old, draw hence (in your affaires)
Your minds set marke, provision for gray haires.

It is that which Epicurus said in the beginning of his letter to Memiceus: "Neither let the youngest shun nor the oldest wearie himselfe in philosophying, for who doth otherwise seemeth to say, that either the season to live happily is not yet come, or is already past." Yet would I not have this young gentleman pent–up, nor carelesly cast–off to the heedlesse choler, or melancholy humour of the hasty Schoole–master. I would not have his budding spirit corrupted with keeping him fast–tied, and as it were labouring fourteene or fifteene houres a day poaring on his booke, as some doe, as if he were a day–labouring man; neither doe I thinke it fit, if at any time, by reason of some solitairie or melancholy complexion, he should be scene with an over–indiscreet application given to his booke, it should be cherished in him; for, that doth often make him both unapt for civill conversation and distracts him from better imployments: How many have I scene in my daies, by an over–greedy desire of knowledge, become as it were foolish? Carneades was so deeply plunged, and as I may say besotted in it, that he could never have leasure to cut his haire, or pare his nailes: nor would I have his noble manners obscured by the incivilitie and barbarisme of others. The French wisdome hath long since proverbially been spoken of as verie apt to conceive study in her youth, but most unapt to keepe it long. In good truth, we see at this day that there is nothing lovelier to behold than the young children of France; but for the most part, they deceive the hope which was fore–apprehended of them: for when they once become men, there is no excellencie at all in them. I have heard men of understanding hold this opinion, that the Colleges to which they are sent (of which there are store) doe thus besot them: whereas to our scholler, a cabinet, a gardin, the table, the bed, a solitarinesse, a companie, morning and evening, and all houres shall be alike unto him, all places shall be a study for him: for Philosophy (as a former of judgements, and modeler of customes) shall be his principall lesson, having the privilege to entermeddle her selfe with all things, and in all places. Isocrates the Orator, being once requested at a great banket to speake of his art, when all thought he had reason to answer, said, "It is not now time to doe what I can, and what should now be done, I cannot doe it; For, to present orations, or to enter into disputation of Rhetorike, before a companie assembled together to be merrie, and make good cheere, would be but a medley of harsh and jarring musicke." The like may

35

be said of all other Sciences. But touching Philosophy, namely, in that point where it treateth of man, and of his duties and offices, it hath been the common judgement of the wisest, that in regard of the pleasantnesse of her conversatione, she ought not to be rejected, neither at banquets nor at sports. And Plato having invited her to his solemne feast, we see how kindly she entertaineth the companie with a milde behaviour, fitly suting her selfe to time and place, notwithstanding it be one of his learned'st and profitable discourses.

AEque pauperibus prodest, locupletibus aque,
Et neglecta aeque pueris senibusque nocebit.
[Footnote: HOR. 1. i. Epist. 125.]

Poore men alike, alike rich men it easeth,
Alike it, scorned, old and young displeaseth.

So doubtlesse he shall lesse be idle than others; for even as the paces we bestow walking in a gallerie, although they be twice as many more, wearie us not so much as those we spend in going a set journey: So our lesson being past over, as it were, by chance, or way of encounter, without strict observance of time or place, being applied to all our actions, shall be digested, and never felt. All sports and exercises shall be a part of his study; running, wrestling, musicke, dancing, hunting, and managing of armes and horses. I would have the exterior demeanor or decencie, and the disposition of his person to be fashioned together with his mind: for, it is not a mind, it is not a body that we erect, but it is a man, and we must not make two parts of him. And as Plato saith, They must not be erected one without another, but equally be directed, no otherwise than a couple of horses matched to draw in one selfe–same teeme. And to heare him, doth he not seeme to imploy more time and care in the exercises of his bodie: and to thinke that the minde is together with the same exercised, and not the contrarie? As for other matters, this institution ought to be directed by a sweet– severe mildnesse; Not as some do, who in lieu of gently–bidding children to the banquet of letters, present them with nothing but horror and crueltie. Let me have this violence and compulsion removed, there is nothing that, in my seeming, doth more bastardise and dizzie a welborne and gentle nature: If you would have him stand in awe of shame and punishment, doe not so much enure him to it: accustome him patiently to endure sweat and cold, the sharpnesse of the wind, the heat of the sunne, and how to despise all hazards. Remove from him all nicenesse and quaintnesse in clothing, in lying, in eating, and in drinking: fashion him to all things, that he prove not a faire and wanton–puling boy, but a lustie and vigorous boy: When I was a child, being a man, and now am old, I have ever judged and believed the same. But amongst other things, I could never away with this kind of discipline used in most of our Colleges. It had peradventure been lesse hurtfull, if they had somewhat inclined to mildnesse, or gentle entreatie. It is a verie prison of captivated youth, and proves dissolute in punishing it before it be so. Come upon them when they are going to their lesson, and you heare nothing but whipping and brawling, both of children tormented, and masters besotted with anger and chafing. How wide are they, which go about to allure a childs mind to go to its booke, being yet but tender and fearefull, with a stearne–frowning countenance, and with hands full of rods? Oh wicked and pernicious manner of teaching! which Quintillian hath very wel noted, that this imperious kind of authoritie, namely, this way of punishing of children, drawes many dangerous inconveniences within. How much more decent were it to see their school–houses and formes strewed with greene boughs and flowers, than with bloudy burchen–twigs? If it lay in me, I would doe as the Philosopher Speusippus did, who caused the pictures of Gladness and Joy, of Flora and of the Graces, to be set up round about his school–house. Where their profit lieth, there should also be their recreation. Those meats ought to be sugred over, that are healthful for childrens stomakes, and those made bitter that are hurtfull for them. It is strange to see how carefull Plato sheweth him selfe in framing of his lawes about the recreation and pastime of the youth of his Citie, and how far he extends him selfe about their exercises, sports, songs, leaping, and dancing, whereof he saith, that severe antiquitie gave the conduct and patronage unto the Gods themselves, namely, to Apollo, to the Muses, and to Minerva. Marke but how far–forth he endevoreth to give a thousand precepts to be kept in his places of exercises both of bodie and mind. As for learned Sciences, he stands not much upon them, and seemeth in particular to commend Poesie, but for Musickes sake. All strangenesse and selfe–particularitie in our manners and conditions, is to be shunned, as an enemie to societie and civill conversation. Who would not be astonished at Demophons complexion, chiefe steward of Alexanders household, who was wont to sweat in the shadow, and quiver for cold in the sunne? I have seene some to startle at the smell of an apple more than at the shot of a peece; some to be frighted with a mouse, some readie to cast their gorge [Footnote: Vomit.] at the sight of a messe of creame, and others to be scared with seeing a fether bed shaken: as Germanicus, who could not abide to see a cock, or heare his crowing. There may haply be some hidden propertie of nature, which in my judgement might easilie be removed, if it were taken in time. Institution hath gotten this upon me (I must confesse with much adoe) for, except beere, all things else that are mans food agree indifferently with my taste. The bodie being yet souple, ought to be accommodated to all fashions and customes; and (alwaies provided, his appetites and desires be kept under) let a yong man boldly be made fit for al Nations and companies; yea, if need be, for al disorders and surfetings; let him acquaint him selfe with al fashions; That he may be able to do al things, and love to do none but those that are commendable. Some strict Philosophers commend not, but rather blame Calisthenes, for losing the good favour of his Master Alexander, only because he would not pledge him as much as he had drunke to him. He shall laugh, jest, dally, and debauch himselfe with his Prince. And in his debauching, I would have him out–go al his fellowes in vigor and constancie, and that he omit not to doe evill, neither for want of strength or knowledge, but for lacke of will. Multum interest utrum peccare quis nolit, aut nesciat: [Footnote: HOR. Epist. xvii. 23.] "There is a great difference, whether one have no will, or no wit to doe amisse." I thought to have honoured a gentleman (as great a stranger, and as far from such riotous disorders as any is in France) by enquiring of him in verie good companie, how many times in all his life he had bin drunke in Germanie during the time of his abode there, about the necessarie affaires of our King; who tooke it even as I meant it, and answered three times, telling the time and manner how. I know some, who for want of that qualitie, have been much perplexed when they have had occasion to converse with that nation. I have often noted with great admiration, that wonderfull nature of Alcibiades, to see how easilie he could sute himselfe to so divers fashions and different humors, without prejudice unto his health; sometimes exceeding the sumptuousnesse and pompe of the Persians, and now and then surpassing. the austeritie and frugalitie of the Lacedemonians; as reformed in Sparta, as voluptuous in Ionia.

Omnis Atistippum decuit color, et status, et res.
[Footnote: HOR. Epist. xvii. 25.]

All colours, states, and things are fit
For courtly Aristippus wit.

Such a one would I frame my Disciple,

—quem duplici panno patientia velat,
  Mirabor, vita via si conversa decebit.

Whom patience clothes with sutes of double kind,
I muse, if he another way will find.

Personavnque feret non inconcinnus utramque.
[Footnote: CIC. Tusc. Qu. 1. iv.]

He not unfitly may,
Both parts and persons play.

Loe here my lessons, wherein he that acteth them, profiteth more than he that but knoweth them, whom if you see, you heare, and if you heare him, you see him. God forbid, saith some bodie in Plato, that to Philosophize, be to learne many things, and to exercise the arts. Hanc amplissimam omnium artium bene vivendi disciplinam, vita magis quant litteris persequntd sunt [Footnote: Ib. 29.] "This discipline of living well, which is the amplest of all other arts, they followed rather in their lives than in their learning or writing." Leo Prince of the Phliasians, enquiring of Heraclides Ponticus, what art he professed, he answered, "Sir, I professe neither art nor science; but I am a Philosopher." Some reproved Diogenes, that being an ignorant man, he did neverthelesse meddle with Philosophie, to whom he replied, "So much the more reason have I and to greater purpose doe I meddle with it." Hegesias praid him upon a time to reade some booke unto him: "You are a merry man," said he: "As you chuse naturall and not painted, right and not counterfeit figges to eat, why doe you not likewise chuse, not the painted and written, but the true and naturall exercises?" He shall not so much repeat, as act his lesson. In his actions shall he make repetition of the same. We must observe, whether there bee wisdome in his enterprises, integritie in his demeanor, modestie in his jestures, justice in his actions, judgement and grace in his speech, courage in his sicknesse, moderation in his sports, temperance in his pleasures, order in the government of his house, and indifference in his taste, whether it be flesh, fish, wine, or water, or whatsoever he feedeth upon. Qui disciplinam suam non ostentationem scientiae sed legem vitae putet: quique obtemperet ipse sibi, et decretis pareat [Footnote: Ib. I. ii.] "Who thinks his learning not an ostentation of knowledge, but a law of life, and himselfe obayes himselfe, and doth what is decreed."

The true mirror of our discourses is the course of our lives. Zeuxidamus answered one that demanded of him, why the Lacedemonians did not draw into a booke, the ordinances of prowesse, that so their yong men might read them; "it is," saith he, "because they would rather accustome them to deeds and actions, than to bookes and writings." Compare at the end of fifteene or sixteene yeares one of these collegiall Latinizers, who hath imployed all that while onely in learning how to speake, to such a one as I meane. The world is nothing but babling and words, and I never saw man that doth not rather speake more than he ought, than lesse. Notwithstanding halfe our age is consumed that way. We are kept foure or five yeares learning to understand bare words, and to joine them into clauses, then as long in proportioning a great bodie extended into foure or five parts; and five more at least ere we can succinctly know how to mingle, joine, and interlace them handsomly into a subtil fashion, and into one coherent orbe. Let us leave it to those whose profession is to doe nothing else. Being once on my journey to Orleans, it was my chance to meet upon that plaine that lieth on this side Clery, with two Masters of Arts, traveling toward Bordeaux, about fiftie paces one from another; far off behind them, I describe a troupe of horsemen, their Master riding formost, who was the Earle of Rochefocault; one of my servants enquiring of the first of those Masters of Arts, what Gentleman he was that followed him; supposing my servant had meant his fellow—scholler, for he had not yet seen the Earles traine, answered pleasantly, "He is no gentleman, Sir, but a Gramarian, and I am a Logitian." Now, we that contrariwise seek not to frame a Gramarian, nor a Logitian, but a compleat gentleman, let us give them leave to mispend their time; we have else—where, and somewhat else of more import to doe. So that our Disciple be well and sufficiently stored with matter; words will follow apace, and if they will hot follow gently, he shall hale them on perforce. I heare some excuse themselves, that they cannot expresse their meaning, and make a semblance that their heads are so full stuft with many goodly things, but for want of eloquence they can neither titter nor make show of them. It is a meere fopperie. And will you know what, in my seeming, the cause is? They are shadows and Chimeraes, proceeding of some formelesse conceptions, which they cannot distinguish or resolve within, and by consequence are not able to produce them in as—much as they understand not themselves: And if you but marke their earnestnesse, and how they stammer and labour at the point of their deliverie, you would deeme that what they go withall, is but a conceiving, and therefore nothing neere downelying; and that they doe but licke that imperfect and shapelesse lump of matter. As for me, I am of opinion, and Socrates would have it so, that he who had a cleare and lively imagination in his mind, may easilie produce and utter the same, although it be in Bergamaske [Footnote: A rustic dialect of the north of Italy.] or Welsh, and if he be dumbe, by signes and tokens.

Verbaque praevisam rem non invita sequentur.
[Footnote: HOR. Art. Poet. 311.]

When matter we fore—know,
Words voluntarie flow.

As one said, as poetically in his prose, Cum res animum occupavere, verba ambiunt; [Footnote: SED. Controv. 1. vii. prae.] "When matter hath possest their minds, they hunt after words:" and another: Ipsa res verba rapiunt: [Footnote: CIC. de Fin. I. iii. c. 5.] "Things themselves will catch and carry words:" He knowes neither Ablative, Conjunctive, Substantive, nor Gramar, no more doth his Lackey, nor any Oyster—wife about the streets, and yet if you have a mind to it he will intertaine you, your fill, and peradventure stumble as little and as seldome against the rules of his tongue, as the best Master of arts in France. He hath no skill in Rhetoricke, nor can he with a preface fore—stall and captivate the Gentle Readers good will: nor careth he greatly to know it. In good sooth, all this garish painting is easilie defaced, by the lustre of an in—bred and simple truth; for these dainties and quaint devices serve but to ammuse the vulgar sort; unapt and incapable to taste the most solid and firme meat: as Afer verie plainly declareth in Cornelius Tacitus. The Ambassadours of Samos being come to Cleomenes King of Sparta, prepared with a long prolix Oration, to stir him up to war against the tyrant Policrates, after he had listned a good while unto them, his answer was: "Touching your Exordium or beginning I have forgotten it; the middle I remember not; and for your conclusion I will do nothing in it." A fit, and (to my thinking) a verie good answer; and the Orators were put to such a shift; as they knew not what to replie. And what said another? the Athenians from out two of their cunning Architects, were to chuse one to erect a notable great frame; the one of them more affected and selfe presuming, presented himselfe before them, with a smooth fore— premeditated discourse, about the subject of that piece of worke, and thereby drew the judgements of the common people unto his liking; but the other in few words spake thus: "Lords of Athens, what this man hath said I will performe." In the greatest earnestnesse of Ciceroes eloquence many were drawn into a kind of admiration; But Cato jesting at it, said, "Have we not a pleasant Consull?" A quicke cunning Argument, and a wittie saying, whether it go before or come after, it is never out of season. If it have no coherence with that which goeth before, nor with what commeth after; it is good and commendable in it selfe. I am none of those that think a good Ryme, to make a good Poeme; let him hardly (if so he please) make a short syllable long, it is no great matter; if the invention be rare and good, and his wit and judgement have cunningly played their part. I will say to such a one; he is a good Poet, but an ill Versifier.

> Emunciae naris, durus componere versus.
> [Footnote: HOR. 1. i. Sat. iv.]

> A man whose sense could finely pierce,
> But harsh and hard to make a verse.

Let a man (saith Horace) make his worke loose all seames, measures, and joynts.

> Tempora certa moddsque, et quod prius ordine verbum est,
> [Footnote: Ib. 58.]
> Posterius facias, praeponens ultima primis:
> Invenias etiam disjecti membra Poetae.
> [Footnote: Ib. 62.]

> Set times and moods, make you the first word last,
> The last word first, as if they were new cast:
> Yet find th' unjoynted Poets joints stand fast.

He shall for all that, nothing gain—say himselfe, every piece will make a good shew. To this purpose answered Menander those that chid him, the day being at hand, in which he had promised a Comedy, and had not begun the same, "Tut—tut," said he, "it is alreadie finished, there wanteth nothing but to adde the verse unto it;" for, having ranged and cast the plot in his mind, he made small accompt of feet, of measures, or cadences of verses, which indeed are but of small import in regard of the rest. Since great Ronsarde and learned Bellay have raised our French Poesie unto that height of honour where it now is: I see not one of these petty ballad—makers, or prentise dogrell rymers, that doth not bombast his labours with high—swelling and heaven—disimbowelling words, and that doth not marshall his cadences verie neere as they doe. Plus sonat quam valet. [Footnote: Sen, Epist. xl.] "The sound is more than the weight or worth." And for the vulgar sort there were never so many Poets, and so few good: but as it hath been easie for them to represent their rymes, so come they far short in imitating the rich descriptions of the one, and rare inventions of the other. But what shall he doe, if he be urged with sophisticall subtilties about a Sillogisme? A gammon of Bacon makes a man drink, drinking quencheth a mans thirst; Ergo, a gammon of bacon quencheth a mans thirst. Let him mock at it, it is more wittie to be mockt at than to be answered. Let him borrow this pleasant counter–craft of Aristippus; "Why shall I unbind that, which being bound doth so much trouble me?" Some one proposed certaine Logicall quiddities against Cleanthes, to whom Chrisippus said; use such jugling tricks to play with children, and divert not the serious thoughts of an aged man to such idle matters. If such foolish wiles, Contorta et aculeata sophismata, [Footnote: Cic. Acad. Qu. 1. iv.] "Intricate and stinged sophismes," must perswade a lie, it is dangerous: but if they proove void of any effect, and move him but to laughter, I see not why he shall beware of them. Some there are so foolish that will go a quarter of a mile out of the way to hunt after a quaint new word, if they once get in chace; Aut qui non verba rebus aptant, sed res extrinsecus arcessunt, quibus verba conveniant: "Or such as fit not words to matter, but fetch matter from abroad, whereto words be fitted." And another, Qui alicujus verbi decore placentis, vocentur ad id quod non proposuerant scribere: [Footnote: Sen. Epist. liii.] "Who are allured by the grace of some pleasing word, to write what they intended not to write." I doe more willingly winde up a wittie notable sentence, that so I may sew it upon me, than unwinde my thread to go fetch it. Contrariwise, it is for words to serve and wait upon the matter, and not for matter to attend upon words, and if the French tongue cannot reach unto it, let the Gaskonie, or any other. I would have the matters to surmount, and so fill the imagination of him that harkeneth, that he have no remembrance at all of the words. It is a naturall, simple, and unaffected speech that I love, so written as it is spoken, and such upon the paper, as it is in the mouth, a pithie, sinnowie, full, strong, compendious and materiall speech, not so delicate and affected as vehement and piercing.

Hac demum sapiet dictio qua feriet.
[Footnote: Epitaph on Lucan, 6.]

In fine, that word is wisely fit,
Which strikes the fence, the marke doth hit.

Rather difficult than tedious, void of affection, free, loose and bold, that every member of it seeme to make a bodie; not Pedanticall, nor Frier–like, nor Lawyer–like, but rather downe right, Souldier–like. As Suetonius calleth that of Julius Caesar, which I see no reason wherefore he calleth it. I have sometimes pleased myselfe in imitating that licenciousnesse or wanton humour of our youths, in wearing of their garments; as carelessly to let their cloaks hang downe over one shoulder; to weare their cloakes scarfe or bawdrikewise, and their stockings loose hanging about their legs. It represents a kind of disdainful fiercenesse of these forraine embellishings, and neglect carelesnesse of art: But I commend it more being imployed in the course and forme of speech. All manner of affectation, namely [Footnote: Especially,] in the livelinesse and libertie of France, is unseemely in a Courtier. And in a Monarchie every Gentleman ought to addresse himselfe unto [Footnote: Aim at] a Courtiers carriage. Therefore do we well somewhat to incline to a native and carelesse behaviour. I like not a contexture, where the seames and pieces may be seen: As in a well compact bodie, what need a man distinguish and number all the bones and veines severally? Quae veritati operam dat oratio, incomposita sit et simplex [Footnote: Sen. Epist. xl] Quis accurate loquitur nisi qui vult putide loqui [Footnote: Ib. Epist. ixxr.] "The speach that intendeth truth must be plaine and unpollisht: Who speaketh elaborately, but he that meanes to speake unfavourably?" That eloquence offereth injurie unto things, which altogether drawes us to observe it. As in apparell, it is a signe of pusillanimitie for one to marke himselfe, in some particular and unusuall fashion: so likewise in common speech, for one to hunt after new phrases, and unaccustomed quaint words, proceedeth of a scholasticall and childish ambition. Let me use none other than are spoken in the hals of Paris. Aristophanes the Gramarian was somewhat out of the way, when he reproved Epicurus, for the simplicitie of his words, and the end of his art oratorie, which was onely perspicuitie in speech. The imitation of speech, by reason of the facilitie of it, followeth presently a whole nation. The imitation of judging and inventing comes more slow. The greater number of Readers, because they have found one self−same kind of gowne, suppose most falsely to holde one like bodie. Outward garments and cloakes may be borrowed, but never the sinews and strength of the bodie. Most of those that converse with me, speake like unto these Essayes; but I know not whether they think alike. The Athenians (as Plato averreth) have for their part great care to be fluent and eloquent in their speech; The Lacedemonians endevour to be short and compendious; and those of Creet labour more to bee plentifull in conceits than in language. And these are the best. Zeno was wont to say, "That he had two sorts of disciples; the one he called [Greek word omitted], curious to learne things, and those were his darlings, the other he termed [Greek word omitted], who respected nothing more than the language." Yet can no man say, but that to speake well, is most gracious and commendable, but not so excellent as some make it: and I am grieved to see how we imploy most part of our time about that onely. I would first know mine owne tongue perfectly, then my neighbours with whom I have most commerce. I must needs acknowledge, that the Greeke and Latine tongues are great ornaments in a gentleman, but they are purchased at over−high a rate. Use it who list, I will tell you how they may be gotten better, cheaper, and much sooner than is ordinarily used, which was tried in myselfe. My late father, having, by all the meanes and industrie that is possible for a man, sought amongst the wisest, and men of best understanding, to find a most exquisite and readie way of teaching, being advised of the inconveniences then in use; was given to understand that the lingring while, and best part of our youth, that we imploy in learning the tongues, which cost them nothing, is the onely cause we can never attaine to that absolute perfection of skill and knowledge of the Greekes and Romanes. I doe not beleeve that to be the onely cause. But so it is, the expedient my father found out was this; that being yet at nurse, and before the first loosing of my tongue, I was delivered to a Germane (who died since, a most excellent Physitian in France) he being then altogether ignorant of the French tongue, but exquisitely readie and skilfull in the Latine. This man, whom my father had sent for of purpose, and to whom he gave verie great entertainment, had me continually in his armes, and was mine onely overseer. There were also joyned unto him two of his countrimen, but not so learned; whose charge was to attend, and now and then to play with me; and all these together did never entertaine me with other than the Latine tongue. As for others of his household, it was an inviolable rule, that neither himselfe, nor my mother, nor man, nor maid−servant, were suffered to speake one word in my companie, except such Latine words as every one had learned to chat and prattle with me. It were strange to tell how every one in the house profited therein. My Father and my Mother learned so much Latine, that for a need they could understand it, when they heard it spoken, even so did all the household servants, namely such as were neerest and most about me. To be short, we were all so Latinized, that the townes round about us had their share of it; insomuch as even at this day, many Latine names both of workmen and of their tooles are yet in use amongst them. And as for myselfe, I was about six years old, and could understand no more French or Perigordine than Arabike; and that without art, without bookes, rules, or grammer, without whipping or whining, I had gotten as pure a Latin tongue as my Master could speake; the rather because I could neither mingle or confound the same with other tongues. If for an Essay they would give me a Theme, whereas the fashion in Colleges is, to give it in French, I had it in bad Latine, to reduce the same into good. And Nicholas Grouchy, who hath written De comitiis Romanorum, William Guerente, who hath commented

Aristotele: George Buchanan, that famous Scottish Poet, and Marke Antonie Muret, whom (while he lived) both France and Italie to this day, acknowledge to have been the best orator: all which have beene my familiar tutors, have often told me, that in mine infancie I had the Latine tongue so readie and so perfect, that themselves feared to take me in hand. And Buchanan, who afterward I saw attending on the Marshall of Brissacke, told me, he was about to write a treatise of the institution of children, and that he tooke the model and patterne from mine: for at that time he had the charge and bringing up of the young Earle of Brissack, whom since we have scene prove so worthy and so valiant a Captaine. As for the Greeke, wherein I have but small understanding, my father purposed to make me learne it by art; But by new and uncustomed meanes, that is, by way of recreation and exercise. We did tosse our declinations and conjugations to and fro, as they doe, who by way of a certaine game at tables learne both Arithmetike and Geometrie. For, amongst other things he had especially beene persuaded to make me taste and apprehend the fruits of dutie and science by an unforced kinde of will, and of mine owne choice; and without any compulsion or rigor to bring me up in all mildnesse and libertie: yea with such kinde of superstition, that, whereas some are of opinion that suddenly to awaken young children, and as it were by violence to startle and fright them out of their dead sleepe in a morning (wherein they are more heavie and deeper plunged than we) doth greatly trouble and distemper their braines, he would every morning cause me to be awakened by the sound of some instrument; and I was never without a servant who to that purpose attended upon me. This example may serve to judge of the rest; as also to commend the judgement and tender affection of so carefull and loving a father: who is not to be blamed, though hee reaped not the fruits answerable to his exquisite toyle and painefull manuring. [Footnote: Cultivation.] Two things hindered the same; first the barrennesse and unfit soyle: for howbeit I were of a sound and strong constitution, and of a tractable and yeelding condition, yet was I so heavie, so sluggish, and so dull, that I could not be rouzed (yea were it to goe to play) from out mine idle drowzinesse. What I saw, I saw it perfectly; and under this heavy, and as it were Lethe–complexion did I breed hardie imaginations, and opinions farre above my yeares. My spirit was very slow, and would goe no further than it was led by others; my apprehension blockish, my invention poore; and besides, I had a marvelous defect in my weake memorie: it is therefore no wonder, if my father could never bring me to any perfection. Secondly, as those that in some dangerous sicknesse, moved with a kind of hope–full and greedie desire of perfect health againe, give eare to every Leach or Emperike, [Footnote: Doctor or quack.] and follow all counsels, the good man being exceedingly fearefull to commit any oversight, in a matter he tooke so to heart, suffered himselfe at last to be led away by the common opinion, which like unto the Cranes, followeth ever those that go before, and yeelded to customer having those no longer about him, that had given him his first directions, and which they had brought out of Italie. Being but six yeares old I was sent to the College of Guienne, then most flourishing and reputed the best in France, where it is impossible to adde any thing to the great care he had, both to chuse the best and most sufficient masters that could be found, to reade unto me, as also for all other circumstances partaining to my education; wherein contrary to usuall customes of Colleges, he observed many particular rules. But so it is, it was ever a College. My Latin tongue was forthwith corrupted, whereof by reason of discontinuance, I afterward lost all manner of use: which new kind of institution stood me in no other stead, but that at my first admittance it made me to overskip some of the lower formes, and to be placed in the highest. For at thirteene yeares of age, that I left the College, I had read over the whole course of Philosophie (as they call it) but with so small profit, that I can now make no account of it. The first taste or feeling I had of bookes, was of the pleasure I tooke in reading the fables of Ovids Metamorphosies; for, being but seven or eight yeares old, I would steale and sequester my selfe from all other delights, only to read them: Forsomuch as the tongue wherein they were written was to me naturall; and it was the easiest booke I knew, and by reason of the matter therein contained most agreeing with my young age. For of King Arthur, of Lancelot du Lake, of Amadis, of Huon of Burdeaux, and such idle time consuming and wit–besotting trash of bookes wherein youth doth commonly ammuse it selfe, I was not so much as acquainted with their names, and to this day know not their bodies, nor what they containe: So exact was my discipline. Whereby I became more carelesse to studie my other prescript lessons. And well did it fall out for my purpose, that I had to deale with a very discreet Master, who out of his judgement could with such dexterite winke at and second my untowardlinesse, and such other faults that were in me. For by that meanes I read over Virgils AEneados, Terence, Plautus, and other Italian Comedies, allured thereunto by the pleasantnesse of their severall subjects: Had he beene so foolishly– severe, or so severely froward as to crosse this course of mine, I thinke verily I had never brought any thing from the College, but the hate and contempt of Bookes, as doth the greatest part of our Nobilitie. Such was his discretion, and so warily did he behave himselfe, that he saw and would not see: hee would foster and increase my longing: suffering me but by stealth and by snatches to glut my selfe with those Bookes, holding ever a gentle hand over me, concerning other regular studies. For, the chiefest thing my father required at their hands (unto whose charge he had committed me) was a kinde of well conditioned mildnesse and facilitie of complexion. [Footnote: Easiness of disposition.] And, to say truth, mine had no other fault, but a certaine dull languishing and heavie slothfullnesse. The danger was not, I should doe ill, but that I should doe nothing.

No man did ever suspect I would prove a bad, but an unprofitable man: foreseeing in me rather a kind of idlenesse than a voluntary craftinesse. I am not so selfe–conceited but I perceive what hath followed. The complaints that are daily buzzed in mine eares are these; that I am idle, cold, and negligent in offices of friendship, and dutie to my parents and kinsfolkes; and touching publike offices, that I am over singular and disdainfull. And those that are most injurious cannot aske, wherefore I have taken, and why I have not paied? but may rather demand, why I doe not quit, and wherefore I doe not give? I would take it as a favour, they should wish such effects of supererogation in me. But they are unjust and over partiall, that will goe about to exact that from me which I owe not, with more vigour than they will exact from themselves that which they owe; wherein if they condemne me, they utterly cancell both the gratifying of the action, and the gratitude, which thereby would be due to me. Whereas the active well doing should be of more consequence, proceeding from my hand, in regard I have no passive at all. Wherefore I may so much the more freely dispose of my fortune, by how much more it is mine, and of my selfe that am most mine owne. Notwithstanding, if I were a great blazoner of mine owne actions, I might peradventure barre such reproches, and justly upraid some, that they are not so much offended, because I doe not enough, as for that I may, and it lies in my power to doe much more than I doe. Yet my minde ceased not at the same time to have peculiar unto it selfe well setled motions, true and open judgements concerning the objects which it knew; which alone, and without any helpe or communication it would digest. And amongst other things, I verily beleeve it would have proved altogether incapable and unfit to yeeld unto force, or stoope unto violence. Shall I account or relate this qualitie of my infancie, which was, a kinde of boldnesse in my lookes, and gentle softnesse in my voice, and affabilitie in my gestures, and a dexterite in conforming my selfe to the parts I undertooke? for before the age of the

Alter ab undecimo turn me vix ceperat annus.

[Footnote: Virg. Buc. Ecl. viii. 39.]

Yeares had I (to make even)
Scarce two above eleven.

I have under–gone and represented the chiefest part in the Latin Tragedies of Buchanan, Guerente, and of Muret; which in great state were acted and plaid in our College of Guienne: wherein Andreas Goveanus our Rector principall; who as in all other parts belonging to his charge, was without comparison the chiefest Rector of France, and my selfe (without ostentation be it spoken) was reputed, if not a chiefe–master, yet a principall Actor in them. It is an exercise I rather commend than disalow in young Gentlemen: and have seene some of our Princes (in imitation of some of former ages) both commendably and honestly, in their proper persons act and play some parts in Tragedies. It hath heretofore been esteemed a lawfull exercise, and a tolerable profession in men of honor, namely in Greece. Aristoni tragico actori rem aperit: huic et genus et fortuna honesta erant: nec ars, quia nihil tale apud Graecos pudori est, ea deformabat. [Footnote: Liv. Deo. iii. 1. iv.] "He imparts the matter to Ariston a Player of tragedies, whose progenie and fortune were both honest; nor did his profession disgrace them, because no such matter is a disparagement amongst the Grecians."

And I have ever accused them of impertinencie, that condemne and disalow such kindes of recreations, and blame those of injustice, that refuse good and honest Comedians, or (as we call them) Players, to enter our good townes, and grudge the common people such publike sports. Politike and wel ordered commonwealths endevour rather carefully to unite and assemble their Citizens together; as in serious offices of devotion, so in honest exercises of recreation. Common societie and loving friendship is thereby cherished and increased. And besides, they cannot have more formal and regular pastimes allowed them, than such as are acted and represented in open view of all, and in the presence of the magistrates themselves; And if I might beare sway, I would thinke it reasonable, that Princes should sometimes, at their proper charges, gratifie the common people with them, as an argument of a fatherly affection, and loving goodnesse towards them: and that in populous and frequented cities, there should be Theatres and places appointed for such spectacles; as a diverting of worse inconveniences, and secret actions. But to come to my intended purpose there is no better way to allure the affection, and to entice the appetite: otherwise a man shall breed but asses laden with Bookes. With jerks of rods they have their satchels full of learning given them to keepe. Which to doe well, one must not only harbor in himselfe, but wed and marry the same with his minde.

OF FRIENDSHIP

Considering the proceeding of a Painters worke I have, a desire hath possessed mee to imitate him: He maketh choice of the most convenient place and middle of everie wall, there to place a picture, laboured with all his skill and sufficiencie; and all void places about it he filleth up with antike Boscage [Footnote: Foliated ornament] or Crotesko [Footnote: Grotesque] works; which are fantasticall pictures, having no grace, but in the variety and strangenesse of them. And what are these my compositions in truth, other than antike workes, and monstrous bodies, patched and hudled up together of divers members, without any certaine or well ordered figure, having neither order, dependencie, or proportion, but casuall and framed by chance?

Definit in piscem mulier formosa superne.
[Footnote: Hon. Art. Poet. 4.]

A woman faire for parts superior,
Ends in a fish for parts inferior.

Touching this second point I goe as farre as my Painter, but for the other and better part I am farre behinde: for my sufficiency reacheth not so farre as that I dare undertake a rich, a polished, and, according to true skill, an art–like table. I have advised myselfe to borrow one of Steven de la Boetie, who with this kinde of worke shall honour all the world. It is a discourse he entitled Voluntary Servitude, but those who have not knowne him, have since very properly rebaptized the same, The Against–one. In his first youth he writ, by way of Essaie, in honour of libertie against Tyrants. It hath long since beene dispersed amongst men of understanding, not without great and well deserved commendations: for it is full of wit, and containeth as much learning as may be: yet doth it differ much from the best he can do. And if in the age I knew him in, he would have undergone my dessigne to set his fantasies downe in writing, we should doubtlesse see many rare things, and which would very neerely approch the honour of antiquity: for especially touching that part of natures gifts, I know none may be compared to him. But it was not long of him, that ever this Treatise came to mans view, and I beleeve he never saw it since it first escaped his hands: with certaine other notes concerning the edict of Januarie, famous by reason of our intestine warre, which haply may in other places finde their deserved praise. It is all I could ever recover of his reliques (whom when death seized, he by his last will and testament, left with so kinde remembrance, heire and executor of his librarie and writings) besides the little booke, I since caused to be published: To which his pamphlet I am particularly most bounden, for so much as it was the instrumentall meane of our first acquaintance. For it was shewed me long time before I saw him; and gave me the first knowledge of his name, addressing, and thus nourishing that unspotted friendship which we (so long as it pleased God) have so sincerely, so entire and inviolably maintained betweene us, that truly a man shall not commonly heare of the like; and amongst our moderne men no signe of any such is scene. So many parts are required to the erecting of such a one, that it may be counted a wonder if fortune once in three ages contract the like. There is nothing to which Nature hath more addressed us than to societie. And Aristotle saith that perfect Law– givers have had more regardfull care of friendship than of justice. And the utmost drift of its perfection is this. For generally, all those amities which are forged and nourished by voluptuousnesse or profit, publike or private need, are thereby so much the lesse faire and generous, and so much the lesse true amities, in that they intermeddle other causes, scope, and fruit with friendship, than it selfe alone: Nor doe those foure ancient kindes of friendships, Naturall, sociall, hospitable, and venerian, either particularly or conjointly beseeme the same. That from children to parents may rather be termed respect: Friendship is nourished by communication, which by reason of the over–great disparitie cannot bee found in them, and would happly offend the duties of nature: for neither all the secret thoughts of parents can be communicated unto children, lest it might engender an unbeseeming familiaritie betweene them, nor the admonitions and corrections (which are the chiefest offices of friendship) could be exercised from children to parents. There have nations beene found, where, by custome, children killed their parents, and others where parents slew their children, thereby to avoid the hindrance of enterbearing [Footnote: Mutually supporting.] one another in after–times: for naturally one dependeth from the ruine of another. There have Philosophers beene found disdaining this naturall conjunction: witnesse Aristippus, who being urged

46

with the affection he ought [Footnote: Owed.] his children, as proceeding from his loyns, began to spit, saying, That also that excrement proceeded from him, and that also we engendred wormes and lice. And that other man, whom Plutarke would have perswaded to agree with his brother, answered, "I care not a straw the more for him, though he came out of the same wombe I did." Verily the name of Brother is a glorious name, and full of loving kindnesse, and therefore did he and I terme one another sworne brother: but this commixture, dividence, and sharing of goods, this joyning wealth to wealth, and that the riches of one shall be the povertie of another, doth exceedingly distemper and distract all brotherly alliance, and lovely conjunction: If brothers should conduct the progresse of their advancement and thrift in one same path and course, they must necessarily oftentimes hinder and crosse one another. Moreover, the correspondencie and relation that begetteth these true and mutually perfect amities, why shall it be found in these? The father and the sonne may very well be of a farre differing complexion, and so many brothers: He is my sonne, he is my kinsman; but he may be a foole, a bad, or a peevish–minded man. And then according as they are friendships which the law and dutie of nature doth command us, so much the lesse of our owne voluntarie choice and libertie is there required unto it: And our genuine libertie hath no production more properly her owne, than that of affection and amitie. Sure I am, that concerning the same I have assaied all that might be, having had the best and most indulgent father that ever was, even to his extremest age, and who from father to sonne was descended of a famous house, and touching this rare–seene vertue of brotherly concord very exemplare:

——et ipse
Notus in fratres animi paterni.
[Footnote: Hor. 1. ii. Qd. li. 6.]

To his brothers knowne so kinde.
As to beare a fathers minde.

To compare the affection toward women unto it, although it proceed from our owne free choice, a man cannot, nor may it be placed in this ranke: Her fire, I confesse it to be more

(——neque enim est dea nescia nostri
Quae dulcem curis miscet amaritiem.)
[Footnote: Catul. Epig. lxvi.]

(Nor is that Goddesse ignorant of me,
Whose bitter–sweets with my cares mixed be.)

active, more fervent, and more sharpe. But it is a rash and wavering fire, waving and divers: the fire of an ague subject to fits and stints, and that hath but slender hold–fast of us. In true friendship, it is a generall and universall heat, and equally tempered, a constant and setled heat, all pleasure and smoothnes, that hath no pricking or stinging in it, which the more it is in lustfull love, the more is it but a raging and mad desire in following that which flies us,

Come segue la lepre il cacciatore
Alfreddo, al caldo, alia montagna, a lito,

Ne pin l'estima poi che presa vede,
E sol dietro a chi fugge affretta il piede.
[Footnote: Ariost. can. x. st. 7.]

Ev'n as the huntsman doth the hare pursue,
In cold, in heat, on mountaines, on the shore,
But cares no more, when he her ta'en espies
Speeding his pace only at that which flies.

As soone as it creepeth into the termes of friendship, that is to say, in the agreement of wits, it languisheth and vanisheth away: enjoying doth lose it, as having a corporall end, and subject to satietie. On the other side, friendship is enjoyed according as it is desired, it is neither bred, nourished, nor increaseth but in jovissance, as being spirituall, and the minde being refined by use custome. Under this chiefe amitie, these fading affections have sometimes found place in me, lest I should speake of him, who in his verses speakes but too much of it. So are these two passions entered into me in knowledge one of another, but in comparison never: the first flying a high, and keeping a proud pitch, disdainfully beholding the other to passe her points farre under it. Concerning marriage, besides that it is a covenant which hath nothing free but the entrance, the continuance being forced and constrained, depending else–where than from our will, and a match ordinarily concluded to other ends: A thousand strange knots are therein commonly to be unknit, able to break the web, and trouble the whole course of a lively affection; whereas in friendship there is no commerce or busines depending on the same, but it selfe. Seeing (to speake truly) that the ordinary sufficiency of women cannot answer this conference and communication, the nurse of this sacred bond: nor seeme their mindes strong enough to endure the pulling of a knot so hard, so fast, and durable. And truly, if without that, such a genuine and voluntarie acquaintance might be contracted, where not only mindes had this entire jovissance, [Footnote: Enjoyment.] but also bodies, a share of the alliance, and where a man might wholly be engaged: It is certaine, that friendship would thereby be more compleat and full: But this sex could never yet by any example attaine unto it, and is by ancient schooles rejected thence. And this other Greeke licence is justly abhorred by our customes, which notwithstanding, because according to use it had so necessarie a disparitie of ages, and difference of offices betweene lovers, did no more sufficiently answer the perfect union and agreement, which here we require: Quis est enim iste amor amicitiae? cur neque deformem adolescentem quisquam amat, neque formosum senem? [Footnote: Cic. Tusc. Qu. lv. c. 33.] "For, what love is this of friendship? why doth no man love either a deformed young man, or a beautifull old man?" For even the picture the Academic makes of it, will not (as I suppose) disavowe mee, to say thus in her behalfe: That the first furie, enspired by the son of Venus in the lovers hart, upon the object of tender youths–flower, to which they allow all insolent and passionate violences, an immoderate heat may produce, was simply grounded upon an externall beauty; a false image of corporall generation: for in the spirit it had no power, the sight whereof was yet concealed, which was but in his infancie, and before the age of budding. For, if this furie did seize upon a base minded courage, the meanes of its pursuit were riches, gifts, favour to the advancement of dignities, and such like vile merchandice, which they reprove. If it fell into a more generous minde, the interpositions [Footnote: Means of approach.] were likewise generous: Philosophicall instructions, documents [Footnote: Teachings.] to reverence religion, to obey the lawes, to die for the good of his countrie: examples of valor, wisdome and justice; the lover endevoring and studying to make himselfe acceptable by the good grace and beauty of his minde (that of his body being long since decayed) hoping by this mentall society to establish a more firme and permanent bargaine. When this pursuit attained the effect in due season (for by not requiring in a lover, he should bring leasure and discretion in his enterprise, they require it exactly in the beloved; forasmuch as he was to judge of an internall beauty, of difficile knowledge, and abstruse discovery) then by the interposition of a spiritual beauty was the desire of a spiritual conception engendred in the beloved. The latter was here chiefest; the corporall, accidentall and second, altogether contrarie to the lover. And therefore doe they preferre the beloved, and verifie that the gods likewise preferre the same: and greatly blame the Poet AEschylus, who in the love betweene Achilles and Patroclus ascribeth the lovers part unto Achilles, who was in the first and beardlesse youth of his adolescency, and the fairest of the Graecians. After this general communitie, the mistris and worthiest part of it, predominant and exercising her offices (they say the most availefull commodity did thereby redound both to the private and publike). That it was the force of countries received the use of it, and the principall defence of equitie and libertie: witnesse the comfortable loves of Hermodius and Aristogiton. Therefore name they it sacred and divine, and it concerns not them whether the violence of tyrants, or the demisnesse of the people be against them: To conclude, all that can be alleged in favour of the Academy, is to say, that it was a love ending in friendship, a thing which hath no bad reference unto the Stoical definition of love: Amorem conatum esse amicitiae faciendae ex pulchritudinis specie: [Footnote: Cic. Tusc. Qu. ir. c. 34.] "That love is an endevour of making friendship, by the shew of beautie." I returne to my description in a more equitable and equall manner. Omnino amicitiae, corroboratis jam confirmatisque ingeniis et aetatibus, judicandae sunt. [Footnote: Cic. Amic.] "Clearly friendships are to be judged by wits, and ages already strengthened and confirmed." As for the rest, those we ordinarily call friendes and amities, are but acquaintances and familiarities, tied together by some occasion or commodities, by meanes whereof our mindes are entertained. In the amitie I speake of, they entermixe and confound themselves one in the other, with so universall a commixture, that they weare out and can no more finde the seame that hath conjoined them together. If a man urge me to tell wherefore I loved him, I feele it cannot be expressed, but by answering; Because it was he, because it was my selfe. There is beyond all my discourse, and besides what I can particularly report of it, I know not what inexplicable and fatall power, a meane and Mediatrix of this indissoluble union. We sought one another before we had scene one another, and by the reports we heard one of another; which wrought a greater violence in us, than the reason of reports may well beare; I thinke by some secret ordinance of the heavens, we embraced one another by our names. And at our first meeting, which was by chance at a great feast, and solemne meeting of a whole towneship, we found our selves so surprized, so knowne, so acquainted, and so combinedly bound together, that from thence forward, nothing was so neer unto us as one unto anothers. He writ an excellent Latyne Satyre since published; by which he excuseth and expoundeth the precipitation of our acquaintance, so suddenly come to her perfection; Sithence it must continue so short a time, and begun so late (for we were both growne men, and he some yeares older than my selfe) there was no time to be lost. And it was not to bee modelled or directed by the paterne of regular and remisse [Footnote: Slight, languid.] friendship, wherein so many precautions of a long and preallable conversation [Footnote: Preceding intercourse.] are required. This hath no other Idea than of it selfe, and can have no reference but to itselfe. It is not one especiall consideration, nor two, nor three, nor foure, nor a thousand: It is I wot not what kinde of quintessence, of all this commixture, which having seized all my will, induced the same to plunge and lose it selfe in his, which likewise having seized all his will, brought it to lose and plunge it selfe in mine, with a mutuall greedinesse, and with a semblable concurrance. I may truly say, lose, reserving nothing unto us, that might properly be called our owne, nor that was either his or mine. When Lelius in the presence of the Romane Consuls, who after the condemnation of Tiberius Gracchus, pursued all those that had beene of his acquaintance, came to enquire of Caius Blosius (who was one of his chiefest friends) what he would have done for him, and that he answered, "All things." "What, all things?" replied he. "And what if he had willed thee to burne our Temples?" Blosius answered, "He would never have commanded such a thing." "But what if he had done it?" replied Lelius. The other answered, "I would have obeyed him." If hee were so perfect a friend to Gracchus as Histories report, he needed not offend the Consuls with this last and bold confession, and should not have departed from the assurance hee had of Gracchus his minde. But yet those who accuse this answer as seditious, understand not well this mysterie: and doe not presuppose in what termes he stood, and that he held Gracchus his will in his sleeve, both by power and knowledge. They were rather friends than Citizens, rather friends than enemies of their countrey, or friends of ambition and trouble. Having absolutely committed themselves one to another, they perfectly held the reines of one anothers inclination: and let this yoke be guided by vertue and conduct of reason (because without them it is altogether impossible to combine and proportion the same). The answer of Blosius was such as it should be. If their affections miscarried, according to my meaning, they were neither friends one to other, nor friends to themselves. As for the rest, this answer sounds no more than mine would doe, to him that would in such sort enquire of me; if your will should command you to kill your daughter, would you doe it? and that I should consent unto it: for, that beareth no witnesse of consent to doe it: because I am not in doubt of my will, and as little of such a friends will. It is not in the power of the worlds discourse to remove me from the certaintie I have of his intentions and judgments of mine: no one of its actions might be presented unto me, under what shape soever, but I would presently finde the spring and motion of it. Our mindes have jumped [Footnote: Agreed.] so unitedly together, they have with so fervent an affection considered of each other, and with like affection so discovered and sounded, even to the very bottome of each others heart and entrails, that I did not only know his, as well as mine owne, but I would (verily) rather have trusted him concerning any matter of mine, than my selfe. Let no man compare any of the other common friendships to this. I have as much knowledge of them as another, yea of the perfectest of their kinde: yet wil I not perswade any man to confound their rules, for so a man might be deceived. In these other strict friendships a man must march with the bridle of wisdome and precaution in his hand: the bond is not so strictly tied but a man may in some sort distrust the same. Love him (said Chilon) as if you should one day hate him againe. Hate him as if you should love him againe. This precept, so abhominable in this soveraigne and mistris Amitie, is necessarie and wholesome in the use of vulgar and customarie friendships: toward which a man must employ the saying Aristotle was wont so often repeat, "Oh you my friends, there is no perfect friend."

In this noble commerce, offices and benefits (nurses of other amities) deserve not so much as to bee accounted of: this confusion so full of our wills is cause of it: for even as the friendship I beare unto my selfe, admits no accrease, [Footnote: Increase.] by any succour I give my selfe in any time of need, whatsoever the Stoickes allege; and as I acknowledge no thanks unto my selfe for any service I doe unto myselfe, so the union of such friends, being truly perfect, makes them lose the feeling of such duties, and hate, and expell from one another these words of division, and difference: benefit, good deed, dutie, obligation, acknowledgement, prayer, thanks, and such their like. All things being by effect common betweene them; wils, thoughts, judgements, goods, wives, children, honour, and life; and their mutual agreement, being no other than one soule in two bodies, according to the fit definition of Aristotle, they can neither lend or give ought to each other. See here the reason why

Lawmakers, to honour marriage with some imaginary resemblance of this divine bond, inhibite donations between husband and wife; meaning thereby to inferre, that all things should peculiarly bee proper to each of them, and that they have nothing to divide and share together. If in the friendship whereof I speake, one might give unto another, the receiver of the benefit should binde his fellow. For, each seeking more than any other thing to doe each other good, he who yeelds both matter and occasion, is the man sheweth himselfe liberall, giving his friend that contentment, to effect towards him what he desireth most. When the Philosopher Diogenes wanted money, he was wont to say that he redemanded the same of his friends, and not that he demanded it: And to show how that is practised by effect, I will relate an ancient singular example. Eudamidas the Corinthiam had two friends: Charixenus a Sycionian, and Aretheus a Corinthian; being upon his death–bed, and very poore, and his two friends very rich, thus made his last will and testament: "To Aretheus, I bequeath the keeping of my mother, and to maintaine her when she shall be old: To Charixenus the marrying of my daughter, and to give her as great a dowry as he may: and in case one of them shall chance to die before, I appoint the survivor to substitute his charge, and supply his place." Those that first saw this testament laughed and mocked at the same; but his heires being advertised thereof, were very well pleased, and received it with singular contentment. And Charixenus, one of them, dying five daies after Eudamidas, the substitution being declared in favour of Aretheus, he carefully and very kindly kept and maintained his mother, and of five talents that he was worth he gave two and a halfe in marriage to one only daughter he had, and the other two and a halfe to the daughter of Eudamidas, whom he married both in one day. This example is very ample, if one thing were not, which is the multitude of friends: For, this perfect amity I speake of, is indivisible; each man doth so wholly give himselfe unto his friend, that he hath nothing left him to divide else–where: moreover he is grieved that he is not double, triple, or quadruple, and hath not many soules, or sundry wils, that he might conferre them all upon this subject. Common friendships may bee divided; a man may love beauty in one, facility of behaviour in another, liberality in one, and wisdome in another, paternity in this, fraternity in that man, and so forth: but this amitie which possesseth the soule, and swaies it in all sovereigntie, it is impossible it should be double. If two at one instant should require helpe, to which would you run? Should they crave contrary offices of you, what order would you follow? Should one commit a matter to your silence, which if the other knew would greatly profit him, what course would you take? Or how would you discharge your selfe? A singular and principall friendship dissolveth all other duties, and freeth all other obligations. The secret I have sworne not to reveale to another, I may without perjurie impart it unto him, who is no other but my selfe. It is a great and strange wonder for a man to double himselfe; and those that talke of tripling know not, nor cannot reach into the height of it. "Nothing is extreme that hath his like." And he who shal presuppose that of two I love the one as wel as the other, and that they enter–love [Footnote: Love mutually.] one another, and love me as much as I love them: he multiplied! in brotherhood, a thing most singular, and a lonely one, and than which one alone is also the rarest to be found in the world. The remainder of this history agreeth very wel with what I said; for, Eudamidas giveth us a grace and favor to his friends to employ them in his need: he leaveth them as his heires of his liberality, which consisteth in putting the meanes into their hands to doe him good. And doubtlesse the force of friendship is much more richly shewen in his deed than in Aretheus. To conclude, they are imaginable effects to him that hath not tasted them; and which makes me wonderfully to honor the answer of that young Souldier to Cyrus, who enquiring of him what he would take for a horse with which he had lately gained the prize of a race, and whether he would change him for a Kingdome? "No surely, my Liege (said he), yet would I willingly forgot him to game a true friend, could I but finde a man worthy of so precious an alliance." He said not ill, in saying "could I but finde." For, a man shall easily finde men fit for a superficiall acquaintance; but in this, wherein men negotiate from the very centre of their harts, and make no spare of any thing, it is most requisite all the wards and springs be sincerely wrought and perfectly true. In confederacies, which hold but by one end, men have nothing to provide for, but for the imperfections, which particularly doe interest and concerne that end and respect. It is no great matter what religion my Physician or Lawyer is of: this consideration hath nothing common with the offices of that friendship they owe mee. So doe I in the familiar acquaintances that those who serve me contract with me. I am nothing inquisitive whether a Lackey be chaste or no, but whether he be diligent: I feare not a gaming Muletier, so much as if he be weake: nor a hot swearing Cooke, as one that is ignorant and unskilfull; I never meddle with saying what a man should doe in the world; there are over many others that doe it; but what my selfe doe in the world.

Mihi sic usus est: Tibi, ut opus est facto, face
[Footnote: Ter. Heau. act. i. sc. i, 28.]

So is it requisite for me:
Doe thou as needfull is for thee.

Concerning familiar table–talke, I rather acquaint my selfe with and follow a merry conceited [Footnote: Fanciful] humour, than a wise man: And in bed I rather prefer beauty than goodnesse; and in society or conversation of familiar discourse, I respect rather sufficiency, though without Preud'hommie, [Footnote: Probity.] and so of all things else. Even as he that was found riding upon an hobby–horse, playing with his children besought him who thus surprized him not to speake of it untill he were a father himselfe, supposing the tender fondnesse and fatherly passion which then would posesse his minde should make him an impartiall judge of such an action; so would I wish to speake to such as had tried what I speake of: but knowing how far such an amitie is from the common use, and how seld scene and rarely found, I looke not to finde a competent judge. For, even the discourses, which sterne antiquitie hath left us concerning this subject, seeme to me but faint and forcelesse in respect of the feeling I have of it; And in that point the effects exceed the very precepts of Philosophie.

Nil ego contulerim jucundo sanus amico.
[Footnote: Hor. 1. i. Sat. vii. 44]

For me, be I well in my wit,
Nought, as a merry friend, so fit.

Ancient Menander accounted him happy that had but met the shadow of a true friend: verily he had reason to say so, especially if he had tasted of any: for truly, if I compare all the rest of my forepassed life, which although I have, by the meere mercy of God, past at rest and ease, and except the losse of so deare a friend, free from all grievous affliction, with an ever–quietnesse of minde, as one that have taken my naturall and originall commodities in good payment, without searching any others: if, as I say, I compare it all unto the foure yeares I so happily enjoied the sweet company and deare– deare society of that worthy man, it is nought but a vapour, nought but a darke and yrkesome light. Since the time I lost him,

quem semper acerbum,
Semper honoratum (sic Dii voluistis) habebo,
[Footnote: Virg. AEn. iii. 49.]

Which I shall ever hold a bitter day,
Yet ever honour'd (so my God t' obey),

I doe but languish, I doe but sorrow: and even those pleasures, all things present me with, in stead of yeelding me comfort, doe but redouble the griefe of his losse. We were copartners in all things. All things were with us at halfe; me thinkes I have stolne his part from him.

—Nee fas esse iilla me voluptate hic frui
Decrevi, tantisper dum ille abest meus particeps.
[Footnote: Ter. Heau. act. i. sc. i, 97.]

I have set downe, no joy enjoy I may,
As long as he my partner is away.

I was so accustomed to be ever two, and so enured [Footnote: Accustomed] to be never single, that me thinks I am but halfe my selfe.

Illam mea si partem animce tulit,
Maturior vis, quid moror altera.
Nec charus aeque nec superstes,
Integer? Ille dies utramque
Duxit ruinam.
[Footnote: Hor. 1. ii. Od. xvii.]

Since that part of my soule riper fate reft me,
Why stay I heere the other part he left me?
Nor so deere, nor entire, while heere I rest:
That day hath in one mine both opprest.

There is no action can betide me, or imagination possesse me, but I heare him saying, as indeed he would have done to me: for even as he did excell me by an infinite distance in all other sufficiencies and vertues, so did he in all offices and duties of friendship.

Quis desiderio sit pudor aut modus,
Tam chari capitis?
[Footnote: Id. 1. i. Od. xxiv.]

What modesty or measure may I beare,
In want and wish of him that was so deare?

O misero frater adempte mihi!

Omnia tecum una perieruni gaudia nostra.
Qua tuus in vita dulcis alebat amor.
[Footnote: CATUL. Eleg. iv. 20, 92, 26, 95.]
Tu mea, tu moriens fregisti commoda frater.
[Footnote: Ib. 21.]
Tecum una tota est nostra sepulta anima,
Cujus ego interitu tota de mente fugavi
Hac studia, atque omnes delicias animi
[Footnote: CATUL. Bl. iv. 94.]
Alloquar? audiero nunquam tua verba loquentem?
[Footnote: Ib. 25.]
Nunquam ego te vita frater amabilior,
Aspiciam posthac? at certe semper amabo.
[Footnote: El. i. 9.]

O brother rest from miserable me,
All our delights are perished with thee,
Which thy sweet love did nourish in my breath.
Thou all my good hast spoiled in thy death:
With thee my soule is all and whole enshrinde,
At whose death I have cast out of my minde
All my mindes sweet–meats, studies of this kinde;
Never shall I, heare thee speake, speake with thee?
Thee brother, than life dearer, never see?
Yet shalt them ever be belov'd of mee.

But let us a little feare this yong man speake, being but sixteene yeares of age.

Because I have found this worke to have since beene published (and to an ill end) by such as seeke to trouble and subvert the state of our common–wealth, nor caring whether they shall reforme it or no; which they have fondly inserted among other writings of their invention, I have revoked my intent, which was to place it here. And lest the Authors memory should any way be interessed with those that could not thoroughly know his opinions and actions, they shall understand that this subject was by him treated of in his infancie, only by way of exercise, as a subject, common, bareworne, and wyer– drawne in a thousand bookes. I will never doubt but he beleeved what he writ, and writ as he thought: for hee was so conscientious that no lie did ever passe his lips, yea were it but in matters of sport or play: and I know, that had it beene in his choyce, he would rather have beene borne at Venice than at Sarlac; and good, reason why: But he had another maxime deepely imprinted in his minde, which was, carefully to obey, and religiously to submit himselfe to the lawes, under which he was borne. There was never a better citizen, nor more affected to the welfare and quietnesse of his countrie, nor a sharper enemie of the changes, innovations, newfangles, and hurly– burlies of his time: He would more willingly have imployed the utmost of his endevours to extinguish and suppresse, than to favour or further them: His minde was modelled to the patterne of other best ages. But yet in exchange of his serious treatise, I will here set you downe another, more pithie, materiall, and of more consequence, by him likewise produced at that tender age.

OF BOOKS

I make no doubt but it shall often befall me to speake of things which are better, and with more truth, handled by such as are their crafts—masters. Here is simply an essay of my natural faculties, and no whit of those I have acquired. And he that shall tax me with ignorance shall have no great victory at my hands; for hardly could I give others reasons for my discourses that give none unto my selfe, and am not well satisfied with them. He that shall make search after knowledge, let him seek it where it is there is nothing I professe lesse. These are but my fantasies by which I endevour not to make things known, but my selfe. They may haply one day be knowne unto me, or have bin at other times, according as fortune hath brought me where they were declared or manifested. But I remember them no more. And if I be a man of some reading, yet I am a man of no remembering, I conceive no certainty, except it bee to give notice how farre the knowledge I have of it doth now reach. Let no man busie himselfe about the matters, but on the fashion I give them. Let that which I borrow be survaied, and then tell me whether I have made good choice of ornaments to beautifie and set foorth the invention which ever comes from mee. For I make others to relate (not after mine owne fantasie but as it best falleth out) what I cannot so well expresse, either through unskill of language or want of judgement. I number not my borrowings, but I weigh them. And if I would have made their number to prevail, I would have had twice as many. They are all, or almost all, of so famous and ancient names, that me thinks they sufficiently name themselves without mee. If in reasons, comparisons, and arguments, I transplant any into my soile, or confound them with mine owne, I purposely conceale the author, thereby to bridle the rashnesse of these hastie censures that are so headlong cast upon all manner of compositions, namely young writings of men yet living; and in vulgare that admit all the world to talke of them, and which seemeth to convince the conception and publike designe alike. I will have them to give Plutarch a barb [Footnote: Thrust, taunt] upon mine own lips, and vex themselves in wronging Seneca in mee. My weaknesse must be hidden under such great credits. I will love him that shal trace or unfeather me; I meane through clearenesse of judgement, and by the onely distinction of the force and beautie of my discourses. For my selfe, who for want of memorie am ever to seeke how to trie and refine them by the knowledge of their country, knowe perfectly, by measuring mine owne strength, that my soyle is no way capable of some over—pretious flowers that therein I find set, and that all the fruits of my increase could not make it amends. This am I bound to answer for if I hinder my selfe, if there be either vanitie or fault in my discourses that I perceive not or am not able to discerne if they be showed me. For many faults do often escape our eyes; but the infirmitie of judgement consisteth in not being able to perceive them when another discovereth them unto us. Knowledge and truth may be in us without judgement, and we may have judgment without them: yea, the acknowledgement of ignorance is one of the best and surest testimonies of judgement that I can finde. I have no other sergeant of band to marshall my rapsodies than fortune. And looke how my humours or conceites present themselves, so I shuffle them up. Sometimes they prease out thicke and three fold, and other times they come out languishing one by one. I will have my naturall and ordinarie pace scene as loose and as shuffling as it is. As I am, so I goe on plodding. And besides, these are matters that a man may not be ignorant of, and rashly and casually to speake of them. I would wish to have a more perfect understanding of things, but I will not purchase it so deare as it cost. My intention is to passe the remainder of my life quietly and not laboriously, in rest and not in care. There is nothing I will trouble or vex myselfe about, no not for science it selfe, what esteeme soever it be of. I doe not search and tosse over books but for an honester recreation to please, and pastime to delight my selfe: or if I studie, I only endevour to find out the knowledge that teacheth or handleth the knowledge of my selfe, and which may instruct me how to die well and how to live well.

Has meus ad metas sudet oportet equus.
[Footnote: Propeet. 1. iv. El. i. 70]

My horse must sweating runne,
That this goale may be wonne.

If in reading I fortune to meet with any difficult points, I fret not my selfe about them, but after I have given them a charge or two, I leave them as I found them. Should I earnestly plod upon them, I should loose both time and my selfe, for I have a skipping wit. What I see not at the first view, I shall lesse see it if I opinionate my selfe upon it. I doe nothing without blithnesse; and an over obstinate continuation and plodding contention doth dazle, dul, and wearie the same: my sight is thereby confounded and diminished. I must therefore withdraw it, and at fittes goe to it againe. Even as to judge well of the lustre of scarlet we are taught to cast our eyes over it, in running over by divers glances, sodaine glimpses and reiterated reprisings. [Footnote: Repeated observations.] If one booke seeme tedious unto me I take another, which I follow not with any earnestnesse, except it be at such houres as I am idle, or that I am weary with doing nothing. I am not greatly affected to new books, because ancient Authors are, in my judgement, more full and pithy: nor am I much addicted to Greeke books, forasmuch as my understanding cannot well rid [Footnote: Accomplish.] his worke with a childish and apprentise intelligence. Amongst moderne bookes meerly pleasant, I esteeme Bocace his Decameron, Rabelais, and the kisses of John the second (if they may be placed under this title), worth the paines–taking to reade them. As for Amadis and such like trash of writings, they had never the credit so much as to allure my youth to delight in them. This I will say more, either boldly or rashly, that this old and heavie–pased minde of mine will no more be pleased with Aristotle, or tickled with good Ovid: his facility and quaint inventions, which heretofore have so ravished me, they can now a days scarcely entertaine me. I speake my minde freely of all things, yea, of such as peradventure exceed my sufficiencie, and that no way I hold to be of my jurisdiction. What my conceit is of them is told also to manifest the proportion of my insight, and not the measure of things. If at any time I finde my selfe distasted of Platoes Axiochus, as of a forceles worke, due regard had to such an Author, my judgement doth nothing beleeve it selfe: It is not so fond–hardy, or selfe–conceited, as it durst dare to oppose it selfe against the authority of so many other famous ancient judgements, which he reputeth his regents and masters, and with whom hee had rather erre. He chafeth with, and condemneth himselfe, either to rely on the superficiall sense, being unable to pierce into the centre, or to view the thing by some false lustre. He is pleased only to warrant himselfe from trouble and unrulinesse: As for weaknesse, he acknowledgeth and ingeniously avoweth the same. He thinks to give a just interpretation to the apparences which his conception presents unto him, but they are shallow and imperfect. Most of AEsopes fables have divers senses, and severall interpretations: Those which Mythologize them, chuse some kinde of colour well suting with the fable; but for the most part, it is no other than the first and superficiall glosse: There are others more quicke, more sinnowie, more essentiall, and more internall, into which they could never penetrate; and thus thinke I with them. But to follow my course, I have ever deemed that in Poesie, Virgil, Lucretius, Catullus, and Horace, doe doubtles by far hold the first ranke: and especially Virgil in his Georgiks, which I esteeme to be the most accomplished peece of worke of Poesie: In comparison of which one may easily discerne, that there are some passages in the AEneidos to which the Author (had he lived) would no doubt have given some review or correction: The fifth booke whereof is (in my mind) the most absolutely perfect. I also love Lucan, and willingly read him, not so much for his stile, as for his owne worth and truth of his opinion and judgement. As for good Terence, I allow the quaintnesse and grace of his Latine tongue, and judge him wonderfull conceited and apt, lively to represent the motions and passions of the minde, and the condition of our manners: our actions make me often remember him. I can never reade him so often but still I discover some new grace and beautie in him. Those that lived about Virgil's time, complained that some would compare Lucretius unto him. I am of opinion that verily it is an unequall comparison; yet can I hardly assure my selfe in this opinion whensoever I finde my selfe entangled in some notable passage of Lucretius. If they were moved at this comparison, what would they say now of the fond, hardy and barbarous stupiditie of those which now adayes compare Ariosto unto him? Nay, what would Ariosto say of it himselfe?

> O seclum insipiens et infacetutn.
> [Footnote: Catul. Epig, xl. 8.]

> O age that hath no wit,
> And small conceit in it.

I thinke our ancestors had also more reason to cry out against those that blushed not to equall Plautus unto Terence (who makes more show to be a Gentleman) than Lucretius unto Virgil. This one thing doth greatly advantage the estimation and preferring of Terence, that the father of the Roman eloquence, of men of his quality doth so often make mention of him; and the censure [Footnote: Opinion.] which the chiefe Judge of the Roman Poets giveth of his companion. It hath often come unto my minde, how such as in our dayes give themselves to composing of comedies (as the Italians who are very happy in them) employ three or foure arguments of Terence and Plautus to make up one of theirs. In one onely comedy they will huddle up five or six of Bocaces tales. That which makes them so to charge themselves with matter, is the distrust they have of their owne sufficiency, and that they are not able to undergoe so heavie a burthen with their owne strength. They are forced to finde a body on which they may rely and leane themselves: and wanting matter of their owne wherewith to please us, they will have the story or tale to busie and ammuse us: where as in my Authors it is cleane contrary: The elegancies, the perfections and ornaments of his manner of speech, make us neglect and lose the longing for his subject. His quaintnesse and grace doe still retaine us to him. He is every where pleasantly conceited, [Footnote: Full of pleasant notions.]

> Liquidus puroque simillimus amni
> [Footnote: Hor. 1. ii. Epist. II. 120.]

> So clearely–neate, so neately–cleare,
> As he a fine–pure River were,

and doth so replenish our minde with his graces that we forget those of the fable. The same consideration drawes me somewhat further. I perceive that good and ancient Poets have shunned the affectation and enquest, not only of fantasticall, new fangled, Spagniolized, and Petrarchisticall elevations, but also of more sweet and sparing inventions, which are the ornament of all the Poeticall workes of succeeding ages. Yet is there no competent Judge that findeth them wanting in those

Ancient ones, and that doth not much more admire that smoothly equall neatnesse, continued sweetnesse, and flourishing comelinesse of Catullus his Epigrams, than all the sharpe quips and witty girds wherewith Martiall doth whet and embellish the conclusions of his. It is the same reason I spake of erewhile, as Martiall of himselfe. Minus illi ingenio laborandum fuit, in cuius locum materia successerat. [Footnote: Mart. Praf. 1. viii.] "He needed the lesse worke with his wit, in place whereof matter came in supply." The former without being moved or pricked cause themselves to be heard lowd enough: they have matter to laugh at every where, and need not tickle themselves; where as these must have foraine helpe: according as they have lesse spirit, they must have more body. They leape on horsebacke, because they are not sufficiently strong in their legs to march on foot. Even as in our dances, those base conditioned men that keepe dancing–schooles, because they are unfit to represent the port and decencie of our nobilitie, endevour to get commendation by dangerous lofty trickes, and other strange tumbler–like friskes and motions. And some Ladies make a better shew of their countenances in those dances, wherein are divers changes, cuttings, turnings, and agitations of the body, than in some dances of state and gravity, where they need but simply to tread a naturall measure, represent an unaffected cariage, and their ordinary grace; And as I have also seene some excellent Lourdans, or Clownes, attired in their ordinary worky–day clothes, and with a common homely countenance, affoord us all the pleasure that may be had from their art: but prentises and learners that are not of so high a forme, besmeare their faces, to disguise themselves, and in motions counterfeit strange visages and antickes, to enduce us to laughter. This my conception is no where better discerned than in the comparison betweene Virgils AEneidos and Orlando Furioso. The first is seene to soare aloft with full–spread wings, and with so high and strong a pitch, ever following his point; the other faintly to hover and flutter from tale to tale, and as it were skipping from bough to bough, always distrusting his owne wings, except it be for some short flight, and for feare his strength and breath should faile him, to sit downe at every fields– end;

Excursusque breves tentat.
[Footnote: Virg. AEn. 1. iv. 194.]

Out–lopes [Footnote: Wanderings out.] sometimes he doth assay,
But very short, and as he may.

Loe here then, concerning this kinde of subjects, what Authors please me best: As for my other lesson, which somewhat more mixeth profit with pleasure, whereby I learne to range my opinions and addresse my conditions, the Bookes that serve me thereunto are Plutarke (since he spake [Footnote: Was translated by Angot] French) and Seneca; both have this excellent commodity for my humour, that the knowledge I seeke in them is there so scatteringly and loosely handled, that whosoever readeth them is not tied to plod long upon them, whereof I am uncapable. And so are Plutarkes little workes and Senecas Epistles, which are the best and most profitable parts of their writings. It is no great matter to draw mee to them, and I leave them where I list. For they succeed not and depend not one of another. Both jumpe [Footnote: Agree] and suit together, in most true and profitable opinions: And fortune brought them both into the world in one age. Both were Tutors unto two Roman Emperours: Both were strangers, and came from farre Countries; both rich and mighty in the common–wealth, and in credit with their masters. Their instruction is the prime and creame of Philosophy, and presented with a plaine, unaffected, and pertinent fashion. Plutarke is more uniforme and constant; Seneca more waving and diverse. This doth labour, force, and extend himselfe, to arme and strengthen vertue against weaknesse, feare, and vitious desires; the other seemeth nothing so much to feare their force or attempt, and in a manner scorneth to hasten or change his pace about them, and to put himselfe upon his guard. Plutarkes opinions are Platonicall, gentle and accommodable unto civill societie: Senecaes Stoicall and Epicurian, further from common use, but in my conceit [Footnote: Opinion.] more proper, particular, and more solid. It appeareth in Seneca that he somewhat inclineth and yeeldeth to the tyrannic of the Emperors which were in his daies; for I verily believe, it is with a forced judgement he condemneth the cause of those noblie— minded murtherers of Caesar; Plutarke is every where free and open hearted; Seneca full–fraught with points and sallies; Plutarke stuft with matters. The former doth move and enflame you more; the latter content, please, and pay you better: This doth guide you, the other drive you on. As for Cicero, of all his works, those that treat of Philosophie (namely morall) are they which best serve my turne, and square with my intent. But boldly to confess the truth (for, since the bars of impudencie were broken downe, all curbing is taken away), his manner of writing seemeth verie tedious unto me, as doth all such like stuffe. For his prefaces, definitions, divisions, and Etymologies consume the greatest part of his works; whatsoever quick, wittie, and pithie conceit is in him is surcharged and confounded by those his long and far–fetcht preambles. If I bestow but one hour in reading them, which is much for me, and let me call to minde what substance or juice I have drawne from him, for the most part I find nothing but wind and ostentation in him; for he is not yet come to the arguments which make for his purpose, and reasons that properly concerne the knot or pith I seek after. These Logicall and Aristotelian ordinances are not avail full for me, who onely endeavour to become more wise and sufficient, and not more wittie or eloquent. I would have one begin with the last point: I understand sufficiently what death and voluptuousnesse are: let not a man busie himselfe to anatomize them. At the first reading of a booke I seeke for good and solid reasons that may instruct me how to sustaine their assaults. It is neither grammaticall subtilties nor logicall quiddities, nor the wittie contexture of choice words or arguments and syllogismes, that will serve my turne. I like those discourses that give the first charge to the strongest part of the doubt; his are but flourishes, and languish everywhere. They are good for schooles, at the barre, or for Orators and Preachers, where we may slumber: and though we wake a quarter of an houre after, we may finde and trace him soone enough. Such a manner of speech is fit for those judges that a man would corrupt by hooke or crooke, by right or wrong, or for children and the common people, unto whom a man must tell all, and see what the event would be. I would not have a man go about and labour by circumlocutions to induce and winne me to attention, and that (as our Heralds or Criers do) they shall ring out their words: Now heare me, now listen, or ho–yes. [Footnote: Oyez, hear.] The Romanes in their religion were wont to say, "Hoc age; [Footnote: Do this.] "which in ours we say, "Sursum corda. [Footnote: Lift up your hearts.] There are so many lost words for me. I come readie prepared from my house. I neede no allurement nor sawce, my stomacke is good enough to digest raw meat: And whereas with these preparatives and flourishes, or preambles, they thinke to sharpen my taste or stir my stomacke, they cloy and make it wallowish. [Footnote: Mawkish.] Shall the privilege of times excuse me from this sacrilegious boldnesse, to deem Platoes Dialogismes to be as languishing, by over–filling and stuffing his matter? And to bewaile the time that a man who had so many thousands of things to utter, spends about so many, so long, so vaine, and idle interloqutions, and preparatives? My ignorance shall better excuse me, in that I see nothing in the beautie of his language. I generally enquire after bookes that use sciences, and not after such as institute them. The two first, and Plinie, with others of their ranke, have no Hoc age in them, they will have to doe with men that have forewarned themselves; or if they have, it is a materiall and substantial! Hoc age, and that hath his bodie apart I likewise love to read the Epistles

59

and ad Atticum, not onely because they containe a most ample instruction of the historic and affaires of his times, but much more because in them I descrie his private humours. For (as I have said elsewhere) I am wonderfull curious to discover and know the minde, the soul, the genuine disposition and naturall judgement of my authors. A man ought to judge their sufficiencie and not their customes, nor them by the shew of their writings, which they set forth on this world's theatre. I have sorrowed a thousand times that ever we lost the booke that Brutus writ of Vertue. Oh it is a goodly thing to learne the Theorike of such as understand the practice well. But forsomuch as the Sermon is one thing and the Preacher an other, I love as much to see Brutus in Plutarke as in himself: I would rather make choice to know certainly what talk he had in his tent with some of his familiar friends, the night fore—going the battell, than the speech he made the morrow after to his Armie; and what he did in his chamber or closet, than what in the senate or market place. As for Cicero, I am of the common judgement, that besides learning there was no exquisite [Footnote: Overelaborate.] eloquence in him: He was a good citizen, of an honest, gentle nature, as are commonly fat and burly men: for so was he: But to speake truly of thim? full of ambitious vanity and remisse niceness. [Footnote: Ineffectual fastidiousness.] And I know not well how to excuse him, in that he deemed his Poesie worthy to be published. It is no great imperfection to make bad verses, but it is an imperfection in him that he never perceived how unworthy they were of the glorie of his name. Concerning his eloquence, it is beyond all comparison, and I verily beleeve that none shall ever equall it. Cicero the younger, who resembled his father in nothing but in name, commanding in Asia, chanced one day to have many strangers at his board, and amongst others, one Caestius sitting at the lower end, as the manner is to thrust in at great mens tables: Cicero inquired of one of his men what he was, who told him his name, but he dreaming on other matters, and having forgotten what answere his man made him, asked him his name twice or thrice more: the servant, because he would not be troubled to tell him one thing so often, and by some circumstance to make him to know him better, "It is," said he, "the same Caestius of whom some have told you that, in respect of his owne, maketh no accompt of your fathers eloquence:" Cicero being suddainly mooved, commanded the said poore Caestius to be presently taken from the table, and well whipt in his presence: Lo heere an uncivill and barbarous host. Even amongst those which (all things considered) have deemed his eloquence matchlesse and incomparable, others there have been who have not spared to note some faults in it. As great Brutus said, that it was an eloquence broken, halting, and disjoynted, fractam et elumbem: "Incoherent and sinnowlesse." Those Orators that lived about his age, reproved also in him the curious care he had of a certaine long cadence at the end of his clauses, and noted these words, esse videatur, which he so often useth. As for me, I rather like a cadence that falleth shorter, cut like Iambikes: yet doth he sometimes confounde his numbers, [Footnote: Confuse his rhythm.] but it is seldome: I have especially observed this one place: "Ego vero me minus diu senem esse mallem, quam esse senem, antequam essem? [Footnote: Cic. De Senect.] "But I had rather not be an old man, so long as I might be, than to be old before I should be." Historians are my right hand, for they are pleasant and easie; and therewithall the man with whom I desire generally to be acquainted may more lively and perfectly be discovered in them than in any other composition: the varietic and truth of his inward conditions, in grosse and by retale: the diversitie of the meanes of his collection and composing, and of the accidents that threaten him. Now those that write of mens lives, forasmuch as they ammuse and busie themselves more about counsels than events, more about that which commeth from within than that which appeareth outward; they are fittest for me: And that's the reason why Plutarke above all in that kind doth best please me. Indeed I am not a little grieved that we have not a dozen of Laertius, or that he is not more knowne, or better understood; for I am no lesse curious to know the fortunes and lives of these great masters of the world than to understand the diversitie of their decrees and conceits. In this kind of studie of historie a man must, without distinction, tosse and turne over all sorts of Authors, both old and new, both French and others, if he will learne the things they so diversly treat of. But me thinkes that Caesar above all doth singularly deserve to be studied, not onely for the understanding of the historie as of himselfe; so much perfection and excellencie is there in him more than in others, although Salust be reckoned one of the number. Verily I read that author with a little more reverence and respects than commonly men reade profane and humane Workes: sometimes considering him by his actions and wonders of his greatnesse, and other times waighing the puritie and inimitable polishing and elegancie of his tongue, which (as Cicero saith) hath not onely exceeded all historians, but haply Cicero himselfe: with such sinceritie in his judgement, speaking of his enemies, that except the false colours wherewith he goeth about to cloake his bad cause, and the corruption and filthinesse of his pestilent ambition, I am perswaded there is nothing in him to be found fault with: and that he hath been over–sparing to speake of himselfe; for so many notable and great things could never be executed by him, unlesse he had put more of his owne into them than he setteth downe. I love those Historians that are either very simple or most excellent. The simple who have nothing of their owne to adde unto the storie and have but the care and diligence to collect whatsoever come to their knowledge, and sincerely and faithfully to register all things, without choice or culling, by the naked truth leave our judgment more entire and better satisfied.

Such amongst others (for examples sake) plaine and well–meaning Froissard, who in his enterprise hath marched with so free and genuine a puritie, that having committed some oversight, he is neither ashamed to acknowledge nor afraid to correct the same, wheresoever he hath either notice or warning of it; and who representeth unto us the diversitie of the newes then current and the different reports that were made unto him. The subject of an historie should be naked, bare, and formelesse; each man according to his capacitie or understanding may reap commoditie out of it. The curious and most excellent have the sufficiencie to cull and chuse that which is worthie to be knowne and may select of two relations that which is most likely: from the condition of Princes and of their humours, they conclude their counsels and attribute fit words to them: they assume a just authoritie and bind our faith to theirs. But truly that belongs not to many. Such as are betweene both (which is the most common fashion), it is they that spoil all; they will needs chew our meat for us and take upon them a law to judge, and by consequence to square and encline the storie according to their fantasie; for, where the judgement bendeth one way, a man cannot chuse but wrest and turne his narration that way. They undertake to chuse things worthy to bee knowne, and now and then conceal either a word or a secret action from us, which would much better instruct us: omitting such things as they understand not as incredible: and haply such matters as they know not how to declare, either in good Latin or tolerable French. Let them boldly enstall their eloquence and discourse: Let them censure at their pleasure, but let them also give us leave to judge after them: And let them neither alter nor dispense by their abridgements and choice anything belonging to the substance of the matter; but let them rather send it pure and entire with all her dimensions unto us. Most commonly (as chiefly in our age) this charge of writing histories is committed unto base, ignorant, and mechanicall kind of people, only for this consideration that they can speake well; as if we sought to learne the Grammer of them; and they have some reason, being only hired to that end, and publishing nothing but their tittle–tattle to aime at nothing else so much. Thus with store of choice and quaint words, and wyre drawne phrases, they huddle up and make a hodge–pot of a laboured contexture of the reports which they gather in the market places or such other assemblies. The only good histories are those that are written by such as commanded or were imploied themselves in weighty affaires or that were partners in the conduct of them, or that at least have had the fortune to manage others of like qualitie. Such in a manner are all the Graecians and Romans. For many eye–witnesses having written of one same subject (as it hapned in those times when Greatnesse and Knowledge did commonly meet) if any fault or over–sight have past them, it must be deemed exceeding light and upon some doubtful accident. What may a man expect at a Phisitians hand that discourseth of warre, or of a bare Scholler treating of Princes secret designes? If we shall but note the religion which the Romans had in that, wee need no other example: Asinius Pollio found some mistaking or oversight in Caesars Commentaries, whereinto he was falne, only because he could not possiblie oversee all things with his owne eyes that hapned in his Armie, but was faine to rely on the reports of particular men, who often related untruths unto him: or else because he had not been curiously advertized [Footnote: Minutely informed.] and distinctly enformed by his Lieutenants and Captaines of such matters as they in his absence had managed or effected. Whereby may be seen that nothing is so hard or so uncertaine to be found out as the certaintie of the truth, sithence [Footnote: Since.] no man can put any assured confidence concerning the truth of a battel, neither in the knowledge of him that was Generall or commanded over it, nor in the soldiers that fought, of anything that hath hapned amongst them; except after the manner of a strict point of law, the severall witnesses are brought and examined face to face, and that all matters be nicely and thorowly sifted by the objects and trials of the successe of every accident. Verily the knowledge we have of our owne affaires is much more barren and feeble. But this hath sufficiently been handled by Bodin, and agreeing with my conception. Somewhat to aid the weaknesse of my memorie and to assist her great defects; for it hath often been my chance to light upon bookes which I supposed to be new and never to have read, which I had not understanding diligently read and run over many years before, and all bescribled with my notes; I have a while since accustomed my selfe to note at the end of my booke (I meane such as I purpose to read but once) the time I made an end to read it, and to set downe what censure or judgement I gave of it; that so it may at least at another time represent unto my mind the aire and generall idea I had conceived of the Author in reading him. I will here set downe the Copie of some of my annotations, and especially what I noted upon my Guicciardine about ten yeares since: (For what language soever my books speake unto me I speake unto them in mine owne.) He is a diligent Historiographer and from whom in my conceit a man may as exactly learne the truth of such affaires as passed in his time, as of any other writer whatsoever: and the rather because himselfe hath been an Actor of most part of them and in verie honourable place. There is no signe or apparance that ever he disguised or coloured any matter, either through hatred, malice, favour, or vanitie; whereof the free and impartiall judgements he giveth of great men, and namely of those by whom he had been advanced or imployed in his important charges, as of Pope Clement the seaventh, beareth undoubted testimony. Concerning the parts wherein he most goeth about to prevaile, which are his digressions and discourses, many of them are verie excellent and enriched with faire ornaments, but he hath too much pleased himselfe in them: for endeavouring to omit nothing that might be spoken, having so full and large a subject, and almost infinite, he proveth somewhat languishing, and giveth a taste of a kind of scholasticall tedious babling. Moreover, I have noted this, that of so severall and divers armes, successes, and effects he judgeth of; of so many and variable motives, alterations, and counsels, that he relateth, he never referreth any one unto vertue, religion or conscience: as if they were all extinguished and banished the world. And of all actions how glorious soever in apparance they be of themselves, he doth ever impute the cause of them to some vicious and blame–worthie occasion, or to some commoditie and profit. It is impossible to imagine that amongst so infinite a number of actions whereof he judgeth, some one have not been produced and compassed by way of reason. No corruption could ever possesse men so universally but that some one must of necessity escape the contagion; which makes me to feare he hath had some distaste or blame in his passion, and it hath haply fortuned that he hath judged or esteemed of others according to himselfe. In my Philip de Comines there is this: In him you shall find a pleasing– sweet and gently–gliding speech, fraught with a purely sincere simplicitie, his narration pure and unaffected, and wherein the Authours unspotted good meaning doth evidently appeare, void of all manner of vanitie or ostentation speaking of himselfe, and free from all affection or envie–speaking of others; his discourses and perswasions accompanied more with a well–meaning zeale and meere [Footnote: Pure.] veritie than with any laboured and exquisite sufficiencie, and allthrough with gravitie and authoritie, representing a man well–borne and brought up in high negotiations. Upon the Memoires and historic of Monsieur du Bellay: It is ever a well–pleasing thing to see matters written by those that have as said how and in what manner they ought to be directed and managed: yet can it not be denied but that in both these Lords there will manifestly appeare a great declination from a free libertie of writing, which clearly shineth in ancient writers of their kind: as in the Lord of louinille, familiar unto Saint Lewis; Eginard, Chancellor unto Charlemaine; and of more fresh memorie in Philip de Comines. This is rather a declamation or pleading for King Francis against the Emperour Charles the fifth, than an Historic. I will not beleeve they have altered or changed any thing concerning the generalitie of matters, but rather to wrest and turne the judgement of the events many times against reason, to our advantage, and to omit whatsoever they supposed to be doubtful or ticklish in their masters life: they have made a business of it: witnesse the recoylings of the Lords of Momorancy and Byron, which therein are forgotten; and which is more, you shall not so much as find the name of the Ladie of Estampes mentioned at all. A man may sometimes colour and haply hide secret actions, but absolutely to conceal that which all the world knoweth, and especially such things as have drawne–on publike effects, and of such consequence, it is an inexcusable defect, or as I may say unpardonable oversight. To conclude, whosoever desireth to have perfect information and knowledge of king Francis the first, and of the things hapned in his time, let him addresse himselfe elsewhere if he will give any credit unto me. The profit he may reap here is by the particular description of the battels and exploits of warre wherein these gentlemen were present; some privie conferences, speeches, or secret actions of some princes that then lived, and the practices managed, or negotiations directed by the Lord of Langeay, in which doubtless are verie many things well worthy to be knowne, and diverse discourses not vulgare.

MONTAIGNE. WHAT IS A CLASSIC?

BY CHARLES–AUGUSTIN SAINTE-BEUVE

TRANSLATED BY E. LEE

INTRODUCTORY NOTE

Charles Augustin Sainte–Beuve, the foremost French critic of the nineteenth century, and, in the view of many, the greatest literary critic of the world, was born at Boulogne–sur–Mer, December 23, 1804. He studied medicine, but soon abandoned it for literature; and before he gave himself up to criticism he made some mediocre attempts in poetry and fiction. He became professor at the College de France and the Ecole Normale and was appointed Senator in 1865. A course of lectures given at Lausanne in 1837 resulted in his great "Histoire de Port–Royal" and another given at Liege in his "Chateaubriand et son groupe litteraire." But his most famous productions were his critical essays published periodically in the "Constitutionnel" the "Moniteur" and the "Temps" later collected in sets under the names of "Critiques et Portraits Litteraires" "Portraits Contemporains" "Causeries du Lundi" and "Nouveaux Lundis." At the height of his vogue, these Monday essays were events of European importance. He died in 1869.

Sainte–Beuve's work was much more than literary criticism as that type of writing had been generally conceived before his time. In place of the mere classification of books and the passing of a judgment upon them as good or bad, he sought to illuminate and explain by throwing light on a literary work from a study of the life, circumstances, and aim of the writer, and by a comparison with the literature of other times and countries. Thus his work was historical, psychological, and ethical, as well as esthetic, and demanded vast learning and a literary outlook of unparalleled breadth. In addition to this equipment he had fine taste and an admirable style; and by his universality, penetration, and balance he raised to a new level the profession of critic.

MONTAIGNE

While the good ship France is taking a somewhat haphazard course, getting into unknown seas, and preparing to double what the pilots (if there is a pilot) call the Stormy Cape, while the look–out at the mast–head thinks he sees the spectre of the giant Adamastor rising on the horizon, many honourable and peaceable men continue their work and studies all the same, and follow out to the end, or as far as they can, their favourite hobbies. I know, at the present time, a learned man who is collating more carefully than has ever yet been done the different early editions of Rabelais—editions, mark you, of which only one copy remains, of which a second is not to be found: from the careful collation of the texts some literary and maybe philosophical result will be derived with regard to the genius of the French Lucian–Aristophanes. I know another scholar whose devotion and worship is given to a very different man—to Bossuet: he is preparing a complete, exact, detailed history of the life and works of the great bishop. And as tastes differ, and "human fancy is cut into a thousand shapes" (Montaigne said that), Montaigne also has his devotees, he who, himself, was so little of one: a sect is formed round him. In his lifetime he had Mademoiselle de Gournay, his daughter of alliance, who was solemnly devoted to him; and his disciple, Charron, followed him closely, step by step, only striving to arrange his thoughts with more order and method. In our time amateurs, intelligent men, practice the religion under another form: they devote themselves to collecting the smallest traces of the author of the Essays, to gathering up the slightest relics, and Dr. Payen may be justly placed at the head of the group. For years he has been preparing a book on Montaigne, of which the title will be—"Michel de Montaigne, a collection of unedited or little known facts about the author of the Essays, his book, and his other writings, about his family, his friends, his admirers, his detractors."

While awaiting the conclusion of the book, the occupation and amusement of a lifetime, Dr. Payen keeps us informed in short pamphlets of the various works and discoveries made about Montaigne.

If we separate the discoveries made during the last five or six years from the jumble of quarrels, disputes, cavilling, quackery, and law–suits (for there have been all those), they consist in this– –

In 1846 M. Mace found in the (then) Royal Library, amongst the "Collection Du Puys," a letter of Montaigne, addressed to the king, Henri IV., September 2, 1590.

In 1847 M. Payen printed a letter, or a fragment of a letter of Montaigne of February 16, 1588, a letter corrupt and incomplete, coming from the collection of the Comtesse Boni de Castellane.

But, most important of all, in 1848, M. Horace de Viel-Castel found in London, at the British Museum, a remarkable letter of Montaigne, May 22, 1585, when Mayor of Bordeaux, addressed to M. de Matignon, the king's lieutenant in the town. The great interest of the letter is that it shows Montaigne for the first time in the full discharge of his office with all the energy and vigilance of which he was capable. The pretended idler was at need much more active than he was ready to own.

M. Detcheverry, keeper of the records to the mayoralty of Bordeaux, found and published (1850) a letter of Montaigne, while mayor, to the Jurats, or aldermen of the town, July 30, 1585.

M. Achille Jubinal found among the manuscripts of the National Library, and published (1850), a long, remarkable letter from Montaigne to the king, Henri IV., January 18, 1590, which happily coincides with that already found by M. Mace.

Lastly, to omit nothing and do justice to all, in a "Visit to Montaigne's Chateau in Perigord," of which the account appeared in 1850, M. Bertrand de Saint-Germain described the place and pointed out the various Greek and Latin inscriptions that may still be read in Montaigne's tower in the third-storey chamber (the ground floor counting as the first), which the philosopher made his library and study.

M. Payen, collecting together and criticising in his last pamphlet the various notices and discoveries, not all of equal importance, allowed himself to be drawn into some little exaggeration of praise; but we cannot blame him. Admiration, when applied to such noble, perfectly innocent, and disinterested subjects, is truly a spark of the sacred fire: it produces research that a less ardent zeal would quickly leave aside, and sometimes leads to valuable results. However, it would be well for those who, following M. Payen's example, intelligently understand and greatly admire Montaigne, to remember, even in their ardour, the advice of the wise man and the master. "There is more to do," said he, speaking of the commentators of his time, "in interpreting the interpretations than in interpreting the things themselves; and more bdoks about books than on any other subject. We do nothing, but everything swarms with commentators; of authors there is a great rarity." Authors are of great price and very scared at all times—that is to say, authors who really increase the sum of human knowledge. I should like all who write on Montaigne, and give us the details of their researches and discoveries, to imagine one thing,—Montaigne himself reading and criticising them. "What would he think of me and the manner in which I am going to speak of him to the public?" If such a question was put, how greatly it would suppress useless phrases and shorten idle discussions! M. Payen's last pamphlet was dedicated to a man who deserves equally well of Montaigne—M. Gustave Brunet, of Bordeaux. He, speaking of M. Payen, in a work in which he pointed out interesting and various corrections of Montaigne's text, said: "May he soon decide to publish the fruits of his researches: he will have left nothing for future Montaignologues" Montaignologues! Great Heaven! what would Montaigne say of such a word coined in his honour? You who occupy yourselves so meritoriously with him, but who have, I think, no claim to appropriate him to yourselves, in the name of him whom you love, and whom we all love by a greater or lesser title, never, I beg of you, use such words; they smack of the brotherhood and the sect, of pedantry and of the chatter of the schools—things utterly repugnant to Montaigne.

Montaigne had a simple, natural, affable mind, and a very happy disposition. Sprung from an excellent father, who, though of no great education, entered with real enthusiasm into the movement of the Renaissance and all the liberal novelties of his time, the son corrected the excessive enthusiasm, vivacity, and tenderness he inherited by a great refinement and justness of reflection; but he did not abjure the original groundwork. It is scarcely more than thirty years ago that whenever the sixteenth century was mentioned it was spoken of as a barbarous epoch, Montaigne only excepted: therein lay error and ignorance. The sixteenth century was a great century, fertile, powerful, learned, refined in parts, although in some aspects it was rough, violent, and seemingly coarse. What it particularly lacked was taste, if by taste is meant the faculty of clear and perfect selection, the extrication of the elements of the beautiful. But in the succeeding centuries taste quickly became distaste. If, however, in literature it was crude, in the arts properly so–called, in those of the hand and the chisel, the sixteenth century, even in France, is, in the quality of taste, far greater than the two succeeding centuries: it is neither meagre nor massive, heavy nor distorted. In art its taste is rich and of fine quality,—at once unrestrained and complex, ancient and modern, special to itself and original. In the region of morals it is unequal and mixed. It was an age of contrasts, of contrasts in all their crudity, an age of philosophy and fanaticism, of scepticism and strong faith. Everything was at strife and in collision; nothing was blended and united. Everything was in ferment; it was a period of chaos; every ray of light caused a storm. It was not a gentle age, or one we can call an age of light, but an age of struggle and combat. What distinguished Montaigne and made a phenomenon of him was, that in such an age he should have possessed moderation, caution, and order.

Born on the last day of February, 1533, taught the ancient languages as a game while still a child, waked even in his cradle by the sound of musical instruments, he seemed less fitted for a rude and violent epoch than for the commerce and sanctuary of the muses. His rare good sense corrected what was too ideal and poetical in his early education; but he preserved the happy faculty of saying everything with freshness and wit. Married, when past thirty, to an estimable woman who was his companion for twenty–eight years, he seems to have put passion only into friendship. He immortalised his love for Etienne de la Boetie, whom he lost after four years of the sweetest and closest intimacy. For some time counsellor in the Parliament of Bordeaux, Montaigne, before he was forty, retired from public life, and flung away ambition to live in his tower of Montaigne, enjoying his own society and his own intellect, entirely given up to his own observations and thoughts, and to the busy idleness of which we know all the sports and fancies. The first edition of the Essays appeared in 1580, consisting of only two books, and in a form representing only the first rough draft of what we have in the later editions. The same year Montaigne set out on a voyage to Switzerland and Italy. It was during that voyage that the aldermen of Bordeaux elected him mayor of their town. At first he refused and excused himself, but warned that it would be well to accept, and enjoined by the king, he took the office, "the more beautiful," he said, "that there was neither renunciation nor gain other than the honour of its performance." He filled the office for four years, from July 1582 to July 1586, being re–elected after the first two years. Thus Montaigne, at the age of fifty, and a little against his will, re– entered public life when the country was on the eve of civil disturbances which, quieted and lulled to sleep for a while, broke out more violently at the cry of the League. Although, as a rule, lessons serve for nothing, since the art of wisdom and happiness cannot be taught, let us not deny ourselves the pleasure of listening to Montaigne; let us look on his wisdom and happiness; let him speak of public affairs, of revolutions and disturbances, and of his way of conducting himself with regard to them. We do not put forward a model, but we offer our readers an agreeable recreation.

Although Montaigne lived in so agitated and stormy a time, a period that a man who had lived through the Terror (M. Daunou) called the most tragic century in all history, he by no means regarded his age as the worst of ages. He was not of those prejudiced and afflicted persons, who, measuring everything by their visual horizon, valuing everything according to their present sensations, alway declare that the disease they suffer from is worse than any ever before experienced by a human being. He was like Socrates, who did not consider himself a citizen of one city but of the world; with his broad and full imagination he embraced the universality of countries and of ages; he even judged more equitably the very evils of which he was witness and victim. "Who is it," he said, "that, seeing the bloody havoc of these civil wars of ours, does not cry out that the machine of the world is near dissolution, and that the day of judgment is at hand, without considering that many worse revolutions have been seen, and that, in the mean time, people are being merry in a thousand other parts of the earth for all this? For my part, considering the license and impunity that always attend such commotions, I admire they are so moderate, and that there is not more mischief done. To him who feels the hailstones patter about his ears, the whole hemisphere appears to be in storm and tempest." And raising his thoughts higher and higher, reducing his own suffering to what it was in the immensity of nature, seeing there not only himself but whole kingdoms as mere specks in the infinite, he added in words which foreshadowed Pascal, in words whose outline and salient points Pascal did not disdain to borrow: "But whoever shall represent to his fancy, as in a picture, that great image of our mother nature, portrayed in her full majesty and lustre, whoever in her face shall read so general and so constant a variety, whoever shall observe himself in that figure, and not himself but a whole kingdom, no bigger than the least touch or prick of a pencil in comparison of the whole, that man alone is able to value things according to their true estimate and grandeur."

Thus Montaigne gives us a lesson, a useless lesson, but I state it all the same, because among the many unprofitable ones that have been written down, it is perhaps of greater worth than most. I do not mean to underrate the gravity of the circumstances in which France is just now involved, for I believe there is pressing need to bring together all the energy, prudence, and courage she possesses in order that the country may come out with honour [Footnote: This essay appeared April 28, 1851]. However, let us reflect, and remember that, leaving aside the Empire, which as regards internal affairs was a period of calm, and before 1812 of prosperity, we who utter such loud complaints, lived in peace from 1815 to 1830, fifteen long years; that the three days of July only inaugurated another order of things that for eighteen years guaranteed peace and in dustrial prosperity; in all, thirty−two years of repose. Stormy days came; tempests burst, and will doubtless burst again. Let us learn how to live through them, but do not let us cry out every day, as we are disposed to do, that never under the sun were such storms known as we are enduring. To get away from the present state of feeling, to restore lucidity and proportion to our judgments, let us read every evening a page of Montaigne.

A criticism of Montaigne on the men of his day struck me, and it bears equally well on those of ours. Our philosopher says somewhere that he knows a fair number of men possessing various good qualities—one, intelligence; another, heart; another, address, conscience or knowledge, or skill in languages, each has his share: "but of a great man as a whole, having so many good qualities together, or one with such a degree of excellence that we ought to admire him, or compare him with those we honour in the past, my fortune has never shown me one." He afterwards made an exception in favour of his friend Etienne de la Boetie, but he belonged to the company of great men dead before attaining maturity, and showing promise without having time to fulfil it. Montaigne's criticism called up a smile. He did not see a true and wholly great man in his time, the age of L'Hopital, Coligny, and the Guises. Well! how does ours seem to you? We have as many great men as in Montaigne's time, one distinguished for his intellect, another for his heart, a third for skill, some (a rare thing) for conscience, many for knowledge and language. But we too lack the perfect man, and he is greatly to be desired. One of the most intelligent observers of our day recognised and proclaimed it some years ago: "Our age," said M. de Remusat, "is wanting in great men." [Footnote: Essais de Philosophie, vol. i, p. 22]

How did Montaigne conduct himself in his duties as first magistrate of a great city? If we take him literally and on a hasty first glance we should believe he discharged them slackly and languidly. Did not Horace, doing the honours to himself, say that in war he one day let his shield fall (relicta non bene parmula)? We must not be in too great a hurry to take too literally the men of taste who have a horror of over−estimating themselves. Minds of a fine quality are more given to vigilance and to action than they are apt to confess. The man who boasts and makes a great noise, will, I am almost sure, be less brave in the combat than Horace, and less vigilant at the council board than Montaigne.

On entering office Montaigne was careful to warn the aldermen of Bordeaux not to expect to find in him more than there really was; he presented himself to them without affectation. "I represented to them faithfully and conscientiously all that I felt myself to be,—a man without memory, without vigilance, without experience, and without energy; but also, without hate, without ambition, without avarice, and without violence." He should be sorry, while taking the affairs of the town in hand, that his feelings should be so strongly affected as those of his worthy father had been, who in the end had lost his place and health. The eager and ardent pledge to satisfy an impetuous desire was not his method. His opinion was "that you must lend yourself to others, and only give yourself to yourself." And repeating his thought, according to his custom in all kinds of metaphors and picturesque forms, he said again that if he some times allowed himself to be urged to the management of other men's affairs, he promised to take them in hand, not "into my lungs and liver." We are thus forewarned, we know what to expect. The mayor and Montaigne were two distinct persons; under his role and office he reserved to himself a certain freedom and secret security. He continued to judge things in his own fashion and impartially, although acting loyally for the cause confided to him. He was far from approving or even excusing all he saw in his party, and he could judge his adversaries and say of them: "He did that thing wickedly, and this virtuously." "I would have," he added, "matters go well on our side; but if they do not, I shall not run mad. I am heartily for the right party; but I do not affect to be taken notice of for an especial enemy to others." And he entered into some details and applications which at that time were piquant. Let us remark, however, in order to explain and justify his somewhat extensive profession of impartiality, that the chiefs of the party then in evidence, the three Henris, were famous and considerable men on several counts: Henri, Duke of Guise, head of the League; Henri, King of Navarre, leader of the Opposition; and the King Henri III. in whose name Montaigne was mayor, who wavered between the two. When parties have neither chief nor head, when they are known by the body only, that is to say, in their hideous and brutal reality, it is more difficult and also more hazardous to be just towards them and to assign to each its share of action.

The principle which guided him in his administration was to look only at the fact, at the result, and to grant nothing to noise and outward show: "How much more a good effect makes a noise, so much I abate of the goodness of it." For it is always to be feared that it was more performed for the sake of the noise than upon the account of goodness: "Being exposed upon the stall, 'tis half sold." That was not Montaigne's way: he made no show; he managed men and affairs as quietly as he could; he employed in a manner useful to all alike the gifts of sincerity and conciliation; the personal attraction with which nature endowed him was a quality of the highest value in the management of men. He preferred to warn men of evil rather than to take on himself the honour of repressing it: "Is there any one who desires to be sick that he may see his physician's practice? And would not that physician deserve to be whipped who should wish the plague amongst us that he might put his art into practice?" Far from desiring that trouble and disorder in the affairs of the city should rouse and honour his govern ment, he had ever willingly, he said, contributed all he could to their tranquillity and ease. He is not of those whom municipal honours intoxicate and elate, those "dignities of office" as he called them, and of which all the noise "goes from one cross–road to another." If he was a man desirous of fame, he recognised that it was of a kind greater than that. I do not know, however, if even in a vaster field he would have changed his method and manner of proceed ing. To do good for the public imperceptibly would always seem to him the ideal of skill and the culminating point of happiness. "He who will not thank me," he said, "for the order and quiet calm that has accompanied my administration, cannot, however, deprive me of the share that belongs to me by the title of my good fortune." And he is inexhaustible in describing in lively and graceful expressions the kinds of effective and imperceptible services he believed he had rendered—services greatly superior to noisy and glorious deeds: "Actions which come from the workman's hand carelessly and noiselessly have most charm, that some honest man chooses later and brings from their obscurity to thrust them into the light for their own sake." Thus fortune served Montaigne to perfection, and even in his administration of affairs, in difficult conjunctures, he never had to belie his maxim, nor to step very far out of the way of life he had planned: "For my part I commend a gliding, solitary, and silent life." He reached the end of his magistracy almost satisfied with himself, having accomplished what he had promised himself, and much more than he had promised others.

The letter lately discovered by M. Horace de Viel–Castel corroborates the chapter in which Montaigne exhibits and criticises himself in the period of his public life. "That letter," says M. Payen, "is entirely on affairs. Montaigne is mayor; Bordeaux, lately disturbed, seems threatened by fresh agitations; the king's lieutenant is away. It is Wednesday, May 22, 1585; it is night, Montaigne is wakeful, and writes to the governor of the province." The letter, which is of too special and local an interest to be inserted here, may be summed up in these words:—Montaigne regretted the absence of Marshal de Matignon, and feared the consequences of its prolongation; he was keeping, and would continue to keep, him acquainted with all that was going on, and begged him to return as soon as his circumstances would permit. "We are looking after our gates and guards, and a little more carefully in your absence. . . . If anything important and fresh occurs, I shall send you a messenger immediately, so that if you hear no news from me, you may consider that nothing has happened." He begs M. de Matignon to remember, however, that he might not have time to warn him, "entreating you to consider that such movements are usually so sudden, that if they do occur they will take me by the throat without any warning." Besides, he will do everything to ascertain the march of events beforehand. "I will do what I can to hear news from all parts, and to that end shall visit and observe the inclinations of all sorts of men." Lastly, after keeping the marshal informed of everything, of the least rumours abroad in the city, he pressed him to return, assuring him "that we spare neither our care, nor, if need be, our lives to preserve everything in obedience to the king." Montaigne was never prodigal of protestations and praises, and what with others was a mere form of speech, was with him a real undertaking and the truth.

Things, however, became worse and worse: civil war broke out; friendly or hostile parties (the difference was not great) infested the country. Montaigne, who went to his country house as often as he could, whenever the duties of his office, which was drawing near its term, did not oblige him to be in Bordeaux, was exposed to every sort of insult and outrage. "I underwent," he said, "the inconveniences that moderation brings along with it in such a disease. I was pitied on all hands; to the Ghibelline I was a Guelph, and to the Guelph a Ghibelline." In the midst of his personal grievances he could disengage and raise his thoughts to reflections on the public misfortunes and on the degradation of men's characters. Considering closely the disorder of parties, and all the abject and wretched things which developed so quickly, he was ashamed to see leaders of renown stoop and debase themselves by cowardly complacency; for in those circumstances we know, like him, "that in the word of command to march, draw up, wheel, and the like, we obey him indeed; but all the rest is dissolute and free." "It pleases me," said Montaigne ironically, "to observe how much pusillanimity and cowardice there is in ambition; by how abject and servile ways it must arrive at its end." Despising ambition as he did, he was not sorry to see it unmasked by such practices and degraded in his sight. However, his goodness of heart overcoming his pride and contempt, he adds sadly, "it displeases me to see good and generous natures, and that are capable of justice, every day corrupted in the management and command of this confusion. . . . We had ill-contrived souls enough without spoiling those that were generous and good." He rather sought in that misfortune an opportunity and motive for fortifying and strengthening himself. Attacked one by one by many disagreeables and evils, which he would have endured more cheerfully in a heap—that is to say, all at once— —pursued by war, disease, by all the plagues (July 1585), in the course things were taking, he already asked himself to whom he and his could have recourse, of whom he could ask shelter and subsistence for his old age; and having looked and searched thoroughly all around, he found himself actually destitute and RUINED. For, "to let a man's self fall plumb down, and from so great a height, it ought to be in the arms of a solid, vigorous, and fortunate friendship. They are very rare, if there be any." Speaking in such a manner, we perceive that La Boetie had been some time dead. Then he felt that he must after all rely on himself in his distress, and must gain strength; now or never was the time to put into practice the lofty lessons he spent his life in collecting from the books of the philosophers. He took heart again, and attained all the height of his virtue: "In an ordinary and quiet time, a man prepares himself for moderate and common accidents; but in the confusion wherein we have been for these thirty years, every Frenchman, whether in particular or in general, sees himself every hour upon the point of the total ruin and overthrow of his fortune." And far from being discouraged and cursing fate for causing him to be born in so stormy an age, he suddenly congratulated himself: "Let us thank fortune that has not made us live in an effeminate, idle and languishing age." Since the curiosity of wise men seeks the past for disturbances in states in order to learn the secrets of history, and, as we should say, the whole physiology of the body social, "so does my curiosity," he declares, "make me in some sort please myself with seeing with my own eyes this notable spectacle of our public death, its forms and symptoms; and, seeing I could not hinder it, am content to be destined to assist in it, and thereby to instruct myself." I shall not suggest a consolation of that sort to most people; the greater part of mankind does not possess the heroic and eager curiosity of Empedocles and the elder Pliny, the two intrepid men who went straight to the volcanoes and the disturbances of nature to examine them at close quarters, at the risk of destruction and death. But to a man of Montaigne's nature, the thought of that stoical observation gave him consolation even amid real evils. Considering the condition of false peace and doubtful truce, the regime of dull and profound corruption which had preceded the last disturbances, he almost congratulated himself on seeing their cessation; for "it was," he said of the regime of Henri III., "an universal juncture of particular members, rotten to emulation of one another, and the most of them with inveterate ulcers, that neither required nor admitted of any cure. This conclusion therefore did really more animate than depress me." Note that his health, usually delicate, is here raised to the level of his morality, although what it had suffered through the various disturbances might have been enough to undermine it. He had the satisfaction of feeling that he had some hold against fortune, and that it would take a greater shock still to crush him.

Another consideration, humbler and more humane, upheld him in his troubles, the consolation arising from a common misfortune, a misfortune shared by all, and the sight of the courage of others. The people, especially the real people, they who are victims and not robbers, the peasants of his district, moved him by the manner in which they endured the same, or even worse, troubles than his. The disease or plague which raged at that time in the country pressed chiefly on the poor; Montaigne learned from them resignation and the practice of philosophy. "Let us look down upon the poor people that we see scattered upon the face of the earth, prone and intent upon their business, that neither know Aristotle nor Cato, example nor precept. Even from these does nature every day extract effects of constancy and patience, more pure and manly than those we so inquisitively study in the schools." And he goes on to describe them working to the bitter end, even in their grief, even in disease, until their strength failed them. "He that is now digging in my garden has this morning buried his father, or his son. . . . They never keep their beds but to die." The whole chapter is fine, pathetic, to the point, evincing noble, stoical elevation of mind, and also the cheerful and affable disposition which Montaigne said, with truth, was his by inheritance, and in which he had been nourished. There could be nothing better as regards "consolation in public calamities," except a chapter of some not more human, but of some truly divine book, in which the hand of God should be everywhere visible, not perfunctorily, as with Montaigne, but actually and lovingly present. In fact, the consolation Montaigne gives himself and others is perhaps as lofty and beautiful as human consolation without prayer can be.

He wrote the chapter, the twelfth of the third book, in the midst of the evils described, and before they were ended. He concluded it in his graceful and poetical way with a collection of examples, "a heap of foreign flowers," to which he furnished only the thread for fastening them together.

There is Montaigne to the life; no matter how seriously he spoke, it was always with the utmost charm. To form an opinion on his style you have only to open him indifferently at any page and listen to his talk on any subject; there is none that he did not enliven and make suggestive. In the chapter "Of Liars," for instance, after enlarging on his lack of memory and giving a list of reasons by which he might console himself, he suddenly added this fresh and delightful reason, that, thanks to his faculty for forgetting, "the places I revisit, and the books I read over again, always smile upon me with a fresh novelty." It is thus that on every subject he touched he was continually new, and created sources of freshness.

Montesquieu, in a memorable exclamation, said: "The four great poets, Plato, Malebranche, Shaftesbury, Montaigne!" How true it is of Montaigne! No French writer, including the poets proper, had so lofty an idea of poetry as he had. "From my earliest childhood," he said, "poetry had power over me to transport and transpierce me." He considered, and therein shows penetration, that "we have more poets than judges and interpreters of poetry. It is easier to write than to understand." In itself and its pure beauty his poetry defies definition; whoever desired to recognise it at a glance and discern of what it actually consisted would see no more than "the brilliance of a flash of lightning." In the constitution and continuity of his style, Montaigne is a writer very rich in animated, bold similes, naturally fertile in metaphors that are never detached from the thought, but that seize it in its very centre, in its interior, that join and bind it. In that respect, fully obeying his own genius, he has gone beyond and some times exceeded the genius of language. His concise, vigorous and always forcible style, by its poignancy, emphasises and repeats the meaning. It may be said of his style that it is a continual epigram, or an ever–renewed metaphor, a style that has only been successfully employed by the French once, by Montaigne himself. If we wanted to imitate him, supposing we had the power and were naturally fitted for it—if we desired to write with his severity, exact proportion, and diverse continuity of figures and turns—it would be necessary to force our language to be more powerful, and poetically more complete, than is usually our custom. Style a la Montaigne, consistent, varied in the series and assortment of the metaphors, exacts the creation of a portion of the tissue itself to hold them. It is absolutely necessary that in places the woof should be enlarged and extended, in order to weave into it the metaphor; but in defining him I come almost to write like him. The French language, French prose, which in fact always savours more or less of conversation, does not, naturally, possess the resources and the extent of canvas necessary for a continued picture: by the side of an animated metaphor it will often exhibit a sudden lacuna and some weak places. In filling this by boldness and invention as Montaigne did, in creating, in imagining the expression and locution that is wanting, our prose should appear equally finished. Style a la Montaigne would, in many respects, be openly at war with that of Voltaire. It could only come into being and flourish in the full freedom of the sixteenth century, in a frank, ingenious, jovial, keen, brave, and refined mind, of an unique stamp, that even for that time, seemed free and somewhat licentious, and that was inspired and emboldened, but not intoxicated by the pure and direct spirit of ancient sources.

Such as he is, Montaigne is the French Horace; he is Horatian in the groundwork, often in the form and expression, although in that he sometimes approaches Seneca. His book is a treasure–house of moral observations and of experience; at whatever page it is opened, and in what ever condition of mind, some wise thought expressed in a striking and enduring fashion is certain to be found. It will at once detach itself and engrave itself on the mind, a beautiful meaning in full and forcible words, in one vigorous line, familiar or great. The whole of his book, said Etienne Pasquier, is a real seminary of beautiful and remarkable sentences, and they come in so much the better that they run and hasten on without thrusting them selves into notice. There is something for every age, for every hour of life: you cannot read in it for any time without having the mind filled and lined as it were, or, to put it better, fully armed and clothed. We have just seen how much useful counsel and actual consolation it contains for an honourable man, born for private life, and fallen on times of disturbance and revolution. To this I shall add the counsel he gave those who, like myself and many men of my acquaintance, suffer from political disturbances without in any way provoking them, or believing ourselves capable of averting them. Montaigne, as Horace would have done, counsels them, while apprehending everything from afar off, not to be too much preoccupied with such matters in advance; to take advantage to the end of pleasant moments and bright intervals. Stroke on stroke come his piquant and wise similes, and he concludes, to my thinking, with the most delightful one of all, and one, besides, entirely appropriate and seasonable: it is folly and fret, he said, "to take out your furred gown at Saint John because you will want it at Christmas."

WHAT IS A CLASSIC?

A delicate question, to which somewhat diverse solutions might be given according to times and seasons. An intelligent man suggests it to me, and I intend to try, if not to solve it, at least to examine and discuss it face to face with my readers, were it only to persuade them to answer it for themselves, and, if I can, to make their opinion and mine on the point clear. And why, in criticism, should we not, from time to time, venture to treat some of those subjects which are not personal, in which we no longer speak of some one but of some thing? Our neighbours, the English, have well succeeded in making of it a special division of literature under the modest title of "Essays." It is true that in writing of such subjects, always slightly abstract and moral, it is advisable to speak of them in a season of quiet, to make sure of our own attention and of that of others, to seize one of those moments of calm moderation and leisure seldom granted our amiable France; even when she is desirous of being wise and is not making revolutions, her brilliant genius can scarcely tolerate them.

A classic, according to the usual definition, is an old author canonised by admiration, and an authority in his particular style. The word classic was first used in this sense by the Romans. With them not all the citizens of the different classes were properly called classici, but only those of the chief class, those who possessed an income of a certain fixed sum. Those who possessed a smaller income were described by the term infra classem, below the preeminent class. The word classicus was used in a figurative sense by Aulus Gellius, and applied to writers: a writer of worth and distinction, classicus assiduusque scriptor, a writer who is of account, has real property, and is not lost in the proletariate crowd. Such an expression implies an age sufficiently advanced to have already made some sort of valuation and classification of literature.

At first the only true classics for the moderns were the ancients. The Greeks, by peculiar good fortune and natural enlightenment of mind, had no classics but themselves. They were at first the only classical authors for the Romans, who strove and contrived to imitate them. After the great periods of Roman literature, after Cicero and Virgil, the Romans in their turn had their classics, who became almost exclusively the classical authors of the centuries which followed. The middle ages, which were less ignorant of Latin antiquity than is believed, but which lacked proportion and taste, confused the ranks and orders. Ovid was placed above Homer, and Boetius seemed a classic equal to Plato. The revival of learning in the fifteenth and sixteenth centuries helped to bring this long chaos to order, and then only was admiration rightly proportioned. Thenceforth the true classical authors of Greek and Latin antiquity stood out in a luminous background, and were harmoniously grouped on their two heights.

Meanwhile modern literatures were born, and some of the more precocious, like the Italian, already possessed the style of antiquity. Dante appeared, and, from the very first, posterity greeted him as a classic. Italian poetry has since shrunk into far narrower bounds; but, whenever it desired to do so, it always found again and preserved the impulse and echo of its lofty origin. It is no indifferent matter for a poetry to derive its point of departure and classical source in high places; for example, to spring from Dante rather than to issue laboriously from Malherbe.

Modern Italy had her classical authors, and Spain had every right to believe that she also had hers at a time when France was yet seeking hers. A few talented writers en dowed with originality and exceptional animation, a few brilliant efforts, isolated, without following, interrupted and recommenced, did not suffice to endow a nation with a solid and imposing basis of literary wealth. The idea of a classic implies something that has continuance and consistence, and which produces unity and tradition fashions and transmits itself, and endures. It was only after the glorious years of Louis XIV. that the nation felt with tremor and pride that such good fortune had happened to her. Every voice in formed Louis XIV. of it with flattery, exaggeration, and emphasis, yet with a certain sentiment of truth. Then arose a singular and striking contradiction: those men of whom Perrauit was the chief, the men who were most smitten with the marvels of the age of Louis the Great, who even went the length of sacrificing the ancients to the moderns, aimed at exalting and canonising even those whom they regarded as inveterate opponents and adversaries. Boileau avenged and angrily upheld the ancients against Perrault, who extolled the moderns—that is to say, Corneille, Moliere, Pascal, and the eminent men of his age, Boileau, one of the first, included. Kindly La Fontaine, taking part in the dispute in behalf of the learned Huet, did not perceive that, in spite of his defects, he was in his turn on the point of being held as a classic himself.

Example is the best definition. From the time France possessed her age of Louis XIV. and could contemplate it at a little distance, she knew, better than by any arguments, what to be classical meant. The eighteenth century, even in its medley of things, strengthened this idea through some fine works, due to its four great men. Read Voltaire's Age of Louis XIV., Montesquieu's Greatness and Fall of the Romans, Buffon's Epochs of Nature, the beautiful pages of reverie and natural description of Rousseau's Savoyard Vicar, and say if the eighteenth century, in these memorable works, did not understand how to reconcile tradition with freedom of development and independence. But at the be ginning of the present century and under the Empire, in sight of the first attempts of a decidedly new and somewhat adventurous literature, the idea of a classic in a few resist ing minds, more sorrowful than severe, was strangely nar rowed and contracted. The first Dictionary of the Academy (1694) merely defined a classical author as "a much−approved ancient writer, who is an authority as regards the subject he treats." The Dictionary of the Academy of 1835 narrows that definition still more, and gives precision and even limit to its rather vague form. It describes classical authors as those "who have become models in any language whatever," and in all the articles which follow, the expressions, models, fixed rules for composition and style, strict rules of art to which men must conform, continually recur. That definition of classic was evidently made by the respectable Academicians, our predecessors, in face and sight of what was then called romantic—that is to say, in sight of the enemy. It seems to me time to renounce those timid and restrictive definitions and to free our mind of them. A true classic, as I should like to hear it defined, is an author who has enriched the human mind, increased its treasure, and caused it to advance a step; who has discovered some moral and not equivocal truth, or revealed some eternal passion in that heart where all seemed known and discovered; who has expressed his thought, observation, or invention, in no matter what form, only provided it be broad and great, refined and sensible, sane and beautiful in itself; who has spoken to all in his own peculiar style, a style which is found to be also that of the whole world, a style new without neologism, new and old, easily contemporary with all time.

Such a classic may for a moment have been revolutionary; it may at least have seemed so, but it is not; it only lashed and subverted whatever prevented the restoration of the balance of order and beauty.

If it is desired, names may be applied to this definition which I wish to make purposely majestic and fluctuating, or in a word, all– embracing. I should first put there Corneille of the Polyeucte, Cinna, and Horaces. I should put Moliere there, the fullest and most complete poetic genius we have ever had in France. Goethe, the king of critics, said:—

"Moliere is so great that he astonishes us afresh every time we read him. He is a man apart; his plays border on the tragic, and no one has the courage to try and imitate him. His Avare, where vice destroys all affection between father and son, is one of the most sublime works, and dramatic in the highest degree. In a drama every action ought to be important in itself, and to lead to an action greater still. In this respect Tartuffe is a model. What a piece of exposition the first scene is! From the beginning everything has an important meaning, and causes something much more important to be foreseen. The exposition in a certain play of Lessing that might be mentioned is very fine, but the world only sees that of Tartuffe once. It is the finest of the kind we possess. Every year I read a play of Moliere, just as from time to time I contemplate some engraving after the great Italian masters."

I do not conceal from myself that the definition of the classic I have just given somewhat exceeds the notion usually ascribed to the term. It should, above all, include conditions of uniformity, wisdom, moderation, and reason, which dominate and contain all the others. Having to praise M. Royer–Collard, M. de Remusat said—"If he derives purity of taste, propriety of terms, variety of expression, attentive care in suiting the diction to the thought, from our classics, he owes to himself alone the distinctive character he gives it all." It is here evident that the part allotted to classical qualities seems mostly to depend on harmony and nuances of expression, on graceful and temperate style: such is also the most general opinion. In this sense the pre–eminent classics would be writers of a middling order, exact, sensible, elegant, always clear, yet of noble feeling and airily veiled strength. Marie–Joseph Chenier has described the poetics of those temperate and accomplished writers in lines where he shows himself their happy disciple:—

"It is good sense, reason which does all,—virtue, genius, soul, talent, and taste.—What is virtue? reason put in practice;—talent? reason expressed with brilliance;—soul? reason delicately put forth;—and genius is sublime reason."

While writing those lines he was evidently thinking of Pope, Boileau, and Horace, the master of them all. The peculiar characteristic of the theory which subordinated imagination and feeling itself to reason, of which Scaliger perhaps gave the first sign among the moderns, is, properly speaking, the Latin theory, and for a long time it was also by preference the French theory. If it is used appositely, if the term reason is not abused, that theory possesses some truth; but it is evident that it is abused, and that if, for instance, reason can be confounded with poetic genius and make one with it in a moral epistle, it cannot be the same thing as the genius, so varied and so diversely creative in its expression of the passions, of the drama or the epic. Where will you find reason in the fourth book of the AEneid and the transports of Dido? Be that as it may, the spirit which prompted the theory, caused writers who ruled their inspiration, rather than those who abandoned themselves to it, to be placed in the first rank of classics; to put Virgil there more surely than Homer, Racine in preference to Corneille. The masterpiece to which the theory likes to point, which in fact brings together all conditions of prudence, strength, tempered boldness, moral elevation, and grandeur, is Athalie. Turenne in his two last campaigns and Racine in Athalie are the great examples of what wise and prudent men are capable of when they reach the maturity of their genius and attain their supremest boldness.

Buffon, in his Discourse on Style, insisting on the unity of design, arrangement, and execution, which are the stamps of true classical works, said:—"Every subject is one, and however vast it is, it can be comprised in a single treatise. Interruptions, pauses, sub– divisions should only be used when many subjects are treated, when, having to speak of great, intricate, and dissimilar things, the march of genius is interrupted by the multiplicity of obstacles, and contracted by the necessity of circumstances: otherwise, far from making a work more solid, a great number of divisions destroys the unity of its parts; the book appears clearer to the view, but the author's design remains obscure." And he continues his criticism, having in view Montesquieu's Spirit of Laws, an excellent book at bottom, but sub–divided: the famous author, worn out before the end, was unable to infuse inspiration into all his ideas, and to arrange all his matter. However, I can scarcely believe that Buffon was not also thinking, by way of contrast, of Bossuet's Discourse on Universal History, a subject vast indeed, and yet of such an unity that the great orator was able to comprise it in a single treatise. When we open the first edition, that of 1681, before the division into chapters, which was introduced later, passed from the margin into the text, very thing is developed in a single series, almost in one breath. It might be said that the orator has here acted like the nature of which Buffon speaks, that "he has worked on an eternal plan from which he has nowhere departed," so deeply does he seem to have entered into the familiar counsels and designs of providence.

Are Athalie and the Discourse on Universal History the greatest masterpieces that the strict classical theory can present to its friends as well as to its enemies? In spite of the admirable simplicity and dignity in the achievement of such unique productions, we should like, nevertheless, in the interests of art, to expand that theory a little, and to show that it is possible to enlarge it without relaxing the tension. Goethe, whom I like to quote on such a subject, said:—

"I call the classical healthy, and the romantic sickly. In my opinion the Nibelungen song is as much a classic as Homer. Both are healthy and vigorous. The works of the day are romantic, not because they are new, but because they are weak, ailing, or sickly. Ancient works are classical not because they are old, but because they are powerful, fresh, and healthy. If we regarded romantic and classical from those two points of view we should soon all agree."

Indeed, before determining and fixing the opinions on that matter, I should like every unbiassed mind to take a voyage round the world and devote itself to a survey of different literatures in their primitive vigour and infinite variety. What would be seen? Chief of all a Homer, the father of the classical world, less a single distinct individual than the vast living expression of a whole epoch and a semi–barbarous civilisation. In order to make him a true classic, it was necessary to attribute to him later a design, a plan, literary invention, qualities of atticism and urbanity of which he had certainly never dreamed in the luxuriant development of his natural inspirations. And who appear by his side? August, venerable ancients, the AEschyluses and the Sophocles, mutilated, it is true, and only there to present us with a debris of themselves, the survivors of many others as worthy, doubtless, as they to survive, but who have succumbed to the injuries of time. This thought alone would teach a man of impartial mind not to look upon the whole of even classical literatures with a too narrow and restricted view; he would learn that the exact and well–proportioned order which has since so largely prevailed in our admiration of the past was only the outcome of artificial circumstances.

And in reaching the modern world, how would it be? The greatest names to be seen at the beginning of literatures are those which disturb and run counter to certain fixed ideas of what is beautiful and appropriate in poetry. For example, is Shakespeare a classic? Yes, now, for England and the world; but in the time of Pope he was not considered so. Pope and his friends were the only pre–eminent classics; directly after their death they seemed so for ever. At the present time they are still classics, as they deserve to be, but they are only of the second order, and are for ever subordinated and relegated to their rightful place by him who has again come to his own on the height of the horizon.

It is not, however, for me to speak ill of Pope or his great disciples, above all, when they possess pathos and naturalness like Goldsmith: after the greatest they are perhaps the most agreeable writers and the poets best fitted to add charm to life. Once when Lord Bolingbroke was writing to Swift, Pope added a postscript, in which he said—"I think some advantage would result to our age, if we three spent three years together." Men who, without boasting, have the right to say such things must never be spoken of lightly: the fortunate ages, when men of talent could propose such things, then no chimera, are rather to be envied. The ages called by the name of Louis XIV. or of Queen Anne are, in the dispassionate sense of the word, the only true classical ages, those which offer protection and a favourable climate to real talent. We know only to well how in our untrammelled times, through the instability and storminess of the age, talents are lost and dissipated. Nevertheless, let us acknowledge our age's part and superiority in greatness. True and sovereign genius triumphs over the very difficulties that cause others to fail: Dante, Shakespeare, and Milton were able to attain their height and produce their imperishable works in spite of obstacles, hardships and tempests. Byron's opinion of Pope has been much discussed, and the explanation of it sought in the kind of contradiction by which the singer of Don Juan and Childe Harold extolled the purely classical school and pronounced it the only good one, while himself acting so differently. Goethe spoke the truth on that point when he remarked that Byron, great by the flow and source of poetry, feared that Shakespeare was more powerful than himself in the creation and realisation of his characters. "He would have liked to deny it; the elevation so free from egoism irritated him; he felt when near it that he could not display himself at ease. He never denied Pope, because he did not fear him; he knew that Pope was only a low wall by his side."

If, as Byron desired, Pope's school had kept the supremacy and a sort of honorary empire in the past, Byron would have been the first and only poet in his particular style; the height of Pope's wall shuts out Shakespeare's great figure from sight, whereas when Shakespeare reigns and rules in all his greatness, Byron is only second.

In France there was no great classic before the age of Louis XIV.; the Dantes and Shakespeares, the early authorities to whom, in times of emancipation, men sooner or later return, were wanting. There were mere sketches of great poets, like Mathurin Regnier, like Rabelais, without any ideal, without the depth of emotion and the seriousness which canonises. Montaigne was a kind of premature classic, of the family of Horace, but for want of worthy surroundings, like a spoiled child, he gave himself up to the unbridled fancies of his style and humour. Hence it happened that France, less than any other nation, found in her old authors a right to demand vehemently at a certain time literary liberty and freedom, and that it was more difficult for her, in enfranchising herself, to remain classical. However, with Moliere and La Fontaine among her classics of the great period, nothing could justly be refused to those who possessed courage and ability.

The important point now seems to me to be to uphold, while extending, the idea and belief. There is no receipt for making classics; this point should be clearly recognised. To believe that an author will become a classic by imitating certain qualities of purity, moderation, accuracy, and elegance, independently of the style and inspiration, is to believe that after Racine the father there is a place for Racine the son; dull and estimable role, the worst in poetry. Further, it is hazardous to take too quickly and without opposition the place of a classic in the sight of one's contemporaries; in that case there is a good chance of not retaining the position with posterity. Fontanes in his day was regarded by his friends as a pure classic; see how at twenty-five years' distance his star has set. How many of these precocious classics are there who do not endure, and who are so only for a while! We turn round one morning and are surprised not to find them standing behind us. Madame de Sevigne would wittily say they possessed but an evanescent colour. With regard to classics, the least expected prove the best and greatest: seek them rather in the vigorous genius born immortal and flourishing for ever. Apparently the least classical of the four great poets of the age of Louis XIV. was Moliere; he was then applauded far more than he was esteemed; men took delight in him without understanding his worth. After him, La Fontaine seemed the least classical: observe after two centuries what is the result for both. Far above Boileau, even above Racine, are they not now unanimously considered to possess in the highest degree the characteristics of an all-embracing morality?

Meanwhile there is no question of sacrificing or depreciating anything. I believe the temple of taste is to be rebuilt; but its reconstruction is merely a matter of enlargement, so that it may become the home of all noble human beings, of all who have permanently increased the sum of the mind's delights and possessions. As for me, who cannot, obviously, in any degree pretend to be the architect or designer of such a temple, I shall confine myself to expressing a few earnest wishes, to submit, as it were, my designs for the edifice. Above all I should desire not to exclude any one among the worthy, each should be in his place there, from Shakespeare, the freest of creative geniuses, and the greatest of classics without knowing it, to Andrieux, the last of classics in little. "There is more than one chamber in the mansions of my Father;" that should be as true of the kingdom of the beautiful here below, as of the kingdom of Heaven. Homer, as always and everywhere, should be first, likest a god; but behind him, like the procession of the three wise kings of the East, would be seen the three great poets, the three Homers, so long ignored by us, who wrote epics for the use of the old peoples of Asia, the poets Valmiki, Vyasa of the Hindoos, and Firdousi of the Persians: in the domain of taste it is well to know that such men exist, and not to divide the human race. Our homage paid to what is recognized as soon as perceived, we must not stray further; the eye should delight in a thousand pleasing or majestic spectacles, should rejoice in a thousand varied and surprising combinations, whose apparent confusion would never be without concord and harmony. The oldest of the wise men and poets, those who put human morality into maxims, and those who in simple fashion sung it, would converse together in rare and gentle speech, and would not be surprised at understanding each other's meaning at the very first word. Solon, Hesiod, Theognis, Job, Solomon, and why not Confucius, would welcome the cleverest moderns, La Rochefoucauld and La Bruyere, who, when listening to them, would say "they knew all that we know, and in repeating life's experiences, we have discovered nothing." On the hill, most easily discernible, and of most accessible ascent, Virgil, surrounded by Menander, Tibullus, Terence, Fenelon, would occupy himself in discoursing with them with great charm and divine enchantment: his gentle countenance would shine with an inner light, and be tinged with modesty; as on the day when entering the theatre at Rome, just as they finished reciting his verses, he saw the people rise with an unanimous movement and pay to him the same homage as to Augustus. Not far from him, regretting the separation from so dear a friend, Horace, in his turn, would preside (as far as so accomplished and wise a poet could preside) over the group of poets of social life who could talk although they sang,—Pope, Boileau, the one become less irritable, the other less fault-finding. Montaigne, a true poet, would be among them, and would give the finishing touch that should deprive that delightful corner of the air of a literary school. There would La Fontaine forget himself, and becoming less volatile would wander no more. Voltaire would be attracted by it, but while finding pleasure in it would not have patience to remain. A little lower down, on the same hill as Virgil, Xenophon, with simple bearing, looking in no way like a general, but rather resembling a priest of the Muses, would be seen gathering round him the Attics of every tongue and of every nation, the Addisons, Pellissons, Vauvenargues—all who feel the value of an easy persuasiveness, an exquisite simplicity, and a gentle negligence mingled with ornament. In the centre of the place, in the portico of the principal temple (for there would be several in the enclosure), three great men would like to meet often, and when they were together, no fourth, however great, would dream of joining their discourse or their silence. In them would be seen beauty, proportion in greatness, and that perfect harmony which appears but once in the full youth of the world. Their three names have become the ideal of art—Plato, Sophocles, and Demosthenes. Those demi-gods honoured, we see a numerous and familiar company of choice spirits who follow, the Cervantes and Molieres, practical painters of life, indulgent friends who are still the first of benefactors, who laughingly embrace all mankind, turn man's experience to gaiety, and know the powerful workings of a sensible, hearty, and legitimate joy. I do not wish to make this description, which if complete would fill a volume, any longer. In the middle ages, believe me, Dante would occupy the sacred heights: at the feet of the singer of Paradise all Italy would be spread out like a garden; Boccaccio and Ariosto would there disport themselves, and Tasso would find again the orange groves of Sorrento. Usually a corner would be reserved for each of the various nations, but the authors would take delight in leaving it, and in their travels would recognise, where we should least expect it, brothers or masters. Lucretius, for example, would enjoy discussing the origin of the world and the reducing of chaos to order with Milton. But both arguing from their own point of view, they would only agree as regards divine pictures of poetry and nature.

Such are our classics; each individual imagination may finish the sketch and choose the group preferred. For it is necessary to make a choice, and the first condition of taste, after obtaining knowledge of all, lies not in continual travel, but in rest and cessation from wandering. Nothing blunts and destroys taste so much as endless journeyings; the poetic spirit is not the Wandering Jew. However, when I speak of resting and making choice, my meaning is not that we are to imitate those who charm us most among our masters in the past. Let us be content to know them, to penetrate them, to admire them; but let us, the late-comers, endeavour to be ourselves. Let us have the sincerity and naturalness of our own thoughts, of our own feelings; so much is always possible. To that let us add what is more difficult, elevation, an aim, if possible, towards an exalted goal; and while speaking our own language, and submitting to the conditions of the times in which we live, whence we derive our strength and our defects, let us ask from time to time, our brows lifted towards the heights and our eyes fixed on the group of honoured mortals: what would that say of us?

But why speak always of authors and writings? Maybe an age is coming when there will be no more writing. Happy those who read and read again, those who in their reading can follow their unrestrained inclination! There comes a time in life when, all our journeys over, our experiences ended, there is no enjoyment more delightful than to study and thoroughly examine the things we know, to take pleasure in what we feel, and in seeing and seeing again the people we love: the pure joys of our maturity. Then it is that the word classic takes its true meaning, and is defined for every man of taste by an irresistible choice. Then taste is formed, it is shaped and definite; then good sense, if we are to possess it at all, is perfected in us. We have neither more time for experiments, nor a desire to go forth in search of pastures newf We cling to our friends, to those proved by long intercourse. Old wine, old books, old friends. We say to ourselves with Voltaire in these delightful lines:—"Let us enjoy, let us write, let us live, my dear Horace!...I have lived longer than you: my verse will not last so long. But on the brink of the tomb I shall make it my chief care—to follow the lessons of your philosophy—to despise death in enjoying life—to read your writings full of charm and good sense—as we drink an old wine which revives our senses."

In fact, be it Horace or another who is the author preferred, who reflects our thoughts in all the wealth of their maturity, of some one of those excellent and antique minds shall we request an interview at every moment; of some one of them shall we ask a friendship which never deceives, which could not fail us; to some one of them shall we appeal for that sensation of serenity and amenity (we have often need of it) which reconciles us with mankind and with ourselves.

THE POETRY OF THE CELTIC RACES

BY ERNEST RENAN

TRANSLATED BY W. G. HUTCHISON

INTRODUCTORY NOTE

Ernest Renan was born in 1823, at Treguier in Brittany. He was educated for the priesthood, but never took orders, turning at first to teaching. He continued his studies in religion and philology, and, after traveling in Syria on a government commission, he returned to Paris and became professor of Hebrew in the College de France, from which he was suspended for a time on account of protests against his heretical teachings. He died in 1892.

Renan's activity divides itself into two parts. The first culminated in his two great works on the "Origins of Christianity" and on the "History of Israel." As to the scientific value of these books there is difference of opinion, as was to be expected in a treatment of such subjects to the exclusion of the miraculous. But the delicacy and vividness of his portraits of the great personalities of Hebrew history, and the acuteness of his analysis of national psychology, are not to be denied.

The other part of his work is more miscellaneous, but most of it is in some sense philosophical or autobiographical. Believing **pro**foundly in scientific method, Renan was unable to find in science a basis for either ethics or **metaph**ysics, and ended in a skepticism often ironical, yet not untinged with mysticism.

"He was an amazing write**r**," says M. Faguet, "and disconcerted criticism by the impossibility of explaining his methods of procedure; he was luminous, supple, naturally pliant and yielding; beneath his apparently effeminate grace an extraordinary strength of character would suddenly make itself felt; he had, more than any nineteenth-century writer, the quality of charm; he exercised a caressing innuence which enveloped, and finally conquered, the reader."

In no kind of writing was Renan's command of style more notable than in the description of scenery; and in his pictures of his native Brittany in the essay on "The Poetry of the Celtic Races," as well as in his analysis of national qualities, two of his most characteristic powers are admirably displayed.

THE POETRY OF THE CELTIC RACES

Every one who travels through the Armorican peninsula experiences a change of the most abrupt description, as soon as he leaves behind the district most closely bordering upon the continent, in which the cheerful but commonplace type of face of Normandy and Maine is continually in evidence, and passes into the true Brittany, that which merits its name by language and race. A cold wind arises full of a vague sadness, and carries the soul to other thoughts; the tree-tops are bare and twisted; the heath with its monotony of tint stretches away into the distance; at every step the granite protrudes from a soil too scanty to cover it; a sea that is almost always sombre girdles the horizon with eternal moaning. The same contrast is manifest in the people: to Norman vulgarity, to a plump and prosperous population, happy to live, full of its own interests, egoistical as are all these who make a habit of enjoyment, succeeds a timid and reserved race living altogether within itself, heavy in appearance but capable of profound feeling, and of an adorable delicacy in its religious instincts. A like change is apparent, I am told, in passing from England into Wales, from the Lowlands of Scotland, English by language and manners, into the Gaelic Highlands; and too, though with a perceptible difference, when one buries oneself in the districts of Ireland where the race has remained pure from all admixture of alien blood. It seems like entering on the subterranean strata of another world, and one experiences in some measure the impression given us by Dante, when he leads us from one circle of his Inferno to another.

Sufficient attention is not given to the peculiarity of this fact of an ancient race living, until our days and almost under our eyes, its own life in some obscure islands and peninsulas in the West, more and more affected, it is true, by external influences, but still faithful to its own tongue, to its own memories, to its own customs, and to its own genius. Especially is it forgotten that this little people, now concentrated on the very confines of the world, in the midst of rocks and mountains whence its enemies have been powerless to force it, is in possession of a literature which, in the Middle Ages, exercised an immense influence, changed the current of European civilisation, and imposed its poetical motives on nearly the whole of Christendom. Yet it is only necessary to open the authentic monuments of the Gaelic genius to be convinced that the race which created them has had its own original manner of feeling and thinking, that nowhere has the eternal illusion clad itself in more seductive hues, and that in the great chorus of humanity no race equals this for penetrative notes that go to the very heart. Alas! it too is doomed to disappear, this emerald set in the Western seas. Arthur will return no more from his isle of faery, and St. Patrick was right when he said to Ossian, "The heroes that thou weepest are dead; can they be born again?" It is high time to note, before they shall have passed away, the divine tones thus expiring on the horizon before the growing tumult of uniform civilisation. Were criticism to set itself the task of calling back these distant echoes, and of giving a voice to races that are no more, would not that suffice to absolve it from the reproach, unreasonably and too frequently brought against it, of being only negative?

Good works now exist which facilitate the task of him who undertakes the study of these interesting literatures. Wales, above all, is distinguished by scientific and literary activity, not always accompanied, it is true, by a very rigorous critical spirit, but deserving the highest praise. There, researches which would bring honour to the most active centres of learning in Europe are the work of enthusiastic amateurs. A peasant called Owen Jones published in 1801–7, under the name of the Myvyrian Archaiology of Wales, the precious collection which is to this day the arsenal of Cymric antiquities. A number of erudite and zealous workers, Aneurin Owen, Thomas Price of Crickhowell, William Rees, and John Jones, following in the footsteps of the Myvyrian peasant, set themselves to finish his work, and to profit from the treasures which he had collected. A woman of distinction, Lady Charlotte Guest, charged herself with the task of acquainting Europe with the collection of the Mabinogion, [Footnote: The Mabinogion, from the Llyfr Coch O Hergest and other ancient Welsh Manuscripts, with an English Translation and Notes. By Lady Charlotte Guest. London and Llandovery, 1837–49. The word Mabinogi (in the plural Mabinogion) designates a form of romantic narrative peculiar to Wales. The origin and primitive meaning of this word are very uncertain, and Lady Guest's right to apply it to the whole of the narratives which she has published is open to doubt.] the pearl of Gaelic literature, the completest expression of the Cymric genius. This magnificent work, executed in twelve years with the luxury that the wealthy English amateur knows how to use in his publications, will one day attest how full of life the consciousness of the Celtic races remained in the present century. Only indeed the sincerest patriotism could inspire a woman to undertake and achieve so vast a literary monument. Scotland and Ireland have in like measure been enriched by a host of studies of their ancient history. Lastly, our own Brittany, though all too rarely studied with the philological and critical rigour now exacted in works of erudition, has furnished Celtic antiquities with her share of worthy research. Does it not suffice to cite M. de la Villemarque, whose name will be henceforth associated among us with these studies, and whose services are so incontestable, that criticism need have no fear of depreciating him in the eyes of a public which has accepted him with so much warmth and sympathy?

I.

If the excellence of races is to be appreciated by the purity of their blood and the inviolability of their national character, it must needs be admitted that none can vie in nobility with the still surviving remains of the Celtic race. [Footnote: To avoid all misunderstanding, I ought to point out that by the word Celtic I designate here, not the whole of the great race which, at a remote epoch, formed the population of nearly the whole of Western Europe, but simply the four groups which, in our days, still merit this name, as opposed to the Teutons and to the Neo–Latin peoples. These four groups are: (i) The inhabitants of Wales or Cambria, and the peninsula of Cornwall, bearing even now the ancient name of Cymry; (2) the Bretons bretonnants, or dwellers in French Brittany speaking Bas–Breton, who represent an emigration of the Cymry from Wales; (3) the Gaels of the North of Scotland speaking Gaelic; (4) the Irish, although a very profound line of demarcation separates Ireland from the rest of the Celtic family. [It is also necessary to point out that Renan in this essay applies the name Breton both to the Bretons proper, i. e. the inhabitants of Brittany, and to the British members of the Celtic race.—Translator's Note.]]

Never has a human family lived more apart from the world, and been purer from all alien admixture. Confined by conquest within forgotten islands and peninsulas, it has reared an impassable barrier against external influences; it has drawn all from itself; it has lived solely on its own capital. From this ersues that powerful individuality, that hatred of the foreigner, which even in our own days has formed the essential feature of the Celtic peoples. Roman civilisation scarcely reached them, and left among them but few traces. The Teutonic invasion drove them back, but did not penetrate them. At the present hour they are still constant in resistance to an invasion dangerous in an altogether different way,– –that of modern civilisation, destructive as it is of local variations and national types. Ireland in particular (and herein we perhaps have the secret of her irremediable weakness) is the only country in Europe where the native can produce the titles of his descent, and designate with certainty, even in the darkness of prehistoric ages, the race from which he has sprung.

It is in this secluded life, in this defiance of all that comes from without, that we must search for the explanation of the chief features of the Celtic character. It has all the failings, and all the good qualities, of the solitary man; at once proud and timid, strong in feeling and feeble in action, at home free and unreserved, to the outside world awkward and embarrassed. It distrusts the foreigner, because it sees in him a being more refined than itself, who abuses its simplicity. Indifferent to the admiration of others, it asks only one thing, that it should be left to itself. It is before all else a domestic race, fitted for family life and fireside joys. In no other race has the bond of blood been stronger, or has it created more duties, or attached man to his fellow with so much breadth and depth. Every social institution of the Celtic peoples was in the beginning only an extension of the family. A common tradition attests, to this very day, that nowhere has the trace of this great institution of relationship been better preserved than in Brittany. There is a widely–spread belief in that country, that blood speaks, and that two relatives, unknown one to the other, in any part of the world wheresoever it may be, recognise each other by the secret and mysterious emotion which they feel in each other's presence. Respect for the dead rests on the same principle. Nowhere has reverence for the dead been greater than among the Briton peoples; nowhere have so many memories and prayers clustered about the tomb. This is because life is not for these people a personal adventure, undertaken by each man on his own account, and at his own risks and perils; it is a link in a long chain, a gift received and handed on, a debt paid and a duty done.

It is easily discernible how little fitted were natures so strongly concentrated to furnish one of those brilliant developments, which imposes the momentary ascendency of a people on the world; and that, no doubt, is why the part played externally by the Cymric race has always been a secondary one. Destitute of the means of expansion, alien to all idea of aggression and conquest, little desirous of making its thought prevail outside itself, it has only known how to retire so far as space has permitted, and then, at bay in its last place of retreat, to make an invincible resistance to its enemies. Its very fidelity has been a useless devotion. Stubborn of submission and ever behind the age, it is faithful to its conquerors when its conquerors are no longer faithful to themselves. It was the last to defend its religious independence against Rome—and it has become the staunchest stronghold of Catholicism; it was the last in France to defend its political independence against the king—and it has given to the world the last royalists.

Thus the Celtic race has worn itself out in resistance to its time, and in the defence of desperate causes. It does not seem as though in any epoch it had any aptitude for political life. The spirit of family stifled within it all attempts at more extended organisation. Moreover, it does not appear that the peoples which form it are by themselves susceptible of progress. To them life appears as a fixed condition, which man has no power to alter. Endowed with little initiative, too much inclined to look upon themselves as minors and in tutelage, they are quick to believe in destiny and resign themselves to it. Seeing how little audacious they are against God, one would scarcely believe this race to be the daughter of Japhet.

Thence ensues its sadness. Take the songs of its bards of the sixth century; they weep more defeats than they sing victories. Its history is itself only one long lament; it still recalls its exiles, its flights across the seas. If at times it seems to be cheerful, a tear is not slow to glisten behind its smile; it does not know that strange forgetfulness of human conditions and destinies which is called gaiety. Its songs of joy end as elegies; there is nothing to equal the delicious sadness of its national melodies. One might call them emanations from on high which, falling drop by drop upon the soul, pass through it like memories of another world. Never have men feasted so long upon these solitary delights of the spirit, these poetic memories which simultaneously intercross all the sensations of life, so vague, so deep, so penetrative, that one might die from them, without being able to say whether it was from bitterness or sweetness.

The infinite delicacy of feeling which characterises the Celtic race is closely allied to its need of concentration. Natures that are little capable of expansion are nearly always those that feel most deeply, for the deeper the feeling, the less it tends to express itself. Thence we have that charming shamefastness, that veiled and exquisite sobriety, equally far removed from the sentimental rhetoric too familiar to the Latin races, and the reflective simplicity of Germany, which are so admirably displayed in the ballads published by M. de la Villemarque. The apparent reserve of the Celtic peoples, often taken for coldness, is due to this inward timidity which makes them believe that a feeling loses half its value if it be expressed; and that the heart ought to have no other spectator than itself.

If it be permitted us to assign sex to nations as to individuals, we should have to say without hesitance that the Celtic race, especially with regard to its Cymric or Breton branch, is an essentially feminine race. No human family, I believe, has carried so much mystery into love. No other has conceived with more delicacy the ideal of woman, or been more fully dominated by it. It is a sort of intoxication, a madness, a vertigo. Read the strange Mabinogi of Peredur, or its French imitation Parceval le Gallois; its pages are, as it were, dewy with feminine sentiment. Woman appears therein as a kind of vague vision, an intermediary between man and the supernatural world. I am acquainted with no literature that offers anything analogous to this. Compare Guinevere or Iseult with those Scandinavian furies Gudrun and Chrimhilde, and you will avow that woman such as chivalry conceived her, an ideal of sweetness and loveliness set up as the supreme end of life, is a creation neither classical, nor Christian, nor Teutonic, but in reality Celtic.

Imaginative power is nearly always proportionate to concentration of feeling, and lack of the external development of life. The limited nature of Greek and Italian imagination is due to the easy expansiveness of the peoples of the South, with whom the soul, wholly spread abroad, reflects but little within itself. Compared with the classical imagination, the Celtic imagination is indeed the infinite contrasted with the finite. In the fine Mabinogi of the Dream of Maxem Wledig, the Emperor Maximus beholds in a dream a young maiden so beautiful, that on waking he declares he cannot live without her. For several years his envoys scour the world in search of her; at last she is discovered in Brittany. So is it with the Celtic race; it has worn itself out in taking dreams for realities, and in pursuing its splendid visions. The essential element in the Celt's poetic life is the adventure—that is to say, the pursuit of the unknown, an endless quest after an object ever flying from desire. It was of this that St. Brandan dreamed, that Peredur sought with his mystic chivalry, that Knight Owen asked of his subterranean journeyings. This race desires the infinite, it thirsts for it, and pursues it at all costs, beyond the tomb, beyond hell itself. The characteristic failing of the Breton peoples, the tendency to drunkenness—a failing which, according to the traditions of the sixth century, was the cause of their disasters—is due to this invincible need of illusion. Do not say that it is an appetite for gross enjoyment; never has there been a people more sober and more alien to all sensuality. No, the Bretons sought in mead what Owen, St. Brandan, and Peredur sought in their own way,—the vision of the invisible world. To this day in Ireland drunkenness forms a part of all Saint's Day festivals—that is to say, the festivals which best have retained their national and popular aspect.

Thence arises the profound sense of the future and of the eternal destinies of his race, which has ever borne up the Cymry, and kept him young still beside his conquerors who have grown old. Thence that dogma of the resurrection of the heroes, which appears to have been one of those that Christianity found most difficulty in rooting out. Thence Celtic Messianism, that belief in a future avenger who shall restore Cambria, and deliver her out of the hands of her oppressors, like the mysterious Leminok promised by Merlin, the Lez– Breiz of the Armoricans, the Arthur of the Welsh. [Footnote: M. Augustin Thierry has finely remarked that the renown attaching to Welsh prophecies in the Middle Ages was due to their steadfastness in affirming the future of their race. (Histoire de la Conquete d'Angleterre.)] The hand that arose from the mere, when the sword of Arthur fell therein, that seized it, and brandished it thrice, is the hope of the Celtic races. It is thus that little peoples dowered with imagination revenge themselves on their conquerors. Feeling themselves to be strong inwardly and weak outwardly, they protest, they exult; and such a strife unloosing their might, renders them capable of miracles. Nearly all great appeals to the supernatural are due to peoples hoping against all hope. Who shall say what in our own times has fermented in the bosom of the most stubborn, the most powerless of nationalities—Poland? Israel in humiliation dreamed of the spiritual conquest of the world, and the dream has come to pass.

II

At a first glance the literature of Wales is divided into three perfectly distinct distinct branches: the bardic or lyric, which shines forth in splendour in the sixth century by the works of Taliessin, of Aneurin, and of Liware'h Hen, and continues through an uninterrupted series of imitations up to modern times; the Mabinogion, or literature of romance, fixed towards the twelfth century, but linking themselves in the groundwork of their ideas with the remotest ages of the Celtic genius; finally, an ecclesiastical and legendary literature, impressed with a distinct stamp of its own. These three literatures seem to have existed side by side, almost without knowledge of one another. The bards, proud of their solemn rhetoric, held in disdain the popular tales, the form of which they considered careless; on the other hand, both bards and romancers appear to have had few relations with the clergy; and one at times might be tempted to suppose that they ignored the existence of Christianity. To our thinking it is in the Mabinogion that the true expression of the Celtic genius is to be sought; and it is surprising that so curious a literature, the source of nearly all the romantic creations of Europe, should have remained unknown until our own days. The cause is doubtless to be ascribed to the dispersed state of the Welsh manuscripts, pursued till last century by the English, as seditious books compromising those who possessed them. Often too they fell into hands of ignorant owners whose caprice or ill—will sufficed to keep them from critical research.

The Mabinogion have been preserved for us in two principal documents—one of the thirteenth century from the library of Hengurt, belonging to the Vaughan family; the other dating from the fourteenth century, known under the name of the Red Book of Hergest, and now in Jesus College, Oxford. No doubt it was some such collection that charmed the weary hours of the hapless Leolin in the Tower of London, and was burned after his condemnation, with the other Welsh books which had been the companions of his captivity. Lady Charlotte Guest has based her edition on the Oxford manuscript; it cannot be sufficiently regretted that paltry considerations have caused her to be refused the use of the earlier manuscript, of which the later appears to be only a copy. Regrets are redoubled when one knows that several Welsh texts, which were seen and copied fifty years ago, have now disappeared. It is in the presence of facts such as these that one comes to believe that revolutions—in general so destructive of the works of the past—are favourable to the preservation of literary monuments, by compelling their concentration in great centres, where their existence, as well as their publicity, is assured.

The general tone of the Mabinogion is rather romantic than epic. Life is treated naively and not too emphatically. The hero's individuality is limitless. We have free and noble natures acting in all their spontaneity. Each man appears as a kind of demi—god characterised by a supernatural gift. This gift is nearly always connected with some miraculous object, which in some measure is the personal seal of him who possesses it. The inferior classes, which this people of heroes necessarily supposes beneath it, scarcely show themselves, except in the exercise of some trade, for practising which they are held in high esteem. The somewhat complicated products of human industry are regarded as living beings, and in their manner endowed with magical properties. A multiplicity of celebrated objects have proper names, such as the drinking—cup, the lance, the sword, and the shield of Arthur; the chess—board of Gwendolen, on which the black pieces played of their own accord against the white; the horn of Bran Galed, where one found whatever liquor one desired; the chariot of Morgan, which directed itself to the place to which one wished to go; the pot of Tyrnog, which would not cook when meat for a coward was put into it; the grindstone of Tudwal, which would only sharpen brave men's swords; the coat of Padarn, which none save a noble could don; and the mantle of Tegan, which no woman could put upon herself were she not above reproach. [Footnote: Here may be recognised the origin of trial by court mantle, one of the most interesting episodes in Lancelot of the Lake.] The animal is conceived in a still more individual way; it has a proper name, personal qualities, and a role which it develops at its own will and with full consciousness. The same hero appears as at once man and animal, without it being possible to trace the line of demarcation between the two natures.

The tale of Kilhwch and Olwen, the most extraordinary of the Mabinogion, deals with Arthur's struggle against the wild–boar king Twrch Trwyth, who with his seven cubs holds in check all the heroes of the Round Table. The adventures of the three hundred ravens of Kerverhenn similarly form the subject of the Dream of Rhonabwy. The idea of moral merit and demerit is almost wholly absent from all these compositions. There are wicked beings who insult ladies, who tyrannise over their neighbours, who only find pleasure in evil because such is their nature; but it does not appear that they incur wrath on that account. Arthur's knights pursue them, not as criminals but as mischievous fellows. All other beings are perfectly good and just, but more or less richly gifted. This is the dream of an amiable and gentle race which looks upon evil as being the work of destiny, and not a product of the human conscience. All nature is enchanted, and fruitful as imagination itself in indefinitely varied creations. Christianity rarely discloses itself; although at times its proximity can be felt, it alters in no respect the purely natural surroundings in which everything takes place. A bishop figures at table beside Arthur, but his function is strictly limited to blessing the dishes. The Irish saints, who at one time present themselves to give their benediction to Arthur and receive favours at his hands, are portrayed as a race of men vaguely known and difficult to understand. No mediaeval literature held itself further removed from all monastic influence. We evidently must suppose that the Welsh bards and story–tellers lived in a state of great isolation from the clergy, and had their culture and traditions quite apart.

The charm of the Mabinogion principally resides in the amiable serenity of the Celtic mind, neither sad nor gay, ever in suspense between a smile and a tear. We have in them the simple recital of a child, unwitting of any distinction between the noble and the common; there is something of that softly animated world, of that calm and tranquil ideal to which Ariosto's stanzas transport us. The chatter of the later mediaeval French and German imitators can give no idea of this charming manner of narration. The skilful Chretien de Troyes himself remains in this respect far below the Welsh story– tellers, and as for Wolfram of Eschenbach, it must be avowed that the joy of the first discovery has carried German critics too far in the exaggeration of his merits. He loses himself in interminable descriptions, and almost completely ignores the art of his recital.

What strikes one at a first glance in the imaginative compositions of the Celtic races, above all when they are contrasted with those of the Teutonic races, is the extreme mildness of manners pervading them. There are none of those frightful vengeances which fill the Edda and the Niebelungen. Compare the Teutonic with the Gaelic hero,—Beowulf with Peredur, for example. What a difference there is! In the one all the horror of disgusting and blood–embrued barbarism, the drunkenness of carnage, the disinterested taste, if I may say so, for destruction and death; in the other a profound sense of justice, a great height of personal pride it is true, but also a great capacity for devotion, an exquisite loyalty. The tyrannical man, the monster, the Black Man, find a place here like the Lestrigons and the Cyclops of Homer only to inspire horror by contrast with softer manners; they are almost what the wicked man is in the naive imagination of a child brought up by a mother in the ideas of a gentle and pious morality. The primitive man of Teutonism is revolting by his purposeless brutality, by a love of evil that only gives him skill and strength in the service of hatred and injury. The Cymric hero on the other hand, even in his wildest flights, seems possessed by habits of kindness and a warm sympathy with the weakv. Sympathy indeed is one of the deepest feelings among the Celtic peoples. Even Judas is not denied a share of their pity. St. Brandan found him upon a rock in the midst of the Polar seas; once a week he passes a day there to refresh himself from the fires of hell. A cloak that he had given to a beggar is hung before him, and tempers his sufferings.

If Wales has a right to be proud of her Mabinogion, she has not less to felicitate herself in having found a translator truly worthy of interpreting them. For the proper understanding of these original beauties there was needed a delicate appreciation of Welsh narration, and an intelligence of the naive order, qualities of which an erudite translator would with difficulty have been capable. To render these gracious imaginings of a people so eminently dowered with feminine tact, the pen of a woman was necessary. Simple, animated, without effort and without vulgarity, Lady Guest's translation is a faithful mirror of the original Cymric. Even supposing that, as regards philology, the labours of this noble Welsh lady be destined to receive improvement, that does not prevent her book from for ever remaining a work of erudition and highly distinguished taste. [Footnote: M. de la Villemarque published in 1843 under the title of Cantes populaires des anciens Bretons, a French translation of the narratives that Guest had already presented in English at that time.]

The Mabinogion, or at least the writings which Lady Guest thought she ought to include under this common name, divide themselves into two perfectly distinct classes—some connected exclusively with the two peninsulas of Wales and Cornwall, and relating to the heroic personality of Arthur; the others alien to Arthur, having for their scene not only the parts of England that have remained Cymric, but the whole of Great Britain, and leading us back by the persons and traditions mentioned in them to the later years of the Roman occupation. The second class, of greater antiquity than the first, at least on the ground of subject, is also distinguished by a much more mythological character, a bolder use of the miraculous, an enigmatical form, a style full of alliteration and plays upon words. Of this number are the tales of Pwyll, of Bramwen, of Manawyddan, of Math the son of Mathonwy, the Dream of the Emperor Maximus, the story of Llud and Llewelys, and the legend of Taliessin. To the Arthurian cycle belong the narratives of Owen, of Geraint, of Peredur, of Kilhwch and Olwen, and the Dream of Rhonabwy. It is also to be remarked that the two last-named narratives have a particularly antique character. In them Arthur dwells in Cornwall, and not as in the others at Caerleon on the Usk. In them he appears with an individual character, hunting and taking a personal part in warfare, while in the more modern tales he is only an emperor all- powerful and impassive, a truly sluggard hero, around whom a pleiad of active heroes groups itself. The Mabinogi of Kilhwch and Olwen, by its entirely primitive aspect, by the part played in it by the wild-boar in conformity to the spirit of Celtic mythology, by the wholly supernatural and magical character of the narration, by innumerable allusions the sense of which escapes us, forms a cycle by itself. It represents for us the Cymric conception in all its purity, before it had been modified by the introduction of any foreign element. Without attempting here to analyse this curious poem, I should like by some extracts to make its antique aspect and high originality apparent.

Kilhwch, the son of Kilydd, prince of Kelyddon, having heard some one mention the name of Olwen, daughter of Yspaddaden Penkawr, falls violently in love, without having ever seen her. He goes to find Arthur, that he may ask for his aid in the difficult undertaking which he meditates; in point of fact, he does not know in what country the fair one of his affection dwells. Yspaddaden is besides a frightful tyrant who suffers no man to go from his castle alive, and whose death is linked by destiny to the marriage of his daughter. [Footnote: The idea of making the death of the father the condition of possession of the daughter is to be found in several romances of the Breton cycle, in Lancelot for example.] Arthur grants Kilhwch some of his most valiant comrades in arms to assist him in this enterprise. After wonderful adventures the knights arrive at the castle of Yspaddaden, and succeed in seeing the young maiden of Kilhwch's dream. Only after three days of persistent struggle do they manage to obtain a response from Olwen's father, who attaches his daughter's hand to conditions apparently impossible of realisation. The performance of these trials makes a long chain of adventures, the framework of a veritable romantic epic which has come to us in a very fragmentary form. Of the thirty−eight adventures imposed on Kilhwch the manuscript used by Lady Guest only relates seven or eight. I choose at random one of these narratives, which appears to me fitted to give an idea of the whole composition. It deals with the finding of Mabon the son of Modron, who was carried away from his mother three days after his birth, and whose deliverance is one of the labours exacted of Kilhwch.

"His followers said unto Arthur, 'Lord, go thou home; thou canst not proceed with thy host in quest of such small adventures as these.' Then said Arthur, 'It were well for thee, Gwrhyr Gwalstawd Ieithoedd, to go upon this quest, for thou knowest all languages, and art familiar with those of the birds and the beasts. Thou, Eidoel, oughtest likewise to go with my men in search of thy cousin. And as for you, Kai and Bedwyr, I have hope of whatever adventure ye are in quest of, that ye will achieve it. Achieve ye this adventure for me.'"

They went forward until they came to the Ousel of Cilgwri. And Gwrhyr adjured her for the sake of Heaven, saying, "Tell me if thou knowest aught of Mabon the son of Modron, who was taken when three nights old from between his mother and the wall." And the Ousel answered, "When I first came here there was a smith's anvil in this place, and I was then a young bird; and from that time no work has been done upon it, save the pecking of my beak every evening, and now there is not so much as the size of a nut remaining thereof; yet all the vengeance of Heaven be upon me, if during all that time I have ever heard of the man for whom you enquire. Nevertheless I will do that which is right, and that which it is fitting I should do for an embassy from Arthur. There is a race of animals who were formed before me, and I will be your guide to them."

So they proceeded to the place where was the Stag of Redynvre. "Stag of Redynvre, behold we are come to thee, an embassy from Arthur, for we have not heard of any animal older than thou. Say, knowest thou aught of Mabon the son of Modron, who was taken from his mother when three nights old?" The Stag said, "When first I came hither there was a plain all around me, without any trees save one oak sapling, which grew up to be an oak with an hundred branches. And that oak has since perished, so that now nothing remains of it but the withered stump; and from that day to this I have been here, yet have I never heard of the man for whom you enquire. Nevertheless, being an embassy from Arthur, I will be your guide to the place where there is an animal which was formed before I was."

So they proceeded to the place where was the Owl of Cwm Cawlwyd. "Owl of Cwm Cawlwyd, here is an embassy from Arthur; knowest thou aught of Mabon the son of Modron, who was taken after three nights from his mother?" "If I knew I would tell you. When first I came hither, the wide valley you see was a wooded glen. And a race of men came and rooted it up. And there grew there a second wood; and this wood is the third. My wings, are they not withered stumps? Yet all this time, even until to−day, I have never heard of the man for whom you enquire. Nevertheless I will be the guide of Arthur's embassy until you come to the place where is the oldest animal in the world, and the one that has travelled most, the Eagle of Gwern Abwy."

Gwrhyr said, "Eagle of Gwern Abwy, we have come to thee an embassy from Arthur, to ask thee if thou knowest aught of Mabon the son of Modron, who was taken from his mother when he was three nights old." The Eagle said, "I have been here for a great space of time, and when I first came hither there was a rock here, from the top of which I pecked at the stars every evening; and now it is not so much as a span high. From that day to this I have been here, and I have never heard of the man for whom you enquire, except once when I went in search of food as far as Llyn Llyw. And when I came there, I struck my talons into a salmon, thinking he would serve me as food for a long time. But he drew me into the deep, and I was scarcely able to escape from him. After that I went with my whole kindred to attack him, and to try to destroy him, but he sent messengers, and made peace with me; and came and besought me to take fifty fish spears out of his back. Unless he know something of him whom you seek, I cannot tell who may. However, I will guide you to the place where he is."

So they went thither; and the Eagle said, "Salmon of Llyn Llyw, I have come to thee with an embassy from Arthur, to ask thee if thou knowest aught concerning Mabon the son of Modron, who was taken away at three nights old from his mother." "As much as I know I will tell thee. With every tide I go along the river upwards, until I come near to the walls of Gloucester, and there have I found such wrong as I never found elsewhere; and to the end that ye may give credence thereto, let one of you go thither upon each of my two shoulders." So Kai and Gwrhyr Gwalstawd Ieithoedd went upon the shoulders of the salmon, and they proceeded until they came unto the wall of the prison, and they heard a great wailing and lamenting from the dungeon. Said Gwrhyr, "Who is it that laments in this house of stone?" "Alas there is reason enough for whoever is here to lament. It is Mabon the son of Modron who is here imprisoned; and no imprisonment was ever so grievous as mine, neither that of Lludd Llaw Ereint, nor that of Greid the son of Eri." "Hast thou hope of being released for gold or for silver, or for any gifts of wealth, or through battle and fighting?" "By fighting will whatever I may gain be obtained."

We shall not follow the Cymric hero through trials the result of which can be foreseen. What, above all else, is striking in these strange legends is the part played by animals, transformed by the Welsh imagination into intelligent beings. No race conversed so intimately as did the Celtic race with the lower creation, and accorded it so large a share of moral life. [Footnote: See especially the narratives of Nennius, and of Giraldus Cambrensis. In them animals have at least as important a part as men.] The close association of man and animal, the fictions so dear to mediaeval poetry of the Knight of the Lion, the Knight of the Falcon, the Knight of the Swan, the vows consecrated by the presence of birds of noble repute, are equally Breton imaginings. Ecclesiastical literature itself presents analogous features; gentleness towards animals informs all the legends of the saints of Brittany and Ireland. One day St. Kevin fell asleep, while he was praying at his window with outstretched arms; and a swallow perceiving the open hand of the venerable monk, considered it an excellent place wherein to make her nest. The saint on awaking saw the mother sitting upon her eggs, and, loth to disturb her, waited for the little ones to be hatched before he arose from his knees.

This touching sympathy was derived from the singular vivacity with which the Celtic races have inspired their feeling for nature. Their mythology is nothing more than a transparent naturalism, not that anthropomorphic naturalism of Greece and India, in which the forces of the universe, viewed as living beings and endowed with consciousness, tend more and more to detach themselves from physical phenomena, and to become moral beings; but in some measure a realistic naturalism, the love of nature for herself, the vivid impression of her magic, accompanied by the sorrowful feeling that man knows, when, face to face with her, he believes that he hears her commune with him concerning his origin and his destiny. The legend of Merlin mirrors this feeling. Seduced by a fairy of the woods, he flies with her and becomes a savage. Arthur's messengers come upon him as he is singing by the side of a fountain; he is led back again to court; but the charm carries him away. He returns to his forests, and this time for ever. Under a thicket of hawthorn Vivien has built him a magical prison. There he prophesies the future of the Celtic races; he speaks of a maiden of the woods, now visible and now unseen, who holds him captive by her spells. Several Arthurian legends are impressed with the same character. Arthur himself in popular belief became, as it were, a woodland spirit. "The foresters on their nightly round by the light of the moon," says Gervais of Tilbury, [Footnote: An English chronicler of the twelfth century.] "often hear a great sound as of horns, and meet bands of huntsmen; when they are asked whence they come, these huntsmen make reply that they are of King Arthur's following." [Footnote: This manner of explaining all the unknown noises of the wood by Arthur's Hunting is still to be found in several districts. To understand properly the cult of nature, and, if I may say so, of landscape among the Celts, see Gildas and Nennius, pp. 131, 136, 137, etc. (Edit. San Marte, Berlin. 1884);] Even the French imitators of the Breton romances keep an impression—although a rather insipid one—of the attraction exercised by nature on the Celtic imagination. Elaine, the heroine of Lancelot, the ideal of Breton perfection, passes her life with her companions in a garden, in the midst of flowers which she tends. Every flower culled by her hands is at the instant restored to life; and the worshippers of her memory are under an obligation, when they cut a flower, to sow another in its place.

The worship of forest, and fountain, and stone is to be explained by this primitive naturalism, which all the Councils of the Church held in Brittany united to proscribe. The stone, in truth, seems the natural symbol of the Celtic races. It is an immutable witness that has no death. The animal, the plant, above all the human figure, only express the divine life under a determinate form; the stone on the contrary, adapted to receive all forms, has been the fetish of peoples in their childhood. Pausanias saw, still standing erect, the thirty square stones of Pharse, each bearing the name of a divinity. The men–hir to be met with over the whole surface of the ancient world, what is it but the monument of primitive humanity, a living witness of its faith in Heaven? [Footnote: It is, however, doubtful whether the monuments known in France at Celtic (men–hir. dot–men, etc.) are the work of the Celts. With M. Worsaae and the Copenhagen archaeologists, I am inclined to think that these monuments belong to a more ancient humanity. Never, in fact, has any branch of the Indo–European race built in this fashion. (See two articles by M. Merimee in L'Athenaum franfais, Sept. 11th, 1852, and April 25th, 1853.)]

It has frequently been observed that the majority of popular beliefs still extant in our different provinces are of Celtic origin. A not less remarkable fact is the strong tinge of naturalism dominant in these beliefs. Nay more, every time that the old Celtic spirit appears in our history, there is to be seen, re−born with it, faith in nature and her magic influences. One of the most characteristic of these manifestations seems to me to be that of Joan of Arc. That indomitable hope, that tenacity in the affirmation of the future, that belief that the salvation of the kingdom will come from a woman,—all those features, far removed as they are from the taste of antiquity, and from Teutonic taste, are in many respects Celtic. The memory of the ancient cult perpetuated itself at Domremy, as in so many other places, under the form of popular superstition. The cottage of the family of Arc was shaded by a beech tree, famed in the country and reputed to be the abode of fairies. In her childhood Joan used to go and hang upon its branches garlands of leaves and flowers, which, so it was said, disappeared during the night. The terms of her accusation speak with horror of this innocent custom, as of a crime against the faith; and indeed they were not altogether deceived, those unpitying theologians who judged the holy maid. Although she knew it not, she was more Celtic than Christian. She has been foretold by Merlin; she knows of neither Pope nor Church,— she only believes the voice that speaks in her own heart. This voice she hears in the fields, in the sough of the wind among the trees, when measured and distant sounds fair upon her ears. During her trial, worn out with questions and scholastic subtleties, she is asked whether she still hears her voices. "Take me to the woods." she says, "and I shall hear them clearly." Her legend is tinged with the same colours; nature loved her, the wolves never touched the sheep of her flock. When she was a little girl, the birds used to come and eat bread from her lap as though they were tame. [Footnote: Since the first publication of these views, on which I should not like more emphasis to be put than what belongs to a passing impression, similar considerations have been developed, in terms that appear a little too positive, by M. H. Martin (History of France, vol. vi., 1856). The objections raised to it are, for the most part, due to the fact that very few people are capable of delicately appreciating questions of this kind, relative to the genius of races. It frequently happens that the resurrection of an old national genius takes place under a very different form from that which one would have expected, and by means of individuals who have no idea of the ethnographical part which they play.]

III

The MABINOGION do not recommend themselves to our study, only as a manifestation of the romantic genius of the Breton races. It was through them that the Welsh imagination exercised its influence upon the Continent, that it transformed, in the twelfth century, the poetic art of Europe, and realised this miracle,—that the creations of a half−conquered race have become the universal feast of imagination for mankind.

Few heroes owe less to reality than Arthur. Neither Gildas nor Aneurin, his contemporaries, speak of him; Bede did not even know his name; Taliessin and Liwarc'h Hen gave him only a secondary place. In Nennius, on the other hand, who lived about 850, the legend has fully unfolded. Arthur is already the exterminator of the Saxons; he has never experienced defeat; he is the suzerain of an army of kings. Finally, in Geoffrey of Monmouth, the epic creation culminates. Arthur reigns over the whole earth; he conquers Ireland, Norway, Gascony, and France. At Caerleon he holds a tournament at which all the monarchs of the world are present; there he puts upon his head thirty crowns, and exacts recognition as the sovereign lord of the universe. So incredible is it that a petty king of the sixth century, scarcely remarked by his contemporaries, should have taken in posterity such colossal proportions, that several critics have supposed that the legendary Arthur and the obscure chieftain who bore that name have nothing in common, the one with the other, and that the son of Uther Pendragon is a wholly ideal hero, a survivor of the old Cymric mythology. As a matter of fact, in the symbols of Neo–Druidism—that is to say, of that secret doctrine, the outcome of Druidism, which prolonged its existence even to the Middle Ages under the form of Freemasonry—we again find Arthur transformed into a divine personage, and playing a purely mythological part. It must at least be allowed that, if behind the fable some reality lies hidden, history offers us no means of attaining it. It cannot be doubted that the discovery of Arthur's tomb in the Isle of Avalon in 1189 was an invention of Norman policy, just as in 1283, the very year in which Edward I. was engaged in crushing out the last vestiges of Welsh independence, Arthur's crown was very conveniently found, and forthwith united to the other crown jewels of England.

We naturally expect Arthur, now become the representative of Welsh nationality, to sustain in the Mabinogion a character analogous to this role, and therein, as in Nennius, to serve the hatred of the vanquished against the Saxons. But such is not the case. Arthur, in the Mabinogion, exhibits no characteristics of patriotic resistance; his part is limited to uniting heroes around him, to maintaining the retainers of his palace, and to enforcing the laws of his order of chivalry. He is too strong for any one to dream of attacking him. He is the Charlemagne of the Carlovingian romances, the Agamemnon of Homer,—one of those neutral personalities that serve but to give unity to the poem. The idea of warfare against the alien, hatred towards the Saxon, does not appear in a single instance. The heroes of the Mabinogion have no fatherland; each fights to show his personal excellence, and satisfy his taste for adventure, but not to defend a national cause. Britain is the universe; no one suspects that beyond the Cymry there may be other nations and other races.

It was by this ideal and representative character that the Arthurian legend had such an astonishing prestige throughout the whole world. Had Arthur been only a provincial hero, the more or less happy defender of a little country, all peoples would not have adopted him, any more than they have adopted the Marco of the Serbs, [Footnote: A Servian ballad–hero.] or the Robin Hood of the Saxons. The Arthur who has charmed the world is the head of an order of equality, in which all sit at the same table, in which a man's worth depends upon his valour and his natural gifts. What mattered to the world the fate of an unknown peninsula, and the strife waged on its behalf? What enchanted it was the ideal court presided over by Gwenhwyvar (Guinevere), where around the monarchical unity the flower of heroes was gathered together, where ladies, as chaste as they were beautiful, loved according to the laws of chivalry, and where the time was passed in listening to stories, and learning civility and beautiful manners.

This is the secret of the magic of that Round Table, about which the Middle Ages grouped all their ideas of heroism, of beauty, of modesty, and of love. We need not stop to inquire whether the ideal of a gentle and polished society in the midst of the barbarian world is, in all its features, a purely Breton creation, whether the spirit of the courts of the Continent has not in some measure furnished the model, and whether the Mabinogion themselves have not felt the reaction of the French imitations;[Footnote: The surviving version of the Mdbinogian has a later date than these imitations, and the Red Book includes several tales borrowed from the French trouveres. But it is out of the question to maintain that the really Welsh narratives have been borrowed in a like manner, since among them are some unknown to the trouveres, which could only possess interest for Breton countries] it suffices for us that the new order of sentiments which we have just indicated was, throughout the whole of the Middle Ages, persistently attached to the groundwork of the Cymric romances. Such an association could not be fortuitous; if the imitations are all so glaring in colour, it is evidently because in the original this same colour is to be found united to particularly strong character. How otherwise shall we explain why a forgotten tribe on the very confines of the world should have imposed its heroes upon Europe, and, in the domain of imagination, accomplished one of the most singular revolutions known to the historian of letters?

If, in fact, one compares European literature before the introduction of the Cymric romances, with what it became when the trouveres set themselves to draw from Breton sources, one recognises readily that with the Breton narratives a new element entered into the poetic conception of the Christian peoples, and modified it profoundly. The Carlovingian poem, both by its structure and by the means which it employs, does not depart from classical ideas. The motives of man's action are the same as in the Greek epic. The essentially romantic element, the life of forests and mysterious adventure, the feeling for nature, and that impulse of imagination which makes the Breton warrior unceasingly pursue the unknown;— nothing of all this is as yet to be observed. Roland differs from the heroes of Homer only by his armour; in heart he is the brother of Ajax or Achilles. Perceval, on the contrary, belongs to another world, separated by a great gulf from that in which the heroes of antiquity live and act.

It was above all by the creation of woman's character, by introducing into mediaeval poetry, hitherto hard and austere, the nuances of love, that the Breton romances brought about this curious metamorphosis. It was like an electric spark; in a few years European taste was changed. Nearly all the types of womankind known to the Middle Ages, Guinevere, Iseult, Enid, are derived from Arthur's court. In the Carlovingian poems woman is a nonentity without character or individuality; in them love is either brutal, as in the romance of "Ferebras," or scarcely indicated, as in the "Song of Roland." In the "Mabinogion," on the other hand, the principal part always belongs to the women. Chivalrous gallantry, which makes the warrior's happiness to consist in serving a woman and meriting her esteem, the belief that the noblest use of strength is to succour and avenge weakness, results, I know, from a turn of imagination which possessed nearly all European peoples in the twelfth century; but it cannot be doubted that this turn of imagination first found literary expression among the Breton peoples. One of the most surprising features in the Mabinogion is the delicacy of the feminine feeling breathed in them; an impropriety or a gross word is never to be met with. It would be necessary to quote at length the two romances of Peredur and Geraint to demonstrate an innocence such as this; but the naive simplicity of these charming compositions forbids us to see in this innocence any underlying meaning. The zeal of the knight in the defence of ladies' honour became a satirical euphemism only in the French imitators, who transformed the virginal modesty of the Breton romances into a shameless gallantry—so far indeed that these compositions, chaste as they are in the original, became the scandal of the Middle Ages, provoked censures, and were the occasion of the ideas of immorality which, for religious people, still cluster about the name of romance.

Certainly chivalry is too complex a fact for us to be permitted to assign it to any single origin. Let us say however that in the idea of envisaging the esteem of a woman as the highest object of human activity, and setting up love as the supreme principle of morality, there is nothing of the antique spirit, or indeed of the Teutonic. Is it in the "Edda" or in the "Niebelungen" that we shall find the germ of this spirit of pure love, of exalted devotion, which forms the very soul of chivalry? As to following the suggestion of some critics and seeking among the Arabs for the beginnings of this institution, surely of all literary paradoxes ever mooted, this is one of the most singular. The idea of conquering woman in a land where she is bought and sold, of seeking her esteem in a land where she is scarcely considered capable of moral merit! I shall oppose the partizans of this hypothesis with one single fact,—the surprise experienced by the Arabs of Algeria when, by a somewhat unfortunate recollection of mediaeval tournaments, the ladies were entrusted with the presentation of prizes at the Beiram races. What to the knight appeared an unparalleled honour seemed to the Arabs a humiliation and almost an insult.

The introduction of the Breton romances into the current of European literature worked a not less profound revolution in the manner of conceiving and employing the marvellous. In the Carlovingian poems the marvellous is timid, and conforms to the Christian faith; the supernatural is produced directly by God or his envoys. Among the Cymry, on the contrary, the principle of the marvel is in nature herself, in her hidden forces, in her inexhaustible fecundity. There is a mysterious swan, a prophetic bird, a suddenly appearing hand, a giant, a black tyrant, a magic mist, a dragon, a cry that causes the hearer to die of terror, an object with extraordinary properties. There is no trace of the monotheistic conception, in which the marvellous is only a miracle, a derogation of eternal laws. Nor are there any of those personifications of the life of nature which form the essential part of the Greek and Indian mythologies. Here we have perfect naturalism, an unlimited faith in the possible, belief in the existence of independent beings bearing within themselves the principle of their strength,—an idea quite opposed to Christianity, which in such beings necessarily sees either angels or fiends. And besides, these strange beings are always presented as being outside the pale of the Church; and when the knight of the Round Table has conquered them, he forces them to go and pay homage to Guinevere, and have themselves baptised.

Now, if in poetry there is a marvellous element that we might accept, surely it is this. Classical mythology, taken in its first simplicity, is too bold, taken as a mere figure of rhetoric, too insipid, to give us satisfaction. As to the marvellous element in Christianity, Boileau is right: no fiction is compatible with such a dogmatism. There remains then the purely naturalistic marvellous, nature interesting herself in action and acting herself, the great mystery of fatality unveiling itself by the secret conspiring of all beings, as in Shakespeare and Ariosto. It would be curious to ascertain how much of the Celt there is in the former of these poets; as for Ariosto he is the Breton poet par excellence. All his machinery, all his means of interest, all his fine shades of sentiment, all his types of women, all his adventures, are borrowed from the Breton romances.

Do we now understand the intellectual role of that little race which gave to the world Arthur, Guinevere, Lancelot, Perceval, Merlin, St. Brandan, St. Patrick, and almost all the poetical cycles of the Middle Ages? What a striking destiny some nations have, in alone possessing the right to cause the acceptance of their heroes, as though for that were necessary a quite peculiar degree of authority, seriousness, and faith! And it is a strange thing that it is to the Normans, of all peoples the one least sympathetically inclined towards the Bretons, that we owe the renown of the Breton fables. Brilliant and imitative, the Norman everywhere became the pre– eminent representative of the nation on which he had at first imposed himself by force. French in France, English in England, Italian in Italy, Russian at Novgorod, he forgot his own language to speak that of the race which he had conquered, and to become the interpreter of its genius. The deeply suggestive character of the Welsh romances could not fail to impress men so prompt to seize and assimilate the ideas of the foreigner. The first revelation of the Breton fables, the Latin Chronicle of Geoffrey of Monmouth, appeared about the year 1137, under the auspices of Robert of Gloucester, natural son of Henry I. Henry II. acquired a taste for the same narratives, and at his request Robert Wace, in 1155, wrote in French the first history of Arthur, thus opening the path in which walked after him a host of poets or imitators of all nationalities, French, Provencal, Italian, Spanish, English, Scandinavian, Greek, and Georgian. We need not belittle the glory of the first trouveres who put into a language, then read and understood from one end of Europe to the other, fictions which, but for them, would have doubtless remained for ever unknown. It is however difficult to attribute to them an inventive faculty, such as would permit them to merit the title of creators. The numerous passages in which one feels that they do not fully understand the original which they imitate, and in which they attempt to give a natural significance to circumstances of which the mythological bearing escaped them, suffice to prove that, as a rule, they were satisfied to make a fairly faithful copy of the work before their eyes.

What part has Armorican Brittany played in the creation or propagation of the legends of the Round Table? It is impossible to say with any degree of precision; and in truth such a question becomes a matter of secondary import once we form a just idea of the close bonds of fraternity, which did not cease until the twelfth century to unite the two branches of the Breton peoples. That the heroic traditions of Wales long continued to live in the branch of the Cymric family which came and settled in Armorica cannot be doubted when we find Geraint, Urien, and other heroes become saints in Lower Brittany; [Footnote: I shall only cite a single proof; it is a law of Edward the Confessor: "Britones vero Armorici quum venerint in regno isto, suscipi debent et in regno protegi sicut probi cives de corpore regni hujus; exierunt quondam de sanguine Britonum regni hujus."—Wilkins, Leges Anglo–Saxonicae, p. 206.]and above all when we see one of the most essential episodes of the Arthurian cycle, that of the Forest of Broceliande, placed in the same country. A large number of facts collected by M. de la Villemarrque [Footnote: "Les Romans de la Table–Ronde et les contes des anciens Bretons" (Paris, 1859), pp. 20 et seq. In the "Contes populaires des anciens Bretons," of which the above may be considered as a new edition, the learned author had somewhat exaggerated the influence of French Brittany. In the present article, when first published, I had, on the other hand, depreciated it too much.] prove, on the other hand, that these same traditions produced a true poetic cycle in Brittany, and even that at certain epochs they must have recrossed the Channel, as though to give new life to the mother country's memories. The fact that Gauthier Calenius, Archdeacon of Oxford, brought back from Brittany to England (about 1125) the very text of the legends which were translated into Latin ten years afterwards by Geoffrey of Monmouth is here decisive. I know that to readers of the Mabinogion such an opinion will appear surprising at a first glance, All is Welsh in these fables, the places, the genealogies, the customs; in them Armorica is only represented by Hoel, an important personage no doubt, but one who has not achieved the fame of the other heroes of Arthur's court. Again, if Armorica saw the birth of the Arthurian cycle, how is it that we fail to find there any traces of that brilliant nativity? [Footnote: M. de la Villemarque makes appeal to the popular songs still extant in Brittany, in which Arthur's deeds are celebrated. In fact, in his Chants populaires de la Bretagne two poems are to be found in which that hero's name figures.]

These objections, I avow, long barred my way, but I no longer find them insoluble. And first of all there is a class of Mabinogion, including those of Owen, Geraint, and Peredur, stories which possess no very precise geographical localisation. In the second place, national written literature being less successfully defended in Brittany than in Wales against the invasion of foreign culture, it may be conceived that the memory of the old epics should be there more obliterated. The literary share of the two countries thus remains sufficiently distinct. The glory of French Brittany is in her popular songs; but it is only in Wales that the genius of the Breton people has succeeded in establishing itself in authentic books and achieved creations.

IV.

In comparing the Breton cycle as the French trouveres knew it, and the same cycle as it is to be found in the text of the Mabinogion, one might be tempted to believe that the European imagination, enthralled by these brilliant fables, added to them some poetical themes unknown to the Welsh. Two of the most celebrated heroes of the continental Breton romances, Lancelot and Tristan, do not figure in the Mabinogion; on the other hand, the characteristics of the Holy Grail are presented in a totally different way from that which we find in the French and German poets. A more attentive study shows that these elements, apparently added by the French poets, are in reality of Cymric origin. And first of all, M. de la Villemarque has demonstrated to perfection that the name of Lancelot is only a translation of that of the Welsh hero Mael, who in point of fact exhibits the fullest analogy with the Lancelot of the French romances. [Footnote: Ancelot is the diminutive of Ancel, and means servant, page, or esquire. To this day in the Cymric dialects Mael has the same signification. The surname of Poursigant, which we find borne by some Welshmen in the French service in the early part of the fourteenth century, is also no doubt a translation of Mael.] The context, the proper names, all the details of the romance of Lancelot also present the most pronounced Breton aspect. As much must be said of the romance of Tristan. It is even to be hoped that this curious legend will be discovered complete in some Welsh manuscript. Dr. Owen states that he has seen one of which he was unable to obtain a copy. As to the Holy Grail, it must be avowed that the mystic cup, the object after which the French Parceval and the German Parsifal go in search, has not nearly the same importance among the Welsh. In the romance of Peredur it only figures in an episodical fashion, and without a well–defined religious intention.

"Then Peredur and his uncle discoursed together, and he beheld two youths enter the hall, and proceed up to the chamber, bearing a spear of mighty size, with three streams of blood flowing from the point to the ground. And when all the company saw this, they began wailing and lamenting. But for all that, the man did not break off his discourse with Peredur. And as he did not tell Peredur the meaning of what he saw, he forbore to ask him concerning it. And when the clamour had a little subsided, behold two maidens entered, with a large salver between them, in which was a man's head, surrounded by a profusion of blood. And thereupon the company of the court made so great an outcry, that it was irksome to be in the same hall with them. But at length they were silent." This strange and wondrous circumstance remains an enigma to the end of the narrative. Then a mysterious young man appears to Peredur, apprises him that the lance from which the blood was dropping is that with which his uncle was wounded, that the vessel contains the blood and the head of one of his cousins, slain by the witches of Kerloiou, and that it is predestined that he, Peredur, should be their avenger. In point of fact, Peredur goes and convokes the Round Table; Arthur and his knights come and put the witches of Kerloiou to death.

If we now pass to the French romance of Parceval, we find that all this phantasmagoria clothes a very different significance. The lance is that with which Longus pierced Christ's side, the Grail or basin is that in which Joseph of Arimathea caught the divine blood. This miraculous vase procures all the good things of heaven and earth; it heals wounds, and is filled at the owner's pleasure with the most exquisite food. To approach it one must be in a state of grace; only a priest can tell of its marvels. To find these sacred relics after the passage of a thousand trials,—such is the object of Peredur's chivalry, at once worldly and mystical. In the end he becomes a priest; he takes the Grail and the lance into his hermitage; on the day of his death an angel bears them up to Heaven. Let us add that many traits prove that in the mind of the French trouvere the Grail is confounded with the eucharist. In the miniatures which occasionally accompany the romance of Parceval, the Grail is in the form of a pyx, appearing at all the solemn moments of the poem as a miraculous source of succour.

Is this strange myth, differing as it does from the simple narrative presented in the Welsh legend of Peredur, really Cymric, or ought we rather to see in it an original creation of the trouveres, based upon a Breton foundation? With M. de la Villemarque we believe that this curious fable is essentially Cymric. [Footnote: See the excellent discussion of this interesting problem in the introduction to "Contes populaires des anciens Bretons" (pp. 181 et seq.).] In the eighth century a Breton hermit had a vision of Joseph of Arimathea bearing the chalice of the Last Supper, and wrote the history called the Gradal. The whole Celtic mythology is full of the marvels of a magic caldron under which nine fairies blow silently, a mysterious vase which inspires poetic genius, gives wisdom, reveals the future, and unveils the secrets of the world. One day as Bran the Blessed was hunting in Ireland upon the shore of a lake, he saw come forth from it a black man bearing upon his back an enormous caldron, followed by a witch and a dwarf. This caldron was the instrument of the supernatural power of a family of giants. It cured all ills, and gave back life to the dead, but without restoring to them the use of speech—an allusion to the secret of the bardic initiation. In the same way Perceval's wariness forms the whole plot of the quest of the Holy Grail. The Grail thus appears to us in its primitive meaning as the pass–word of a kind of free–masonry which survived in Wales long after the preaching of the Gospel, and of which we find deep traces in the legend of Taliessin. Christianity grafted its legend upon the mythological data, and a like transformation was doubtless made by the Cymric race itself. If the Welsh narrative of Peredur does not offer the same developments as the French romance of Parceval, it is because the Red Book of Hergest gives us an earlier version than that which served as a model for Chretien de Troyes. It is also to be remarked that, even in Parceval, the mystical idea is not as yet completely developed, that the trouvere seems to treat this strange theme as a narrative which he has found already complete, and the meaning of which he can scarcely guess. The motive that sets Parceval a–field in the French romance, as well as in the Welsh version, is a family motive; he seeks the Holy Grail as a talisman to cure his uncle the Fisherman– King, in such a way that the religious idea is still subordinated to the profane intention. In the German version, on the other hand, full as it is of mysticism and theology, the Grail has a temple and priests. Parsifal, who has become a purely ecclesiastical hero, reaches the dignity of King of the Grail by his religious enthusiasm and his chastity. [Footnote: It is indeed remarkable that all the Breton heroes in their last transformation are at once gallant and devout. One of the most celebrated ladies of Arthur's court, Luned, becomes a saint and a martyr for her chastity, her festival being celebrated on August 1st. She it is who figures in the French romances under the name of Lunette. See Lady Guest, vol. i., pp. 113, 114.] Finally, the prose versions, more modern still, sharply distinguish the two chivalries, the one earthly, the other mystical. In them Parceval becomes the model of the devout knight. This was the last of the metamorphoses which that all–powerful enchantress called the human imagination made him undergo; and it was only right that, after having gone through so many dangers, he should don a monkish frock, wherein to take his rest after his life of adventure.

V.

When we seek to determine the precise moment in the history of the Celtic races at which we ought to place ourselves in order to appreciate their genius in its entirety, we find ourselves led back to the sixth century of our era. Races have nearly always a predestined hour at which, passing from simplicity to reflection, they bring forth to the light of day, for the first time, all the treasures of their nature. For the Celtic races the poetic moment of awakening and primal activity was the sixth century. Christianity, still young amongst them, has not completely stifled the national cult; the religion of the Druids defends itself in its schools and holy places; warfare against the foreigner, without which a people never achieves a full consciousness of itself, attains its highest degree of spirit. It is the epoch of all the heroes of enduring fame, of all the characteristic saints of the Breton Church; finally, it is the great age of bardic literature, illustrious by the names of Taliessin, of Aneurin, of Liwarc'h Hen.

To such as would view critically the historical use of these half– fabulous names and would hesitate to accept as authentic, poems that have come down to us through so long a series of ages, we reply that the objections raised to the antiquity of the bardic literature— objections of which W. Schlegel made himself the interpreter in opposition to M. Fauriel—have completely disappeared under the investigations of an enlightened and impartial criticism. [Footnote: This evidently does not apply to the language of the poems in question. It is well known that mediaeval scribes, alien as they were to all ideas of archaeology, modernised the texts, in measure as they copied them; and that a manuscript in the vulgar tongue, as a rule, only attests the language of him who transcribed it.] By a rare exception sceptical opinion has for once been found in the wrong. The sixth century is in fact for the Breton peoples a perfectly historical century. We touch this epoch of their history as closely and with as much certainty as Greek or Roman antiquity. It is indeed known that, up to a somewhat late period, the bards continued to compose pieces under the names—which had become popular—of Aneurin, Taliessin, and Liwarc'h Hen; but no confusion can be made between these insipid rhetorical exercises and the really ancient fragments which bear the names of the poets cited— fragments full of personal traits, local circumstances, and individual passions and feelings.

Such is the literature of which M. de la Villemarque has attempted to unite the most ancient and authentic monuments in his "Breton Bards of the Sixth Century." Wales has recognised the service that our learned compatriot has thus rendered to Celtic studies. We confess, however, to much preferring to the "Bards" the "Popular Songs of Brittany." It is in the latter that M. de la Villemarque has best served Celtic studies, by revealing to us a delightful literature, in which, more clearly than anywhere else, are apparent these features of gentleness, fidelity, resignation, and timid reserve which form the character of the Breton peoples. [Footnote: This interesting collection ought not, however, to be accepted unreservedly; and the absolute confidence with which it has been quoted is not without its inconveniences. We believe that when M. de la Villemarque comments on the fragments which, to his eternal honour, he has been the first to bring to light, his criticism is far from being proof against all reproach, and that several of the historical allusions which he considers that he finds in them are hypotheses more ingenious than solid. The past is too great, and has come down to us in too

99

fragmentary a manner, for such coincidences to be probable. Popular celebrities are rarely those of history, and when the rumours of distant centuries come to us by two channels, one popular, the other historical, it is a rare thing for these two forms of tradition to be fully in accord with one another. M. de la Villemarque is also too ready to suppose that the people repeats for centuries songs that it only half understands. When a song ceases to be intelligible, it is nearly always altered by the people, with the end of approximating it to the sounds farmliar and significant to their ears. Is it not also to be feared that in this case the editor, in entire good faith, may lend some slight inflection to the text, so as to find in it the sense that he desires, or has in his mind?]

The theme of the poetry of the bards of the sixth century is simple and exclusively heroic; it ever deals with the great motives of patriotism and glory. There is a total absence of all tender feeling, no trace of love, no well–marked religious idea, but only a vague and naturalistic mysticism,—a survival of Druidic teaching,— and a moral philosophy wholly expressed in Triads, similar to that taught in the half–bardic, half–Christian schools of St. Cadoc and St. Iltud. The singularly artificial and highly wrought form of the style suggests the existence of a system of learned instruction possessing long traditions. A more pronounced shade, and there would be a danger of falling into a pedantic and mannered rhetoric. The bardic literature, by its lengthened existence through the whole of the Middle Ages, did not escape this danger. It ended by being no more than a somewhat insipid collection of unoriginalities in style, and conventional metaphors. [Footnote: A Welsh scholar, Mr. Stephens, in his History of Cymric Literature (Llandovery, 1849), has demonstrated these successive transformations very well.]

The opposition between bardism and Christianity reveals itself in the pieces translated by M. de la Villemarque by many features of original and pathetic interest. The strife which rent the soul of the old poets, their antipathy to the grey men of the monastery, their sad and painful conversion, are to be found in their songs. The sweetness and tenacity of the Breton character can alone explain how a heterodoxy so openly avowed as this maintained its position in face of the dominant Christianity, and how holy men, Kolumkill for example, took upon themselves the defence of the bards against the kings who desired to stamp them out. The strife was the longer in its duration, in that Christianity among the Celtic peoples never employed force against rival religions, and, at the worst, left to the vanquished the liberty of ill humour. Belief in prophets, indestructible among these peoples, created, in despite of faith the Anti–Christian type of Merlin, and caused his acceptance by the whole of Europe. Gildas and the orthodox Bretons were ceaseless in their thunderings against the prophets, and opposed to them Elias and Samuel, two bards who only foretold good; even in the twelfth century Giraldus Cambrensis saw a prophet in the town of Caerleon.

Thanks to this toleration bardism lasted into the heart of the Middle Ages, under the form of a secret doctrine, with a conventional language, and symbols almost wholly borrowed from the solar divinity of Arthur. This may be termed Neo–Druidism, a kind of Druidism subtilised and reformed on the model of Christianity, which may be seen growing more and more obscure and mysterious, until the moment of its total disappearance. A curious fragment belonging to this school, the dialogue between Arthur and Eliwlod, has transmitted to us the latest sighs of this latest protestation of expiring naturalism. Under the form of an eagle Eliwlod introduces the divinity to the sentiment of resignation, of subjection, and of humility, with which Christianity combated pagan pride. Hero–worship recoils step by step before the great formula, which Christianity ceases not to repeat to the Celtic races to

100

sever them from their memories: There is none greater than God. Arthur allows himself to be persuaded to abdicate from his divinity, and ends by reciting the Pater.

I know of no more curious spectacle than this revolt of the manly sentiments of hero–worship against the feminine feeling which flowed so largely into the new faith. What, in fact, exasperates the old representatives of Celtic society are the exclusive triumph of the pacific spirit and the men, clad in linen and chanting psalms, whose voice is sad, who preach asceticism, and know the heroes no more. [Footnote: The antipathy to Christianity attributed by the Armorican people to the dwarfs and korigans belongs in like measure to traditions of the opposition encountered by the Gospel in its beginnings. The korigans in fact are, for the Breton peasant, great princesses who would not accept Christianity when the apostles came to Brittany. They hate the clergy and the churches, the bells of which make them take to flight. The Virgin above all is their great enemy; she it is who has hounded them forth from their fountains, and on Saturday, the day consecrated to her, whosoever beholds them combing their hair or counting their treasures is sure to perish. (Villemarque, Chants populaires, Introduction.)] We know the use that Ireland has made of this theme, in the dialogues which she loves to imagine between the representatives of her profane and religious life, Ossian and St. Patrick. [Footnote: See Miss Brooke's Reliques of Irish Poetry, Dublin, 1789, pp. 37 et seq., PP. 75 et seq.] Ossian regrets the adventures, the chase, the blast of the horn, and the kings of old time. "If they were here," he says to St. Patrick, "thou should'st not thus be scouring the country with the psalm–singing flock." Patrick seeks to calm him by soft words, and sometimes carries his condescension so far as to listen to his long histories, which appear to interest the saint but slightly. "Thou hast heard my story," says the old bard in conclusion; "albeit my memory groweth weak, and I am devoured with care, yet I desire to continue still to sing the deeds of yore, and to live upon ancient glories. Now am I stricken with years, my life is frozen within me, and all my joys are fleeting away. No more can my hand grasp the sword, nor mine arm hold the lance in rest. Among priests my last sad hour lengtheneth out, and psalms take now the place of songs of victory." "Let thy songs rest," says Patrick, "and dare not to compare thy Finn to the King of Kings, whose might knoweth no bounds: bend thy knees before Him, and know Him for thy Lord." It was indeed necessary to surrender, and the legend relates how the old bard ended his days in the cloister, among the priests whom he had so often used rudely, in the midst of these chants that he knew not. Ossian was too good an Irishman for any one to make up his mind to damn him utterly. Merlin himself had to cede to the new spell. He was, it is said, converted by St. Columba; and the popular voice in the ballads repeats to him unceasingly this sweet and touching appeal: "Merlin, Merlin, be converted; there is no divinity save that of God."

VI.

We should form an altogether inadequate idea of the physiognomy of the Celtic races, were we not to study them under what is perhaps the most singular aspect of their development—that is to say, their ecclesiastical antiquities and their saints. Leaving on one side the temporary repulsion which Christian mildness had to conquer in the classes of society which saw their influence diminished by the new order of things, it can be truly said, that the gentleness of manners and the exquisite sensibility of the Celtic races, in conjunction with the absence of a formerly existing religion of strong organisation, predestined them to Christianity. Christianity in fact, addressing itself by preference to the more humble feelings in human nature, met here with admirably prepared disciples; no race has so delicately understood the charm of littleness, none has placed the simple creature, the innocent, nearer God. The ease with which the new religion took possession of these peoples is also remarkable. Brittany and Ireland between them scarce count two or three martyrs; they are reduced to venerating as such those of their compatriots who were slain in the Anglo–Saxon and Danish invasions. Here comes to light the profound difference dividing the Celtic from the Teutonic race. The Teutons only received Christianity tardily and in spite of themselves, by scheming or by force, after a sanguinary resistance, and with terrible throes, Christianity was in fact on several sides repugnant to their nature; and one understands the regrets of pure Teutonists who, to this day, reproach the new faith with having corrupted their sturdy ancestors.

Such was not the case with the Celtic peoples; that gentle little race was naturally Christian. Far from changing them, and taking away some of their qualities, Christianity finished and perfected them. Compare the legends relating to the introduction of Christianity into the two countries, the Kristni Saga for instance, and the delightful legends of Lucius and St. Patrick. What a difference we find! In Iceland the first apostles are pirates, converted by some chance, now saying mass, now massacring their enemies, now resuming their former profession of sea–rovers; everything is done in accord with expediency, and without any serious faith.

In Ireland and Brittany grace operates through women, by I know not what charm of purity and sweetness. The revolt of the Teutons was never effectually stifled; never did they forget the forced baptisms, and the sword–supported Carlovingian missionaries, until the day when Teutonism took its revenge, and Luther through seven centuries gave answer to Witikind. On the other hand, the Celts were, even in the third century, perfect Christians. To the Teutons Christianity was for long nothing but a Roman institution, imposed from without. They entered the Church only to trouble it; and it was not without very great difficulty that they succeeded in forming a national clergy. To the Celts, on the contrary, Christianity did not come from Rome; they had their native clergy, their own peculiar usages, their faith at first hand. It cannot, in fact, be doubted that in apostolic times Christianity was preached in Brittany; and several historians, not without justification, have considered that it was borne there by Judaistic Christians, or by disciples of the school of St. John. Everywhere else Christianity found, as a first substratum, Greek or Roman civilisation. Here it found a virgin soil of a nature analogous to its own, and naturally prepared to receive it.

Few forms of Christianity have offered an ideal of Christian perfection so pure as the Celtic Church of the sixth, seventh, and eighth centuries. Nowhere, perhaps, has God been better worshipped in spirit than in those great monastic communities of Hy, or of Iona, of Bangor, of Clonard, or of Lindisfarne. One of the most distinguished developments of Christianity—doubtless too distinguished for the popular and practical mission which the Church had to undertake—Pelagianism, arose from it. The true and refined morality, the simplicity, and the wealth of invention which give distinction to the legends of the Breton and Irish saints are indeed admirable. No race adopted Christianity with so much originality, or, while subjecting itself to the common faith, kept its national characteristics more persistently. In religion, as in all else, the Bretons sought isolation, and did not willingly fraternise with the rest of the world. Strong in their moral superiority, persuaded that they possessed the veritable canon of faith and religion, having received their Christianity from an apostolic and wholly primitive preaching, they experienced no need of feeling themselves in communion with Christian societies less noble than their own. Thence arose that long struggle of the Breton churches against Roman pretensions, which is so admirably narrated by M. Augustin Thierry, [Footnote: In his History of the Conquest. The objections raised by M. Varin and some other scholars to M. Thierry's narrative only affect some secondary details, which were rectified in the edition published after the illustrious historian's death.] thence those inflexible characters of Columba and the monks of Iona, defending their usages and institutions against the whole Church, thence finally the false position of the Celtic peoples in Catholicism, when that mighty force, grown more and more aggressive, had drawn them together from all quarters, and compelled their absorption in itself. Having no Catholic past, they found themselves unclassed on their entrance into the great family, and were never able to succeed in creating for themselves an Archbishopric. All their efforts and all their innocent deceits to attribute that title to the Churches of Dol and St. Davids were wrecked on the overwhelming divergence of their past; their bishops had to resign themselves to being obscure suffragans of Tours and Canterbury.

It remains to be said that, even in our own days, the powerful originality of Celtic Christianity is far from being effaced. The Bretons of France, although they have felt the consequences of the revolutions undergone by Catholicism on the Continent, are, at the present hour, one of the populations in which religious feeling has retained most independence. The new devotions find no favour with it; the people are faithful to the old beliefs and the old saints; the psalms of religion have for them an ineffable harmony. In the same way, Ireland keeps, in her more remote districts, quite unique forms of worship from those of the rest of the world, to which nothing in other parts of Christendom can be compared. The influence of modern Catholicism, elsewhere so destructive of national usages, has had here a wholly contrary effect, the clergy having found it incumbent on them to seek a vantage ground against Protestantism, in attachment to local practices and the customs of the past.

It is the picture of these Christian institutions, quite distinct from those of the remainder of the West, of this sometimes strange worship, of these legends of the saints marked with so distinct a seal of nationality, that lends an interest to the ecclesiastical antiquities of Ireland, of Wales, and of Armorican Brittany. No hagiology has remained more exclusively natural than that of the Celtic peoples; until the twelfth century those peoples admitted very few alien saints into their martyrology. None, too, includes so many naturalistic elements. Celtic Paganism offered so little resistance to the new religion, that the Church did not hold itself constrained to put in force against it the rigour with which elsewhere it pursued the slightest traces of mythology. The conscientious essay by W. Rees on the "Saints of Wales", and that by the Rev. John Williams, an extremely learned ecclesiastic of the diocese of St. Asaph, on the "Ecclesiastical Antiquities of the Cymry", suffice to make one understand the immense value which a complete and intelligent history of the Celtic Churches, before their absorption in the Roman Church, would possess. To these might be added the learned work of Dom Lobineau on the Saints of Brittany, re–issued in our days by the Abbe Tresvaux, had not the half– criticism of the Benedictine, much worse than a total absence of criticism, altered those naive legends and cut away from them, under the pretext of good sense and religious reverence, that which to us gives them interest and charm.

Ireland above all would offer a religious physiognomy quite peculiar to itself, which would appear singularly original, were history in a position to reveal it in its entirety. When we consider the legions of Irish saints who in the sixth, seventh, and eighth centuries inundated the Continent and arrived from their isle bearing with them their stubborn spirit, their attachment to their own usages, their subtle and realistic turn of mind, and see the Scots (such was the name given to the Irish) doing duty, until the twelfth century, as instructors in grammar and literature to all the West, we cannot doubt that Ireland, in the first half of the Middle Ages, was the scene of a singular religious movement. Studious philologists and daring philosophers, the Hibernian monks were above all indefatigable copyists; and it was in part owing to them that the work of the pen became a holy task. Columba, secretly warned that his last hour is at hand, finishes the page of the psalter which he has commenced, writes at the foot that he bequeaths the continuation to his successor, and then goes into the church to die. Nowhere was monastic life to find such docile subjects. Credulous as a child, timid, indolent, inclined to submit and obey, the Irishman alone was capable of lending himself to that complete self−abdication in the hands of the abbot, which we find so deeply marked in the historical and legendary memorials of the Irish Church. One easily recognises the land where, in our own days, the priest, without provoking the slightest scandal, can, on a Sunday before quitting the altar, give the orders for his dinner in a very audible manner, and announce the farm where he intends to go and dine, and where he will hear his flock in confession. In the presence of a people which lived by imagination and the senses alone, the Church did not consider itself under the necessity of dealing severely with the caprices of religious fantasy. It permitted the free action of the popular instinct; and from this freedom emerged what is perhaps of all cults the most mythological and most analogous to the mysteries of antiquity, presented in Christian annals, a cult attached to certain places, and almost exclusively consisting in certain acts held to be sacramental.

Without contradiction the legend of St. Brandan is the most singular product of this combination of Celtic naturalism with Christian spiritualism. The taste of the Hibernian monks for making maritime pilgrimages through the archipelago of the Scottish and Irish seas, everywhere dotted with monasteries, [Footnote: The Irish saints literally covered the Western seas. A very considerable number of the saints of Brittany, St. Tenenan, St. Renan, etc., were emigrants from Ireland. The Breton legends of St. Malo, St. David, and of St. Pol of Leon are replete with similar stories of voyages to the distant isles of the West.] and the memory of yet more distant voyages in Polar seas, furnished the framework of this curious composition, so rich in local impressions. From Pliny (IV. xxx. 3) we learn that, even in his time, the Bretons loved to venture their lives upon the high seas, in search of unknown isles. M. Letronne has proved that in 795, sixty−five years consequently before the Danes, Irish monks landed in Iceland and established themselves on the coast. In this island the Danes found Irish books and bells; and the names of certain localities still bear witness to the sojourn of those monks, who were known by the name of Papae (fathers). In the Faroe Isles, in the Orkneys, and the Shetlands, indeed in all parts of the Northern seas, the Scandinavians found themselves preceded by those Papas, whose habits contrasted so strangely with their own. [Footnote: On this point see the careful researches of Humboldt in his History of the Geography of the New Continent, vol. ii.] Did they not have a glimpse too of that great land, the vague memory of which seems to pursue them, and which Columbus was to discover, following the traces of their dreams? It is only known that the existence of an island, traversed by a great river and situated to the west of Ireland, was, on the faith of the Irish, a dogma for mediaeval geographers.

The story went that, towards the middle of the sixth century, a monk called Barontus, on his return from voyaging upon the sea, came and craved hospitality at the monastery of Clonfert. Brandan the abbot besought him to give pleasure to the brothers by narrating the marvels of God that he had seen on the high seas. Barontus revealed to them the existence of an island surrounded by fogs, where he had left his disciple Mernoc; it is the Land of Promise that God keeps for his saints. Brandan with seventeen of his monks desired to go in quest of this mysterious land. They set forth in a leather boat, bearing with them as their sole provision a utensil of butter, wherewith to grease the hides of their craft. For seven years they lived thus in their boat, abandoning to God sail and rudder, and only stopping on their course to celebrate the feasts of Christmas and Easter on the back of the king of fishes, Jasconius. Every step of this monastic Odyssey is a miracle, on every isle is a monastery, where the wonders of a fantastical universe respond to the extravagances of a wholly ideal life. Here is the Isle of Sheep, where these animals govern themselves according to their own laws; elsewhere the Paradise of Birds, where the winged race lives after the fashion of monks, singing matins and lauds at the canonical hours. Brandan and his companions celebrate mass here with the birds, and remain with them for fifty days, nourishing themselves with nothing but the singing of their hosts. Elsewhere there is the Isle of Delight, the ideal of monastic life in the midst of the seas. Here no material necessity makes itself felt; the lamps light of themselves for the offices of religion, and never burn out, for they shine with a spiritual light. An absolute stillness reigns in the island; every one knows precisely the hour of his death; one feels neither cold, nor heat, nor sadness, nor sickness of body or soul. All this has endured since the days of St. Patrick, who so ordained it. The Land of Promise is more marvellous still; there an eternal day reigns; all the plants have flowers, all the trees bear fruits. Some privileged men alone have visited it. On their return a perfume is perceived to come from them, which their garments keep for forty days.

In the midst of these dreams there appears with a surprising fidelity to truth the feeling for the picturesque in Polar voyages,— —the transparency of the sea, the aspect of bergs and islands of ice melting in the sun, the volcanic phenomena of Iceland, the sporting of whales, the characteristic appearance of the Norwegian fiords, the sudden fogs, the sea calm as milk, the green isles crowned with grass which grows down to the very verge of the waves. This fantastical nature created expressly for another humanity, this strange topography at once glowing with fiction and speaking of truth, make the poem of St. Brandan one of the most extraordinary creations of the human mind, and perhaps the completest expression of the Celtic ideal. All is lovely, pure, and innocent; never has a gaze so benevolent and so gentle been cast upon the earth; there is not a single cruel idea, not a trace of frailty or repentance. It is the world seen through the crystal of a stainless conscience, one might almost say a human nature, as Pelagius wished it, that has never sinned. The very animals participate in this universal mildness. Evil appears under the form of monsters wandering on the deep, or of Cyclops confined in volcanic islands; but God causes them to destroy one another, and does not permit them to do hurt to the good.

We have just seen how, around the legend of a monk the Irish imagination grouped a whole cycle of physical and maritime myths. The Purgatory of St. Patrick became the framework of another series of fables, embodying the Celtic ideas concerning the other life and its different conditions. [Footnote: See Thomas Wright's excellent dissertation, Saint Patrick's Purgatory (London, 1844), and Calderon's The Well of Saint Patrick.] Perhaps the profoundest instinct of the Celtic peoples is their desire to penetrate the unknown. With the sea before them, they wish to know what lies beyond; they dream of a Promised Land. In the face of the unknown that lies beyond the tomb, they dream of that great journey which the pen of Dante has celebrated. The legend tells how, while St. Patrick was preaching about Paradise and Hell to the Irish, they confessed that they would feel more assured of the reality of these places, if he would allow one of them to descend there, and then come back with information

St. Patrick consented. A pit was dug, by which an Irishman set out upon the subterranean journey. Others wished to attempt the journey after him. With the consent of the abbot of the neighbouring monastery, they descended into the shaft, they passed through the torments of Hell and Purgatory, and then each told of what he had seen. Some did not emerge again; those who did laughed no more, and were henceforth unable to join in any gaiety. Knight Owen made a descent in 1153, and gave a narrative of his travels which had a prodigious success.

Other legends related that when St. Patrick drove the goblins out of Ireland, he was greatly tormented in this place for forty days by legions of black birds. The Irish betook themselves to the spot, and experienced the same assaults which gave them an immunity from Purgatory. According to the narrative of Giraldus Cambrensis, the isle which served as the theatre of this strange superstition was divided into two parts. One belonged to the monks, the other was occupied by evil spirits, who celebrated religious rites in their own manner, with an infernal uproar. Some people, for the expiation of their sins, voluntarily exposed themselves to the fury of those demons. There were nine ditches in which they lay for a night, tormented in a thousand different ways. To make the descent it was necessary to obtain the permission of the bishop. His duty it was to dissuade the penitent from attempting the adventure, and to point out to him how many people had gone in who had never come out again. If the devotee persisted, he was ceremoniously conducted to the shaft. He was lowered down by means of a rope, with a loaf and a vessel of water to strengthen him in the combat against the fiend which he proposed to wage. On the following morning the sacristan offered the rope anew to the sufferer. If he mounted to the surface again, they brought him back to the church, bearing the cross and chanting psalms. If he were not to be found, the sacristan closed the door and departed. In more modern times pilgrims to the sacred isles spent nine days there. They passed over to them in a boat hollowed out of the trunk of a tree. Once a day they drank of the water of the lake; processions and stations were performed in the beds or cells of the saints. Upon the ninth day the penitents entered into the shaft. Sermons were preached to them warning them of the danger they were about to run, and they were told of terrible examples. They forgave their enemies and took farewell of one another, as though they were at their last agony. According to contemporary accounts, the shaft was a low and narrow kiln, into which nine entered at a time, and in which the penitents passed a day and a night, huddled and tightly pressed against one another. Popular belief imagined an abyss underneath, to swallow up the unworthy and the unbelieving. On emerging from the pit they went and bathed in the lake, and so their Purgatory was accomplished. It would appear from the accounts of eye-witnesses that, to this day, things happen very nearly after the same fashion.

The immense reputation of the Purgatory of St. Patrick filled the whole of the Middle Ages. Preachers made appeal to the public notoriety of this great fact, to controvert those who had their doubts regarding Purgatory. In the year 1358 Edward III. gave to a Hungarian of noble birth, who had come from Hungary expressly to visit the sacred well, letters patent attesting that he had undergone his Purgatory. Narratives of those travels beyond the tomb became a very fashionable form of literature; and it is important for us to remark the wholly mythological, and as wholly Celtic, characteristics dominant in them. It is in fact evident that we are dealing with a mystery or local cult, anterior to Christianity, and probably based upon the physical appearance of the country. The idea of Purgatory, in its final and concrete form, fared specially well amongst the Bretons and the Irish. Bede is one of the first to speak of it in a descriptive manner, and the learned Mr. Wright very justly observes that nearly all the descriptions of Purgatory come from Irishmen, or from Anglo-Saxons who have resided in Ireland, such as St. Fursey, Tundale, the Northumbrian Dryhthelm, and Knight Owen. It is likewise a remarkable thing that only the Irish were able to behold the marvels of their Purgatory. A canon from Hemstede in Holland, who descended in 1494, saw nothing at all. Evidently this idea of travels in the other world and its infernal categories, as the Middle Ages accepted it, is Celtic. The belief in the three circles of existence is again to be found in the Triads, [Footnote: A series of aphorisms under the form of triplets, which give us, with numerous interpolations, the ancient teaching of the bards, and that traditional wisdom which, according to the testimony of the ancients, was transmitted by means of mnemonic verses in the schools of the Druids. under an aspect which does not permit one to see any Christian interpolation.]

The soul's peregrinations after death are also the favourite theme of the most ancient Armorican poetry. Among the features by which the Celtic races most impressed the Romans were the precision of their ideas upon the future life, their inclination to suicide, and the loans and contracts which they signed with the other world in view. The more frivolous peoples of the South saw with awe in this assurance the fact of a mysterious race, having an understanding of the future and the secret of death. Through the whole of classical antiquity runs the tradition of an Isle of Shadows, situated on the confines of Brittany, and of a folk devoted to the passage of souls, which lives upon the neighbouring coast. In the night they hear dead men prowling about their cabin, and knocking at the door. Then they rise up; their craft is laden with invisible beings; on their return it is lighter. Several of these features reproduced by Plutarch, Claudian, Procopius, [Footnote: A Byzantine historian of the fifth and sixth centuries.] and Tzetzes [Footnote: A Greek poet and grammarian of the twelfth century.] would incline one to believe that the renown of the Irish myths made its way into classical antiquity about the first or second century. Plutarch, for example, relates, concerning the Cronian Sea, fables identical with those which fill the legend of St. Malo. Procopius, describing the sacred Island of Brittia, which consists of two parts separated by the sea, one delightful, the other given over to evil spirits, seems to have read in advance the description of the Purgatory of St. Patrick, which Giraldus Cambrensis was to give seven centuries later. It cannot be doubted for a moment, after the able researches of Messrs. Ozanam, Labitte, and Wright, that to the number of poetical themes which Europe owes to the genius of the Celts, is to be added the framework of the Divine Comedy.

One can understand how greatly this invincible attraction to fables must have discredited the Celtic race in the eyes of nationalities that believed themselves to be more serious. It is in truth a strange thing, that the whole of the mediaeval epoch, whilst submitting to the influence of the Celtic imagination, and borrowing from Brittany and Ireland at least half of its poetical subjects, believed itself obliged, for the saving of its own honour, to slight and satirise the people to which it owed them. Even Chretien de Troyes, for example, who passed his life in exploiting the Breton romances for his own purposes, originated the saying—

"Les Gallois sont tous par nature
Plus sots que betes de pature."

Some English chronicler, I know not who, imagined he was making a charming play upon words when he described those beautiful creations, the whole world of which deserved to live, as "the childish nonsense with which those brutes of Bretons amuse themselves." The Bollandists [Footnote: A group of Jesuits who issued a collection of "Lives of the Saints". The first five volumes were edited by John Bolland.] found it incumbent to exclude from their collection, as apocryphal extravagances, those admirable religious legends, with which no Church has anything to compare. The decided leaning of the Celtic race towards the ideal, its sadness, its fidelity, its good faith, caused it to be regarded by its neighbours as dull, foolish, and superstitious. They could not understand its delicacy and refined manner of feeling. They mistook for awkwardness the embarrassment experienced by sincere and open natures in the presence of more artificial natures. The contrast between French frivolity and Breton stubbornness above all led, after the fourteenth century, to most deplorable conflicts, whence the Bretons ever emerged with a reputation for wrong–headedness.

It was still worse, when the nation that most prides itself on its practical good sense found confronting it the people that, to its own misfortune, is least provided with that gift. Poor Ireland, with her ancient mythology, with her Purgatory of St. Patrick, and her fantastic travels of St. Brandan, was not destined to find grace in the eyes of English puritanism. One ought to observe the disdain of English critics for these fables, and their superb pity for the Church which dallies with Paganism, so far as to keep up usages which are notoriously derived from it. Assuredly we have here a praiseworthy zeal, arising from natural goodness; and yet, even if these flights of imagination did no more than render a little more supportable many sufferings which are said to have no remedy, that after all would be something. Who shall dare to say where, here on earth, is the boundary between reason and dreaming? Which is worth more, the imaginative instinct of man, or the narrow orthodoxy that pretends to remain rational, when speaking of things divine? For my own part, I prefer the frank mythology, with all its vagaries, to a theology so paltry, so vulgar, and so colourless, that it would be wronging God to believe that, after having made the visible world so beautiful he should have made the invisible world so prosaically reasonable.

In presence of the ever–encroaching progress of a civilisation which is of no country, and can receive no name, other than that of modern or European, it would be puerile to hope that the Celtic race is in the future to succeed in obtaining isolated expression of its originality. And yet we are far from believing that this race has said its last word. After having put in practice all chivalries, devout and worldly, gone with Peredur in quest of the Holy Grail and fair ladies, and dreamed with St. Brandan of mystical Atlantides, who knows what it would produce in the domain of intellect, if it hardened itself to an entrance into the world, and subjected its rich and profound nature to the conditions of modern thought? It appears to me that there would result from this combination, productions of high originality, a subtle and discreet manner of taking life, a singular union of strength and weakness, of rude simplicity and mildness. Few races have had so complete a poetic childhood as the Celtic; mythology, lyric poetry, epic, romantic imagination, religious enthusiasm—none of these failed them; why should reflection fail them? Germany, which commenced with science and criticism, has come to poetry; why should not the Celtic races, which began with poetry, finish with criticism? There is not so great a distance from one to the other as is supposed; the poetical races are the philosophic races, and at bottom philosophy is only a manner of poetry. When one considers how Germany, less than a century ago, had her genius revealed to her, how a multitude of national individualities, to all appearance effaced, have suddenly risen again in our own days, more instinct with life than ever, one feels persuaded that it is a rash thing to lay down any law on the intermittence and awakening of nations; and that modern civilisation, which appeared to be made to absorb them, may perhaps be nothing more than their united fruition.

THE EDUCATION OF THE HUMAN RACE

BY GOTTHOLD EPHRAIM LESSINO

TRANSLATED BY F. W. ROBERTSON

INTRODUCTORY NOTE

Lessing's life has been sketched in the introduction to his "Minna von Barnhelm" in the volume of Continental Dramas in The Harvard Classics.

"The Education of the Human Race" is the culmination of a bitter theological controversy which began with the publication by Lessing, in 1774–1778, of a series of fragments of a work on natural religion by the German deist, Reimarus. This action brought upon Lessing the wrath of the orthodox German Protestants, led by J. M. Goeze, and in the battle that followed Lessing did his great work for the liberalising of religious thought in Germany. The present treatise is an extraordinarily condensed statement of the author's attitude towards the fundamental questions of religion, and gives his view of the signification of the previous religious history of mankind, along with his faith And hope for the future.

As originally issued, the essay purported to be merely edited by Lessing; but there is no longer any doubt as to his having been its author. It is an admirable and characteristic expression of the serious and elevated spirit in which he dealt with matters that had then, as often, been degraded by the virulence of controversy.

THE EDUCATION OF THE HUMAN RACE

1

That which Education is to the Individual, Revelation is to the Race.

2

Education is Revelation coming to the Individual Man; and Revelation is Education which has come, and is yet coming, to the Human Race.

3

Whether it can be of any advantage to the science of instruction to contemplate Education in this point of view, I will not here inquire; but in Theology it may unquestionably be of great advantage, and may remove many difficulties, if Revelation be conceived of as the Educator of Humanity.

4

Education gives to Man nothing which he might not educe out of himself; it gives him that which he might educe out of himself, only quicker and more easily. In the same way too, Revelation gives nothing to the human species, which the human reason left to itself might not attain; only it has given, and still gives to it, the most important of these things earlier.

5

And just as in Education, it is not a matter of indifference in what order the powers of a man are developed, as it cannot impart to a man all at once; so was God also necessitated to maintain a certain order, and a certain measure in His Revelation.

6

Even if the first man were furnished at once with a conception of the One God; yet it was not possible that this conception, imparted, and not gained by thought, should subsist long in its clearness. As soon as the Human Reason, left to itself, began to elaborate it, it broke up the one Immeasurable into many Measurables, and gave a note or sign of mark to every one of these parts.

7

Hence naturally arose polytheism and idolatry. And who can say how many millions of years human reason would have been bewildered in these errors, even though in all places and times there were individual men who recognized them as errors, had it not pleased God to afford it a better direction by means of a new Impulse?

8

But when He neither could nor would reveal Himself any more to each individual man, He selected an individual People for His special education; and that exactly the most rude and the most unruly, in order to begin with it from the very commencement.

9

This was the Hebrew People, respecting whom we do not in the least know what kind of Divine Worship they had in Egypt. For so despised a race of slaves was not permitted to take part in the worship of the Egyptians; and the God of their fathers was entirely unknown to them.

10

It is possible that the Egyptians had expressly prohibited the Hebrews from having a God or Gods, perhaps they had forced upon them the belief that their despised race had no God, no Gods, that to have a God or Gods was the prerogative of the superior Egyptians only, and this may have been so held in order to have the power of tyrannising over them with a greater show of fairness. Do Christians even now do much better with their slaves?

11

To this rude people God caused Himself to be announced first, simply as "the God of their fathers," in order to make them acquainted and familiar with the idea of a God belonging to them also, and to begin with confidence in Him.

12

Through the miracles with which He led them out of Egypt, and planted them in Canaan, He testified of Himself to them as a God mightier than any other God.

13

And as He proceeded, demonstrating Himself to be the Mightiest of all, which only One can be, He gradually accustomed them thus to the idea of THE ONE.

14

But how far was this conception of The One, below the true transcendental conception of the One which Reason learnt to derive, so late with certainty, from the conception of the Infinite One?

15

Although the best of the people were already more or less approaching the true conception of the One only, the people as a whole could not for a long time elevate themselves to it. And this was the sole true reason why they so often abandoned their one God, and expected to find the One, i. e., as they meant, the Mightiest, in some God or other, belonging to another people.

16

But of what kind of moral education was a people so raw, so incapable of abstract thoughts, and so entirely in their childhood capable? Of none other but such as is adapted to the age of children, an education by rewards and punishments addressed to the senses.

17

Here too Education and Revelation meet together. As yet God could give to His people no other religion, no other law than one through obedience to which they might hope to be happy, or through disobedience to which they must fear to be unhappy. For as yet their regards went no further than this earth. They knew of no immortality of the soul; they yearned after no life to come. But now to reveal these things to one whose reason had as yet so little growth, what would it have been but the same fault in the Divine Rule as is committed by the schoolmaster, who chooses to hurry his pupil too rapidly, and boast of his progress, rather than thoroughly to ground him?

18

But, it will be asked, to what purpose was this education of so rude a people, a people with whom God had to begin so entirely from the beginning? I reply, in order that in the process of time He might employ particular members of this nation as the Teachers of other people. He was bringing up in them the future Teachers of the human race. It was the Jews who became their teachers, none but Jews; only men out of a people so brought up, could be their teachers.

19

For to proceed. When the Child by dint of blows and caresses had grown and was now come to years of understanding, the Father sent it at once into foreign countries: and here it recognised at once the Good which in its Father's house it had possessed, and had not been conscious of.

20.

While God guided His chosen people through all the degrees of a child–like education, the other nations of the earth had gone on by the light of reason. The most part had remained far behind the chosen people. Only a few had got before them. And this too, takes place with children, who are allowed to grow up left to themselves: many remain quite raw, some educate themselves even to an astonishing degree.

21

But as these more fortunate few prove nothing against the use and necessity of Education, so the few heathen nations, who even appear to have made a start in the knowledge of God before the chosen people, prove nothing against a Revelation. The Child of Education begins with slow yet sure footsteps; it is late in overtaking many a more happily organised child of nature; but it does overtake it; and thenceforth can never be distanced by it again.

22

Similarly—Putting aside the doctrine of the Unity of God, which in a way is found, and in a way is not found, in the books of the Old Testament—that the doctrine of immortality at least is not discoverable in it, is wholly foreign to it, that all doctrine connected therewith of reward and punishment in a future life, proves just as little against the Divine origin of these books. Notwithstanding the absence of these doctrines, the account of miracles and prophecies may be perfectly true. For let us suppose that these doctrines were not only wanting therein, but even that they were not at all true; let us suppose that for mankind all was over in this life; would the Being of God be for this reason less demonstrated? Would God be for this less at liberty, would it less become Him to take immediate charge of the temporal fortunes of any people out of this perishable race? The miracles which He performed for the Jews, the prophecies which He caused to be recorded through them, were surely not for the few mortal Jews, in whose time they had happened and been recorded: He had His intentions therein in reference to the whole Jewish people, to the entire Human Race, which, perhaps, is destined to remain on earth forever, though every individual Jew and every individual man die forever.

23

Once more, The absence of those doctrines in the writings of the Old Testament proves nothing against their Divinity. Moses was sent from God even though the sanction of his law only extended to this life. For why should it extend further? He was surely sent only to the Israelitish people of that time, and his commission was perfectly adapted to the knowledge, capacities, yearnings of the then existing Israelitish people, as well as to the destination of that which belonged to the future. And this is sufficient.

24

So far ought Warburton to have gone, and no further. But that learned man overdrew his bow. Not content that the absence of these doctrines was no discredit to the Divine mission of Moses, it must even be a proof to him of the Divinity of the mission. And if he had only sought this proof in the adaptation of such a law to such a people!

But he betook himself to the hypothesis of a miraculous system continued in an unbroken line from Moses to Christ, according to which, God had made every individual Jew exactly happy or unhappy, in the proportion to his obedience or disobedience to the law deserved. He would have it that this miraculous system had compensated for the want of those doctrines (of eternal rewards and punishments, without which no state can subsist; and that such a compensation even proved what that want at first sight appeared to negative.

25

How well it was that Warburton could by no argument prove or even make likely this continuous miracle, in which he placed the existence of Israelitish Theocracy! For could he have done so, in truth, he could then, and not till then, have made the difficulty really insuperable, to me at least. For that which was meant to prove the Divine character of the Mission of Moses, would have rendered the matter itself doubtful, which God, it is true, did not intend then to reveal; but which on the other hand, He certainly would not render unattainable.

26

I explain myself by that which is a picture of Revelation. A Primer for children may fairly pass over in silence this or that important piece of knowledge or art which it expounds, respecting which the Teacher judged, that it is not yet fitted for the capacities of the children for whom he was writing. But it must contain absolutely nothing which blocks up the way towards the knowledge which is held back, or misleads the children from it. Rather far, all the approaches towards it must be carefully left open; and to lead them away from even one of these approaches, or to cause them to enter it later than they need, would alone be enough to change the mere imperfection of such a Primer into an actual fault.

27

In the same way, in the writings of the Old Testament those primers for the rude Israelitish people, unpractised in thought, the doctrines of the immortality of the soul, and future recompenses, might be fairly left out: but they were bound to contain nothing which could have even procrastinated the progress of the people, for whom they were written, in their way to this grand truth. And to say but a small thing, what could have more procrastinated it than the promise of such a miraculous recompense in this life? A promise made by Him who promises nothing that He does not perform.

28

For although unequal distribution of the goods of this life, Virtue and Vice seem to be taken too little into consideration, although this unequal distribution docs not exactly afford a strong proof of the immortality of the soul and of a life to come, in which this difficulty will be reserved hereafter, it is certain that without this difficulty the human understanding would not for a long time, perhaps never, have arrived at better or firmer proofs. For what was to impel it to seek for these better proofs? Mere curiosity?

29

An Israelite here and there, no doubt, might have extended to every individual member of the entire commonwealth, those promises and threatenings which belong to it as a whole, and be firmly persuaded that whosoever should be pious must also be happy, and that whoever was unhappy must be bearing the penalty of his wrong–doing, which penalty would forthwith change itself into blessing, as soon as he abandoned his sin. Such a one appears to have written Job, for the plan of it is entirely in this spirit.

30

But daily experience could not possibly be permitted to confirm this belief, or else it would have been all over, for ever, with people who had this experience, so far as all recognition and reception was concerned of the truth as yet unfamiliar to them. For if the pious were absolutely happy, and it also of course was a necessary part of his happiness that his satisfaction should be broken by no uneasy thoughts of death, and that he should die old, and satisfied with life to the full: how could he yearn after another life? and how could he reflect upon a thing after which he did not yearn? But if the pious did not reflect thereupon, who then should reflect? The transgressor? he who felt the punishments of his misdeeds, and if he cursed this life, must have so gladly renounced that other existence?

31

Much less would it signify if an Israelite here and there directly and expressly denied the immortality of the soul and future recompense, on account of the law having no reference thereto. The denial of an individual, had it even been a Solomon, did not arrest the progress of the general reason, and was even in itself a proof that the nation had now come a great step nearer the truth For individuals only deny what the many are bringing into consideration; and to bring into consideration that, concerning which no one troubled himself at all before, is half way to knowledge.

32

Let us also acknowledge that it is a heroic obedience to obey the laws of God simply because they are God's laws, and not because He has promised to reward the obedience to them here and there; to obey them even though there be an entire despair of future recompense, and uncertainty respecting a temporal one.

33

Must not a people educated in this heroic obedience towards God have been destined, must they not have been capable beyond all others of executing Divine purpose? of quite a special character? Let the soldier, who pays blind obedience to his leader, become also convinced of his leader's wisdom, and then say what that leader may not undertake to achieve with him.

34

As yet the Jewish people had reverenced in their Jehovah rather the mightiest than the wisest of all Gods; as yet they had rather feared Him as a Jealous God than loved Him: a proof this too, that the conception which they had of their eternal One God was not exactly the right conception which we should have of God. However, now the time was come that these conceptions of theirs were to be expanded, ennobled, rectified, to accomplish which God availed Himself of a quite natural means, a better and more correct measure, by which it got the opportunity of appreciating Him.

35

Instead of, as hitherto, appreciating Him in contrast with the miserable idols of the small neighboring peoples, with whom they lived in constant rivalry, they began, in captivity under the wise Persians, to measure Him against the "Being of all Beings" such as a more disciplined reason recognized and reverenced.

36

Revelation had guided their reason, and now, all at once, reason gave clearness to their Revelation.

37

This was the first reciprocal influence which these two (Reason and Revelation) exercised on one another; and so far is the mutual influence from being unbecoming to the Author of them both, that without it either of them would have been useless.

38

The child, sent abroad, saw other children who knew more, who lived more becomingly, and asked itself, in confusion, "Why do I not know that too? Why do I not live so too? Ought I not to have been taught and admonished of all this in my father's house?" Thereupon it again sought out its Primer, which had long been thrown into a corner, in order to throw off a blame upon the Primer. But behold, it discovers that the blame does not rest upon the books, that the shame is solely its own, for not having long ago, known this very thing, and lived in this very way.

39

Since the Jews, by this time, through the medium of the pure Persian doctrine, recognized in their Jehovah, not simply the greatest of all national deities, but GOD; and since they could, the more readily find Him and indicate Him to others in their sacred writings, inasmuch as He was really in them; and since they manifested as great an aversion for sensuous representations, or at all events, were instructed in these Scriptures, to have an aversion to them as great as the Persians had always felt; what wonder that they found favor in the eyes of Cyrus, with a Divine Worship which he recognized as being, no doubt, far below pure Sabeism, but yet far above the rude idolatries which in its stead had taken possession of the forsaken land of the Jews.

40

Thus enlightened respecting the treasures which they had possessed, without knowing it, they returned, and became quite another people, whose first care it was to give permanency to this illumination amongst themselves. Soon an apostacy and idolatry among them was out of the question. For it is possible to be faithless to a national deity, but never to God, after He has once been recognised.

The theologians have tried to explain this complete change in the Jewish people in a different way; and one, who has well demonstrated the insufficiency of these explanations, at last was for giving us, as a true account—"the visible fulfilment of the prophecies which had been spoken and written respecting the Babylonish captivity and the restoration from it." But even this reason can be only so far the true one, as it presupposes the, by this time, exalted ideas of God. The Jews must by this time have recognised that to do miracles, and to predict the future, belonged only to God, both of which they had ascribed formerly to false idols, by which it came to pass that even miracles and prophecies had hitherto made so weak an impression upon them.

42

Doubtless, the Jews were made more acquainted with the doctrine of immortality among the Chaldeans and Persians. They became more familiar with it too in the schools of the Greek Philosophers in Egypt.

43

However, as this doctrine was not in the same condition in reference to their Scriptures that the doctrines of God's Unity and Attributes were—since the former were entirely overlooked by that sensual people, while the latter would be sought for:—and since too, for the former, previous exercising was necessary, and as yet there had been only hints and allusions, the faith in the immortality of the soul could naturally never be the faith of the entire people. It was and continued to be only the creed of a certain section of them.

44

An example of what I mean by "previous exercising" for the doctrine of immortality, is the Divine threatenings of punishing the misdeeds of the fathers upon the children unto the third and fourth generation. This accustomed the fathers to live in thought with their remotest posterity, and to feel, as it were, beforehand, the misfortune which they had brought upon these guiltless ones.

45

By an allusion I mean that which was intended only to excite curiosity and to occasion questions. As, for instance, the oft– recurring mode of expression, describing death by "he was gathered to his fathers."

By a "hint" I mean that which already contains any germ, out of which the, as yet, held back truth allows itself to be developed. Of this character was the inference of Christ from the naming of God "the God of Abraham, Isaac, and Jacob." This hint appears to me to be unquestionably capable of being worked out into a strong proof.

47

In such previous exercitations, allusions, hints, consists the positive perfection of a Primer; just as the above–mentioned peculiarity of not throwing difficulties or hindrances in the way to the suppressed truth constitutes the negative perfection of such a book.

48

Add to all this the clothing and style.

1. The clothing of abstract truths, which were not entirely to be passed over, in allegories and instructive single circumstances, which were narrated as actual occurrences. Of this character are the Creation under the image of growing Day; the Origin of Evil in the story of the Forbidden Tree; the source of the variety of languages in the history of the Tower of Babel,

49 2. The style—sometimes plain and simple, sometimes poetical, throughout full of tautologies, but of such a kind as practised sagacity, since they sometimes appear to be saying something else, and yet the same thing; sometimes the same thing over again, and yet to signify or to be capable of signifying at the bottom, something else:—

50

And then you have all the properties of excellence which belong to a Primer for a childlike people, as well as for children.

51

But every Primer is only for a certain age. To delay the child, that has outgrown it, longer in it than it was intended for, is hurtful. For to be able to do this is a way in any sort profitable, you must insert into it more than there is really in it, and extract from it more than it can contain. You must look for and make too much of allusions and hints; squeeze allegories too closely; interpret examples too circumstantially; press too much upon words. This gives the child a petty, crooked, hair splitting understanding: it makes him full of mysteries, superstitions; full of contempt for all that is comprehensible and easy.

52

The very way in which the Rabbins handled their sacred books! The very character which they thereby imparted to the character of their people!

53

A Better Instructor must come and tear the exhausted Primer from the child's hands. CHRIST came!

54

That portion of the human race which God had willed to comprehend in one Educational plan, was ripe for the Second step of Education. He had, however, only willed to comprehend on such a plan, one which by language, mode of action, government, and other natural and political relationships, was already united in itself.

55

That is, this portion of the human race was come so far in the exercise of its reason, as to need, and to be able to make use of nobler and worthier motives of moral action than temporal rewards and punishments, which had hitherto been its guides. The child had become a youth. Sweetmeats and toys have given place to the budding desire to go as free, as honored, and as happy as its elder brother.

56

For a long time, already, the best individuals of that portion of the human race (called above the elder brother); had been accustomed to let themselves be ruled by the shadow of such nobler motives. The Greek and Roman did everything to live on after this life, even if it were only in the remembrance of their fellow–citizens.

57

It was time that another true life to be expected after this should gain an influence over the youth's actions.

58

And so Christ was the first certain practical Teacher of the immortality of the soul.

59

The first certain Teacher. Certain, through the prophecies which were fulfilled in Him; certain, through the miracles which He achieved; certain, through His own revival after a death through which He had sealed His doctrine. Whether we can still prove this revival, these miracles, I put aside, as I leave on one side who the Person of Christ was. All that may have been at that time of great weight for the reception of His doctrine, but it is now no longer of the same importance for the recognition of the truth of His doctrine.

60

The first practical Teacher. For it is one thing to conjecture, to wish, and to believe the immortality of the soul, as a philosophic speculation: quite another thing to direct the inner and outer acts by it.

61

And this at least Christ was the first to teach. For although, already before Him, the belief had been introduced among many nations, that bad actions have yet to be punished in that life; yet they were only such actions as were injurious to civil society, and consequently, too, had already had their punishment in civil society. To enforce an inward purity of heart in reference to another life, was reserved for Him alone.

62

His disciples have faithfully propagated these doctrines: and if they had even had no other merit, than that of having effected a more general publication, among other nations, of a Truth which Christ had appeared to have destined only for the Jews, yet would they have even on that account alone, to be reckoned among the Benefactors and Fosterers of the Human Race.

63

If, however, they transplanted this one great Truth together with other doctrines, whose truth was less enlightening, whose usefulness was of a less exalted character, how could it be otherwise. Let us not blame them for this, but rather seriously examine whether these very commingled doctrines have not become a new impulse of directions for human reason.

64

At least, it is already clear that the New Testament Scriptures, in which these doctrines after some time were found preserved, have afforded, and still afford, the second better Primer for the race of man.

65

For seven hundred years past they have exercised human reason more than all other books, and enlightened it more, were it even only through the light which the human reason itself threw into them.

66

It would have been impossible for any other book to become so generally known among different nations: and indisputably, the fact that modes of thought so diverse from each other have been occupied on the same book, has helped on the human reason more than if every nation had had its own Primer specially for itself.

67

It was also highly necessary that each people for a period should hold this Book as the ne plus ultra of their knowledge. For the youth must consider his Primer as the first of all books, that the impatience to finish this book, may not hurry him on to things for which he has, as yet, laid no basis.

68

And one thing is also of the greatest importance even now. Thou abler spirit, who art fretting and restless over the last page of the Primer, beware! Beware of letting thy weaker fellow scholars mark what thou perceivest afar, or what thou art beginning to see!

Until these weaker fellow scholars are up with thee, rather return once more into this Primer, and examine whether that which thou takest only for duplicates of the method, for a blunder in the teaching, is not perhaps something more.

70

Thou hast seen in the childhood of the human race, respecting the doctrine of God's unity, that God makes immediate revelations of mere truths of reason, or has permitted and caused pure truths of reason to be taught, for some time, as truths of immediate revelation, in order to promulgate them the more rapidly, and ground them the more firmly.

71

Thou experiencest in the boyhood of the Race the same thing in reference to the doctrine of the immortality of the soul. It is preached in the better Primer as a Revelation, instead of taught as a result of human reason.

72

As we by this time can dispense with the Old Testament, in reference to the doctrine of the unity of

God, and as we are by degrees beginning also to be less dependent on the New Testament, in reference to the immortality of the soul: might there not in this Book also be other truths of the same sort prefigured, mirrored, as it were, which we are to marvel at, as revelations, exactly so long as until the time shall come when reason shall have learned to educe them, out of its other demonstrated truths and bind them up with them?

73

For instance, the doctrine of the Trinity. How if this doctrine should at last, after endless errors, right and left, only bring men on the road to recognise that God cannot possibly be One in the sense in which finite things are one, that even His unity must be a transcendental unity, which does not exclude a sort of purality? Must not God at least have the most perfect conception of Himself, i. e., a conception in which is found everything which is in Him? But would everything be found in it which is in Him, if a mere conception, a mere possibility, were found even of his necessary Reality as well as of His other qualities? This possibility exhausts the being of His other qualities. Does it that of His necessary Reality? I think not. Consequently God can either have no perfect conception of himself at all, or this perfect conception is just as necessarily real, i. e., actually existent, as He Himself is. Certainly the image of myself in the mirror is nothing but an empty representation of me, because it only has that of me upon the surface of which beams of light fall. But now if this image had everything, everything without exception, which I have myself, would it then still be a mere empty representation, or not rather a true reduplication of myself? When I believe that I recognise in God a familiar reduplication, I perhaps do not so much err, as that my language is insufficient for my ideas: and so much at least for ever incontrovertible, that they who wish to make the idea thereof popular for comprehension, could scarcely have expressed themselves more intelligibly and suitably than by giving the name of a Son begotten from Eternity.

74

And the doctrine of Original Sin. How, if at last everything were to convince us that man standing on the first and lowest step of his humanity, is not so entirely master of his actions as to be able to obey moral laws?

75

And the doctrine of the Son's satisfaction. How, if at last, all compelled us to assume that God, in spite of that original incapacity of man, chose rather to give him moral laws, and forgive him all transgressions in consideration of His Son, i. e., in consideration of the self–existent total of all His own perfections, compared with which, and in which, all imperfections of the individual disappear, than not to give him those laws, and then to exclude him from all moral blessedness, which cannot be conceived of without moral laws.

Let it not be objected that speculations of this description upon the mysteries of religion are forbidden. The word mystery signified, in the first ages of Christianity, something quite different from what it means now: and the cultivation of revealed truths into truths of reason, is absolutely necessary, if the human race is to be assisted by them. When they were revealed they were certainly no truths of reason, but they were revealed in order to become such. They were like the "that makes"—of the ciphering master, which he says to the boys, beforehand, in order to direct them thereby in their reckoning. If the scholars were to be satisfied with the "that makes," they would never learn to calculate, and would frustrate the intention with which their good master gave them a guiding clue in their work.

77

And why should not we too, by the means of a religion whose historical truth, if you will, looks dubious, be conducted in a familiar way to closer and better conceptions of the Divine Being, our own nature, our relation to God, truths at which the human reason would never have arrived of itself?

78

It is not true that speculations upon these things have ever done harm or become injurious to the body politic. You must reproach, not the speculations, but the folly and the tyranny of checking them. You must lay the blame on those who would not permit men having their own speculations to exercise them.

79

On the contrary, speculations of this sort, whatever the result, are unquestionably the most fitting exercises of the human heart, generally, so long as the human heart, generally, is at best only capable of loving virtue for the sake of its eternal blessed consequences.

80

For in this selfishness of the human heart, to will to practice the understanding too, only on that which concerns our corporal needs, would be to blunt rather than to sharpen it. It absolutely will be exercised on spiritual objects, if it is to attain its perfect illumination, and bring out that purity of heart which makes us capable of loving virtue for its own sake alone.

81

Or, is the human species never to arrive at this highest step of illumination and purity?—Never?

82

Never?—Let me not think this blasphemy, All Merciful! Education has its goal, in the Race, no less than in the Individual. That which is educated is educated for something.

83

The flattering prospects which are open to the people, the Honor and Well—being which are painted to him, what are they more than the means of educating him to become a man, who, when these prospects of Honor and Well—being have vanished, shall be able to do his Duty?

84

This is the aim of human education, and should not the Divine education extend as far? Is that which is successful in the way of Art with the individual, not to be successful in the way of Nature with the whole? Blasphemy! Blasphemy!!

85

No! It will come! it will assuredly come! the time of the perfecting, when man, the more convinced his understanding feels itself of an ever better Future, will nevertheless not be necessitated to borrow motives of action from this Future; for he will do the Right because it is right, not because arbitrary rewards are annexed thereto, which formerly were intended simply to fix and strengthen his unsteady gaze in recognising the inner, better, rewards of well—doing.

86

It will assuredly come! the time of a new eternal Gospel, which is promised us in the Primer of the New Testament itself!

87

Perhaps even some enthusiasts of the thirteenth and fourteenth centuries had caught a glimpse of a beam of this new eternal Gospel, and only erred in that they predicted its outburst at so near to their own time.

88

Perhaps their "Three Ages of the World" were not so empty a speculation after all, and assuredly they had no contemptible views when they taught that the New Covenant must become as much antiquated as the old has been. There remained by them the similarity of the economy of the same God. Ever, to let them speak my words, ever the self—same plan of the Education of the Race.

89

Only they were premature. Only they believed that they could make their contemporaries, who had scarcely outgrown their childhood, without enlightenment, without preparation, men worthy of their Third Age.

90

And it was just this which made them enthusiasts. The enthusiast often casts true glances into the future, but for this future he cannot wait. He wishes this future accelerated, and accelerated through him. That for which nature takes thousands of years is to mature itself in the moment of his existence.

For what possession has he in it if that which he recognises as the Best does not become the best in his lifetime? Does he come back? Does he expect to come back? Marvellous only that this enthusiastic expectation does not become more the fashion among enthusiasts. 91

Go thine inscrutable way, Eternal Providence! Only let me not despair in Thee, because of this inscrutableness. Let me not despair in Thee, even if Thy steps appear to me to be going back. It is not true that the shortest line is always straight.

92

Thou hast on Thine Eternal Way so much to carry on together, so much to do! So many aside steps to take! And what if it were as good as proved that the vast flow wheel which brings mankind nearer to this perfection is only put in motion by smaller, swifter wheels, each of which contributes its own individual unit thereto?

93

It is so! The very same Way by which the Race reaches its perfection, must every individual man—one sooner—another later— have travelled over. Have travelled over in one and the same life? Can he have been, in one and the self–same life, a sensual Jew and a spiritual Christian? Can he in the self–same life have overtaken both?

94

Surely not that! But why should not every individual man have existed more than once upon this World?

95

Is this hypothesis so laughable merely because it is the oldest? Because the human understanding, before the sophistries of the Schools had dissipated and debilitated it, lighted upon it at once?

Why may not even I have already performed those steps of my perfecting which bring to man only temporal punishments and rewards?

97

And once more, why not another time all those steps, to perform which the views of Eternal Rewards so powerfully assist us?

Why should I not come back as often as I am capable of acquiring fresh knowledge, fresh expertness? Do I bring away so much from once, that there is nothing to repay the trouble of coming back?

99

Is this a reason against it? Or, because I forget that I have been here already? Happy is it for me that I do forget. The recollection of my former condition would permit me to make only a bad use of the present. And that which even I must forget now, is that necessarily forgotten for ever?

100

Or is it a reason against the hypothesis that so much time would have been lost to me? Lost?—And how much then should I miss?—Is not a whole Eternity mine?

LETTERS UPON THE AESTHETIC EDUCATION OF MAN

BY J. C. FRIEDRICH VON SCHILLER

INTRODUCTORY NOTE

An outline of the life of Schiller will be found prefixed to the translation of "Wilhelm Tell" in the volume of Continental Dramas in The Harvard Classics.

Schiller's importance in the intellectual history of Germany is by no means confined to his poetry and dramas. He did notable work in history and philosophy, and in the department of esthetics especially, he made significant contributions, modifying and developing in important respects the doctrines of Kant. In the letters on "Esthetic Education" which are here printed, he gives the philosophic basis for his doctrine of art, and indicates clearly and persuasively his view of the place of beauty in human life.

LETTERS UPON THE AESTHETIC EDUCATION OF MAN

LETTER I.

By your permission I lay before you, in a series of letters, the results of my researches upon beauty and art. I am keenly sensible of the importance as well as of the charm and dignity of this undertaking. I shall treat a subject which is closely connected with the better portion of our happiness and not far removed from the moral nobility of human nature. I shall plead this cause of the Beautiful before a heart by which her whole power is felt and exercised, and which will take upon itself the most difficult part of my task in an investigation where one is compelled to appeal as frequently to feelings as to principles.

That which I would beg of you as a favour, you generously impose upon me as a duty; and, when I solely consult my inclination, you impute to me a service. The liberty of action you prescribe is rather a necessity for me than a constraint little exercised in formal rules, I shall scarcely incur the risk of sinning against good taste by any undue use of them; my ideas, drawn rather from within than from reading or from an intimate experience with the world, will not disown their origin; they would rather incur any reproach than that of a sectarian bias, and would prefer to succumb by their innate feebleness than sustain themselves by borrowed authority and foreign support.

In truth, I will not keep back from you that the assertions which follow rest chiefly upon Kantian principles; but if in the course of these researches you should be reminded of any special school of philosophy, ascribe it to my incapacity, not to those principles. No; your liberty of mind shall be sacred to me; and the facts upon which I build will be furnished by your own sentiments; your own unfettered thought will dictate the laws according to which we to proceed.

With regard to the ideas which predominate in the practical part of Kant's system, philosophers only disagree, whilst mankind, I am confident of proving, have never done so. If stripped of their technical shape, they will appear as the verdict of reason pronounced from time immemorial by common consent, and as facts of the moral instinct which nature, in her wisdom, has given to man in order to serve as guide and teacher until his enlightened intelligence gives him maturity. But this very technical shape which renders truth visible to the understanding conceals it from the feelings; for, unhappily, understanding begins by destroying the object of the inner sense before it can appropriate the object. Like the chemist, the philosopher finds synthesis only by analysis, or the spontaneous work of nature only through the torture of art. Thus, in order to detain the fleeting apparition, he must enchain it in the fetters of rule, dissect its fair proportions into abstract notions, and preserve its living spirit in a fleshless skeleton of words. Is it surprising that natural feeling should not recognise itself in such a copy, and if in the report of the analyst the truth appears as paradox?

Permit me therefore to crave your indulgence if the following researches should remove their object from the sphere of sense while endeavouring to draw it towards the understanding. That which I before said of moral experience can be applied with greater truth to the manifestation of "the beautiful." It is the mystery which enchants, and its being is extinguished with the extinction of the necessary combination of its elements.

LETTER II.

But I might perhaps make a better use of the opening you afford me if I were to direct your mind to a loftier theme than that of art. It would appear to be unseasonable to go in search of a code for the aesthetic world, when the moral world offers matter of so much higher interest, and when the spirit of philosophical inquiry is so stringently challenged by the circumstances of our times to occupy itself with the most perfect of all works of art—the establishment and structure of a true political freedom.

It is unsatisfactory to live out of your own age and to work for other times. It is equally incumbent on us to be good members of our own age as of our own state or country. If it is conceived to be unseemly and even unlawful for a man to segregate himself from the customs and manners of the circle in which he lives, it would be inconsistent not to see that it is equally his duty to grant a proper share of influence to the voice of his own epoch, to its taste and its requirements, in the operations in which he engages.

But the voice of our age seems by no means favorable to art, at all events to that kind of art to which my inquiry is directed. The course of events has given a direction to the genius of the time that threatens to remove it continually further from the ideal of art. For art has to leave reality, it has to raise itself bodily above necessity and neediness for art is the daughter of freedom, and it requires its prescriptions and rules to be furnished by the necessity of spirits and not by that of matter. But in our day it is necessity, neediness, that prevails, and bends a degraded humanity under its iron yoke. Utility is the great idol of the time, to which all powers do homage and all subjects are subservient. In this great balance of utility, the spiritual service of art has no weight, and, deprived of all encouragement, it vanishes from the noisy Vanity Fair of our time. The very spirit of philosophical inquiry itself robs the imagination of one promise after another, and the frontiers of art are narrowed, in proportion as the limits of science are enlarged.

The eyes of the philosopher as well as of the man of the world are anxiously turned to the theatre of political events, where it is presumed the great destiny of man is to be played out. It would almost seem to betray e culpable indifference to the welfare of society if we did not share this general interest. For this great commerce in social and moral principles is of necessity a matter of the greatest concern to every human being, on the ground both of its subject and of its results. It must accordingly be of deepest moment to every man to think for himself. It would seem that now at length a question that formerly was only settled by the law of the stronger is to be determined by the calm judgment of the reason, and every man who is capable of placing himself in a central position, and raising his individuality into that of his species, can look upon himself as in possession of this judicial faculty of reason; being moreover, as man and member of the human family, a party in the case under trial and involved more or less in its decisions. It would thus appear that this great political process is not only engaged with his individual case, it has also to pronounce enactments, which he as a rational spirit is capable of enunciating and entitled to pronounce.

It is evident that it would have been most attractive to me to inquire into an object such as this, to decide such a question in conjunction with a thinker of powerful mind, a man of liberal sympathies, and a heart imbued with a noble enthusiasm for the weal of humanity. Though so widely separated by worldly position, it would have been a delightful surprise to have found your unprejudiced mind arriving at the same result as my own in the field of ideas, Nevertheless, I think I can not only excuse, but even justify by solid grounds, my step in resisting this attractive purpose and in preferring beauty to freedom. I hope that I shall succeed in convincing you that this matter of art is less foreign to the needs than to the tastes of our age; nay, that, to arrive at a solution even in the political problem, the road of aesthetics must be pursued, because it is through beauty that we arrive at freedom. But I cannot carry out this proof without my bringing to your remembrance the principles by which the reason is guided in political legislation.

LETTER III.

Man is not better treated by nature in his first start than her other works are; so long as he is unable to act for himself as an independent intelligence, she acts for him. But the very fact that constitutes him a man is, that he does not remain stationary, where nature has placed him, that he can pass with his reason, retracing the steps nature had made him anticipate, that he can convert the work of necessity into one of free solution, and elevate physical necessity into a moral law.

When man is raised from his slumber in the senses, he feels that he is a man, he surveys his surroundings, and finds that he is in a state. He was introduced into this state, by the power of circumstances, before he could freely select his own position. But as a moral being he cannot possibly rest satisfied with a political condition forced upon him by necessity, and only calculated for that condition; and it would be unfortunate if this did satisfy him. In many cases man shakes off this blind law of necessity, by his free spontaneous action, of which among many others we have an instance, in his ennobling by beauty and suppressing by moral influence the powerful impulse implanted in him by nature in the passion of love. Thus, when arrived at maturity, he recovers his childhood by an artificial process, he founds a state of nature in his ideas, not given him by any experience, but established by the necessary laws and conditions of his reason, and he attributes to this ideal condition an object, an aim, of which he was not cognisant in the actual reality of nature. He gives himself a choice of which he was not capable before, and sets to work just as if he were beginning anew, and were exchanging his original state of bondage for one of complete independence, doing this with complete insight and of his free decision. He is justified in regarding this work of political thraldom as non-existing, though a wild and arbitrary caprice may have founded its work very artfully; though it may strive to maintain it with great arrogance and encompass it with a halo of veneration. For the work of blind powers possesses no authority, before which freedom need bow, and all must be made to adapt itself to the highest end which reason has set up in his personality. It is in this wise that a people in a state of manhood is justified in exchanging a condition of thraldom for one of moral freedom.

Now the term natural condition can be applied to every political body which owes its establishment originally to forces and not to laws, and such a state contradicts the moral nature of man, because lawfulness can alone have authority over this. At the same time this natural condition is quite sufficient for the physical man, who only gives himself laws in order to get rid of brute force. Moreover, the physical man is a reality, and the moral man problematical. Therefore when the reason suppresses the natural condition, as she must if she wishes to substitute her own, she weighs the real physical man against the problematical moral man, she weighs the existence of society against a possible, though morally necessary, ideal of society. She takes from man something which he really possesses, and without which he possesses nothing, and refers him as a substitute to something that he ought to possess and might possess; and if reason had relied too exclusively on him, she might, in order to secure him a state of humanity in which he is wanting and can want without injury to his life, have robbed him even of the means of animal existence which is the first necessary condition of his being a man. Before he had opportunity to hold firm to the law with his will, reason would have withdrawn from his feet the ladder of nature.

The great point is therefore to reconcile these two considerations: to prevent physical society from ceasing for a moment in time, while the moral society is being formed in the idea; in other words, to prevent its existence from being placed in jeopardy, for the sake of the moral dignity of man. When the mechanic has to mend a watch, he lets the wheels run out, but the living watchworks of the state have to be repaired while they act, and a wheel has to be exchanged for another during its revolutions. Accordingly props must be sought for to support society and keep it going while it is made independent of the natural condition from which it is sought to emancipate it.

This prop is not found in the natural character of man, who, being selfish and violent, directs his energies rather to the destruction than to the preservation of society. Nor is it found in his moral character, which has to be formed, which can never be worked upon or calculated on by the lawgiver, because it is free and never appears. It would seem therefore that another measure must be adopted. It would seem that the physical character of the arbitrary must be separated from moral freedom; that it is incumbent to make the former harmonise with the laws and the latter dependent on impressions; it would be expedient to remove the former still farther from matter and to bring the latter somewhat more near to it; in short to produce a third character related to both the others—the physical and the moral—paving the way to a transition from the sway of mere force to that of law, without preventing the proper development of the moral character, but serving rather as a pledge in the sensuous sphere of a morality in the unseen.

LETTER IV.

Thus much is certain. It is only when a third character, as previously suggested, has preponderance that a revolution in a state according to moral principles can be free from injurious consequences; nor can anything else secure its endurance. In proposing or setting up a moral state, the moral law is relied upon as a real power, and free will is drawn into the realm of causes, where all hangs together, mutually with stringent necessity and rigidity. But we know that the condition of the human will always remains contingent, and that only in the Absolute Being physical coexists with moral necessity. Accordingly if it is wished to depend on the moral conduct of man as on natural results, this conduct must become nature, and he must be led by natural impulse to such a course of action as can only and invariably have moral results. But the will of man is perfectly free between inclination and duty, and no physical necessity ought to enter as a sharer in this magisterial personality. If therefore he is to retain this power of solution, and yet become a reliable link in the causal concatenation of forces, this can only be effected when the operations of both these impulses are presented quite equally in the world of appearances. It is only possible when, with every difference of form, the matter of man's volition remains the same, when all his impulses agreeing with his reason are sufficient to have the value of a universal legislation.

It may be urged that every individual man carries, within himself, at least in his adaptation and destination, a purely ideal man. The great problem of his existence is to bring all the incessant changes of his outer life into conformity with the unchanging unity of this ideal. This pure ideal man, which makes itself known more or less clearly in every subject, is represented by the state, which is the objective and, so to speak, canonical form in which the manifold differences of the subjects strive to unite. Now two ways present themselves to the thought, in which the man of time can agree with the man of idea, and there are also two ways in which the state can maintain itself in individuals. One of these ways is when the pure ideal man subdues the empirical man, and the state suppresses the individual, or again when the individual BECOMES the state, and the man of time is ENNOBLED to the man of idea.

I admit that in a one–sided estimate from the point of view of morality this difference vanishes, for the reason is satisfied if her law prevails unconditionally. But when the survey taken is complete and embraces the whole man (anthropology), where the form is considered together with the substance, and a living feeling has a voice, the difference will become far more evident. No doubt the reason demands unity, and nature variety, and both legislations take man in hand. The law of the former is stamped upon him by an incorruptible consciousness, that of the latter by an ineradicable feeling. Consequently education will always appear deficient when the moral feeling can only be maintained with the sacrifice of what is natural; and a political administration will always be very imperfect when it is only able to bring about unity by suppressing variety. The state ought not only to respect the objective and generic but also the subjective and specific in individuals; and while diffusing the unseen world of morals, it must not depopulate the kingdom of appearance, the external world of matter.

When the mechanical artist places his hand on the formless block, to give it a form according to his intention, he has not any scruples in doing violence to it. For the nature on which he works does not deserve any respect in itself, and he does not value the whole for its parts, but the parts on account of the whole. When the child of the fine arts sets his hand to the same block, he has no scruples either in doing violence to it, he only avoids showing this violence. He does not respect the matter in which he works, any more than the mechanical artist; but he seeks by an apparent consideration for it to deceive the eye which takes this matter under its protection. The political and educating artist follows a very different course, while making man at once his material and his end. In this case the aim or end meets in the material, and it is only because the whole serves the parts that the parts adapt themselves to the end. The political artist has to treat his material—man—with a very different kind of respect from that shown by the artist of fine art to his work. He must spare man's peculiarity and personality, not to produce a deceptive effect on the senses, but objectively and out of consideration for his inner being.

But the state is an organisation which fashions itself through itself and for itself, and for this reason it can only be realised when the parts have been accorded to the idea of the whole. The state serves the purpose of a representative, both to pure ideal and to objective humanity, in the breast of its citizens, accordingly it will have to observe the same relation to its citizens in which they are placed to it, and it will only respect their subjective humanity in the same degree that it is ennobled to an objective existence. If the internal man is one with himself, he will be able to rescue his peculiarity, even in the greatest generalisation of his conduct, and the state will only become the exponent of his fine instinct, the clearer formula of his internal legislation. But if the subjective man is in conflict with the objective and contradicts him in the character of the people, so that only the oppression of the former can give the victory to the latter, then the state will take up the severe aspect of the law against the citizen, and in order not to fall a sacrifice, it will have to crush under foot such a hostile individuality, without any compromise.

Now man can be opposed to himself in a twofold manner: either as a savage, when his feelings rule over his principles; or as a barbarian, when his principles destroy his feelings. The savage despises art, and acknowledges nature as his despotic ruler; the barbarian laughs at nature, and dishonours it, but he often proceeds in a more contemptible way than the savage, to be the slave of his senses. The cultivated man makes of nature his friend, and honours its friendship, while only bridling its caprice.

Consequently, when reason brings her moral unity into physical society, she must not injure the manifold in nature. When nature strives to maintain her manifold character in the moral structure of society, this must not create any breach in moral unity; the victorious form is equally remote from uniformity and confusion. Therefore, TOTALITY of character must be found in the people which is capable and worthy to exchange the state of necessity for that of freedom.

LETTER V.

Does the present age, do passing events, present this character? I direct my attention at once to the most prominent object in this vast structure.

It is true that the consideration of opinion is fallen, caprice is unnerved, and, although still armed with power, receives no longer any respect. Man has awaked from his long lethargy and self– deception, and he demands with impressive unanimity to be restored to his imperishable rights. But he does not only demand them; he rises on all sides to seize by force what, in his opinion, has been unjustly wrested from him. The edifice of the natural state is tottering, its foundations shake, and a physical possibility seems at length granted to place law on the throne, to honour man at length as an end, and to make true freedom the basis of political union. Vain hope! The moral possibility is wanting, and the generous occasion finds an unsusceptible rule.

Man paints himself in his actions, and what is the form depicted in the drama of the present time? On the one hand, he is seen running wild, on the other in a state of lethargy; the two extremest stages of human degeneracy, and both seen in one and the same period.

In the lower larger masses, coarse, lawless impulses come to view, breaking loose when the bonds of civil order are burst asunder, and hastening with unbridled fury to satisfy their savage instinct. Objective humanity may have had cause to complain of the state; yet subjective man must honour its institutions. Ought he to be blamed because he lost sight of the dignity of human nature, so long as he was concerned in preserving his existence? Can we blame him that he proceeded to separate by the force of gravity, to fasten by the force of cohesion, at a time when there could be no thought of building or raising up? The extinction of the state contains its justification. Society set free, instead of hastening upward into organic life, collapses into its elements.

On the other hand, the civilized classes give us the still more repulsive sight of lethargy, and of a depravity of character which is the more revolting because it roots in culture. I forget who of the older or more recent philosophers makes the remark, that what is more noble is the more revolting in its destruction. The remark applies with truth to the world of morals. The child of nature, when he breaks loose, becomes a madman; but the art scholar, when he breaks loose, becomes a debased character. The enlightenment of the understanding, on which the more refined classes pride themselves with some ground, shows on the whole so little of an ennobling influence on the mind that it seems rather to confirm corruption by its maxims. We deny nature in her legitimate field and feel her tyranny in the moral sphere, and while resisting her impressions, we receive our principles from her. While the affected decency of our manners does not even grant to nature a pardonable influence in the initial stage, our materialistic system of morals allows her the casting vote in the last and essential stage. Egotism has founded its system in the very bosom of a refined society, and without developing even a sociable character, we feel all the contagions and miseries of society. We subject our free judgment to its despotic opinions, our feelings to its bizarre customs, and our will to its seductions. We only maintain our caprice against her holy rights. The man of the world has his heart contracted by a proud self– complacency, while that of the man of nature often beats in sympathy; and every man seeks for nothing more than to save his wretched property from the general destruction, as it were from some great conflagration. It is conceived that the only way to find a shelter against the aberrations of sentiment is by completely foregoing its indulgence, and mockery, which is often a useful chastener of mysticism, slanders in the same breath the noblest aspirations. Culture, far from giving us freedom, only develops, as it advances, new necessities; the fetters of the physical close more tightly around us, so that the fear of loss quenches even the ardent impulse toward improvement, and the maxims of passive obedience are held to be the highest wisdom of life. Thus the spirit of the time is seen to waver between perversions and savagism, between what is unnatural and mere nature, between superstition and moral unbelief, and it is often nothing but the equilibrium of evils that sets bounds to it.

LETTER VI.

Have I gone too far in this portraiture of our times? I do not anticipate this stricture, but rather another—that I have proved too much by it. You will tell me that the picture I have presented resembles the humanity of our day, but it also bodies forth all nations engaged in the same degree of culture, because all, without exception, have fallen off from nature by the abuse of reason, before they can return to it through reason.

But if we bestow some serious attention to the character of our times, we shall be astonished at the contrast between the present and the previous form of humanity, especially that of Greece. We are justified in claiming the reputation of culture and refinement, when contrasted with a purely natural state of society, but not so comparing ourselves with the Grecian nature. For the latter was combined with all the charms of art and with all the dignity of wisdom, without, however, as with us, becoming a victim to these influences. The Greeks put us to shame not only by their simplicity, which is foreign to our age; they are at the same time our rivals, nay, frequently our models, in those very points of superiority from which we seek comfort when regretting the unnatural character of our manners. We see that remarkable people uniting at once fulness of form and fulness of substance, both philosophising and creating, both tender and energetic, uniting a youthful fancy; to the virility of reason in a glorious humanity.

At the period of Greek culture, which was an awakening of the powers of the mind, the senses and the spirit had no distinctly separated property; no division had yet torn them asunder, leading them to partition in a hostile attitude, and to mark off their limits with precision. Poetry had not yet become the adversary of wit, nor had speculation abused itself by passing into quibbling. In cases of necessity both poetry and wit could exchange parts, because they both honoured truth only in their special way. However high might be the flight of reason, it drew matter in a loving spirit after it, and, while sharply and stiffly defining it, never mutilated what it touched. It is true the Greek mind displaced humanity, and recast it on a magnified scale in the glorious circle of its gods; but it did this not by dissecting human nature, but by giving it fresh combinations, for the whole of human nature was represented in each of the gods. How different is the course followed by us moderns! We also displace and magnify individuals to form the image of the specks, but we do this in a fragmentary way, not by altered combinations, so that it is necessary to gather up from different individuals the elements that form the species in its totality. It would almost appear is if the powers of mind express themselves with us in real life or empirically as separately as the psychologist distinguishes them in the representation. For we see not only individual subjects, but whole classes of men, uphold their capacities only in part, while the rest of their faculties scarcely show a germ of activity, as in the case of the stunted growth of plants.

I do not overlook the advantages to which the present race, regarded as a unity and in the balance of the understanding, may lay claim over what is best in the ancient world; but it is obliged to engage in the contest as a compact mass, and measure itself as a whole against a whole. Who among the moderns could step forth, man against man, and strive with an Athenian for the prize of higher humanity?

Whence comes this disadvantageous relation of individuals coupled with great advantages of the race? Why could the individual Greek be qualified as the type of his time? and why can no modern dare to offer himself as such? Because all–uniting nature imparted its forms to the Greek, and an all–dividing understanding gives our forms to us.

It was culture itself that gave these wounds to modern humanity. The inner union of human nature was broken, and a destructive contest divided its harmonious forces directly; on the one hand, an enlarged experience and a more distinct thinking necessitated a sharper separation of the sciences, while on the other hand, the more complicated machinery of states necessitated a stricter sundering of ranks and occupations. Intuitive and speculative understanding took up a hostile attitude in opposite fields, whose borders were guarded with jealousy and distrust; and by limiting its operation to a narrow sphere, men have made unto themselves a master who is wont not unfrequently to end by subduing and oppressing all the other faculties. Whilst on the one hand a luxuriant imagination creates ravages in the plantations that have cost the intelligence so much labour, on the other hand a spirit of abstraction suffocates the fire that might have warmed the heart and inflamed the imagination.

This subversion, commenced by art and learning in the inner man, was carried out to fulness and finished by the spirit of innovation in government. It was, no doubt, reasonable to expect that the simple organisation of the primitive republics should survive the quaintness of primitive manners and of the relations of antiquity. But, instead of rising to a higher and nobler degree of animal life, this organisation degenerated into a common and coarse mechanism. The zoophyte condition of the Grecian states, where each individual enjoyed an independent life, and could, in cases of necessity, become a separate whole and unit in himself, gave way to an ingenious mechanism, when, from the splitting up into numberless parts, there results a mechanical life in the combination. Then there was a rupture between the state and the church, between laws and customs; enjoyment was separated from labour, the means from the end, the effort from the reward. Man himself eternally chained down to a little fragment of the whole, only forms a kind of fragment; having nothing in his ears but the monotonous sound of the perpetually revolving wheel, he never develops the harmony of his being; and instead of imprinting the seal of humanity on his being, he ends by being nothing more than the living impress of the craft to which he devotes himself, of the science that he cultivates. This very partial and paltry relation, linking the isolated members to the whole, does not depend on forms that are given spontaneously; for how could a complicated machine, which shuns the light, confide itself to the free will of man? This relation is rather dictated, with a rigorous strictness, by a formulary in which the free intelligence of man is chained down. The dead letter takes the place of a living meaning, and a practised memory becomes a safer guide than genius and feeling.

If the community or state measures man by his function, only asking of its citizens memory, or the intelligence of a craftsman, or mechanical skill, we cannot be surprised that the other faculties of the mind are neglected, for the exclusive culture of the one that brings in honour and profit. Such is the necessary result of an organisation that is indifferent about character, only looking to acquirements, whilst in other cases it tolerates the thickest darkness, to favour a spirit of law and order; it must result if it wishes that individuals in the exercise of special aptitudes 'should gain in depth what they are permitted to lose in extension. We are aware, no doubt, that a powerful genius does not shut up its activity within the limits of its functions; but mediocre talents consume in the craft fallen to their lot the whole of their feeble energy; and if some of their energy is reserved for matters of preference, without prejudice to its functions, such a state of things at once bespeaks a spirit soaring above the vulgar. Moreover, it is rarely a recommendation in the eye of a state to have a capacity superior to your employment, or one of those noble intellectual cravings of a man of talent which contend in rivalry with the duties of office. The state is so jealous of the exclusive possession of its servants that it would prefer—nor can it be blamed in this—for functionaries to show their powers with the Venus of Cytherea rather than the Uranian Venus.

It is thus that concrete individual life is extinguished, in order that the abstract whole may continue its miserable life, and the state remains for ever a stranger to its citizens, because feeling does not discover it anywhere. The governing authorities find themselves compelled to classify, and thereby simplify, the multiplicity of citizens, and only to know humanity in a representative form and at second hand. Accordingly they end by entirely losing sight of humanity, and by confounding it with a simple artificial creation of the understanding, whilst on their part the subject classes cannot help receiving coldly laws that address themselves so little to their personality. At length society, weary of having a burden that the state takes so little trouble to lighten, falls to pieces and is broken up—a destiny that has long since attended most European states. They are dissolved in what may be called a state of moral nature, in which public authority is only one function more, hated and deceived by those who think it necessary, respected only by those who can do without it.

Thus compressed between two forces, within and without, could humanity follow any other course than that which it has taken? The speculative mind, pursuing imprescriptible goods and rights in the sphere of ideas, must needs have become a stranger to the world of sense, and lose sight of matter for the sake of form. On its part, the world of public affairs, shut up in a monotonous circle of objects, and even there restricted by formulas, was led to lose sight of the life and liberty of the whole, while becoming impoverished at the same time in its own sphere. Just as the speculative mind was tempted to model the real after the intelligible, and to raise the subjective of its imagination into laws constituting the existence of things, so the state spirit rushed into the opposite extreme, wished to make a particular and fragmentary experience the measure of all observation, and to apply without exception to all affairs the rules of its own particular craft. The speculative mind had necessarily to become the prey of a vain subtlety, the state spirit of a narrow pedantry; for the former was placed too high to see the individual, and the latter too low to survey the whole. But the disadvantage of this direction of mind was not confined to knowledge and mental production; it extended to action and feeling. We know that the sensibility of the mind depends, as to degree, on the liveliness, and for extent on the richness of the imagination. Now the predominance of the faculty of analysis must necessarily deprive the imagination of its warmth and energy, and a restricted sphere of objects must diminish its wealth. It is for this reason that the abstract thinker has very often a cold heart, because he analyses impressions, which only move the mind by their combination or totality; on the other hand, the man of business, the statesman, has very often a narrow heart, because shut up in the narrow circle of his employment his imagination can neither expand nor adapt itself to another manner of viewing things.

My subject has led me naturally to place in relief the distressing tendency of the character of our own times to show the sources of the evil, without its being my province to point out the compensations offered by nature. I will readily admit to you that, although this splitting up of their being was unfavourable for individuals, it was the only road open for the progress of the race. The point at which we see humanity arrived among the Greeks was undoubtedly a maximum; it could neither stop there nor rise higher. It could not stop there, for the sum of notions acquired forced infallibly the intelligence to break with feeling and intuition, and to lead to clearness of knowledge. Nor could it rise any higher; for it is only in a determinate measure that clearness can be reconciled with a certain degree of abundance and of warmth. The Greeks had attained this measure, and to continue their progress in culture, they, as we, were obliged to renounce the totality of their being, and to follow different and separate roads in order to seek after truth.

There was no other way to develop the manifold aptitudes of man than to bring them in opposition with one another. This antagonism of forces is the great instrument of culture, but it is only an instrument; for as long as this antagonism lasts, man is only on the road to culture. It is only because these special forces are isolated in man, and because they take on themselves to impose an exclusive legislation, that they enter into strife with the truth of things, and oblige common sense, which generally adheres imperturbably to external phaenomena, to dive into the essence of things. While pure understanding usurps authority in the world of sense, and empiricism attempts to subject this intellect to the conditions of experience, these two rival directions arrive at the highest possible development, and exhaust the whole extent of their sphere. While on the one hand imagination, by its tyranny, ventures to destroy the order of the world, it forces reason, on the other side, to rise up to the supreme sources of knowledge, and to invoke against this predominance of fancy the help of the law of necessity.

By an exclusive spirit in the case of his faculties, the individual is fatally led to error; but the species is led to truth. It is only by gathering up all the energy of our mind in a single focus, and concentrating a single force in our being, that we give in some sort wings to this isolated force, and that we draw it on artificially far beyond the limits that nature seems to have imposed upon it. If it be certain that all human individuals taken together would never have arrived, with the visual power given them by nature, to see a satellite of Jupiter, discovered by the telescope of the astronomer, it is just as well established that never would the human understanding have produced the analysis of the infinite, or the critique of pure reason, if in particular branches, destined for this mission, reason had not applied itself to special researches, and if, after having, as it were, freed itself from all matter, it had not by the most powerful abstraction given to the spiritual eye of man the force necessary, in order to look into the absolute. But the question is, if a spirit thus absorbed in pure reason and intuition will be able to emancipate itself from the rigorous fetters of logic, to take the free action of poetry, and seize the individuality of things with a faithful and chaste sense? Here nature imposes even on the most universal genius a limit it cannot pass, and truth will make martyrs as long as philosophy will be reduced to make its principal occupation the search for arms against errors.

But whatever may be the final profit for the totality of the world, of this distinct and special perfecting of the human faculties, it cannot be denied that this final aim of the universe, which devotes them to this kind of culture, is a cause of suffering, and a kind of malediction for individuals. I admit that the exercises of the gymnasium form athletic bodies; but beauty is only developed by the free and equal play of the limbs. In the same way the tension of the isolated spiritual forces may make extraordinary men; but it is only the well–tempered equilibrium of these forces that can produce happy and accomplished men. And in what relation should we be placed with past and future ages if the perfecting of human nature made such a sacrifice indispensable? In that case we should have been the slaves of humanity, we should have consumed our forces in servile work for it during some thousands of years, and we should have stamped on our humiliated, mutilated nature the shameful brand of this slavery—all this in order that future generations, in a happy leisure, might consecrate themselves to the cure of their moral health, and develop the whole of human nature by their free culture.

But can it be true that man has to neglect himself for any end whatever? Can nature snatch from us; for any end whatever, the perfection which is prescribed to us by the aim of reason? It must be false that the perfecting of particular faculties renders the sacrifice of their totality necessary; and even if the law of nature had imperiously this tendency, we must have the power to reform by a superior art this totality of our being, which art has destroyed.

LETTER VII.

Can this effect of harmony be attained by the state? That is not possible, for the state, as at present constituted, has given occasion to evil, and the state as conceived in the idea, instead of being able to establish this more perfect humanity, ought to be based upon it. Thus the researches in which I have indulged would have brought me back to the same point from which they had called me off for a time. The present age, far from offering us this form of humanity, which we have acknowledged as a necessary condition of an improvement of the state, shows us rather the diametrically opposite form. If therefore the principles I have laid down are correct, and if experience confirms the picture I have traced of the present time, it would be necessary to qualify as unseasonable every attempt to effect a similar change in the state, and all hope as chimerical that would be based on such an attempt, until the division of the inner man ceases, and nature has been sufficiently developed to become herself the instrument of this great change and secure the reality of the political creation of reason.

In the physical creation, nature shows us the road that we have to follow in the moral creation. Only when the Struggle of elementary forces has ceased in inferior organisations, nature rises to the noble form of the physical man. In like manner, the conflict of the elements of the moral man and that of blind instincts must have ceased, and a coarse antagonism in himself, beiore the attempt can be hazarded. On the other hand, the independence of man's character must be secured, and his submission to despotic forms must have given place to a suitable liberty, before the variety in his constitution can be made subordinate to the unity of the ideal. When the man of nature still makes such an anarchical abuse of his will, his liberty ought hardly to be disclosed to him. And when the man fashioned by culture makes so little use of his freedom, his free will ought not to be taken from him. The concession of liberal principles becomes a treason to social order when it is associated with a force still in fermentation, and increases the already exuberant energy of its nature. Again, the law of conformity under one level becomes tyranny to the individual when it is allied to a weakness already holding sway and to natural obstacles, and when it comes to extinguish the last spark of spontaneity and of originality.

The tone of the age must therefore rise from its profound moral degradation; on the one hand it must emancipate itself from the blind service of nature, and on the other it must revert to its simplicity, its truth, and its fruitful sap; a sufficient task for more than a century. However, I admit readily, more than one special effort may meet with success, but no improvement of the whole will result from it, and contradictions in action will be a continual protest against the unity of maxims. It will be quite possible, then, that in remote corners of the world humanity may be honoured in the person of the negro, while in Europe it may be degraded in the person of the thinker. The old principles will remain, but they will adopt the dress of the age, and philosophy will lend its name to an oppression that was formerly authorised by the Church. In one place, alarmed at the liberty which in its opening efforts always shows itself an enemy, it will cast itself into the arms of a convenient servitude. In another place, reduced to despair by a pedantic tutelage, it will be driven into the savage license of the state of nature. Usurpation will invoke the weakness of human nature, and insurrection will invoke its dignity, till at length the great sovereign of all human things, blind force, shall come in and decide, like a vulgar pugilist, this pretended contest of principles.

LETTER VIII.

Must philosophy therefore retire from this field, disappointed in its hopes? Whilst in all other directions the dominion of forms is extended, must this the most precious of all gifts be abandoned to a formless chance? Must the contest of blind forces last eternally in the political world, and is social law never to triumph over a hating egotism?

Not in the least. It is true that reason herself will never attempt directly a struggle with this brutal force which resists her arms, and she will be as far as the son of Saturn in the 'Iliad' from descending into the dismal field of battle, to fight them in person. But she chooses the most deserving among the combatants, clothes him with divine arms as Jupiter gave them to his son−in−law, and by her triumphing force she finally decides the victory.

Reason has done all that she could in finding the law and promulgating it; it is for the energy of the will and the ardour of feeling to carry it out. To issue victoriously from her contest with force, truth herself must first become a force, and turn one of the instincts of man into her champion in the empire of phenomena. For instincts are the only motive forces in the material world. If hitherto truth has so little manifested her victorious power, this has not depended on the understanding, which could not have unveiled it, but on the heart which remained closed to it, and on instinct which did not act with it.

Whence, in fact, proceeds this general sway of prejudices, this might of the understanding in the midst of the light disseminated by philosophy and experience? The age is enlightened, that is to say, that knowledge, obtained and vulgarised, suffices to set right at least our practical principles. The spirit of free inquiry has dissipated the erroneous opinions which long barred the access to truth, and has undermined the ground on which fanaticism and deception had erected their throne. Reason has purified itself from the il lusions of the senses and from a mendacious sophistry, and philosophy herself raises her voice and exhorts us to return to the bosom of nature, to which she had first made us unfaithful. Whence then is it that we remain still barbarians?

There must be something in the spirit of man—as it is not in the objects themselves—which prevents us from receiving the truth, notwithstanding the brilliant light she diffuses, and from accepting her, whatever may be her strength for producing conviction. This something was perceived and expressed by an ancient sage in this very significant maxim: sapere aude [Footnote: Dare to be wise].

Dare to be wise! A spirited courage is required to triumph over the impediments that the indolence of nature as well as the cowardice of the heart oppose to our in struction. It was not without reason that the ancient Mythos made Minerva issue fully armed from the head of Jupiter, for it is with warfare that this instruction com mences. From its very outset it has to sustain a hard fight against the senses, which do not like to be roused from their easy slumber. The greater part of men are much too exhausted and enervated by their struggle with want to be able to engage in a new and severe contest with error. Satisfied if they themselves can escape from the hard labour of thought, they willingly abandon to others the guardianship of their thoughts. And if it happens that nobler necessities agitate their soul, they cling with a greedy faith to the formulas that the state and the church hold in reserve for such cases. If these unhappy men deserve our compassion, those others deserve our just contempt, who, though set free from those necessities by more fortunate circumstances, yet willingly bend to their yoke. These latter persons prefer this twilight of obscure ideas; where the feelings have more intensity, and the imagination can at will create convenient chimeras, to the rays of truth which put to flight the pleasant illusions of their dreams. They have founded the whole structure of their happiness on these very illusions, which ought to be combated and dissipated by the light of knowledge, and they would think they were paying too dearly for a truth which begins by robbing them of all that has value in their sight. It would be necessary that they should be already sages to love wisdom: a truth that was felt at once by him to whom philosophy owes its name. [Footnote: The Greek word means, as is known, love of wisdom.]

It is therefore not going far enough to say that the light of the understanding only deserves respect when it reacts on the character; to a certain extent it is from the character that this light proceeds; for the road that terminates in the head must pass through the heart. Accordingly, the most pressing need of the present time is to educate the sensibility, because it is the means, not only to render efficacious in practice the improvement of ideas, but to call this improvement into existence.

LETTER IX.

But perhaps there is a vicious circle in our previous reasoning? Theoretical culture must it seems bring along with it practical culture, and yet the latter must be the condition of the former. All improvement in the political sphere must proceed from the ennobling of the character. But, subject to the influence of a social constitution still barbarous, how can character become ennobled? It would then be necessary to seek for this end an instrument that the state does not furnish, and to open sources that would have preserved themselves pure in the midst of political corruption.

I have now reached the point to which all the considerations tended that have engaged me up to the present time. This instrument is the art of the beautiful; these sources are open to us in its immortal models.

Art, like science, is emancipated from all that is positive, and all that is humanly conventional; both are completely independent of the arbitrary will of men. The political legislator may place their empire under an interdict, but he cannot reign there. He can proscribe the friend of truth, but truth subsists; he can degrade the artist, but he cannot change art. No doubt, nothing is more common than to see science and art bend before the spirit of the age, and creative taste receive its law from critical taste. When the character becomes stiff and hardens itself, we see science severely keeping her limits, and art subject to the harsh restraint of rules; when the character is relaxed and softened, science endeavours to please and art to rejoice. For whole ages philosophers as well as artists show themselves occupied in letting down truth and beauty to the depths of vulgar humanity. They themselves are swallowed up in it; but, thanks to their essential vigour and indestructible life, the true and the beautiful make a victorious fight, and issue triumphant from the abyss.

No doubt the artist is the child of his time, but unhappy for him if he is its disciple or even its favourite. Let a beneficent deity carry off in good time the suckling from the breast of its mother, let it nourish him on the milk of a better age, and suffer him to grow up and arrive at virility under the distant sky of Greece. When he has attained manhood, let him come back, presenting a face strange to his own age; let him come, not to delight it with his apparition, but rather to purify it, terrible as the son of Agamemnon. He will, indeed, receive his matter from the present time, but he will borrow the form from a nobler time and even beyond all time, from the essential, absolute, immutable unity. There, issuing from the pure ether of its heavenly nature, flows the source of all beauty, which was never tainted by the corruption of generations or of ages, which roll along far beneath it in dark eddies. Its matter may be dishonoured as well as ennobled by fancy, but the ever chaste form escapes from the caprices of imagination. The Roman had already bent his knee for long years to the divinity of the emperors, and yet the statues of the gods stood erect; the temples retained their sanctity for the eye long after the gods had become a theme for mockery, and the noble architecture of the palaces that shielded the infamies of Nero and of Commodus were a protest against them. Humanity has lost its dignity, but art has saved it, and preserves it in marbles full of meaning; truth continues to live in illusion, and the copy will serve to re– establish the model. If the nobility of art has survived the nobility of nature, it also goes before it like an inspiring genius, forming and awakening minds. Before truth causes her triumphant light to penetrate into the depth of the heart, poetry intercepts her rays, and the summits of humanity shine in a bright light, while a dark and humid night still hangs over the valleys.

But how will the artist avoid the corruption of his time which encloses him on all hands? Let him raise his eyes to his own dignity, and to law; let him not lower them to necessity and fortune. Equally exempt from a vain activity which would imprint its trace on the fugitive moment, and from the dreams of an impatient enthusiasm which applies the measure of the absolute to the paltry productions of time, let the artist abandon the real to the understanding, for that is its proper field. But let the artist endeavour to give birth to the ideal by the union of the possible and of the necessary. Let him stamp illusion and truth with the effigy of this ideal; let him apply it to the play of his imagination and his most serious actions, in short, to all sensuous and spiritual forms; then let him quietly launch his work into infinite time.

But the minds set on fire by this ideal have not all received an equal share of calm from the creative genius—that great and patient temper which is required to impress the ideal on the dumb marble, or to spread it over a page of cold, sober letters, and then entrust it to the faithful hands of time. This divine instinct, and creative force, much too ardent to follow this peaceful walk, often throws itself immediately on the present, on active life, and strives to transform the shapeless matter of the moral world. The misfortune of his brothers, of the whole species, appeals loudly to the heart of the man of feeling; their abasement appeals still louder; enthusiasm is inflamed, and in souls endowed with energy the burning desire aspires impatiently to action and facts. But has this innovator examined himself to see if these disorders of the moral world wound his reason, or if they do not rather wound his self–love? If he does not determine this point at once, he will find it from the impulsiveness with which he pursues a prompt and definite end. A pure, moral motive has for its end the absolute; time does not exist for it, and the future becomes the present to it directly, by a necessary development, it has to issue from the present. To a reason having no limits the direction towards an end becomes confounded with the accomplishment of this end, and to enter on a course is to have finished it.

If, then, a young friend of the true and of the beautiful were to ask me how, notwithstanding the resistance of the times, he can satisfy the noble longing of his heart, I should reply: Direct the world on which you act towards that which is good, and the measured and peaceful course of time will bring about the results. You have given it this direction if by your teaching you raise its thoughts towards the necessary and the eternal; if, by your acts or your creations, you make the necessary and the eternal the object of your leanings. The structure of error and of all that is arbitrary, must fall, and it has already fallen, as soon as you are sure that it is tottering. But it is important that it should not only totter in the external but also in the internal man. Cherish triumphant truth in the modest sanctuary of your heart; give it an incarnate form through beauty, that it may not only be the understanding that does homage to it, but that feeling may lovingly grasp its appearance. And that you may not by any chance take from external reality the model which you yourself ought to furnish, do not venture into its dangerous society before you are assured in your own heart that you have a good escort furnished by ideal nature. Live with your age, but be not its creation; labour for your contemporaries, but do for them what they need, and not what they praise. Without having shared their faults, share their punishment with a noble resignation, and bend under the yoke which they find is as painful to dispense with as to bear. By the constancy with which you will despise their good fortune, you will prove to them that it is not through cowardice that you submit to their sufferings. See them in thought such as they ought to be when you must act upon them; but see them as they are when you are tempted to act for them. Seek to owe their suffrage to their dignity; but to make them happy keep an account of their unworthiness; thus, on the one hand, the nobleness of your heart will kindle theirs, and, on the other, your end will not be reduced to nothingness by their unworthiness. The gravity of your principles will keep them off from you, but in play they will still endure them. Their taste is purer than their heart, and it is by their taste you must lay hold of this suspicious fugitive. In vain will you combat their maxims, in vain will you condemn their actions; but you can try your moulding hand on their leisure. Drive away caprice, frivolity, and coarseness, from their pleasures, and you will banish them imperceptibly from their acts, and at length from their feelings. Everywhere that you meet them, surround them with great, noble, and ingenious forms; multiply around them the symbols of perfection, till appearance triumphs over reality, and art over nature.

LETTER X.

Convinced by my preceding letters, you agree with me on this point, that man can depart from his destination by two opposite roads, that our epoch is actually moving on these two false roads, and that it has become the prey, in one case, of coarseness, and elsewhere of exhaustion and de pravity. It is the beautiful that must bring it back from this twofold departure. But how can the cultivation of the fine arts remedy, at the same time, these opposite defects, and unite in itself two contradictory qualities? Can it bind nature in the savage, and set it free in the barbarian? Can it at once tighten a spring and loose it, and if it cannot produce this double effect, how will it be reasonable to expect from it so important a result as the education of man?

It may be urged that it is almost a proverbial adage that the feeling developed by the beautiful refines manners, and any new proof offered on the subject would appear superfluous. Men base this maxim on daily experience, which shows us almost always clearness of intellect, deli cacy of feeling, liberality and even dignity of conduct, associated with a cultivated taste, while an uncultivated taste is almost always accompanied by the opposite qualities. With considerable assurance, the most civilised nation of antiquity is cited as an evidence of this, the Greeks, among whom the perception of the beautiful attained its highest development, and, as a contrast, it is usual to point to nations in a partial savage state, and partly barbarous, who expiate their insensibility to the beautiful by a coarse or, at all events, a hard austere character. Nevertheless, some thinkers are tempted occasionally to deny either the fact itself or to dispute the legitimacy of the consequences that are derived from it. They do not entertain so unfavourable an opinion of that savage coarseness which is made a reproach in the case of certain nations; nor do they form so advantageous an opinion of the refinement so highly lauded in the case of cultivated nations. Even as far back as in antiquity there were men who by no means regarded the culture of the liberal arts as a benefit, and who were consequently led to forbid the entrance of their republic to imagination.

I do not speak of those who calumniate art, because they have never been favoured by it. These persons only appreciate a possession by the trouble it takes to acquire it, and by the profit it brings; and how could they properly appreciate the silent labour of taste in the exterior and in terior man? How evident it is that the accidental disadvantages attending liberal culture would make them lose sight of its essential advantages! The man deficient in form despises the grace of diction as a means of corruption, courtesy in the social relations as dissimulation, delicacy and generosity in conduct as an affected exaggeration. He cannot forgive the favourite of the Graces for having enlivened all assemblies as a man of the world, of having directed all men to his views like a statesman, and of giving his impress to the whole century as a writer; while he, the victim of labour, can only obtain, with all his learning, the least attention or overcome the least difficulty. As he cannot learn from his fortunate rival the secret of pleasing, the only course open to him is to deplore the corruption of human nature, which adores rather the appearance than the reality.

But there are also opinions deserving respect, that pronounce themselves adverse to the effects of the beautiful, and find formidable arms in experience, with which to wage war against it. "We are free to admit"—such is their language—"that the charms of the beautiful can further honourable ends in pure hands; but it is not repugnant to its nature to produce, in impure hands, a directly contrary effect, and to employ in the service of injustice and error the power that throws the soul of man into chains. It is exactly because taste only attends to the form and never to the substance; it ends by placing the soul on the dangerous incline, leading it to neglect all reality and to sacrifice truth and morality to an attractive envelope. All the real difference of things vanishes, and it is only the appearance that determines their value! How many men of talent"—thus these arguers proceed—"have been turned aside from all effort by the seductive power of the beautiful, or have been led away from all serious exercise of their activity, or have been induced to use it very feebly? How many weak minds have been impelled to quarrel with the organisation of society, simply because it has pleased the imagination of poets to present the image of a world constituted differently, where no propriety chains down opinion and no artifice helds nature in thraldom? What a dangerous logic of the passions they have learned since the poets have painted them in their pictures in the most brilliant colours and since, in the contest with law and duty, they have commonly re mained masters of the battlefield. What has society gained by the relations of society, formerly under the sway of truth, being now subject to the laws of the beautiful, or by the external impression deciding the estimation in which merit is to be held? We admit that all virtues whose appearance produces an agreeable effect are now seen to flourish, and those which, in society, give a value to the man who possesses them. But, as a compensation, all kinds of excesses are seen to prevail, and all vices are in vogue that can be reconciled with a graceful exterior." It is certainly a matter entitled to reflection that, at almost all the periods of history when art flourished and taste held sway, humanity is found in a state of decline; nor can a single instance be cited of the union of a large diffusion of aesthetic culture with political liberty and social virtue, of fine manners associated with good morals, and of politeness fraternising with truth and loyalty of character and life.

As long as Athens and Sparta preserved their independence, and as long as their institutions were based on respect for the laws, taste did not reach its maturity, art remained in its infancy, and beauty was far from exer cising her empire over minds. No doubt, poetry had already taken a sublime flight, but it was on the wings of genius, and we know that genius borders very closely on savage coarseness, that it is a light which shines readily in the midst of darkness, and which therefore often argues against rather than in favour of the taste of the time. When the golden age of art appears under Pericles and Alexander, and the sway of taste becomes more general, strength and liberty have abandoned Greece; eloquence corrupts the truth, wisdom offends it on the lips of Socrates, and virtue in the life of Phocion. It is well known that the Romans had to exhaust their energies in civil wars, and, corrupted by Oriental luxury, to bow their heads under the yoke of a fortunate despot, before Grecian art triumphed over the stiffness of their character. The same was the case with the Arabs: civilisation only dawned upon them when the vigour of their military spirit became softened under the sceptre of the Abbassides. Art did not appear in modern Italy till the glorious Lombard League was dissolved, Florence submitting to the Medici, and all those brave cities gave up the spirit of independ ence for an inglorious resignation. It is almost super fluous to call to mind the example of modern nations, with whom refinement has increased in direct proportion to the decline of their liberties. Wherever we direct our eyes in past times, we see taste and freedom mutually avoiding each other. Everywhere we see that the beautiful only founds its sway on the ruins of heroic virtues.

And yet this strength of character, which is commonly sacrificed to establish aesthetic culture, is the most power ful spring of all that is great and excellent in man, and no other advantage, however great, can make up for it. Accordingly, if we only keep to the experiments hitherto made, as to the influence of the beautiful, we cannot certainly be much encouraged in developing feelings so dangerous to the real culture of man. At the risk of being hard and coarse, it will seem preferable to dispense with this dissolving force of the beautiful, rather than see human nature a prey to its enervating influence, notwithstanding all its refining advantages. However, experience is perhaps not the proper tribunal at which to decide such a question; before giving so much weight to its testimony, it would be well to inquire if the beauty we have been discussing is the power that is condemned by the previous examples. And the beauty we are discussing seems to assume an idea of the beautiful derived from a source different from experience, for it is this higher notion of the beautiful which has to decide if what is called beauty by experience is entitled to the name.

This pure and rational idea of the beautiful—supposing it can be placed in evidence—cannot be taken from any real and special case, and must, on the contrary, direct and give sanction to our judgment in each special case. It must therefore be sought for by a process of abstraction, and it ought to be deduced from the simple possibility of a nature both sensuous and rational; in short, beauty ought to present itself as a necessary condition of humanity. It is therefore essential that we should rise to the pure idea of humanity, and as experience shows us nothing but individuals, in particular cases, and never humanity at large, we must endeavour to find in their individual and variable mode of being the absolute and the permanent, and to grasp the necessary conditions of their existence, suppressing all accidental limits. No doubt this transcendental procedure will remove us for some time from the familiar circle of phaenomena and the living presence of objects, to keep us on the unproductive ground of abstract ideas; but we are engaged in the search after a principle of knowledge solid enough not to be shaken by anything, and the man who does not dare to rise above reality will never conquer this truth.

LETTER XI.

If abstraction rises to as great an eievation as possible, it arrives at two primary ideas, before which it is obliged to stop and to recognise its limits. It distinguishes in man something that continues, and something that changes in cessantly. That which continues it names his person; that which changes his position, his condition.

The person and the condition, I and my determinations, which we represent as one and the same thing in the neces sary being, are eternally distinct in the finite being. Not withstanding all continuance in the person, the condition changes; in spite of all change of condition, the person remains. We pass from rest to activity, from emotion to indifference, from assent to contradiction, but we are always we ourselves, and what immediately springs from ourselves remains. It is only in the absolute subject that all his determinations continue with his personality. All that Divinity is, it is because it is so; consequently it is eternally what it is, because it is eternal.

As the person and the condition are distinct in man, be cause he is a finite being, the condition cannot be founded on the person, nor the person on the condition. Admitting the second case, the person would have to change; and in the former case, the condition would have to continue. Thus in either supposition either the personality or the quality of a finite being would necessarily cease. It is not because we think, feel, and will, that we are; it is not because we are that we think, feel, and will. We are because we are. We feel, think, and will, because there is out of us something that is not ourselves.

Consequently the person must have its principle of exist ence in itself because the permanent cannot be derived from the changeable, and thus we should be at once in possession of the idea of the absolute being, founded on itself; that is to say, of the idea of freedom. The condition must have a foundation, and as it is not through the person, and is not therefore absolute, it must be a sequence and a result; and thus, in the second place, we should have arrived at the condition of every dependent being, of everything in the process of becoming something else: that is, of the idea of time. "Time is the necessary condition of all processes, of becoming (werden);" this is an indentical proposition, for it says nothing but this: "That something may follow, there must be a succession."

The person which manifests itself in the eternally continuing Ego, or I myself, and only in him, cannot become something or begin in time, because it is much rather time that must begin with him, because the permanent must serve as basis to the changeable. That change may take place, something must change; this something cannot therefore be the change itself. When we say the flower opens and fades, we make of this flower a permanent being in the midst of this transformation; we lend it, in some sort, a personality, in which these two conditions are manifested. It cannot be objected that man is born, and becomes something; for man is not only a person simply, but he is a person finding himself in a determinate condition. Now our determinate state of condition springs up in time, and it is thus that man, as a phenomenon or appearance, must have a beginning, though in him pure intelligence is eternal. Without time, that is, without a becoming, he would not be a determinate being; his personality would exist virtually, no doubt, but not in action. It is not by the succession of its perceptions that the immutable Ego or person manifests himself to himself.

Thus, therefore, the matter of activity, or reality, that the supreme intelligence draws from its own being, must be received by man; and he does, in fact, receive it, through the medium of perception, as something which is outside him in space, and which changes in him in time. This matter which changes in him is always accompanied by the Ego, the personality, that never changes; and the rule prescribed for man by his rational nature is to remain immutably himself in the midst of change, to refer all perceptions to experience, that is, to the unity of knowledge, and to make of each of its manifestations of its modes in time the law of all time. The matter only exists in as far as it changes; he, his personality, only exists in as far as he does not change. Consequently, represented in his perfection, man would be the permanent unity, which remains always the same, among the waves of change.

Now, although an infinite being, a divinity could not become (or be subject to time), still a tendency ought to be named divine which has for its infinite end the most characteristic attribute of the divinity; the absolute manifestation of power—the reality of all the possible—and the absolute unity of the manifestation (the necessity of all reality). It cannot be disputed that man bears within himself, in his personality, a predisposition for divinity. The way to divinity—if the word "way" can be applied to what never leads to its end–is open to him in every direction.

Considered in itself and independently of all sensuous matter, his personality is nothing but the pure virtuality of a possible infinite manifestation, and so long as there is neither intuition nor feeling, it is nothing more than a form, an empty power. Considered in itself, and independently of all spontaneous activity of the mind, sensuousness can only make a material man; without it, it is a pure form; but it cannot in any way establish a union between matter and it. So long as he only feels, wishes, and acts under the influence of desire, he is nothing more than the world, if by this word we point out only the formless contents of time. Without doubt, it is only his sensuousness that makes his strength pass into efficacious acts, but it is his personality alone that makes this activity his own. Thus, that he may not only be a world, he must give form to matter, and in order not to be a mere form, he must give reality to the virtuality that he bears in him. He gives matter to form by creating time, and by opposing the immutable to change, the diversity of the world to the eternal unity of the Ego. He gives a form to matter by again suppressing time, by maintaining permanence in change, and by placing the diversity of the world under the unity of the Ego.

Now from this source issue for man two opposite exigencies, the two fundamental laws of sensuous–rational nature. The first has for its object absolute reality; it must make a world of what is only form, manifest all that in it is only a force. The second law has for its object absolute formality; it must destroy in him all that is only world, and carry out harmony in all changes. In other terms, he must manifest all that is internal, and give form to all that is external. Considered in its most lofty accomplishment, this twofold labour brings us back to the idea of humanity which was my starting–point.

LETTER XII.

This twofold labour or task, which consists in making the necessary pass into reality in us and in making out of us reality subject to the law of necessity, is urged upon us as a duty by two opposing forces, which are justly styled impulsions or instincts, because they impel us to realise their object. The first of these impulsions, which I shall call the sensuous instinct, issues from the physical existence of roan, or from sensuous nature; and it is this instinct which tends to enclose him in the limits of time and to make of him a material being; I do not say to give him matter, for to do that a certain free activity of the personality would be necessary, which, receiving matter, distinguishes it from the Ego, or what is permanent. By matter I only understand in this place the change or reality that fills time. Consequently the instinct requires that there should be change, and that time should contain something. This simply filled state of time is named sensation, and it is only in this state that physical existence manifests itself.

As all that is in time is successive, it follows by that fact alone that something is: all the remainder is excluded. When one note on an instrument is touched, among all those that it virtually offers, this note alone is real. When man is actually modified, the infinite possibility of all his modifications is limited to this single mode of existence. Thus, then, the exclusive action of sensuous impulsion has for its necessary consequence the narrowest limitation. In this state man is only a unity of magnitude, a complete moment in time; or, to speak more correctly, he is not, for his personality is suppressed as long as sensation holds sway over him and carries time along with it.

This instinct extends its domains over the entire sphere of the finite in man, and as form is only revealed in matter, and the absolute by means of its limits, the total manifestation of human nature is connected on a close analysis with the sensuous instinct. But though it is only this instinct that awakens and develops what exists virtually in man, it is nevertheless this very instinct which renders his perfection impossible. It binds down to the world of sense by indestructible ties the spirit that tends higher and it calls back to the limits of the present, abstraction Which had its free development in the sphere of the infinite. No doubt, thought can escape it for a moment, and a firm will victoriously resists its exigencies; but soon compressed nature resumes her rights to give an imperious reality to our existence, to give it contents, substance, knowledge, and an aim for our activity.

The second impulsion, which may be named the formal instinct, issues from the absolute existence of man, or from his rational nature, and tends to set free, and bring harmony into the diversity of its manifestations, and to maintain personality notwithstanding all the changes of state. As this personality, being an absolute and indivisible unity, can never be in contradiction with itself, as we are ourselves for ever, this impulsion, which tends to maintain personality, can never exact in one time anything but what it exacts and requires for ever. It therefore decides for always what it decides now, and orders now what it orders for ever. Hence it embraces the whole series of times, or what comes to the same thing, it suppresses time and change. It wishes the real to be necessary and eternal, and it wishes the eternal and the necessary to be real; in other terms, it tends to truth and justice.

If the sensuous instinct only produces ACCIDENTS, the formal instinct gives laws, laws for every judgment when it is a question of knowledge, laws for every will when it is a question of action. Whether, therefore, we recognise an object or conceive an objective value to a state of the subject, whether we act in virtue of knowledge or make of the objective the determining principle of our state; in both cases we withdraw this state from the jurisdiction of time, and we attribute to it reality for all men and for all time, that is, universality and necessity. Feeling can only say: "That is true FOR THIS SUBJECT AND AT THIS MOMENT," and there may come another moment, another subject, which withdraws the affirmation from the actual feeling. But when once thought pronounces and says: "THAT IS" it decides for ever and ever, and the validity of its decision is guaranteed by the personality itself, which defies all change. Inclination can only say: "That is good FOR YOUR INDIVIDUALITY and PRESENT NECESSITY?" but the changing current of affairs will sweep them away, and what you ardently desire to-day will form the object of your aversion to-morrow. But when the moral feeling says: "That ought to be," it decides for ever. If you confess the truth because it is the truth, and if you practice justice because it is justice, you have made of a particular case the law of all possible cases, and treated one moment of your life as eternity.

Accordingly, when the formal impulse holds sway and the pure object acts in us, the being attains its highest expansion, all barriers disappear, and from the unity of magnitude in which man was enclosed by a narrow sensuousness, he rises to the UNITY OF IDEA, which embraces and keeps subject the entire sphere of phenomena. During this operation we are no longer in time, but time is in us with its infinite succession. We are no longer individuals but a species; the judgment of all spirits is expressed by our own, and the choice of all hearts is represented by our own act.

LETTER XIII.

On a first survey, nothing appears more opposed than these two impulsions; one having for its object change, the other immutability, and yet it is these two notions that exhaust the notion of humanity, and a third FUNDAMENTAL IMPULSION, holding a medium between them, is quite inconceivable. How then shall we re- establish the unity of human nature, a unity that appears completely destroyed by this primitive and radical opposition?

I admit these two tendencies are contradictory, but it should be noticed that they are not so in the SAME OBJECTS. But things that do not meet cannot come into collision. No doubt the sensuous impulsion desires change; but it does not wish that it should extend to personality and its field, nor that there should be a change of principles. The formal impulsion seeks unity and permanence, but it does not wish the condition to remain fixed with the person, that there should be identity of feeling. Therefore these two impulsions are not divided by nature, and if, nevertheless, they appear so, it is because they have become divided by transgressing nature freely, by ignoring themselves, and by confounding their spheres. The office of culture is to watch over them and to secure to each one its proper LIMITS; therefore culture has to give equal justice to both, and to defend not only the rational impulsion against the sensuous, but also the latter against the former. Hence she has to act a twofold part: first, to protect sense against the attacks of freedom; secondly, to secure personality against the power of sensations. One of these ends is attained by the cultivation of the sensuous, the other by that of the reason.

Since the world is developed in time, or change, the perfection of the faculty that places men in relation with the world will necessarily be the greatest possible mutability and extensiveness. Since personality is permanence in change, the perfection of this faculty, which must be opposed to change, will be the greatest possible freedom of action (autonomy) and intensity. The more the receptivity is developed under manifold aspects, the more it is movable and offers surfaces to phaenomena, the larger is the part of the world seized upon by man, and the more virtualities he develops in himself. Again, in proportion as man gains strength and depth, and depth and reason gain in freedom, in that proportion man TAKES IN a larger share of the world, and throws out forms outside himself. Therefore his culture will consist, first, in placing his receptivity on contact with the world in the greatest number of points possible, and is raising passivity to the highest exponent on the side of feeling; secondly, in procuring for the determining faculty the greatest possible amount of independence, in relation to the receptive power, and in raising activity to the highest degree on the side of reason. By the union of these two qualities man will associate the highest degree of self–spontaneity (autonomy) and of freedom with the fullest plenitude of existence, and instead of abandoning himself to the world so as to get lost in it, he will rather absorb it in himself, with all the infinitude of its phenomena, and subject it to the unity of his reason.

But man can invert this relation, and thus fail in attaining his destination in two ways. He can hand over to the passive force the intensity demanded by the active force; he can encroach by material impulsion on the formal impulsion, and convert the receptive into the determining power. He can attribute to the active force the extensiveness belonging to the passive force, he can encroach by the formal impulsion on the material impulsion, and substitute the determining for the receptive power. In the former case, he will never be an Ego, a personality; in the second case, he will never be a Non–Ego, and hence in both cases he will be NEITHER ONE NOR THE OTHER, consequently he will nothing.

In fact, if the sensuous impulsion becomes determining, if the senses become law–givers, and if the world stifles personality, he loses as object what he gains in force. It may be said of man that when he is only the contents of time, he is not and consequently HE HAS no other contents. His condition is destroyed at the same time as his personality, because these are two correlative ideas, because change presupposes permanence, and a limited reality implies an infinite reality. If the formal impulsion becomes receptive, that is, if thought anticipates sensation, and the person substitutes itself in the place of the world, it loses as a subject and autonomous force what it gains as object, because immutability implies change, and that to manifest itself also absolute reality requires limits. As soon as man is only form, he has no form, and the personality vanishes with the condition. In a word, it is only inasmuch as he is spontaneous, autonomous, that there is reality out of him, that he is also receptive; and it is only inasmuch as he is receptive that there is reality in him, that he is a thinking force.

Consequently these two impulsions require limits, and looked upon as forces, they need tempering; the former that it may not encroach on the field of legislation, the latter that it may not invade the ground of feeling. But this tempering and moderating the sensuous impulsion ought not to be the effect of physical impotence or of a blunting of sensations, which is always a matter for contempt. It must be a free act, an activity of the person, which by its moral intensity moderates the sensuous intensity, and by the sway of impressions takes from them in depth what it gives them in surface or breadth. The character must place limits to temperament, for the senses have only the right to lose elements if it be to the advantage of the mind. In its turn, the tempering of the formal impulsion must not result from moral impotence, from a relaxation of thought and will, which would degrade humanity. It is necessary that the glorious source of this second tempering should be the fulness of sensations; it is necessary that sensuousness itself should defend its field with a victorious arm and resist the violence that the invading activity of the mind would do to it. In a word, it is necessary that the material impulsion should be contained in the limits of propriety by personality, and the formal impulsion by receptivity or nature.

LETTER XIV.

We have been brought to the idea of such a correlation between the two impulsions that the action of the one establishes and limits at the same time the action of the other, and that each of them, taken in isolation, does arrive at its highest manifestation just because the other is active.

No doubt this correlation of the two impulsions is simply a problem advanced by reason, and which man will only be able to solve in the perfection of his being. It is in the strictest signification of the term: the idea of his humanity; accordingly, it is an infinite to which he can approach nearer and nearer in the course of time, but without ever reaching it. "He ought not to aim at form to the injury of reality, nor to reality to the detriment of the form. He must rather seek the absolute being by means of a determinate being, and the determinate being by means of an infinite being. He must set the world before him because he is a person, and he must be a person because he has the world before him. He must feel because he has a consciousness of himself, and he must have a consciousness of himself because he feels." It is only in conformity with this idea that he is a man in the full sense of the word; but he cannot be convinced of this so long as he gives himself up exclusively to one of these two impulsions, or only satisfies them one after the other. For as long as he only feels, his absolute personality and existence remain a mystery to him, and as long as he only thinks, his condition or existence in time escapes him. But if there were cases in which he could have at once this twofold experience in which he would have the consciousness of his freedom and the feeling of his existence together, in which he would simultaneously feel as matter and know himself as spirit, in such cases, and in such only, would he have a complete intuition of his humanity, and the object that would procure him this intuition would be a symbol of his accomplished destiny, and consequently serve to express the infinite to him—since this destination can only be fulfilled in the fulness of time.

Presuming that cases of this kind could present themselves in experience, they would awake in him a new impulsion, which, precisely because the two other impulsions would co–operate in it, would be opposed to each of them taken in isolation, and might, with good grounds, be taken for a new impulsion. The sensuous impulsion requires that there should be change, that time should have contents; the formal impulsion requires that time should be suppressed, that there should be no change. Consequently, the impulsion in which both of the others act in concert—allow me to call it the instinct of play, till I explain the term—the instinct of play would have as its object to suppress time in time to conciliate the state of transition or becoming with the absolute being, change with identity.

The sensuous instinct wishes to be determined, it wishes to receive an object; the formal instinct wishes to determine itself, it wishes to produce an object. Therefore the instinct of play will endeavor to receive as it would itself have produced, and to produce as it aspires to receive.

The sensuous impulsion excludes from its subject all autonomy and freedom; the formal impulsion excludes all dependence and passivity. But the exclusion of freedom is physical necessity; the exclusion of passivity is moral necessity. Thus the two impulsions subdue the mind: the former to the laws of nature, the latter to the laws of reason. It results from this that the instinct of play, which unites the double action of the two other instincts, will content the mind at once morally and physically. Hence, as it suppresses all that is contingent, it will also suppress all coercion, and will set man free physically and morally. When we welcome with effusion some one who deserves our contempt, we feel painfully that nature is constrained. When we have a hostile feeling against a person who commands our esteem, we feel painfully the constraint of reason. But if this person inspires us with interest, and also wins our esteem, the constraint of feeling vanishes together with the constraint of reason, and we begin to love him, that is to say, to play, to take recreation, at once with our inclination and our esteem.

Moreover, as the sensuous impulsion controls us physically, and the formal impulsion morally, the former makes our formal constitution contingent, and the latter makes our material constitution contingent, that is to say, there is contingence in the agreement of our happiness with our perfection, and reciprocally. The instinct of play, in which both act in concert, will render both our formal and our material constitution contingent; accordingly, our perfection and our happiness in like manner. And on the other hand, exactly because it makes both of them contingent, and because the contingent disappears with necessity, it will suppress this contingence in both, and will thus give form to matter and reality to form. In proportion that it will lessen the dynamic influence of feeling and passion, it will place them in harmony with rational ideas, and by taking from the laws of reason their moral constraint, it will reconcile them with the interest of the senses.

LETTER XV.

I approach continually nearer to the end to which I lead you, by a path offering few attractions. Be pleased to follow me a few steps further, and a large horizon will open up to you and a delightful prospect will reward you for the labour of the way.

The object of the sensuous instinct, expressed in a universal conception, is named Life in the widest acceptation: a conception that expresses all material existence and all that is immediately present in the senses. The object of the formal instinct, expressed in a universal conception, is called shape or form, as well in an exact as in an inexact acceptation; a conception that embraces all formal qualities of things and all relations of the same to the thinking powers. The object of the play instinct, represented in a general statement, may therefore bear the name of living form; a term that serves to describe all aesthetic qualities of phaenomena, and what people style, in the widest sense, beauty.

Beauty is neither extended to the whole field of all living things nor merely enclosed in this field. A marble block, though it is and remains lifeless, can nevertheless become a living form by the architect and sculptor; a man, though he lives and has a form, is far from being a living form on that account. For this to be the case, it is necessary that his form should be life, and that his life should be a form. As long as we only think of his form, it is lifeless, a mere abstraction; as long as we only feel his life, it is without form, a mere impression. It is only when his form lives in our feeling, and his life in our understanding, he is the living form, and this will everywhere be the case where we judge him to be beautiful.

But the genesis of beauty is by no means declared because we know how to point out the component parts, which in their combination produce beauty. For to this end it would be necessary to comprehend that combination itself, which continues to defy our exploration, as well as all mutual operation between the finite and the infinite. The reason, on transcendental grounds, makes the following demand: There shall be a communion between the formal impulse and the material impulse—that is, there shall be a play instinct—because it is only the unity of reality with the form, of the accidental with the necessary, of the passive state with freedom, that the conception of humanity is completed. Reason is obliged to make this demand, because her nature impels her to completeness and to the removal of all bounds; while every exclusive activity of one or the other impulse leaves human nature incomplete and places a limit in it. Accordingly, as soon as reason issues the mandate, "a humanity shall exist," it proclaims at the same time the law, "there shall be a beauty." Experience can answer us if there is a beauty, and we shall know it as soon as she has taught us if a humanity can exist. But neither reason nor experience can tell us how beauty can be, and how a humanity is possible.

We know that man is neither exclusively matter nor exclusively spirit. Accordingly, beauty, as the consummation of humanity, can neither be exclusively mere life, as has been asserted by sharp–sighted observers, who kept too close to the testimony of experience, and to which the taste of the time would gladly degrade it; Nor can beauty be merely form, as has been judged by speculative sophists, who departed too far from experience, and by philosophic artists, who were led too much by the necessity of art in explaining beauty; it is rather the common object of both impulses, that is, of the play instinct. The use of language completely justifies this name, as it is wont to qualify with the word play what is neither subjectively nor objectively accidental, and yet does not impose necessity either externally or internally. As the mind in the intuition of the beautiful finds itself in a happy medium between law and necessity, it is, because it divides itself between both, emancipated from the pressure of both. The formal impulse and the material impulse are equally earnest in their demands, because one relates in its cognition to things in their reality and the other to their necessity; because in action the first is directed to the preservation of life, the second to the preservation of dignity, and therefore both to truth and perfection. But life becomes more indifferent when dignity is mixed up with it, and duty no longer coerces when inclination attracts. In like manner the mind takes in the reality of things, material truth, more freely and tranquilly as soon as it encounters formal truth, the law of necessity; nor does the mind find itself strung by abstraction as soon as immediate intuition can accompany it. In one word, when the mind comes into communion with ideas, all reality loses its serious value because it becomes small; and as it comes in contact with feeling, necessity parts also with its serious value because it is easy.

But perhaps the objection has for some time occurred to you, Is not the beautiful degraded by this, that it is made a mere play? and is it not reduced to the level of frivolous objects which have for ages passed under that name? Does it not contradict the conception of the reason and the dignity of beauty, which is nevertheless regarded as an instrument of culture, to confine it to the work of being a mere play? and does it not contradict the empirical conception of play, which can coexist with the exclusion of all taste, to confine it merely to beauty?

But what is meant by a MERE PLAY, when we know that in all conditions of humanity that very thing is play, and only that is play which makes man complete and develops simultaneously his twofold nature? What you style LIMITATION, according to your representation of the matter, according to my views, which I have justified by proofs, I name ENLARGEMENT. Consequently, I should have said exactly the reverse: man is serious ONLY with the agreeable, with the good, and with the perfect, but he PLAYS with beauty. In saying this we must not indeed think of the plays that are in vogue in real life, and which commonly refer only to his material state. But in real life we should also seek in vain for the beauty of which we are here speaking. The actually present beauty is worthy of the really, of the actually, present play–impulse; but by the ideal of beauty, which is set up by the reason, an ideal of the play–instinct is also presented, which man ought to have before his eyes in all his plays.

Therefore, no error will ever be incurred if we seek the ideal of beauty on the same road on which we satisfy our play–impulse. We can immediately understand why the ideal form of a Venus, of a Juno, and of an Apollo, is to be sought not at Rome, but in Greece, if we contrast the Greek population, delighting in the bloodless athletic contests of boxing, racing, and intellectual rivalry at Olympia, with the Roman people gloating over the agony of a gladiator. Now the reason pronounces that the beautiful must not only be life and form, but a living form, that is, beauty, inasmuch as it dictates to man the twofold law of absolute formality and absolute reality. Reason also utters the decision that man shall only PLAY with beauty, and he SHALL ONLY PLAY with BEAUTY.

For, to speak out once for all, man only plays when in the full meaning of the word he is a man, and HE IS ONLY COMPLETELY A MAN WHEN HE PLAYS. This proposition, which at this moment perhaps appears paradoxical, will receive a great and deep meaning if we have advanced far enough to apply it to the twofold seriousness of duty and of destiny. I promise you that the whole edifice of aesthetic art and the still more difficult art of life will be supported by this principle. But this proposition is only unexpected in science; long ago it lived and worked in art and in the feeling of the Greeks, her most accomplished masters; only they removed to Olympus what ought to have been preserved on earth. Influenced by the truth of this principle, they effaced from the brow of their gods the earnestness and labour which furrow the cheeks of mortals, and also the hollow lust that smoothes the empty face. They set free the ever serene from the chains of every purpose, of every duty, of every care, and they made INDOLENCE and INDIFFERENCE the envied condition of the godlike race; merely human appellations for the freest and highest mind. As well the material pressure of natural laws as the spiritual pressure of moral laws lost itself in its higher idea of necessity, which embraced at the same time both worlds, and out of the union of these two necessities issued true freedom. Inspired by this spirit, the Greeks also effaced from the features of their ideal, together with DESIRE or INCLINATION, all traces of VOLITION, or, better still, they made both unrecognisable, because they knew how to wed them both in the closest alliance. It is neither charm nor is it dignity which speaks from the glorious face of the Juno Ludovici; it is neither of these, for it is both at once. While the female god challenges our veneration, the godlike woman at the same time kindles our love. But while in ecstacy we give ourselves up to the heavenly beauty, the heavenly self-repose awes us back. The whole form rests and dwells in itself—a fully complete creation in itself—and as if she were out of space, without advance or resistance; it shows no force contending with force, no opening through which time could break in. Irresistibly carried away and attracted by her womanly charm, kept off at a distance by her godly dignity, we also find ourselves at length in the state of the greatest repose, an4 the result is a wonderful impression, for which the understanding has no idea and language no name.

LETTER XVI.

From the antagonism of the two impulsions, and from the association of two opposite principles, we have seen beauty to result, of which the highest ideal must therefore be sought in the most perfect union and equilibrium possible of the reality and of the form. But this equilibrium remains always an idea that reality can never completely reach. In reality, there will always remain a preponderance of one of these elements over the other, and the highest point to which experience can reach will consist in an oscillation between two principles, when sometimes reality and at others form will have the advantage. Ideal beauty is therefore eternally one and indivisible, because there can only be one single equilibrium; on the contrary, experimental beauty will be eternally double, because in the oscillation the equilibrium may be destroyed in two ways—this side and that.

I have called attention in the foregoing letters to a fact that can also be rigorously deduced from the considerations that have engaged our attention to the present point; this fact is that an exciting and also a moderating action may be expected from the beautiful. The TEMPERING action is directed to keep within proper limits the sensuous and the formal impulsions; the EXCITING, to maintain both of them in their full force. But these two modes of action of beauty ought to be completely identified in the idea. The beautiful ought to temper while uniformly exciting the two natures, and it ought also to excite while uniformly moderating them. This result flows at once from the idea of a correlation, in virtue of which the two terms mutually imply each other, and are the reciprocal condition one of the other, a correlation of which the purest product is beauty. But experience does not offer an example of so perfect a correlation. In the field of experience it will always happen more or less that excess on the one side will give rise to deficiency on the other, and deficiency will give birth to excess. It results from this that what in the beau-ideal is only distinct in the idea, is different in reality in empirical beauty, The beau-ideal, though simple and indivisible, discloses, when viewed in two different aspects, on the one hand a property of gentleness and grace, and on the other an energetic property; in experience there is a gentle and graceful beauty, and there is an energetic beauty. It is so, and it will be always so, so long as the absolute is enclosed in the limits of time, and the ideas of reason have to be realised in humanity. For example, the intellectual man has the idea of virtue, of truth, and of happiness; but the active man will only practise VIRTUES, will only grasp TRUTHS, and enjoy HAPPY DAYS. The business of physical and moral education is to bring back this multiplicity to unity, to put morality in the place of manners, science in the place of knowledge; the business of aesthetic education is to make out of beauties the beautiful.

Energetic beauty can no more preserve a man from a certain residue of savage violence and harshness than graceful beauty can secure him against a certain degree of effeminacy and weakness. As it is the effect of the energetic beauty to elevate the mind in a physical and moral point of view and to augment its momentum, it only too often happens that the resistance of the temperament and of the character diminishes the aptitude to receive impressions, that the delicate part of humanity suffers an oppression which ought only to affect its grosser part, and that this course nature participates in an increase of force that ought only to tun? to the account of free personality. It is for this reason that at the periods when we find much strength and abundant sap in humanity, true greatness of thought is seen associated with what is gigantic and extravagant, and the sublimest feeling is found coupled with the most horrible excess of passion. It is also the reason why, in the periods distinguished for regularity and form, nature is as often oppressed as it is governed, as often outraged as it isi surpassed. And as the action of gentle and graceful beauty is to relax the mind in the moral sphere as well as the physical, it happens quite as easily that the energy of feelings is extinguished with the violence of desires, and that character shares in the loss of strength which ought only to affect the passions. This is the reason why, in ages assumed to be refined, it is not a rare thing to see gentleness degenerate into effeminacy, politeness into platitude, correctness into empty sterility, liberal ways into arbitrary caprice, ease into frivolity, calm into apathy, and, lastly, a most miserable caricature treads on the heels of the noblest, the most beautiful type of humanity. Gentle and graceful beauty is therefore a want to the man who suffers the constraint of matter and of forms, for he is moved by grandeur and strength long before he becomes sensible to harmony and grace. Energetic beauty is a necessity to the man who is under the indulgent sway of taste, for in his state of refinement he is only too much disposed to make light of the strength that he retained in his state of rude savagism.

I think I have now answered and also cleared up the contradiction commonly met in the judgments of men respecting the influence of the beautiful, and the appreciation of aesthetic culture. This contradiction is explained directly we remember that there are two sorts of experimental beauty, and that on both hands an affirmation is extended to the entire race, when it can only be proved of one of the species. This contradiction disappears the moment we distinguish a twofold want in humanity to which two kinds of beauty correspond. It is therefore probable that both sides would make good their claims if they come to an understanding respecting the kind of beauty and the form of humanity that they have in view.

Consequently in the sequel of my researches I shall adopt the course that nature herself follows with man considered from the point of view of sesthetics, and setting out from the two kinds of beauty, I shall rise to the idea of the genus. I shall examine the effects produced on man by the gentle and graceful beauty when its springs of action are in full play, and also those produced by energetic beauty when they are relaxed. I shall do this to confound these two sorts of beauty in the unity of the beau—ideal, in the same way that the two opposite forms and modes of being of humanity are absorbed in the unity of the ideal man.

LETTER XVII.

While we were only engaged in deducing the universal idea of beauty from the conception of human nature in general, we had only to consider in the latter the limits established essentially in itself, and inseparable from the notion of the finite. Without attending to the contingent restrictions that human nature may undergo in the real world of phenomena, we have drawn the conception of this nature directly from reason, as a source of every necessity, and the ideal of beauty has been given us at the same time with the ideal of humanity.

But now we are coming down from the region of ideas to the scene of reality, to find man in a DETERMINATE STATE, and consequently in limits which are not derived from the pure conception of humanity, but from external circumstances and from an accidental use of his freedom. But although the limitation of the idea of humanity may be very manifold in the individual, the contents of this idea suffice to teach us that we can only depart from it by TWO opposite roads. For if the perfection of man consist in the harmonious energy of his sensuous and spiritual forces, he can only lack this perfection through the want of harmony and the want of energy. Thus then, before having received on this point the testimony of experience, reason suffices to assure us that we shall find the real and consequently limited man in a state of tension or relaxation, according as the exclusive activity of isolated forces troubles the harmony of his being, or as the unity of his nature is based on the uniform relaxation of his physical and spiritual forces. These opposite limits are, as we have now to prove, suppressed by the beautiful, which re—establishes harmony in man when excited, and energy in man when relaxed; and which, in this way, in conformity with the nature of the beautiful, restores the state of limitation to an absolute state, and makes of man a whole, complete in himself.

Thus the beautiful by no means belies in reality the idea which we have made of it in speculation; only its action is much less free in it than in the field of theory, where we were able to apply it to the pure conception of humanity. In man, as experience shows him to us, the beautiful finds a matter, already damaged and resisting, which robs him in IDEAL perfection of what it communicates to him of its individual mode of being. Accordingly in reality the beautiful will always appear a peculiar and limited species, and not as the pure genus; in excited minds in the state of tension, it will lose its freedom and variety; in relaxed minds, it will lose its vivifying force; but we, who have become familiar with the true character of this contradictory phenomenon, cannot be led astray by it. We shall not follow the great crowd of critics, in determining their conception by separate experiences, and to make them answerable for the deficiencies which man shows under their influence. We know rather that it is man who transfers the imperfections of his individuality over to them, who stands perpetually in the way of their perfection by his subjective limitation, and lowers their absolute ideal to two limited forms of phenomena.

It was advanced that soft beauty is for an unstrung mind, and the energetic beauty for the tightly strung mind. But I apply the term unstrung to a man when he is rather under the pressure of feelings than under the pressure of conceptions. Every exclusive sway of one of his two fundamental impulses is for man a state of compulsion and violence, and freedom only exists in the co–operation of his two natures. Accordingly, the man governed preponderately by feelings, or sensuously unstrung, is emancipated and set free by matter. The soft and graceful beauty, to satisfy this twofold problem, must therefore show herself under two aspects—in two distinct forms. First as a form in repose, she will tone down savage life, and pave the way from feeling to thought. She will, secondly, as a living image equip the abstract form with sensuous power, and lead back the conception to intuition and law to feeling. The former service she does to the man of nature, the second to the man of art. But because she does not in both cases hold complete sway over her matter, but depends on that which is furnished either by formless nature or unnatural art, she will in both cases bear traces of her origin, and lose herself in one place in material life and in another in mere abstract form.

To be able to arrive at a conception how beauty can become a means to remove this twofold relaxation, we must explore its source in the human mind. Accordingly, make up your mind to dwell a little longer in the region of speculation, in order then to leave it for ever, and to advance with securer footing on the ground of experience.

LETTER XVIII.

By beauty the sensuous man is led to form and to thought; by beauty the spiritual man is brought back to matter and restored to the world of sense. From this statement it would appear to follow that between matter and form, between passivity and activity, there must be a middle state, and that beauty plants us in this state. It actually happens that the greater part of mankind really form this conception of beauty as soon as they begin to reflect on its operations, and all experience I seems to point to this conclusion. But, on the other hand, nothing is more unwarrantable and contradictory than such a conception, because the aversion of matter and form, the passive and the active, feeling and thought, is eternal and I cannot be mediated in any way. How can we remove this contradiction? Beauty weds the two opposed conditions of feeling and thinking, and yet there is absolutely no medium between them. The former is immediately certain through experience, the other through the reason.

This is the point to which the whole question of beauty leads, and if we succeed in settling this point in a satisfactory way, we have at length found the clue that will conduct us through the whole labyrinth of aesthetics.

But this requires two very different operations, which must necessarily support each other in this inquiry. Beauty it is said, weds two conditions with one another which are opposite to each other, and can never be one. We must start from this opposition; we must grasp and recognise them in their entire purity and strictness, so that both conditions are separated in the most definite matter; otherwise we mix, but we do not unite them. Secondly, it is usual to say, beauty unites those two opposed conditions, and therefore removes the opposition. But because both conditions remain eternally opposed to one another, they cannot be united in any other way than by being suppressed. Our second business is therefore to make this connection perfect, to carry them out with such purity and perfection that both conditions disappear entirely in a third one, and no trace of separation remains in the whole; otherwise we segregate, but do not unite. All the disputes that have ever prevailed and still prevail in the philosophical world respecting the conception of beauty have no other origin than their commencing without a sufficiently strict distinction, or that it is not carried out fully to a pure union. Those philosophers who blindly follow their feeling in reflecting on this topic can obtain no other conception of beauty, because they distinguish nothing separate in the totality of the sensuous impression. Other philosophers, who take the understanding as their exclusive guide, can never obtain a conception of beauty, because they never see anything else in the whole than the parts, and spirit and matter remain eternally separate, even in their most perfect unity. The first fear to suppress beauty dynamically, that is, as a working power, if they must separate what is united in the feeling. The others fear to suppress beauty logically, that is, as a conception, when they have to hold together what in the understanding is separate. The former wish to think of beauty as it works; the latter wish it to work as it is thought. Both therefore must miss the truth; the former because they try to follow infinite nature with their limited thinking power; the others, because they wish to limit unlimited nature according to their laws of thought The first fear to rob beauty of its freedom by a too strict dissection, the others fear to destroy the distinctness of the conception by a too violent union. But the former do not reflect that the freedom in which they very properly place the essence of beauty is not lawlessness, but harmony of laws; not caprice, but the highest internal necessity. The others do not remember that distinctness, which they with equal right demand from beauty, does not consist in the exclusion of certain realities, but the absolute including of all; that is not therefore limitation, but infinitude. We shall avoid the quicksands on which both have made shipwreck if we begin from the two elements in which beauty divides itself before the understanding, but then afterwards rise to a pure aesthetic unity by which it works on feeling, and in which both those conditions completely disappear.

LETTER XIX.

Two principal and different states of passive and active capacity of being determined [Footnote: Bestimmbarkeit] can be distinguished in man; in like manner two states of passive and active determination. [Footnote: Bestimmung.] The explanation of this proposition leads us most readily to our end.

The condition of the state of man before destination or direction is given him by the impressions of the senses is an unlimited capacity of being determined. The infinite of time and space is given to his imagination for its free use; and, because nothing is settled in this kingdom of the possible, and therefore nothing is excluded from it, this state of absence of determination can be named an empty infiniteness, which must not by any means be confounded with an infinite void.

Now it is necessary that his sensuous nature should be modified, and that in the indefinite series of possible determinations one alone should become real. One perception must spring up in it. That which, in the previous state of determinableness, was only an empty potency becomes now an active force, and receives contents; but at the same time, as an active force it receives a limit, after having been, as a simple power, unlimited. Reality exists now, but the infinite has disappeared. To describe a figure in space, we are obliged to limit infinite space; to represent to ourselves a change in time, we are obliged to divide the totality of time. Thus we only arrive at reality by limitation, at the positive, at a real position, by negation or exclusion; to determination, by the suppression of our free determinableness.

But mere exclusion would never beget a reality, nor would a mere sensuous impression ever give birth to a perception, if there were not something from which it was excluded, if by an absolute act of the mind the negation were not referred to something positive, and if opposition did not issue out of non–position. This act of the mind is styled judging or thinking, and the result is named thought.

Before we determine a place in space, there is no space for us; but without absolute space we could never determine a place. The same is the case with time. Before we have an instant, there is no time to us; but without infinite time—eternity—we should never have a representation of the instant. Thus, therefore, we can only arrive at the whole by the part, to the unlimited through limitation; but reciprocally we only arrive at the part through the whole, at limitation through the unlimited.

It follows from this, that when it is affirmed of beauty that it mediates for man, the transition from feeling to thought, this must not be understood to mean that beauty can fill up the gap that separates feeling from thought, the passive from the active. This gap is infinite; and, without the interposition of a new and independent faculty, it is impossible for the general to issue from the individual, the necessary from the contingent. Thought is the immediate act of this absolute power, which, I admit, can only be manifested in connection with sensuous impressions, but which in this manifestation depends so little on the sensuous that it reveals itself specially in an opposition to it. The spontaneity or autonomy with which it acts excludes every foreign influence; and it is not in as far as it helps thought—which comprehends a manifest contradiction—but only in as far as it procures for the intellectual faculties the freedom to manifest themselves in conformity with their proper laws. It does it only because the beautiful can become a means of leading man from matter to form, from feeling to laws, from a limited existence to an absolute existence.

But this assumes that the freedom of the intellectual faculties can be balked, which appears contradictory to the conception of an autonomous power. For a power which only receives the matter of its activity from without can only be hindered in its action by the privation of this matter, and consequently by way of negation; it is therefore a misconception of the nature of the mind, to attribute to the sensuous passions the power of oppressing positively the freedom of the mind. Experience does indeed present numerous examples where the rational forces appear compressed in proportion to the violence of the sensuous forces. But instead of deducing this spiritual weakness from the energy of passion, this passionate energy must rather be explained by the weakness of the human mind. For the sense can only have a sway such as this over man when the mind has spontaneously neglected to assert its power.

Yet in trying by these explanations to move one objection, I appear to have exposed myself to another, and I have only saved the autonomy of the mind at the cost of its unity. For how can the mind derive at the same time from itself the principles of inactivity and of activity, if it is not itself divided, and if it is not in opposition with itself?

Here we must remember that we have before us, not the infinite mind, but the finite. The finite mind is that which only becomes active through the passive, only arrives at the absolute through limitation, and only acts and fashions in as far as it receives matter. Accordingly, a mind of this nature must associate with the impulse towards form or the absolute, an impulse towards matter or limitation, conditions without which it could not have the former impulse nor satisfy it. How can two such opposite tendencies exist together in the same being? This is a problem that can no doubt embarrass the metaphysician, but not the transcendental philosopher. The latter does not presume to explain the possibility of things, but he is satisfied with giving a solid basis to the knowledge that makes us understand the possibility of experience. And as experience would be equally impossible without this autonomy in the mind, and without the absolute unity of the mind, it lays down these two conceptions as two conditions of experience equally necessary without troubling itself any more to reconcile them. Moreover, this immanence of two fundamental impulses does not in any degree contradict the absolute unity of the mind, as soon as the mind itself, its selfhood, is distinguished from these two motors. No doubt, these two impulses exist and act in it, but itself is neither matter nor form, nor the sensuous nor reason, and this is a point that does not seem always to have occurred to those who only look upon the mind as itself acting when its acts are in harmony with reason, and who declare it passive when its acts contradict reason.

Arrived at its development, each of these two fundamental impulsions tends of necessity and by its nature to satisfy itself; but precisely because each of them has a necessary tendency, and both nevertheless have an opposite tendency, this twofold constraint mutually destroys itself, and the will preserves an entire freedom between them both. It is therefore the will that conducts itself like a power—as the basis of reality—with respect to both these impulses; but neither of them can by itself act as a power with respect to the other. A violent man, by his positive tendency to justice, which never fails in him, is turned away from injustice; nor can a temptation of pleasure, however strong, make a strong character violate its principles. There is in man no other power than his will; and death alone, which destroys man, or some privation of self–consciousness, is the only thing that can rob man of his internal freedom.

An external necessity determines our condition, our existence in time, by means of the sensuous. The latter is quite involuntary, and directly it is produced in us, we are necessarily passive. In the same manner an internal necessity awakens our personality in connection with sensations, and by its antagonism with them; for consciousness cannot depend on the will, which presupposes it. This primitive manifestation of personality is no more a merit to us than its privation is a defect in us. Reason can only be required in a being who is self–conscious, for reason is an absolute consecutiveness and universality of consciousness; before this is the case, he is not a man, nor can any act of humanity be expected from him. The metaphysician can no more explain the limitation imposed by sensation on a free and autonomous mind than the natural philosopher can understand the infinite, which is revealed in consciousness in connection with these limits. Neither abstraction nor experience can bring us back to the source whence issue our ideas of necessity and of universality; this source is concealed in its origin in time from the observer, and its super–sensuous origin from the researches of the metaphysician. But, to sum up in a few words, consciousness is there, and, together with its immutable unity, the law of all that is for man is established, as well as of all that is to be by man, for his understanding and his activity. The ideas of truth and of right present themselves inevitable, incorruptible, immeasurable, even in the age of sensuousness; and without our being able to say why or how, we see eternity in time, the necessary following the contingent. It is thus that, without any share on the part of the subject, the sensation and self–consciousness arise, and the origin of both is beyond our volition, as it is out of the sphere of our knowledge.

But as soon as these two faculties have passed into action, and man has verified by experience, through the medium of sensation, a determinate existence, and through the medium of consciousness, its absolute existence, the two fundamental impulses exert their influence directly their object is given. The sensuous impulse is awakened with the experience of life—with the beginning of the individual; the rational impulsion with the experience of law—with the beginning of his personality; and it is only when these two inclinations have come into existence that the human type is realised. Up to that time, everything takes place in man according to the law of necessity; but now the hand of nature lets him go, and it is for him to keep upright humanity which nature places as a germ in his heart. And thus we see that directly the two opposite and fundamental impulses exercise their influence in him, both lose their constraint, and the autonomy of two necessities gives birth to freedom.

LETTER XX.

That freedom Is an active and not a passive principle results from its very conception; but that liberty itself should be an effect of nature (taking this word in its widest sense), and not the work of man, and therefore that it can be favoured or thwarted by natural means, is the necessary consequence of that which precedes. It begins only when man is complete, and when these two fundamental impulsions have been developed. It will then be wanting whilst he is incomplete, and while one of these impulsions is excluded, and it will be re–established by all that gives back to man his integrity.

Thus it is possible, both with regard to the entire species as to the individual, to remark the moment when man is yet incomplete, and when one of the two exclusions acts solely in him. We know that man commences by life simply, to end by form; that he is more of an individual than a person, and that he starts from the limited or finite to approach the infinite. The sensuous impulsion comes into play therefore before the rational impulsion, because sensation precedes consciousness; and in this priority of sensuous impulsion we find the key of the history of the whole of human liberty.

There is a moment, in fact, when the instinct of life, not yet opposed to the instinct of form, acts as nature and as necessity; when the sensuous is a power because man has not begun; for even in man there can be no other power than his will. But when man shall have attained to the power of thought, reason, on the contrary, will be a power, and moral or logical necessity will take the place of physical necessity. Sensuous power must then be annihilated before the law which must govern it can be established. It is not enough that something shall begin which as yet was not; previously something must end which had begun. Man cannot pass immediately from sensuousness to thought. He must step backwards, for it is only when one determination is suppressed that the contrary determination can take place. Consequently, in order to exchange passive against active liberty, a passive determination against an active, he must be momentarily free from all determination, and must traverse a state of pure determinability. He has then to return in some degree to that state of pure negative indetermination in which he was before his senses were affected by anything. But this state was absolutely empty of all contents, and now the question is to reconcile an equal determination and a determinability equally without limit, with the greatest possible fulness, because from this situation something positive must immediately follow. The determination which man received by sensation must be preserved, because he should not lose the reality; but at the same time, in so far as finite, it should be suppressed, because a determinability without limit would take place. The problem consists then in annihilating the determination of the mode of existence, and yet at the same time in preserving it, which is only possible in one way: in opposing to it another. The two sides of a balance are in equilibrium when empty; they are also in equilibrium when their contents are of equal weight.

Thus, to pass from sensation to thought, the soul traverses a medium position, in which sensibility and reason are at the same time active, and thus they mutually destroy their determinant power, and by their antagonism produce a negation. This medium situation in which the soul is neither physically nor morally constrained, and yet is in both ways active, merits essentially the name of a free situation; and if we call the state of sensuous determination physical, and the state of rational determination logical or moral, that state of real and active determination should be called the aesthetic.

LETTER XXI.

I have remarked in the beginning of the foregoing letter that there is a twofold condition of determinableness and a twofold condition of determination. And now I can clear up this proposition.

The mind can be determined—is determinate—only in as far as it is not determined; it is, however, determinable also, in as far as it is not exclusively determined; that is, if it is not confined in its determination. The former is only a want of determination—it is without limits, because it is without reality; but the latter, the aesthetic determinableness, has no limits, because it unites all reality.

The mind is determined, inasmuch as it is only limited; but it is also determined because it limits itself of its own absolute capacity. It is situated in the former position when it feels, in the second when it thinks. Accordingly the aesthetic constitution is in relation to determinableness what thought is in relation to determination. The latter is a negative from internal and infinite completeness, the former a limitation from internal infinite power. Feeling and thought come into contact in one single point, the mind is determined in both conditions, the man becomes something and exists—either as individual or person—by exclusion; in other cases these two faculties stand infinitely apart. Just in the same manner, the aesthetic determinableness comes in contact with the mere want of determination in a single point, by both excluding every distinct determined existence, by thus being in all other points nothing and all, and hence by being infinitely different. Therefore, if the latter, in the absence of determination from deficiency, is represented as an empty infiniteness, the aesthetic freedom of determination, which forms the proper counterpart to the former, can be considered, as a completed infiniteness; a representation which exactly agrees with the teachings of the previous investigations.

Man is therefore nothing in the aesthetic state, if attention is given to the single result, and not to the whole faculty, and if we regard only the absence or want of every special determination. We must therefore do justice to those who pronounce the beautiful, and the disposition in which it places the mind, as entirely indifferent and unprofitable, in relation to knowledge and feeling. They are perfectly right; for it is certain that beauty gives no separate, single result, either for the understanding or for the will; it does not carry out a single intellectual or moral object; it discovers no truth, does not help us to fulfil a single duty, and, in one word, is equally unfit to found the character or to clear the head. Accordingly, the personal worth of a man, or his dignity, as far as this can only depend on himself, remains entirely undetermined by aesthetic culture, and nothing further is attained than that, on the part of nature, it is made profitable for him to make of himself what he will; that the freedom to be what he ought to be is restored perfectly to him.

But by this, something infinite is attained. But as soon as we remember that freedom is taken from man by the one–sided compulsion of nature in feeling, and by the exclusive legislation of the reason in thinking, we must consider the capacity restored to him by the aesthetical disposition, as the highest of all gifts, as the gift of humanity. I admit that he possesses this capacity for humanity, before every definite determination in which he may be placed. But as a matter of fact, he loses it with every determined condition, into which he may come, and if he is to pass over to an opposite condition, humanity must be in every case restored to him by the aesthetic life.

It is therefore not only a poetical license, but also philosophically correct, when beauty is named our second creator. Nor is this inconsistent with the fact that she only makes it possible for us to attain and realise humanity, leaving this to our free will. For in this she acts in common with our original creator, nature, which has imparted to us nothing further than this capacity for humanity, but leaves the use of it to our own determination of will.

LETTER XXII.

Accordingly, if the aesthetic disposition of the mind must be looked upon in one respect as nothing—that is, when we confine our view to separate and determined operations—it must be looked upon in another respect as a state of the highest reality, in as far as we attend to the absence of all limits and the sum of powers which are commonly active in it. Accordingly we cannot pronounce them, again, to be wrong who describe the aesthetic state to be the most productive in relation to knowledge and morality. They are perfectly right, for a state of mind which comprises the whole of humanity in itself must of necessity include in itself also—necessarily and potentially—every separate expression of it. Again, a disposition of mind that removes all limitation from the totality of human nature must also remove it from every social expression of the same. Exactly because its "aesthetic disposition" does not exclusively shelter any separate function of humanity, it is favourable to all without distinction, nor does it favour any particular functions, precisely because it is the foundation of the possibility of all. All other exercises give to the mind some special aptitude, but for that very reason give it some definite limits; only the aesthetical leads him to the unlimited. Every other condition, in which we can live, refers us to a previous condition, and requires for its solution a following condition; only the aesthetic is a complete whole in itself, for it unites in itself all conditions of its source and of its duration. Here alone we feel ourselves swept out of time, and our humanity expresses itself with purity and integrity as if it had not yet received any impression or interruption from the operation of external powers.

That which flatters our senses in immediate sensation opens our weak and volatile spirit to every impression, but makes us in the same degree less apt for exertion. That which stretches our thinking power and invites to abstract conceptions strengthens our mind for every kind of resistance, but hardens it also in the same proportion, and deprives us of susceptibility in the same ratio that it helps us to greater mental activity. For this very reason, one as well as the other brings us at length to exhaustion, because matter cannot long do without the shaping, constructive force, and the force cannot do without the constructible material. But on the other hand, if we have resigned ourselves to the enjoyment of genuine beauty, we are at such a moment of our passive and active powers in the same degree master, and we shall turn with ease from grave to gay, from rest to movement, from submission to resistance, to abstract thinking and intuition.

This high indifference and freedom of mind, united with power and elasticity, is the disposition in which a true work of art ought to dismiss us, and there is no better test of true aesthetic excellence. If after an enjoyment of this kind we find ourselves specially impelled to a particular mode of feeling or action, and unfit for other modes, this serves as an infallible proof that we have not experienced any pure aesthetic effect, whether this is owing to the object, to our own mode of feeling—as generally happens—or to both together.

As in reality no purely aesthetical effect can be met with—for man can never leave his dependence on material forces—the excellence of a work of art can only consist in its greater approximation to its ideal of aesthetic purity, and however high we may raise the freedom of this effect, we shall always leave it with a particular disposition and a particular bias. Any class of productions or separate work in the world of art is noble and excellent in proportion to the universality of the disposition and the unlimited character of the bias thereby presented to our mind. This truth can be applied to works in various branches of art, and also to different works in the same branch. We leave a grand musical performance with our feelings excited, the reading of a noble poem with a quickened imagination, a beautiful statue or building with an awakened understanding; but a man would not choose an opportune moment who attempted to invite us to abstract thinking after a high musical enjoyment, or to attend to a prosaic affair of common life after a high poetical enjoyment, or to kindle our imagination and astonish our feelings directly after inspecting a fine statue or edifice. The reason of this is that music, BY ITS MATTER, even when most spiritual, presents a greater affinity with the senses than is permitted by aesthetic liberty; it is because even the most happy poetry, having FOR TIS MEDIUM the arbitrary and contingent play of the imagination, always shares in it more than the intimate necessity of the really beautiful allows; it is because the best sculpture touches on severe science BY WHAT IS DETERMINATE IN ITS CONCEPTION. However, these particular affinities are lost in proportion as the works of these three kinds of art rise to a greater elevation, and it is a natural and necessary consequence of their perfection, that, without confounding their objective limits, the different arts come to resemble each other more and more, in the action WHICH THEY EXERCISE ON THE MIND. At its highest degree of ennobling, music ought to become a form, and act on us with the calm power of an antique statue; in its most elevated perfection, the plastic art ought to become music and move us by the immediate action exercised on the mind by the senses; in its most complete developmentment, poetry ought both to stir us powerfully like music and like plastic art to surround us with a peaceful light. In each art, the perfect style consists exactly in knowing how to remove specific limits, while sacrificing at the same time the particular advantages of the art, and to give it by a wise use of what belongs to it specially a more general character.

Nor is it only the limits inherent in the specific character of each kind of art that the artist ought to overstep in putting his hand to the work; he must also triumph over those which are inherent in the particular subject of which he treats. In a really beautiful work of art, the substance ought to be inoperative, the form should do everything; for by the form, the whole man is acted on; the substance acts on nothing but isolated forces. Thus, however vast and sublime it may be, the substance always exercises a restrictive action on the mind, and true aesthetic liberty can only be expected from the form. Consequently the true search of the master consists in destroying matter by the form; and the triumph of art is great in proportion as it overcomes matter and maintains its sway over those who enjoy its work. It is great particularly in destroying matter when most imposing, ambitious, and attractive, when therefore matter has most power to produce the effect proper to it, or, again, when it leads those who consider it more closely to enter directly into relation with it. The mind of the spectator and of the hearer must remain perfectly free and intact; it must issue pure and entire from the magic circle of the artist, as from the hands of the Creator. The most frivolous subject ought to be treated in such a way that we preserve the faculty to exchange it immediately for the most serious work. The arts which have passion for their object, as a tragedy for example, do not present a difficulty here; for, in the first place these arts are not entirely free, because they are in the service of a particular end (the pathetic), and then no connoisseur will deny that even in this class a work is perfect in proportion as amidst the most violent storms of passion it respects the liberty of the soul. There is a fine art of passion, but an impassioned fine art is a contradiction in terms, for the infallible effect of the beautiful is emancipation from the passions. The idea of an instructive fine art (didactic art) or improving (moral) art is no less contradictory, for nothing agrees less with the idea of the beautiful than to give a determinate tendency to the mind.

However, from the fact that a work produces effects only by its substance, it must not always be inferred that there is a want of form in this work; this conclusion may quite as well testify to a want of form in the observer. If his mind is too stretched or too relaxed, if it is only accustomed to receive things either by the senses or the intelligence, even in the most perfect combination, it will only stop to look at the parts, and it will only see matter in the most beautiful form. Only sensible of the coarse elements, he must first destroy the aesthetic organisation of a work to find enjoyment in it, and carefully disinter the details which genius has caused to vanish, with infinite art, in the harmony of the whole. The interest he takes in the work is either solely moral or exclusively physical; the only thing wanting to it is to be exactly what it ought to be—aesthetical. The readers of this class enjoy a serious and pathetic poem as they do a sermon; a simple and playful work, as an inebriating draught; and if on the one hand they have so little taste as to demand edification from a tragedy or from an epos, even such as the "Messias," on the other hand they will be infallibly scandalised by a piece after the fashion of Anacreon and Catullus.

LETTER XXIII.

I take up the thread of my researches, which I broke off only to apply the principles I laid down to practical art and the appreciation of its works.

The transition from the passivity of sensuousness to the activity of thought and of will can be effected only by the intermediary state of aesthetic liberty; and though in itself this state decides nothing respecting our opinions and our sentiments, and therefore leaves our intellectual and moral value entirely problematical, it is, however, the necessary condition without which we should never attain to an opinion or a sentiment. In a word, there is no other way to make a reasonable being out of a sensuous man than by making him first aesthetic.

But, you might object: Is this mediation absolutely indispensable? Could not truth and duty, one or the other, in themselves and by themselves, find access to the sensuous man? To this I reply: Not only is it possible, but it is I absolutely necessary that they owe solely to themselves their determining force, and nothing would be more contradictory to our preceding affirmations than to appear to defend the contrary opinion. It has been expressly proved that the beautiful furnishes no result, either for the comprehension or for the will; that it mingles with no operations, either of thought or of resolution; and that it confers this double power without determining anything with regard to the real exercise of this power. Here all foreign help disappears, and the pure logical form, the idea, would speak immediately to the intelligence, as the pure moral form, the law, immediately to the will.

But that the pure form should be capable of it, and that there is in general a pure form for sensuous man, is that, I maintain, which should be rendered possible by the aesthetic disposition of the soul. Truth is not a thing which can be received from without like reality or the visible existence of objects. It is the thinking force, in his own liberty and activity, which produces it, and it is just this liberty proper to it, this liberty which we seek in vain in sensuous man. The sensuous man is already determined physically, and thenceforth he has no longer his free determinability; he must necessarily first enter into possession of this lost determinability before he can exchange the passive against an active determination. Therefore, in order to recover it, he must either lose the passive determination that he had, or he should enclose already in Himself the active determination to which he should pass. If he confined himself to lose passive determination, he would at the same time lose with it the possibility of an active determination, because thought needs a body, and form can only be realised through matter. He must therefore contain already in himself the active determination that he may be at once both actively and passively determined, that is to say, he becomes necessarily aesthetic.

Consequently, by the aesthetic disposition of the soul the proper activity of reason is already revealed in the sphere of sensuousness, the power of sense is already broken within its own boundaries, and the ennobling of physical man carried far enough, for spiritual man has only to develop himself according to the laws of liberty. The transition from an aesthetic state to a logical and moral state (from the beautiful to truth and duty) is then infinitely more easy than the transition from the physical state to the aesthetic state (from life pure and blind to form). This transition man can effectuate alone by his liberty, whilst he has only to enter into possession of himself not to give it himself; but to separate the elements of his nature, and not to enlarge it. Having attained to the aesthetic disposition, man will give to his judgments and to his actions a universal value as soon as he desires it This passage from brute nature to beauty, in which an entirely new faculty would awaken in him, nature would render easier, and his will has no power over a disposition which, we know, itself gives birth to the will. To bring the aesthetic man to profound views, to elevated sentiments, he requires nothing more than important occasions; to obtain the same thing from the sensuous man, his nature must at first be changed. To make of the former a hero, a sage, it is often only necessary to meet with a sublime situation, which exercises upon the faculty of the will the more immediate action; for the second, it must first be transplanted under another sky.

One of the most important tasks of culture, then, is to submit man to form, even in a purely physical life, and to render it aesthetic as far as the domain of the beautiful can be extended, for it is alone in the aesthetic state, and not in the physical state, that the moral state can be developed. If in each particular case man ought to possess the power to make his judgment and his will the judgment of the entire species; if he ought to find in each limited existence the transition to an infinite existence; if, lastly, he ought from every dependent situation to take his flight to rise to autonomy and to liberty, it must be observed that at no moment is he only individual and solely obeys the law of nature. To be apt and ready to raise himself from the narrow circle of the ends of nature, to rational ends, in the sphere of the former he must already have exercised himself in the second; he must already have realised his physical destiny with a certain liberty that belongs only to spiritual nature, that is to say, according to the laws of the beautiful.

And that he can effect without thwarting in the least degree his physical aim. The exigencies of nature with regard to him turn only upon what he does—upon the substance of his acts; but the ends of nature in no degree determine the way in which he acts, the form of his actions. On the contrary, the exigencies of reason have rigorously the form of his activity for its object. Thus, so much as it is necessary for the moral destination of man, that he be purely moral, that he shows an absolute personal activity, so much is he indifferent that his physical destination be entirely physical, that he acts in a manner entirely passive. Henceforth with regard to this last destination, it entirely depends on him to fulfil it solely as a sensuous being and natural force (as a force which acts only as it diminishes) or, at the same time, as absolute force, as a rational being. To which of these does his dignity best respond? Of this, there can be no question. It is as disgraceful and contemptible for him to do under sensuous impulsion that which he ought to have determined merely by the motive of duty, as it is noble and honourable for him to incline towards conformity with laws, harmony, independence; there even where the vulgar man only satisfies a legitimate want. In a word, in the domain of truth and morality, sensuousness must have nothing to determine; but in the sphere of happiness, form may find a place, and the instinct of play prevail.

Thus then, in the indifferent sphere of physical life, man ought to already commence his moral life; his own proper activity ought already to make way in passivity, and his rational liberty beyond the limits of sense; he ought already to impose the law of his will upon his inclinations; he ought—if you will permit me the expression—to carry into the domain of matter the war against matter, in order to be dispensed from combatting this redoubtable enemy upon the sacred field of liberty; he ought to learn to have nobler desires, not to be forced to have sublime volitions. This is the fruit of aesthetic culture, which submits to the laws of the beautiful, in which neither the laws of nature nor those of reason suffer, which does not force the will of man, and which by the form it gives to exterior life already opens internal life.

LETTER XXIV.

Accordingly three different moments or stages of development can be distinguished, which the individual man, as well as the whole race, must of necessity traverse in a determinate order if they are to fulfil the circle of their determination. No doubt, the separate periods can be lengthened or shortened, through accidental causes which are inherent either in the influence of external things or under the free caprice of men; but neither of them can be overstepped, and the order of their sequence cannot be inverted either by nature or by the will. Man, in his PHYSICAL condition, suffers only the power of nature; he gets rid of this power in the aesthetical condition, and he rules them in the moral state.

What is man before beauty liberates him from free pleasure, and the serenity of form tames down the savageness of life? Eternally uniform in his aims, eternally changing in his judgments, self- seeking without being himself, unfettered without being free, a slave without serving any rule. At this period, the world is to him only destiny, not yet an object; all has existence for him only in as far as it procures existence to him; a thing that neither seeks from nor gives to him is non−existent. Every phenomenon stands out before him, separate and cut off, as he finds himself in the series of beings.

All that is, is to him through the bias of the moment; every change is to him an entirely fresh creation, because with the necessary IN HIM, the necessary OUT OF HIM is wanting, which binds together all the changing forms in the universe, and which holds fast the law on the theatre of his action, while the individual departs. It is in vain that nature lets the rich variety of her forms pass before him; he sees in her glorious fulness nothing but his prey, in her power and greatness nothing but his enemy. Either he encounters objects, and wishes to draw them to himself in desire, or the objects press in a destructive manner upon him, and he thrusts them away in dismay and terror. In both cases his relation to the world of sense is immediate CONTACT; and perpetually anxious through its pressure, restless and plagued by imperious wants, he nowhere finds rest except in enervation, and nowhere limits save in exhausted desire.

> "True, his is the powerful breast and the mighty hand of the
>   Titans...
> A certain inheritance; yet the god welded
> Round his forehead a brazen band;
> Advice, moderation, wisdom, and patience,—
> Hid it from his shy, sinister look.
> Every desire is with him a rage,
> And his rage prowls around limitless."—"Iphigenia in Tauris"

Ignorant of his own human dignity, he is far removed from honouring it in others, and conscious of his own savage greed, he fears it in every creature that he sees like himself. He never sees others in himself, only himself in others, and human society, instead of enlarging him to the race, only shuts him up continually closer in his individuality. Thus limited, he wanders through his sunless life, till favouring nature rolls away the load of matter from his darkened senses, reflection separates him from things, and objects show themselves at length in the after–glow of the consciousness.

It is true we cannot point out this state of rude nature as we have here portrayed it in any definite people and age. It is only an idea, but an idea with which experience agrees most closely in special features. It may be said that man was never in this animal condition, but he has not, on the other hand, ever entirely escaped from it. Even in the rudest subjects, unmistakable traces of rational freedom can be found, and even in the most cultivated, features are not wanting that remind us of that dismal natural condition. It is possible for man, at one and the same time, to unite the highest and the lowest in his nature; and if his DIGNITY depends on a strict separation of one from the other, his HAPPINESS depends on a skilful removal of this separation. The culture which is to bring his dignity into agreement with his happiness will therefore have to provide for the greatest purity of these two principles in their most intimate combination.

Consequently the first appearance of reason in man is not the beginning of humanity. This is first decided by his freedom, and reason begins first by making his sensuous dependence boundless; a phenomenon that does not appear to me to have been sufficiently elucidated, considering its importance and universality. We know that the reason makes itself known to man by the demand for the absolute—the self–dependent and necessary. But as this want of the reason cannot be satisfied in any separate or single state of his physical life, he is obliged to leave the physical entirely and to rise from a limited reality to ideas. But although the true meaning of that demand of the reason is to withdraw him from the limits of time and to lead him up from the world of sense to an ideal world, yet this same demand of reason, by a misapplication—scarcely to be avoided in this age, prone to sensuousness—can direct him to physical life, and, instead of making man free, plunge him in the most terrible slavery.

Facts verify this supposition. Man raised on the wings of imagination leaves the narrow limits of the present, in which mere animality is enclosed, in order to strive on to an unlimited future. But while the limitless is unfolded to his dazed IMAGINATION, his heart has not ceased to live in the separate, and to serve the moment. The impulse towards the absolute seizes him suddenly in the midst of his animality, and as in this cloddish condition all his efforts aim only at the material and temporal, and are limited by his individuality, he is only led by that demand of the reason to extend his individuality into the infinite, instead of to abstract from it. He will be led to seek instead of form an inexhaustible matter, instead of the unchangeable an everlasting change and an absolute securing of his temporal existence. The same impulse which, directed to his thought and action, ought to lead to truth and morality, now directed to his passion and emotional state, produces nothing but an unlimited desire and an absolute want. The first fruits, therefore, that he reaps in the world of spirits, are cares and fear—both operations of the reason; not of sensuousness, but of a reason that mistakes its object and applies its categorical imperative to matter. All unconditional systems of happiness are fruits of this tree, whether they have for their object the present day or the whole of life, or what does not make them any more respectable, the whole of eternity, for their object. An unlimited duration of existence and of well–being is only an ideal of the desires; hence a demand which can only be put forth by an animality striving up to the absolute. Man, therefore, without gaining anything for his humanity by a rational expression of this sort, loses the happy limitation of the animal over which he now only possesses the unenviable superiority of losing the present for an endeavour after what is remote, yet without seeking in the limitless future anything but the present.

But even if the reason does not go astray in its object, or err in the question, sensuousness will continue to falsify the answer for a long time. As soon as man has begun to use his understanding and to knit together phenomena in cause and effect, the reason, according to its conception, presses on to an absolute knitting together and to an unconditional basis. In order merely to be able to put forward this demand man must already have stepped beyond the sensuous, but the sensuous uses this very demand to bring back the fugitive.

In fact it is now that he ought to abandon entirely the world of sense in order to take his flight into the realm of ideas; for the intelligence temains eternally shut up in the finite and in the contingent, and does not cease putting questions without reaching the last link of the chain. But as the man with whom we are engaged is not yet capable of such an abstraction, and does not find it in the sphere of sensuous knowledge, and because he does not look for it in pure reason, he will seek for it below in the region of sentiment, and will appear to find it. No doubt the sensuous shows him nothing that has its foundation in itself, and that legislates for itself, but it shows him something that does not care for foundation or law; therefore thus not being able to quiet the intelligence by showing it a final cause, he reduces it to silence by the conception which desires no cause; and being incapable of understanding the sublime necessity of reason, he keeps to the blind constraint of matter. As sensuousness knows no other end than its interest, and is determined by nothing except blind chance, it makes the former the motive of its actions, and the latter the master of the world.

Even the divine part in man, the moral law, in its first manifestation in the sensuous cannot avoid this perversion, As this moral law is only prohibited and combats in man the interest of sensuous egotism, it must appear to him as something strange until he has come to consider this self–love as the stranger, and the voice of reason as his true self. Therefore he confines himself to feeling the fetters which the latter imposes on him, without having the consciousness of the infinite emancipation which it procures for him. Without suspecting in himself the dignity of lawgiver, he only experiences the constraint and the impotent revolt of a subject fretting under the yoke, because in this experience the sensuous impulsion precedes the moral impulsion, he gives to the law of necessity a beginning in him, a positive origin, and by the most unfortunate of all mistakes he converts the immutable and the eternal in himself into a transitory accident He makes up his mind to consider the notions of the just and the unjust as statutes which have been introduced by a will, and not as having in themselves an eternal value. Just as in the explanation of certain natural phenomena he goes beyond nature and seeks out of her what can only be found in her, in her own laws; so also in the explanation of moral phenomena he goes beyond reason and makes light of his humanity, seeking a god in this way. It is not wonderful that a religion which he has purchased at the cost of his humanity shows itself worthy of this origin, and that he only considers as absolute and eternally binding laws that have never been binding from all eternity. He has placed himself in relation with, not a holy being, but a powerful. Therefore the spirit of his religion, of the homage that he gives to God, is a fear that abases him, and not a veneration that elevates him in his own esteem.

Though these different aberrations by which man departs from the ideal of his destination cannot all take place at the same time, because several degrees have to be passed over in the transition from the obscure of thought to error, and from the obscure of will to the corruption of the will; these degrees are all, without exception, the consequence of his physical state, because in all the vital impulsion sways the formal impulsion. Now, two cases may happen: either reason may not yet have spoken in man, and the physical may reign over him with a blind necessity, or reason may not be sufficiently purified from sensuous impressions, and the moral may still be subject to the physical; in both cases the only principle that has a real power over him is a material principle, and man, at least as regards his ultimate tendency, is a sensuous being. The only difference is, that in the former case he is an animal without reason, and in the second case a rational animal. But he ought to be neither one nor the other: he ought to be a man. Nature ought not to rule him exclusively; nor reason conditionally. The two legislations ought to be completely independent and yet mutually complementary.

LETTER XXV.

Whilst man, in his first physical condition, is only passively affected by the world of sense, he is still entirely identified with it; and for this reason the external world, as yet, has no objective existence for him. When he begins in his aesthetic state of mind to regard the world objectively, then only is his personality severed from it, and the world appears to him an objective reality, for the simple reason that he has ceased to form an identical portion of it.

That which first connects man with the surrounding universe is the power of reflective contemplation. Whereas desire seizes at once its object, reflection removes it to a distance and renders it inalienably her own by saving it from the greed of passion. The necessity of sense which he obeyed during the period of mere sensations, lessens during the period of reflection; the senses are for the time in abeyance; even ever–fleeting time stands still whilst the scattered rays of consciousness are gathering and shape themselves; an image of the infinite is reflected upon the perishable ground. As soon as light dawns in man, there is no longer night outside of him; as soon as there is peace within him the storm lulls throughout the universe, and the contending forces of nature find rest within prescribed limits. Hence we cannot wonder if ancient traditions allude to these great changes in the inner man as to a revolution in surrounding nature, and symbolise thought triumphing over the laws of time, by the figure of Zeus, which terminates the reign of Saturn.

As long as man derives sensations from a contact with nature, he is her slave; but as soon as he begins to reflect upon her objects and laws he becomes her lawgiver. Nature, which previously ruled him as a power, now expands before him as an object. What is objective to him can have no power over him, for in order to become objective it has to experience his own power. As far and as long as he impresses a form upon matter, he cannot be injured by its effect; for a spirit can only be injured by that which deprives it of its freedom. Whereas he proves his own freedom by giving a form to the formless; where the mass rules heavily and without shape, and its undefined outlines are for ever fluctuating between uncertain boundaries, fear takes up its abode; but man rises above any natural terror as soon as he knows how to mould it, and transform it into an object of his art. As soon as he upholds his independence toward phaenomenal nature, he maintains his dignity toward her as a thing of power and with a noble freedom he rises against his gods. They throw aside the mask with which they had kept him in awe during his infancy, and to his surprise his mind perceives the reflection of his own image. The divine monster of the Oriental, which roams about changing the world with the blind force of a beast of prey, dwindles to the charming outline of humanity in Greek fable; the empire of the Titans is crushed, and boundless force is tamed by infinite form.

But whilst I have been merely searching for an issue from the material world and a passage into the world of mind, the bold flight of my imagination has already taken me into the very midst of the latter world. The beauty of which we are in search we have left behind by passing from the life of mere sensations to the pure form and to the pure object. Such a leap exceeds the condition of human nature; in order to keep pace with the latter we must return to the world of sense. Beauty is indeed the sphere of unfettered contemplation and reflection; beauty conducts us into the world of ideas, without however taking us from the world of sense, as occurs when a truth is perceived and acknowledged. This is the pure product of a process of abstraction from everything material and accidental, a pure object free from every subjective barrier, a pure state of self–activity without any admixture of passive sensations. There is indeed a way back to sensation from the highest abstraction; for thought teaches the inner sensation, and the idea of logical and moral unity passes into a sensation of sensual accord. But if we delight in knowledge we separate very accurately our own conceptions from our sensations; we look upon the latter as something accidental, which might have been omitted without the knowledge being impaired thereby, without truth being less true. It would, however, be a vain attempt to suppress this connection of the faculty of feeling with the idea of beauty, consequently, we shall not succeed in representing to ourselves one as the effect of the other, but we must look upon them both together and reciprocally as cause and effect. In the pleasure which we derive from knowledge we readily distinguish the passage from the active to the passive state, and we clearly perceive that the first ends when the second begins. On the contrary, from the pleasure which we take in beauty, this transition from the active to the passive is not perceivable, and reflection is so intimately blended with feeling that we believe we feel the form immediately. Beauty is then an object to us, it is true, because reflection is the condition of the feeling which we have of it; but it is also a state of our personality (our Ego), because the feeling is the condition of the idea we conceive of it: beauty is therefore doubtless form, because we contemplate it, but it is equally life because we feel it. In a word, it is at once our state and our act. And precisely because it is at the same time both a state and an act, it triumphantly proves to us that the passive does not exclude the active, neither matter nor form, neither the finite nor the infinite; and that consequently the physical dependence to which man is necessarily devoted does not in any way destroy his moral liberty. This is the proof of beauty, and I ought to add that this ALONE can prove it. In fact, as in the possession of truth or of logical unity, feeling is not necessarily one with the thought, but follows it accidentally; it is a fact which only proves that a sensitive nature can succeed a rational nature, and vice versa; not that they co–exist, that they exercise a reciprocal action one over the other, and lastly that they ought to be united in an absolute and necessary manner. From this exclusion of feeling as long as there is thought, and of thought so long as there is feeling, we should on the contrary conclude that the two natures are incompatible, so that in order to demonstrate that pure reason is to be realised in humanity, the best proof given by the analysis is that this realisation is demanded. But, as in the realisation of beauty or of aesthetic unity, there is a real union, mutual substitution of matter and of form, of passive and of active, by this alone is proved the compatibility of the two natures, the possible realisation of the infinite in the finite, and consequently also the possibility of the most sublime humanity.

Henceforth we need no longer be embarrassed to find a transition from dependent feeling to moral liberty, because beauty reveals to us the fact that they can perfectly co–exist, and that to show himself a spirit, man need not escape from matter. But if on one side he is free, even in his relation with a visible world, as the fact of beauty teaches, and if on the other side freedom is something absolute and super–sensuous, as its idea necessarily implies, the question is no longer how man succeeds in raising himself from the finite to the absolute, and opposing himself in his thought and will to sensuality, as this has already been produced in the fact of beauty. In a word, we have no longer to ask how he passes from virtue to truth, which is already included in the former, but how he opens a way for himself from vulgar reality to aesthetic reality, and from the ordinary feelings of life to the perception of the beautiful.

LETTER XXVI.

I have shown in the previous letters that it is only the aesthetic disposition of the soul that gives birth to liberty, it cannot therefore be derived from liberty nor have a moral origin. It must be a gift of nature; the favour of chance alone can break the bonds of the physical state and bring the savage to duty. The germ of the beautiful will find an equal difficulty in developing itself in countries where a severe nature forbids man to enjoy himself, and in those where a prodigal nature dispenses him from all effort; where the blunted senses experience no want, and where violent desire can never be satisfied. The delightful flower of the beautiful will never unfold itself in the case of the Troglodyte hid in his cavern always alone, and never finding humanity outside himself; nor among nomads, who, travelling in great troops, only consist of a multitude, and have no individual humanity. It will only flourish in places where man converses peacefully with himself in his cottage, and with the whole race when he issues from it. In those climates where a limpid ether opens the senses to the lightest impression, whilst a life–giving warmth develops a luxuriant nature, where even in the inanimate creation the sway of inert matter is overthrown, and the victorious form ennobles even the most abject natures; in this joyful state and fortunate zone, where activity alone leads to enjoyment, and enjoyment to activity, from life itself issues a holy harmony, and the laws of order develope life, a different result takes place. When imagination incessantly escapes from reality, and does not abandon the simplicity of nature in its wanderings: then and there only the mind and the senses, the receptive force and the plastic force, are developed in that happy equilibrium which is the soul of the beautiful and the condition of humanity.

What phaenomenon accompanies the initiation of the savage into humanity? However far we look back into history the phaenomenon is identical among all people who have shaken off the slavery of the animal state, the love of appearance, the inclination for dress and for games.

Extreme stupidity and extreme intelligence have a certain affinity in only seeking the real and being completely insensible to mere appearance. The former is only drawn forth by the immediate presence of an object in the senses, and the second is reduced to a quiescent state only by referring conceptions to the facts of experience. In short, stupidity cannot rise above reality, nor the intelligence descend below truth. Thus, in as far as the want of reality and attachment to the real are only the consequence of a want and a defect, indifference to the real and an interest taken in appearances are a real enlargement of humanity and a decisive step towards culture. In the first place it is the proof of an exterior liberty, for as long as necessity commands and want solicits, the fancy is strictly chained down to the real; it is only when want is satisfied that it developes without hindrance. But it is also the proof of an internal liberty, because it reveals to us a force which, independent of an external substratum, sets itself in motion, and has sufficient energy to remove from itself the solicitations of nature. The reality of things is effected by things, the appearance of things is the work of man, and a soul that takes pleasure in appearance does not take pleasure in what it receives but in what it makes.

It is self–evident that I am speaking of aesthetical evidence different from reality and truth, and not of logical appearance identical with them. Therefore if it is liked it is because it is an appearance, and not because it is held to be something better than it is: the first principle alone is a play whilst the second is a deception. To give a value to the appearance of the first kind can never injure truth, because it is never to be feared that it will supplant it—the only way in which truth can be injured. To despise this appearance is to despise in general all the fine arts of which it is the essence. Nevertheless, it happens sometimes that the understanding carries its zeal for reality as far as this intolerance, and strikes with a sentence of ostracism all the arts relating to beauty in appearance, because it is only an appearance. However, the intelligence only shows this vigorous spirit when it calls to mind the affinity pointed out further back. I shall find some day the occasion to treat specially of the limits of beauty in its appearance.

It is nature herself which raises man from reality to appearance by endowing him with two senses which only lead him to the knowledge of the real through appearance. In the eye and the ear the organs of the senses are already freed from the persecutions of nature, and the object with which we are immediately in contact through the animal senses is remoter from us. What we see by the eye differs from what we feel; for the understanding to reach objects overleaps the light which separates us from them. In truth, we are passive to an object; in sight and hearing the object is a form we create. While still a savage, man only enjoys through touch merely aided by sight and sound. He either does not rise to perception through sight, or does not rest there. As soon as he begins to enjoy through sight, vision has an independent value, he is aesthetically free, and the instinct of play is developed.

The instinct of play likes appearance, and directly it is awakened it is followed by the formal imitative instinct which treats appearance as an independent thing. Directly man has come to distinguish the appearance from the reality, the form from the body, he can separate, in fact he has already done so. Thus the faculty of the art of imitation is given with the faculty of form in general. The inclination that draws us to it reposes on another tendency I have not to notice here. The exact period when the aesthetic instinct, or that of art, developes, depends entirely on the attraction that mere appearance has for men.

As every real existence proceeds from nature as a foreign power, whilst every appearance comes in the first place from man as a percipient subject, he only uses his absolute sight in separating semblance from essence, and arranging according to subjective law. With an unbridled liberty he can unite what nature has severed, provided he can imagine his union, and he can separate what nature has united, provided this separation can take place in his intelligence. Here nothing can be sacred to him but his own law: the only condition imposed upon him is to respect the border which separates his own sphere from the existence of things or from the realm of nature.

This human right of ruling is exercised by man in the art of appearance; and his success in extending the empire of the beautiful, and guarding the frontiers of truth, will be in proportion with the strictness with which he separates form from substance: for if he frees appearance from reality he must also do the converse.

But man possesses sovereign power only in the world of appearance, in the unstibstantial realm of imagination, only by abstaining from giving being to appearance in theory, and by giving it being in practice. It follows that the poet transgresses his proper limits when he attributes being to his ideal, and when he gives this ideal aim as a determined existence. For he can only reach this result by exceeding his right as a poet, that of encroaching by the ideal on the field of experience, and by pretending to determine real existence in virtue of a simple possibility, or else he renounces his right as poet by letting experience encroach on the sphere of the ideal, and by restricting possibility to the conditions of reality.

It is only by being frank or disclaiming all reality, and by being independent or doing without reality, that the appearance is aesthetical. Directly it apes reality or needs reality for effect it is nothing more than a vile instrument for material ends, and can prove nothing for the freedom of the mind. Moreover, the object in which we find beauty need not be unreal if pur judgment disregards this reality; nor if it regards this the judgment is no longer aesthetical. A beautiful woman if living would no doubt please us as much and rather more than an equally beautiful woman seen in painting; but what makes the former please men is not her being an independent appearance; she no longer pleases the pure aesthetic feeling. In the painting, life must only attract as an appearance, and reality as an idea. But it is certain that to feel in a living object only the pure appearance, requires a greatly higher aesthetic culture than to do without life in the appearance.

When the frank and independent appearance is found in man separately, or in a whole people, it may be inferred they have mind, taste, and all prerogatives connected with them. In this case, the ideal will be seen to govern real life, honour triumphing over fortune, thought over enjoyment, the dream of immortality over a transitory existence.

In this case public opinion will no longer be feared and an olive crown will be more valued than a purple mantle. Impotence and perversity alone have recourse to false and paltry semblance, and individuals as well as nations who lend to reality the support of appearance, or to the aesthetical appearance the support of reality, show their moral unworthiness and their aesthetical impotence. Therefore, a short and conclusive answer can be given to this question—How far will appearance be permitted in the moral world? It will run thus in proportion as this appearance will be sesthetical, that is, an appearance that does not try to make up for reality, nor requires to be made up for by it. The aesthetical appearance can never endanger the truth of morals: wherever it seems to do so the appearance is not aesthetical. Only a stranger to the fashionable world can take the polite assurances, which are only a form, for proofs of affection, and say he has been deceived; but only a clumsy fellow in good society calls in the aid of duplicity and flatters to become amiable. The former lacks the pure sense for independent appearance; therefore he can only give a value to appearance by truth. The second lacks reality, and wishes to replace it by appearance. Nothing is more common than to hear depreciators of the times utter these paltry complaints—that all solidity has disappeared from the world, and that essence is neglected for semblance. Though I feel by no means called upon to defend this age against these reproaches, I must say that the wide application of these criticisms shows that they attach blame to the age, not only on the score of the falsez but also of the frank appearance. And even the exceptions they admit in favour of the beautiful have for their object less the independent appearance than the needy appearance. Not only do they attack the artificial colouring that hides truth and replaces reality, but also the beneficent appearance that fills a vacuum and clothes poverty; and they even attack the ideal appearance that ennobles a vulgar reality. Their strict sense of truth is rightlyl offended by the falsity of manners; unfortunately, they class politeness in this category. It displeases them that the noisy and showy so often eclipse true merit, but they are no less shocked that appearance is also demanded from merit, and that a real substance does not dispense with an agreeable form. They regret the cordiality, the energy, and solidity of ancient times; they would restore with them ancient coarseness, heaviness, and the old Gothic profusion. By judgments of this kind they show an esteem for the matter itself unworthy of humanity, which ought only to value tne matter inasmuch as it can receive a form and enlarge the empire of ideas. Accordingly, the taste of the age need not much fear these criticisms, if it can clear itself before better judges. Our defect is not to grant a value to aesthetic appearance (we do not do this enough): a severe judge of the beautiful might rather reproach us with not having arrived at pure appearance, with not having separated clearly enough existence from the phaenomenon, and thus established their limits. We shall deserve this reproach so long as we cannot enjoy the beautiful in living nature without desiring it; as long as we cannot admire the beautiful in the imitative arts without having an end in view; as long as we do not grant to imagination an absolute legislation of its own; and as long as we do not inspire it with care for its dignity by the esteem we testify for its works.

LETTER XXVII.

Do not fear for reality and truth. Even if the elevated idea of aesthetic appearance became general, it would not become so, as long as man remains so little cultivated as to abuse it; and if it became general, this would result from a culture that would prevent all abuse of it. The pursuit of independent appearance requires more power of abstraction, freedom of heart, and energy of will than man requires to shut himself up in reality; and he must have left the latter behind him if he wishes to attain to aesthetic appearance. Therefore a man would calculate very badly who took the road of the ideal to save himself that of reality. Thus reality would not have much to fear from appearance, as we understand it; but, on the other hand, appearance would have more to fear from reality. Chained to matter, man uses appearance for his purposes before he allows it a proper personality in the art of the ideal: to come to that point a complete revolution must take place in his mode of feeling, otherwise he would not be even on the way to the ideal. Consequently, when we find in man the signs of a pure and disinterested esteem, we can infer that this revolution has taken place in his nature, and that humanity has really begun in him. Signs of this kind are found even in the first and rude attempts that he makes to embellish his existence, even at the risk of making it worse in its material conditions. As soon as he begins to prefer form to substance and to risk reality for appearance (known by him to be such), the barriers of animal life fall, and he finds himself on a track that has no end.

Not satisfied with the needs of nature, he demands the superfluous. First, only the superfluous of matter, to secure his enjoyment beyond the present necessity; but afterwards he wishes a superabundance in matter, an aesthetical supplement to satisfy the impulse for the formal, to extend enjoyment beyond necessity. By piling up provisions simply for a future use, and anticipating their enjoyment in the imagination, he outsteps the limits of the present moment, but not those of time in general. He enjoys more; he does not enjoy differently. But as soon as he makes form enter into his enjoyment, and he keeps in view the forms of the objects which satisfy his desires, he has not only increased his pleasure in extent and intensity, but he has also ennobled it in mode and species.

No doubt nature has given more than is necessary to unreasoning beings; she has caused a gleam of freedom to shine even in the darkness of animal life. When the lion is not tormented by hunger, and when no wild beast challenges him to fight, his unemployed energy creates an object for himself; full of ardour, he fills the re−echoing desert with his terrible roars, and his exuberant force rejoices in itself, showing itself without an object. The insect flits about rejoicing in life in the sunlight, and it is certainly not the cry of want that makes itself heard in the melodious song of the bird; there is undeniably freedom in these movements, though it is not emancipation from want in general, but from a determinate external necessity.

The animal works, when a privation is the motor of its activity, and it plays when the plenitude of force is this motor, when an exuberant life is excited to action. Even in inanimate nature a luxury of strength and a latitude of determination are shown, which in this material sense might be styled play. The tree produces numberless germs that are abortive without developing, and it sends forth more roots, branches and leaves, organs of nutrition, than are used for the preservation of the species. Whatever this tree restores to the elements of its exuberant life, without using it, or enjoying it, may be expended by life in free and joyful movements. It is thus that nature offers in her material sphere a sort of prelude to the limitless, and that even there she suppresses partially the chains from which she will be completely emancipated in the realm of form. The constraint of superabundance or physical play, answers as a transition from the constraint of necessity, or of physical seriousness, to aesthetical play; and before shaking off, in the supreme freedom of the beautiful, the yoke of any special aim, nature already approaches, at least remotely, this independence, by the free movement which is itself its own end and means.

The imagination, like the bodily organs, has in man its free movement and its material play, a play in which, without any reference to form, it simply takes pleasure in its arbitrary power and in the absence of all hindrance. These plays of fancy, inasmuch as form is not mixed up with them, and because a free succession of images makes all their charm, though confined to man, belong exclusively to animal life, and only prove one thing—that he is delivered from all external sensuous constraint—without our being entitled to infer that there is in it an independent plastic force.

From this play of free association of ideas, which is still quite material in nature and is explained by simple natural laws, the imagination, by making the attempt of creating a free form, passes at length at a jump to the aesthetic play: I say at one leap, for quite a new force enters into action here; for here, for the first time, the legislative mind is mixed with the acts of a blind instinct, subjects the arbitrary march of the imagination to its eternal and immutable unity, causes its independent permanence to enter in that which is transitory, and its infinity in the sensuous. Nevertheless, as long as rude nature, which knows of no other law than running incessantly from change to change, will yet retain too much strength, it will oppose itself by its different caprices to this necessity; by its agitation to this permanence; by its manifold needs to this independence, and by its insatiability to this sublime simplicity. It will be also troublesome to recognise the instinct of play in its first trials, seeing that the sensuous impulsion, with its capricious humour and its violent appetites, constantly crosses. It is on that account that we see the taste, still coarse, seize that which is new and startling, the disordered, the adventurous and the strange, the violent and the savage, and fly from nothing so much as from calm and simplicity. It invents grotesque figures, it likes rapid transitions, luxurious forms, sharply marked changes, acute tones, a pathetic song. That which man calls beautiful at this time, is that which excites him, that which gives him matter; but that which excites him to give his personality to the object, that which gives matter to a possible plastic operation, for otherwise it would not be the beautiful for him. A remarkable change has therefore taken place in the form of his judgments; he searches for these objects, not because they affect him, but because they furnish him with the occasion of acting; they please him, not because they answer to a want, but because they satisfy a law, which speaks in his breast, although quite low as yet.

Soon it will not be sufficient for things to please him; he will wish to please: in the first place, it is true, only by that which belongs to him; afterwards by that which he is. That which he possesses, that which he produces, ought not merely to bear any more the traces of servitude, nor to mark out the end, simply and scrupulously, by the form. Independently of the use to which it is destined, the object ought also to reflect the enlightened intelligence which imagines it, the hand which shaped it with affection, the mind free and serene which chose it and exposed it to view. Now, the ancient German searches for more magnificent furs, for more splendid antlers of the stag, for more elegant drinking horns; and the Caledonian chooses the prettiest shells for his festivals. The arms themselves ought to be no longer only objects of terror, but also of pleasure; and the skilfully worked scabbard will not attract less attention than the homicidal edge of the sword. The instinct of play, not satisfied with bringing into the sphere of the necessary an aesthetic superabundance for the future more free, is at last completely emancipated from the bonds of duty, and the beautiful becomes of itself an object of man's exertions. He adorns himself. The free pleasure comes to take a place among his wants, and the useless soon becomes the best part of his joys. Form, which from the outside gradually approaches him, in his dwelling, his furniture, his clothing, begins at last to take possession of the man himself, to transform him, at first exteriorly, and afterwards in the interior. The disordered leaps of joy become the dance, the formless gesture is changed into an amiable and harmonious pantomime, the confused accents of feeling are developed, and begin to obey measure and adapt themselves to song. When, like the flight of cranes, the Trojan army rushes on to the field of battle with thrilling cries, the Greek army approaches in silence and with a noble and measured step. On the one side we see but the exuberance of a blind force, on the other; the triumph of form and the simple majesty of law.

Now, a nobler necessity binds the two sexes mutually, and the interests of the heart contribute in rendering durable an alliance which was at first capricious and changing like the desire that knits it. Delivered from the heavy fetters of desire, the eye, now calmer, attends to the form, the soul contemplates the soul, and the interested exchange of pleasure becomes a generous exchange of mutual inclination. Desire enlarges and rises to love, in proportion as it sees humanity dawn in its object; and, despising the vile triumphs gained by the senses, man tries to win a nobler victory over the will. The necessity of pleasing subjects the powerful nature to the gentle laws of taste; pleasure may be stolen, but love must be a gift. To obtain this higher recompense, it is only through the form and not through matter that it can carry on the contest. It must cease to act on feeling as a force, to appear in the intelligence as a simple phenomenon; it must respect liberty, as it is liberty it wishes to please. The beautiful reconciles the contrast of different natures in its simplest and purest expression. It also reconciles the eternal contrast of the two sexes, in the whole complex framework of society, or at all events it seeks to do so; and, taking as its model the free alliance it has knit between manly strength and womanly gentleness, it strives to place in harmony, in the moral world, all the elements of gentleness and of violence. Now, at length, weakness becomes sacred, and an unbridled strength disgraces; the injustice of nature is corrected by the generosity of chivalrous manners. The being whom no power can make tremble, is disarmed by the amiable blush of modesty, and tears extinguish a vengeance that blood could not have quenched. Hatred itself hears the delicate voice of honour, the conqueror's sword spares the disarmed enemy, and a hospitable hearth smokes for the stranger on the dreaded hill–side where murder alone awaited him before.

In the midst of the formidable realm of forces, and of the sacred empire of laws, the aesthetic impulse of form creates by degrees a third and a joyous realm, that of play and of the appearance, where she emancipates man from fetters, in all his relations, and from all that is named constraint, whether physical or moral.

If in the dynamic state of rights men mutually move and come into collision as forces, in the moral (ethical) state of duties, man opposes to man the majesty of the laws, and chains down his will. In this realm of the beautiful or the aesthetic state, man ought to appear to man only as a form, and an object of free play. To give freedom through freedom is the fundamental law of this realm.

The dynamic state can only make society simply possible by subduing nature through nature; the moral (ethical) state can only make it morally necessary by submitting the will of the individual to the general will. The aesthetic state alone can make it real, because it carries out the will of all through the nature of the individual. If necessity alone forces man to enter into society, and if his reason engraves on his soul social principles, it is beauty only that can give him a social character; taste alone brings harmony into society, because it creates harmony in the individual. All other forms of perception divide the man, because they are based exclusively either in the sensuous or in the spiritual part of his being. It is only the perception of beauty that makes of him an entirety, because it demands the co-operation of his two natures. All other forms of communication divide society, because they apply exclusively either to the receptivity or to the private activity of its members, and therefore to what distinguishes men one from the other. The aesthetic communication alone unites society, because it applies to what is common to all its members. We only enjoy the pleasures of sense as individuals, without the nature of the race in us sharing in it; accordingly, we cannot generalise our individual pleasures, because we cannot generalise our individuality. We enjoy the pleasures of knowledge as a race, dropping the Individual in our judgment; but we cannot generalise the pleasures of the understanding, because we cannot eliminate individuality from the judgments of others as we do from our own. Beauty alone can we enjoy both as individuals and as a race, that is, as representing a race. Good appertaining to sense can only make one person happy, because it is founded on inclination, which is always exclusive; and it can only make a man partially happy, because his real personality does not share in it. Absolute good can only render a man happy conditionally, for truth is only the reward of abnegation, and a pure heart alone has faith in a pure will. Beauty alone confers happiness on all, and under its influence every being forgets that he is limited.

Taste does not suffer any superior or absolute authority, and the sway of beauty is extended over appearance. It extends up to the seat of reason's supremacy, suppressing all that is material. It extends down to where sensuous impulse rules with blind compulsion, and form is undeveloped. Taste ever maintains its power on these remote borders, where legislation is taken from it. Particular desires must renounce their egotism, and the agreeable, otherwise tempting the senses, must in matters of taste adorn the mind with the attractions of grace.

Duty and stern necessity must change their forbidding tone, only excused by resistance, and do homage to nature by a nobler trust in her. Taste leads our knowledge from the mysteries of science into the open expanse of common sense, and changes a narrow scholasticism into the common property of the human race. Here the highest genius must leave its particular elevation, and make itself familiar to the comprehension even of a child. Strength must let the Graces bind it, and the arbitrary lion must yield to the reins of love. For this purpose taste throws a veil over physical necessity, offending a free mind by its coarse nudity, and dissimulating our degrading parentage with matter by a delightful illusion of freedom. Mercenary art itself rises from the dust; and the bondage of the bodily, at its magic touch, falls off from the inanimate and animate. In the aesthetic state the most slavish tool is a free citizen, having the same rights as the noblest; and the intellect which shapes the mass to its intent must consult it concerning its destination. Consequently in the realm of aesthetic appearance, the idea of equality is realised, which the political zealot would gladly see carried out socially. It has often been said that perfect politeness is only found near a throne. If thus restricted in the material, man has, as elsewhere appears, to find compensation in the ideal world.

Does such a state of beauty in appearance exist, and where? It must be in every finely harmonised soul; but as a fact, only in select circles, like the pure ideal of the church and state—in circles where manners are not formed by the empty imitations of the foreign, but by the very beauty of nature; where man passes through all sorts of complications in all simplicity and innocence, neither forced to trench on another's freedom to preserve his own, nor to show grace at the cost of dignity.

FUNDAMENTAL PRINCIPLES OF THE METAPHYSIC OF MORALS

BY IMMANUEL KANT

TRANSLATED BY T. K. ABBOTT

INTRODUCTORY NOTE

Immanuel Kant was born in Konigsberg, East Prussia, April 22, 1724, the son of a saddler of Scottish descent. The family was pietist, and the future philosopher entered the university of his native city in 1740, with a view to studying theology. He developed, however, a many-sided interest in learning, and his earlier publications were in the field of speculative physics. After the close of his period of study at the university he became a private tutor; then In 1755, privat-docent; and in 1770, professor. During the first eleven years of his professorship Kant published little, spending his energies in the meditation that was to result in the philosophical system of which the first part was given to the world in his "Critique of Pure Reason" in 1781. From that time till near the end of the century he issued volume after volume; yet when he died In 1804 he regarded his statement of his system as fragmentary.

Of the enormous importance of Kant in the history of philosophy, no idea can be given here. The important document which follows was published in 1785, and forms the basis of the moral system on which he erected the whole structure of belief in God, Freedom, and Immortality. Kant is often difficult and obscure, and became more so as he grew older; but the present treatise can be followed, in its main lines, by any intelligent person who is interested enough in the fundamental problems of human life and conduct to give it serious and concentrated attention. To such a reader the subtle yet clear distinctions, and the lofty and rigorous principles of action, which it lays down, will prove an intellectual and moral tonic such as hardly any other modern writer affords.

PREFACE

Ancient Greek philosophy was divided into three sciences: Physics, Ethics, and Logic. This division is perfectly suitable to the nature of the thing, and the only improvement that can be made in it is to add the principle on which it is based, so that we may both satisfy ourselves of its completeness, and also be able to determine correctly the necessary subdivisions.

All rational knowledge is either material or formal: the former considers some object, the latter is concerned only with the form of the understanding and of the reason itself, and with the universal laws of thought in general without distinction of its objects. Formal philosophy is called Logic. Material philosophy, however, which has to do with determinate objects and the laws to which they are subject, is again two-fold; for these laws are either laws of nature or of freedom. The science of the former is Physics, that of the latter, Ethics; they are also called natural philosophy and moral philosophy respectively.

Logic cannot have any empirical part; that is, a part in which the universal and necessary laws of thought should rest on grounds taken from experience; otherwise it would not be logic, i. e. a canon for the understanding or the reason, valid for all thought, and capable of demonstration. Natural and moral philosophy, on the contrary, can each have their empirical part, since the former has to determine the laws of nature as an object of experience; the latter the laws of the human will, so far as it is affected by nature: the former, however, being laws according to which everything does happen; the latter, laws according to which everything ought to happen. [Footnote: The word "law" is here used in two different senses, on which see Whately's Logic, Appendix, Art. "Law."] Ethics, however, must also consider the conditions under which what ought to happen frequently does not.

We may call all philosophy empirical, so far as it is based on grounds of experience: on the other hand, that which delivers its doctrines from a priori principles alone we may call pure philosophy. When the latter is merely formal it is logic; if it is restricted to definite objects of the understanding it is metaphysic.

In this way there arises the idea of a two–fold metaphysic—a metaphysic of nature and a metaphysic of morals. Physics will thus have an empirical and also a rational part. It is the same with Ethics; but here the empirical part might have the special name of practical anthropology, the name morality being appropriated to the rational part.

All trades, arts, and handiworks have gained by division of labour, namely, when, instead of one man doing everything, each confines himself to a certain kind of work distinct from others in the treatment it requires, so as to be able to perform it With greater facility and. in the greatest perfection. Where the different kinds of work are not so distinguished and divided, where everyone is a jack–of–all–trades, there manufactures remain still in the greatest barbarism. It might deserve to be considered whether pure philosophy in all its parts does not require a man specially devoted to it, and whether it would not be better for the whole business of science if those who, to please the tastes of the public, are wont to blend the rational and empirical elements together, mixed in all sorts of proportions unknown to themselves, and who call themselves independent thinkers, giving the name of minute philosophers to those who apply themselves to the rational part only—if these, I say, were warned not to carry on two employments together which differ widely in the treatment they demand, for each of which perhaps a special talent is required, and the combination of which in one person only produces bunglers. But I only ask here whether the nature of science does not require that we should always carefully separate the empirical from the rational part, and prefix to Physics proper (or empirical physics) a metaphysic of nature, and to practical anthropology a metaphysic of morals, which must be carefully cleared of everything empirical, so that we may know how much can be accomplished by pure reason in both cases, and from whnat sources it draws this its a priori teaching, and that whether the latter inquiry is conducted by all moralists (whose name is legion), or only by some who feel a calling thereto.

As my concern here is with moral philosophy, I limit the question suggested to this: Whether it is not of the utmost necessity to construct a pure moral philosophy, perfectly cleared of everything which is only empirical, and which belongs to anthropology? for that such a philosophy must be possible is evident from the common idea of duty and of the moral laws. Every one must admit that if a law is to have moral force, i. e. to be the basis of an obligation, it must carry with it absolute necessity; that, for example, the precept, "Thou shalt not lie," is not valid for men alone, as if other rational beings had no need to observe it; and so with all the other moral laws properly so called; that, therefore, the basis of obligation must not be sought in the nature of man, or in the circumstanced in the world in which he is placed, but a priori simply in the conceptions of pure reason; and although any other precept which is founded on principles of mere experience may be in certain respects universal, yet in as far as it rests even in the least degree on an empirical basis, perhaps only as to a motive, such a precept, while it may be a practical rule, can never be called a moral law.

Thus not only are moral laws with their principles essentially distinguished from every other kind of practical knowledge in which there is anything empirical, but all moral philosophy rests wholly on its pure part. When applied to man, it does not borrow the least thing from the knowledge of man himself (anthropology), but gives laws a priori to him as a rational being. No doubt these laws require a judgment sharpened by experience, in order on the one hand to distinguish in what cases they are applicable, and on the other to procure for them access to the will of the man, and effectual influence on conduct; since man is acted on by so many inclinations that, though capable of the idea of a practical pure reason, he is not so easily able to make it effective in concrete in his life.

A metaphysic of morals is therefore indispensably necessary, not merely for speculative reasons, in order to investigate the sources of the practical principles which are to be found a priori in our reason, but also because morals themselves are liable to all sorts of corruption, as long as we are without that clue and supreme canon by which to estimate them correctly. For in order that an action should be morally good, it is not enough that it conform to the moral law, but it must also be done for the sake of the law, otherwise that conformity is only very contingent and uncertain; since a principle which is not moral, although it may now and then produce actions conformable to the law, will also often produce actions which contradict it. Now it is only in a pure philosophy that we can look for the moral law in its purity and genuineness (and, in a practical matter, this is of the utmost consequence): we must, therefore, begin with pure philosophy (metaphysic), and without it there cannot be any moral philosophy at all. That which mingles these pure principles with the empirical does not deserve the name of philosophy (for what distinguishes philosophy from common rational knowledge is, that it treats in separate sciences what the latter only comprehends confusedly); much less does it deserve that of moral philosophy, since by this confusion it even spoils the purity of morals themselves, and counteracts its own end.

Let it not be thought, however, that what is here demanded is already extant in the propaedeutic prefixed by the celebrated Wolf [Footnote: Johann Christian Von Wolf (1679–1728) was the author of treatises on philosophy, mathematics, which were for a long time the standard text–books in the German Universities. His philosophy was founded on that of Leibnitz.] to his moral philosophy, namely, his so–called general practical philosophy, and that, therefore, we have not to strike into an entirely new field. Just because it was to be a general practical philosophy, it has not taken into consideration a will of any particular kind–say one which should be determined solely from a priori principles without any empirical motives, and which we might call a pure will, but volition in general, with all the actions and conditions which belong to it in this general signification. By this it is distinguished from a metaphysic of morals, just as general logic, which treats of the acts and canons of thought in general, is distinguished from transcendental philosophy, which treats of the particular acts and canons of pure thought, i. e. that whose cognitions are altogether a priori. For the metaphysic of morals has to examine the idea and the principles of a possible pure will, and not the acts and conditions of human volition generally, which for the most part are drawn from psychology. It is true that moral laws and duty are spoken of in the general practical philosophy (contrary indeed to all fitness). But this is no objection, for in this respect, also the authors of that science remain true to their idea of it; they do not distinguish the motives which are prescribed as such by reason alone altogether a priori, and which are properly moral, from the empirical motives which the understanding raises to general conceptions merely by comparison of experiences; but without noticing the difference of their sources, and looking on them all as homogeneous, they consider only their greater or less amount. It is in this way they frame their notion of obligation, which though anything but moral, is all that can be asked for in a philosophy which passes no judgment at all on the origin of all possible practical concepts, whether they are a priori, or only a posteriori.

Intending to publish hereafter a metaphysic of morals, I issue in the first instance these fundamental principles. Indeed there is properly no other foundation for it than the critical examination of a pure practical reason; just as that of metaphysics is the critical examination of the pure speculative reason, already published. But in the first place the former is not so absolutely necessary as the latter, because in moral concerns human reason can easily be brought to a high degree of correctness and completeness, even in the commonest understanding, while on the contrary in its theoretic but pure use it is wholly dialectical; and in the second place if the critique of a pure practical reason is to be complete, it must be possible at the same time to show its identity with the speculative reason in a common principle, for it can ultimately be only one and the same reason which has to be distinguished merely in its application. I could not, however, bring it to such completeness here, without introducing considerations of a wholly different kind, which would be perplexing to the reader. On this account I have adopted the title of Fundamental Principles of the Metaphysic of Morals, instead of that of a Critical Examination of the pure practical Reason.

But in the third place, since a metaphysic of morals, in spite of the; discouraging title, is yet capable of being presented in a popular form, and one adapted to the common understanding, I find it useful to separate from it this preliminary treatise on its fundamental principles, in order that I may not hereafter have need to introduce these necessarily subtle discussions into a book of a more simple character.

The present treatise is, however, nothing more than the investigation and establishment of the supreme principle of morality, and this alone constitutes a study complete in itself, and one which ought to be kept apart from every other moral investigation. No doubt my conclusions on this weighty question, which has hitherto been very unsatisfactorily examined, would receive much light from the application of the same principle to the whole system, and would be greatly confirmed by the adequacy which it exhibits throughout; but I must forego this advantage, which indeed would be after all more gratifying than useful, since the easy applicability of a principle and its apparent adequacy give no very certain proof of its soundness, but rather inspire a certain partiality, which prevents us from examining and estimating it strictly in itself, and without regard to consequences.

I have adopted in this work the method which I think most suitable, proceeding analytically from common knowledge to the determination of its ultimate principle, and again descending synthetically from the examination of this principle and its sources to the common knowledge in which we find it employed. The division will, therefore, be as follows:—

1. First section.—Transition from the common rational knowledge of morality to the philosophical.

2. Second section.—Transition from popular moral philosophy to the metaphysic of morals.

3. Third section.—Final step from the metaphysic of morals to the critique of the pure practical reason.

FUNDAMENTAL PRINCIPLES OF THE METAPHYSIC OF MORALS

FIRST SECTION. TRANSITION FROM THE COMMON RATIONAL KNOWLEDGE OF MORALITY TO THE PHILOSOPHICAL

Nothing can possibly be conceived in the world, of even out of it, which can be called good without qualification, except a Good Will Intelligence, wit, judgment, and the other talents of the mind, however they may be named, or courage, resolution, perseverance, as qualities of temperament, are undoubtedly good and desirable in many respects; but these gifts of nature may also become extremely bad and mischievous if the will which is to make use of them, and which, therefore, constitutes what is called character, is not good. It is the same with the gifts of fortune. Power, riches, honour, even health, and the general well–being and contentment with one's condition which is called happiness, inspire pride, and often presumption, if there is not a good will to correct the influence of these on the mind, and with this also to rectify the whole principle of acting, and adapt it to its end. The sight of a Deing who is not adorned with a single feature of a pure and good will, enjoying unbroken prosperity, can never give pleasure to an impartial rational spectator. Thus a good will appears to constitute the indispensable condition even of being worthy of happiness.

There are even some qualities which are of service to this good will itself, and may facilitate its action, yet which have no intrinsic unconditional value, but always presuppose a good will, and this qualifies the esteem that we justly have for them, and does not permit us to regard them as absolutely good. Moderation in the affections and passions, self–control and calm deliberation are not only good in many respects, but even seem to constitute part of the intrinsic worth of the person; but they are far from deserving to be called good without qualification, although they have been so unconditionally praised by the ancients. For without the principles of a good will, they may become extremely bad, and the coolness of a villain not only makes him far more dangerous, but also directly makes him more abominable in our eyes than he would have been without it.

A good will is good not because of what it performs or effects, not by its aptness for the attainment of some proposed end, but simply by virtue of the volition, that is, it is good in itself, and considered by itself is to be esteemed much higher than all that can be brought about by it in favour of any inclination, nay, even of the sum total of all inclinations. Even if it should happen that, owing to special disfavour of fortune, or the niggardly provision of a stepmotherly nature, this will should wholly lack power to accomplish its purpose, if with its greatest efforts it should yet achieve nothing, and there should remain only the good will (not, to be sure, a mere wish, but the summoning of all means in our power), then, like a jewel, it would still shine by its own light, as a thing which has its whole value in itself. Its usefulness or fruitfulness can neither add to nor take away anything from this value. It would be, as it were, only the setting to enable us to handle it the more conveniently in common commerce, or to attract to it the attention of those who are not yet connoisseurs, but not to recommend it to true connoisseurs, or to determine its value.

There is, however, something so strange in this idea of the absolute value of the mere will, in which no account is taken of its utility, that notwithstanding the thorough assent of even common reason to the idea, yet a suspicion must arise that it may perhaps really be the product of mere high–flown fancy, and that we may have misunderstood the purpose of nature in assigning reason as the governor of our will. Therefore we will examine this idea from this point of view.

In the physical constitution of an organized being, that is, a being adapted suitably to the purposes of life, we assume it as a fundamental principle that no organ for any purpose will be found but what is also the fittest and best adapted for that purpose. Now in a being which has reason and a will, if the proper object of nature were its conservation, its welfare, in a word, its happiness, then nature would have hit upon a very bad arrangement in selecting the reason of the creature to carry out this purpose. For all the actions which the creature has to perform with a view to this purpose, and the whole rule of its conduct, would be far more surely prescribed to it by instinct, and that end would have been attained thereby much more certainly than it ever can be by reason. Should reason have been communicated to this favoured creature over and above, it must only have served it to contemplate the happy constitution of its nature, to admire it, to congratulate itself thereon, and to feel thankful for it to the beneficent cause, but not that it should subject its desires to that weak and delusive guidance, and meddle bunglingly with the purpose of nature. In a word, nature would have taken care that reason should not break forth into practical exercise, nor have the presumption, with its weak insight, to think out for itself the plan of happiness, and of the means of attaining it. Nature would not only have taken on herself the choice of the ends, but also of the means, and with wise foresight would have entrusted both to instinct.

And, in fact, we find that the more a cultivated reason applies itself with deliberate purpose to the enjoyment of life and happiness, so much the more does the man fail of true satisfaction. And from this circumstance there arises in many, if they are candid enough to confess it, a certain degree of misology, that is, hatred of reason, especially in the case of those who are most experienced in the use of it, because after calculating all the advantages they derive, I do not say from the invention of all the arts of common luxury, but even from the sciences (which seem to them to be after all only a luxury of the understanding), they find that they have, in fact, only brought more trouble on their shoulders, rather than gained in happiness; and they end by envying, rather than despising, the more common stamp of men who keep closer to the guidance of mere instinct, and do not allow their reason much influence on their conduct. And this we must admit, that the judgment of those who would very much lower the lofty eulogies of the advantages which reason gives us in regard to the happiness and satisfaction of life, or who would even reduce them below zero, is by no means morose or ungrateful to the goodness with which the world is governed, but that there lies at the root of these judgments the idea that our existence has a different and far nobler end, for which, and not for happiness, reason is properly intended, and which must, therefore, be regarded as the supreme condition to which the private ends of man must, for the most part, be postponed. For as reason is not competent to guide the will with certainty in regard to its objects and the satisfaction of all our wants (which it to some extent even multiplies), this being an end to which an implanted instinct would have led with much greater certainty; and since, nevertheless, reason is imparted to us as a practical faculty, i. e. as one which is to have influence on the will, therefore, admitting that nature generally in the distribution of her capacities has adapted the means to the end, its true destination must be to produce a will, not merely good as a means to something else, but good in itself, for which reason was absolutely necessary. This will then, though not indeed the sole and complete good, must be the supreme good and the condition of every other, even of the desire of happiness. Under these circumstances, there is nothing inconsistent with the wisdom of nature in the fact that the cultivation of the reason, which is requisite for the first and unconditional purpose, does in many ways interfere, at least in this life, with the attainment of the second, which is always conditional, namely, happiness. Nay, it may even reduce it to nothing, without nature thereby failing of her purpose. For reason recognises the establishment of a good will as its highest practical destination, and in attaining this purpose is capable only of a satisfaction of its own proper kind, namely, that from the attainment of an end, which end again is determined by reason only, notwithstanding that this may involve many a disappointment to the ends of inclination.

We have then to develop the notion of a will which deserves to be highly esteemed for itself, and is good without a view to anything further, a notion which exists already in the sound natural understanding, requiring rather to be cleared up than to be taught, and which in estimating the value of our actions always takes the first place, and constitutes the condition of all the rest. In order to do this we will take the notion of duty, which includes that of a good will, although implying certain subjectve restrictions and hindrances. These, however, far from concealing it, or rendering it unrecognisable, rather bring it out by contrast, and make it shine forth so much the brighter.

I omit here all actions which are already recognised as inconsistent with duty, although they may be useful for this or that purpose, for with these the question whether they are done from duty cannot arise at all, since they even conflict with it. I also set aside those actions which really conform to duty, but to which men have no direct inclination, performing them because they are impelled thereto by some other inclination. For in this case we can readily distinguish whether the action which agrees with duty is done from duty, or from a selfish view. It is much harder to make this distinction when the action accords with duty, and the subject has besides a direct inclination to it. For example, it is always a matter of duty that a dealer should not overcharge an inexperienced purchaser, and wherever there is much commerce the prudent tradesman does not overcharge, but keeps a fixed price for everyone, so that a child buys of him as well as any other. Men are thus honestly served; but this is not enough to make us believe that the tradesman has so acted from duty and from principles of honesty: his own advantage required it; it is out of the question in this case to suppose that he might besides have a direct inclination in favour of the buyers, so that, as it were, from love he should give no advantage to one over another. Accordingly the action was done neither from duty nor from direct inclination, but merely with a selfish view.

On the other hand, it is a duty to maintain one's life; and, in addition, everyone has also a direct inclination to do so. But on this account the often anxious care which most men take for it has no intrinsic worth, and their maxim has no moral import. They preserve their life as duty requires, no doubt, but not because duty requires. On the other hand, if adversity and hopeless sorrow have completely taken away the relish for life; if the unfortunate one, strong in mind, indignant at his fate rather than desponding or dejected, wishes for death, and yet preserves his life without loving it—not from inclination or fear, but from duty—then his maxim has a moral worth.

To be beneficent when we can is a duty; and besides this, there are many minds so sympathetically constituted that, without any other motive of vanity or self-interest, they find a pleasure in spreading joy around them and can take delight in the satisfaction of others so far as it is their own work. But I maintain that in such a case an action of this kind, however proper, however amiable it may be, has nevertheless no true moral worth, but is on a level with other inclinations, e. g. the inclination to honour, which, if it is happily directed to that which is in fact of public utility and accordant with duty, and consequently honourable, deserves praise and encouragement, but not esteem. For the maxim lacks the moral import, namely, that such actions be done from duty, not from inclination. Put the case that the mind of that philanthropist were clouded by sorrow of his own, extinguishing all sympathy with the lot of others, and that while he still has the power to benefit others in distress, he is not touched oy their trouble because he is absorbed with his own; and now suppose that he tears himself out of this dead insensibility, and performs the action without any inclination to it, but simply from duty, then first has his action its genuine moral worth. Further still; if nature has put little sympathy in the heart of this or that man; if he, supposed to be an upright man, is by temperament cold and indifferent to the sufferings of others, perhaps because in respect of his own he is provided with the special gift of patience and fortitude, and supposes, or even requires, that others should have the same—and such a man would certainly not be the meanest product of nature—but if nature had not specially framed him for a philanthropist, would he not still find in himself a source from whence to give himself a far higher worth than that of a good-natured temperament could be? Unquestionably. It is just in this that the moral worth of the character is brought out which is incomparably the highest of all, namely, that he is beneficent, not from inclination, but from duty.

To secure one's own happiness is a duty, at least indirectly; for discontent with one's condition, under a pressure of many anxieties and amidst unsatisfied wants, might easily become a great temptation to transgression of duty. But here again, without looking to duty, all men have already the strongest and most intimate inclination to happiness, because it is just in this idea that all inclinations are combined in one total. But the precept of happiness is often of such a sort that it greatly interferes with some inclinations, and yet a man cannot form any definite and certain conception of the sum of satisfaction of all of them which is called happiness. It is not then to be wandered at that a single inclination, definite both as to what it promises and as to the time within which it can be gratified, is often able to overcome such a fluctuating idea, and that a gouty patient, for instance, can choose to enjoy what he likes, and to suffer what he may, since, according to his calculation, on this occasion at least, he has [only] not sacrificed the enjoyment of the present moment to a possibly mistaken expectation of a happiness which is supposed to be found in health. But even in this case, if the general desire for happiness did not influence his will, and supposing that in his particular case health was not a necessary element in this calculation, there yet remains in this, sas in all other cases, this law, namely, that he should promote his happiness not from inclination but from duty, land by this would his conduct first acquire true moral worth.

It is in this manner, undoubtedly, that we are to understand those passages of Scripture also in which we are commanded to love our neighbour, even our enemy. For love, as an affection, cannot be commanded, but beneficence for duty's sake may; even though we are not impelled to it by any inclination—nay, are even repelled by a natural and unconquerable aversion. This is practical love, and not pathological—a love which is seated in the will, and not in the propensions of sense—in principles of action and not of tender sympathy; and it is this love alone which can be commanded.

The second [Footnote: The first proposition was that to have moral worth an action must be done from duty.] proposition is: That an action done from duty derives its moral worth, not from the purpose which is to be attained by it, but from the maxim by which it is determined, and therefore does not depend on the realization of the object of the action, but merely on the principle of volition by which the action has taken place, without regard to any object of desire. It is clear from what precedes that the purposes which we may have in view in our actions, or their effects regarded as ends and springs of the will, cannot give to actions any unconditional or moral worth. In what, then, can their worth lie, if it is not to consist in the will and in reference to its expected effect? It cannot lie anywhere but in the principle of the will without regard to the ends which can be attained by the action. For the will stands between its a priori principle, which is formal, and its a posteriori spring, which is material, as between two roads, and as it must be determined by something, it follows that it must be determined by the formal principle of volition when an action is done from duty, in which case every material principle has been withdrawn from it.

The third proposition, which is a consequence of the two preceding, I would express thus: Duty is the necessity "of acting from respect for the law." I may have inclination for an object as the effect of my proposed action, but I cannot have respect for it, just for this reason, that it is an effect and not an energy of will. Similarly, I cannot have respect for inclination, whether my own or another's; I can at most, if my own, approve it; if another's, sometimes even love it; i.e. look on it as favourable to my own interest. It is only what is connected with my will as a principle, by no means as an effect—what does not subserve my inclination, but overpowers it, or at least in case of choice excludes it from its calculation—in other words, simply the law of itself, which can be an object of respect, and hence a command. Now an action done from duty must wholly exclude the influence of inclination, and with it every object of the will, so that nothing remains which can determine the will except objectively the LAW, and subjectively PURE RESPECT for this practical law, and consequently the maxim [Footnote: A MAXIM is the subjective principle of volition. The objective principle (i. e. that which would also serve subjectively as a practical principle to all rational beings if reason had full power over the faculty of desire) is the practical LAW.] that I should follow this law even to the thwarting of all my inclinations.

Thus the moral worth of an action does not lie in the effect expected from it, nor in any principle of action which requires to borrow its motive from this expected effect. For all these effects—agreeableness of one's condition, and even the promotion of the happiness of others—could have been also brought about by other causes, so that for this there would have been no need of the will of a rational being; whereas it is in this alone that the supreme and unconditional good can be found. The pre-eminent good which we call moral can therefore consist in nothing else than THE CONCEPTION OF LAW in itself, WHICH CERTAINLY IS ONLY POSSIBLE IN A RATIONAL BEING, in so far as this conception, and not the expected effect, determines the will. This is a good which is already present in the person who acts accordingly, and we have not to wait for it to appear first in the result. [Footnote: It might be here objected to me that I take refuge behind the word RESPECT in an obscure feeling, instead of giving a distinct solution of the question by a concept of the reason. But although respect is a feeling, it is not a feeling RECEIVED through influence, but is SELF–WROUGHT by a rational concept, and, therefore, is specifically distinct from all feelings of the former kind, which may be referred either to inclination or fear, What I recognise immediately as a law for me, I recognise with respect. This merely signifies the consciousness that my will is SUBORDINATE to a law, without the intervention of other influences on my sense. The immediate determination of the will by the law, and the consciousness of this is called RESPECT, so that this is regarded as an EFFECT of the law on the subject, and not as the CAUSE of it. Respect is properly the conception of a worth which thwarts my self–love. Accordingly it is something which is considered neither as am object of inclination nor of fear, although it has something analogous to both. The OBJECT of respect is the LAW only, and that, the law which we impose on OURSELVES, and yet recognise as necessary in itself. As a law, we are subjected to it without consulting self–love; as imposed by us on ourselves, it is a result of our will. In the former aspect it has an analogy to fear, in the latter to inclination. Respect for a person is properly only respect for the law (of honesty, of which he gives us an example. Since we also look on the improvement of our talents as a duty, we consider that we see in a person of talents, as it were, the EXAMPLE OF A LAW (viz. to become like him in this by exercise), and this constitutes our respect. All so–called moral INTEREST consists simply in RESPECT for the law.]

But what sort of law can that be, the conception of which must determine the will, even without paying any regard to the effect expected from it, in order that this will may be called good absolutely and without qualification? As I have deprived the will of every impulse which could arise to it from obedience to any law, there remains nothing but the universal conformity of its actions to law in general, which alone is to serve the will as a principle, i. e. I am never to act otherwise than so THAT *I* COULD ALSO WILL THAT MY MAXIM SHOULD BECOME A UNIVERSAL LAW. Here now, it is the simple conformity to law in general, without assuming any particular law applicable to certain actions, that serves the will as its principle, and must so serve it, if duty is not to be a vain delusion and a chimerical notion. The common reason of men in its practical judgments perfectly coincides with this, and always has in view the principle here suggested. Let the question be, for example: May I when in distress make a promise with the intention not to keep it? I readily distinguish here between the two significations which the question may have. Whether it is prudent, or whether it is right, to make a false promise. The former may undoubtedly often be the case. I see clearly indeed that it is not enough to extricate myself from a present difficulty by means of this subterfuge, but it must be well considered whether there may not hereafter spring from this lie much greater inconvenience than that from which I now free myself, and as, with all my supposed CUNNING, the consequences cannot be so easily foreseen but that credit once lost may be much more injurious to me than any mischief which I seek to avoid at present, it should be considered whether it would not be more prudent to act herein according to a universal maxim, and to make it a habit to promise nothing except with the intention of keeping it. But it is soon clear to me that such a maxim will still only be based on the fear of consequences. Now it is a wholly different thing to be truthful from duty, and to be so from apprehension of injurious consequences. In the first case, the very notion of the action already implies a law for me; in the second case, I must first look about elsewhere to see what results may be combined with it which would affect myself. For to deviate from the principle of duty is beyond all doubt wicked; but to be unfaithful to my maxim of prudence may often be very advantageous to me, although to abide by it is certainly safer. The shortest way, however, and an unerring one, to discover the answer to this question whether a lying promise is consistent with duty, is to ask myself, Should I be content that my maxim (to extricate myself from difficulty by a false promise) should hold good as a universal law, for myself as well as for others? and should I be able to say to myself, "Every one may make a deceitful promise when he finds himself in a difficulty from which he cannot otherwise extricate himself"? Then I presently become aware that while I can will the lie, I can by no means will that lying should be a universal law. For with such a law there would be no promises at all, since it would be in vain to allege my intention in regard to my future actions to those who would not believe this allegation, or if they overhastily did so, would pay me back in my own coin. Hence my maxim, as soon as it should be made a universal law, would necessarily destroy itself.

I do not, therefore, need any far–reaching penetration to discern what I have to do in order that my will may be morally good. Inexperienced in the course of the world, incapable of being prepared for all its contingencies, I only ask myself: Canst thou also will that thy maxim should be a universal law? If not, then it must be rejected, and that not because of a disadvantage accruing from it to myself or even to others, but because it cannot enter as a principle into a possible universal legislation, and reason extorts from me immediate respect for such legislation. I do not indeed as yet discern on what this respect is based (this the philosopher may inquire), but at least I understand this, that it is an estimation of the worth which far outweighs all worth of what is recommended by inclination, and that the necessity of acting from pure respect for the practical law is what constitutes duty, to which every other motive must give place, because it is the condition of a will being good in itself, and the worth of such a will is above everything.

Thus, then, without quitting the moral knowledge of common human reason, we have arrived at its principle. And although, no doubt, common men do not conceive it in such an abstract and universal form, yet they always have it really before their eyes, and use it as the standard of their decision. Here it would be easy to show how, with this compass in hand, men are well able to distinguish, in every case that occurs, what is good, what bad, conformably to duty or inconsistent with it, if, without in the least teaching them anything new, we only, like Socrates, direct their attention to the principle they themselves employ; and that therefore we do not need science and philosophy to know what we should do to be honest and good, yea, even wise and virtuous. Indeed we might well have conjectured beforehand that the knowledge of what every man is bound to do, and therefore also to know, would be within the reach of every man, even the commonest. [Footnote: Compare the note to the Preface to the Critique of the Practical Reason, p. 111. A specimen of Kant's proposed application of the Socratic method may be found in Mr. Semple'a translation of the Metaphysic of Ethics, p. 290.] Here we cannot forbear admiration when we see how great an advantage the practical judgment has over the theoretical in the common understanding of men. In the latter, if common reason ventures to depart from the laws of experience and from the perceptions of the senses it falls into mere inconceivabilities and self–contradictions, at least into chaos of uncertainty, obscurity, and instability. But in the practical sphere it is just when the common understanding excludes all sensible springs from practical laws that its power of judgment begins to show itself to advantage. It then becomes even subtle, whether it be that it chicanes with its own conscience or with other claims respecting what is to be called right, or whether it desires for its own instruction to determine honestly the worth of actions; and, in the latter case, it may even have as good a hope of hitting the mark as any philosopher whatever can promise himself. Nay, it is almost more sure of doing so, because the philosopher cannot have any other principle, while he may easily perplex his judgment by a multitude of considerations foreign to the matter, and so turn aside from the right way. Would it not therefore be wiser in moral concerns to acquiesce in the judgment of common reason or at most only to call in philosophy for the purpose of rendering the system of morals more complete and intelligible, and its rules more convenient for use (especially for disputation), but not so as to draw off the common understanding from its happy simplicity, or to bring it by means of philosophy into a new path of inquiry and instruction?

Innocence is indeed a glorious thing, only, on the other hand, it is very sad that it cannot well maintain itself, and is easily seduced. On this account even wisdom—which otherwise consists more in conduct than in knowledge—yet has need of science, not in order to learn from it, but to secure for its precepts admission and permanence. Against all the commands of duty which reason represents to man as so deserving of respect, he feels in himself a powerful counterpoise in his wants and inclinations, the entire satisfaction of which he sums up under the name of happiness. Now reason issues its commands unyieldingly, without promising anything to the inclinations, and, as it were, with disregard and contempt for these claims, which are so impetuous, and at the same time so plausible, and which will not allow themselves to be suppressed by any command. Hence there arises a natural dialectic, i. e. a disposition, to argue against these strict laws of duty and to question their validity, or at least their purity and strictness; and, if possible, to make them more accordant with our wishes and inclinations, that is to say, to corrupt them at their very source, and entirely to destroy their worth—a thing which even common practical reason cannot ultimately call good.

Thus is the common reason of man compelled to go out of its sphere, and to take a step into the field of a practical philosophy, not to satisfy any speculative want (which never occurs to it as long as it is content to be mere sound reason), but even on practical grounds, in order to attain in it information and clear instruction respecting the source of its principle, and the correct determination of it in opposition to the maxims which are based on wants and inclinations, so that it may escape from the perplexity of opposite claims, and not run the risk of losing all genuine moral principles through the equivocation into which it easily falls. Thus, when practical reason cultivates itself, there insensibly arises in it a dialectic which forces it to seek aid in philosophy, just as happens to it in its theoretic use; and in this case, therefore, as well as in the other, it will find rest nowhere but in a thorough critical examination of our reason.

SECOND SECTION. TRANSITION FROM POPULAR MORAL PHILOSOPHY TO THE METAPHYSIC OF MORALS

If we have hitherto drawn our notion of duty from the common use of our practical reason, it is by no means to be inferred that we have treated it as an empirical notion. On the contrary, if we attend to the experience of men's conduct, we meet frequent and, as we ourselves allow, just complaints that one cannot find a single certain example of the disposition to act from pure duty. Although many things are done in conformity with what duty prescribes, it is nevertheless always doubtful whether they are done strictly from duty, so as to have a moral worth. Hence there have, at all times, been philosophers who have altogether denied that this disposition actually exists at all in human actions, and have ascribed everything to a more or less refined self–love. Not that they have on that account questioned the soundness of the conception of morality; on the contrary, they spoke with sincere regret of the frailty and corruption of human nature, which thought noble enough to take as its rule an idea so worthy of respect, is yet too weak to follow it, and employs reason, which ought to give it the law only for the purpose of providing for the interest of the inclinations, whether singly or at the best in the greatest possible harmony with one another.

In fact, it is absolutely impossible to make out by experience with complete certainty a single case in which the maxim of an action, however right in itself, rested simply on moral grounds and on the conception of duty. Sometimes it happens that with the sharpest self–examination we can find nothing beside the moral principle of duty which could have been powerful enough to move us to this or that action and to so great a sacrifice; yet we cannot from this infer with certainty that it was not really some secret impulse of self–love, under the false appearance of duty, that was the actual determining cause of the will. We like then to flatter ourselves by falsely taking credit for a more noble motive; whereas in fact we can never, even by the strictest examination, get completely behind the secret springs of action; since, when the question is of moral worth, it is not with the actions which we see that we are concerned, but with those inward principles of them which we do not see.

Moreover, we cannot better serve the wishes of those who ridicule all morality as a mere chimera of human imagination overstepping itself from vanity, than by conceding to them that notions of duty must be drawn only from experience (as from indolence, people are ready to think is also the case with all other notions); for this is to prepare for them a certain triumph. I am willing to admit out of love of humanity that even most of our actions are correct, but if we look closer at them we everywhere come upon the dear self which is always prominent, and it is this they have in view, and not the strict command of duty which would often require self–denial. Without being an enemy of virtue, a cool observer, one that does not mistake the wish for good, however lively, for its reality, may sometimes doubt whether true virtue is actually found anywhere in the world, and this especially as years increase and the judgment is partly made wiser by experience, and partly also more acute in observation. This being so, nothing can secure us from falling away altogether from our ideas of duty, or maintain in the soul a well– grounded respect for its law, but the clear conviction that although there should never have been actions which really sprang from such pure sources, yet whether this or that takes place is not at all the question; but that reason of itself, independent on all experience, ordains what ought to take place, that accordingly actions of which perhaps the world has hitherto never given an example, the feasibility even of which might be very much doubted by one who founds everything on experience, are nevertheless inflexibly commanded by reason; that, ex. gr. even though there might never yet have been a sincere friend, yet not a whit the less is pure sincerity in friendship required of every man, because, prior to all experience, this duty is involved as duty in the idea of a reason determining the will by a priori principles.

When we add further that, unless we deny that the notion of morality has any truth or reference to any possible object, we must admit that its law must be valid, not merely for men, but for all rational creatures generally, not merely under certain contingent conditions or with exceptions, but with absolute necessity, then it is clear that no experience could enable us to infer even the possibility of such apodictic laws. For with what right could we bring into unbounded respect as a universal precept for every rational nature that which perhaps holds only under the contingent conditions of humanity? Or how could laws of the determination of OUR will be regarded as laws of the determination of the will of rational beings generally, and for us only as such, if they were merely empirical, and did not take their origin wholly a priori from pure but practical reason?

Nor could anything be more fatal to morality than that we should wish to derive it from examples. For every example of it that is set before me must be first itself tested by principles of morality, whether it is worthy to serve as an original example, i. e., as a pattern, but by no means can it authoritatively furnish the conception of morality. Even the Holy One of the Gospels must first be compared with our ideal of moral perfection before we can recognise Him as such; and so He says of Himself, "Why call ye Me (whom you see) good; none is good (the model of good) but God only (whom ye do not see)?" But whence have we the conception of God as the supreme good? Simply from the IDEA of moral perfection, which reason frames a priori, and connects inseparably with the notion of a free–will. Imitation finds no place at all in morality, and examples serve only for encouragement, i. e. they put beyond doubt the feasibility of what the law commands, they make visible that which the practical rule expresses more generally, but they can never authorise us to set aside the true original which lies in reason, and to guide ourselves by examples.

If then there is no genuine supreme principle of morality but what must rest simply on pure reason, independent on all experience, I think it is not necessary even to put the question, whether it is good to exhibit these concepts in their generality (in abstracto) as they are established a priori along with the principles belonging to them, if our knowledge is to be distinguished from the vulgar, and to be called philosophical. In our times indeed this might perhaps be necessary; for if we collected votes, whether pure rational knowledge separated from everything empirical, that is to say, metaphysic of morals, or whether popular practical philosophy is to be preferred, it is easy to guess which side would preponderate.

This descending to popular notions is certainly very commendable, if the ascent to the principles of pure reason has first taken place and been satisfactorily accomplished. This implies that we first found Ethics on Metaphysics, and then, when it is firmly established, procure a hearing for it by giving it a popular character. But it is quite absurd to try to be popular in the first inquiry, on which the soundness of the principles depends. It is not only that this proceeding can never lay claim to the very rare merit of a true philosophical popularity, since there is no art in being intelligible if one renounces all thoroughness of insight; but also it produces a disgusting medley of compiled observations and half– reasoned principles. Shallow pates enjoy this because it can be used for every–day chat, but the sagacious find in it only confusion, and being unsatisfied and unable to help themselves, they turn away their eyes, while philosophers, who see quite well through this delusion, are little listened to when they call men off for a time from this pretended popularity, in order that they might be rightfully popular after they have attained a definite insight.

We need only look at the attempts of moralists in that favourite fashion, and we shall find at one time the Special constitution of human nature (including, however, the idea of a rational nature generally), at one time perfection, at another happiness, here moral sense, there fear of God, a little of this, and a little of that, in marvellous mixture, without its occurring to them to ask whether the principles of morality are to be sought in the knowledge of human nature at all (which we can have only from experience); and, if this is not so, if these principles are to be found altogether a priori free from everything empirical, in pure rational concepts only, and nowhere else, not even in the smallest degree; then rather to adopt the method of making this a separate inquiry, as pure practical philosophy, or (if one may use a name so decried) as metaphysic of morals, [Footnote: Just as pure mathematics are distinguished from applied, pure logic from applied, so if we choose we may also

191

distinguish pure philosophy of morals (metaphysic) from applied (viz. applied to human nature). By this designation we are also at once reminded that moral principles are not based on properties of human nature, but must subsist a priori of themselves while from such principles practical rules must be capable of being deduced for every rational nature, and accordingly for that of man.] to bring it by itself to completeness, and to require the public, which wishes for popular treatment, to await the issue of this undertaking.

Such a metaphysic of morals, completely isolated, not mixed with any anthropology, theology, physics, or hyperphysics, and still less with occult qualities (which we might call hypophysical), is not only an indispensable substratum of all sound theoretical knowledge of duties, but is at the same time a desideratum of the highest importance to the actual fulfilment of their precepts. For the pure conception of duty, unmixed with any foreign addition of empirical attractions, and, in a word, the conception of the moral law, exercises on the human heart, by way of reason alone (which first becomes aware with this that it can of itself be practical), an influence so much more powerful than all other springs [Footnote: I have a letter from the late excellent Sulzer, in which he asks me what can be the reason that moral instruction, although containing much that is convincing for the reason, yet accomplishes so little? My answer was postponed in order that I might make it complete. But it is simply this, that the teachers themselves have not got their own notions clear, and when they endeavour to make up for this by raking up motives of moral goodness from every quarter, trying to make their physic right strong, they spoil it. For the commonest understanding shows that if we imagine, on the one hand, an act of honesty done with steadfast mind, apart from every view to advantage of any kind in this world or another, and even under the greatest temptations of necessity or allurement, and, on the other hand, a similar act which was affected, in however low a degree, by a foreign motive, the former leaves far behind and eclipses the second; it elevates the soul, and inspires the wish to be able to act in like manner oneself. Even moderately young children feel this impression, and one should never represent duties to them in any other light.] which may be derived from the field of experience, that in the consciousness of its worth, despises the latter, and can by degrees become their master; whereas a mixed ethics, compounded partly of motives drawn from feelings and inclinations, and partly also of conceptions of reason, must make the mind waver between motives which cannot be brought under any principle, which lead to good only by mere accident, and very often also to evil.

From what has been said, it is clear that all moral conceptions have their seat and origin completely a priori in the reason, and that, moreover, in the commonest reason just as truly as in that which is in the highest degree speculative; that they cannot be obtained by abstraction from any empirical, and therefore merely contingent knowledge; that it is just this purity of their origin that makes them worthy to serve as our supreme practical principle, and that just in proportion as we add anything empirical, we detract from their genuine influence, and from the absolute value of actions; that it is not only of the greatest necessity, in a purely speculative point of view, but is also of the greatest practical importance to derive these notions and laws from pure reason, to present them pure and unmixed, and even to determine the compass of this practical or pure rational knowledge, i. e. to determine the whole faculty of pure practical reason; and, in doing so, we must not make its principles dependent on the particular nature of human reason, though in speculative philosophy this may be permitted, or may even at times be necessary; but since moral laws ought to hold good for every rational creature, we must derive them from the general concept of a rational being. In this way, although for its application to man morality has need of anthropology, yet, in the first instance, we must treat it independently as pure philosophy, i. e. as metaphysic, complete in itself (a thing which in such distinct branches of science is easily done); knowing well that unless we are in possession of this, it would not only be vain to determine the moral element of duty in right actions for purposes of speculative criticism, but it would be impossible to base morals on their genuine principles, even for common practical purposes, especially of moral instruction, so as to produce pure moral dispositions, and to engraft them on men's minds to the promotion of the greatest possible good in the world.

But in order that in this study we may not merely advance by the natural steps from the common moral judgment (in this case very worthy of respect) to the philosophical, as has been already done, but also from a popular philosophy, which goes no further than it can reach by groping with the help of examples, to metaphysic (which does not allow itself to be checked by anything empirical, and as it must measure the whole extent of this kind of rational knowledge, goes as far as ideal conceptions, where even examples fail us), we must follow and clearly describe the practical faculty of reason, from the general rules of its determination to the point where the notion of duty springs from it.

Everything in nature works according to laws. Rational beings alone have the faculty of acting according to the conception of laws, that is according to principles, i. e., have a will. Since the deduction of actions from principles requires reason, the will is nothing but practical reason. If reason infallibly determines the will, then the actions of such a being which are recognised as objectively necessary are subjectively necessary also, i. e., the will is a faculty to choose that only which reason independent on inclination recognises as practically necessary, i. e., as good. But if reason of itself does not sufficiently determine the will, if the latter is subject also to subjective conditions (particular impulses) which do not always coincide with the objective conditions; in a word, if the will does not in itself completely accord with reason (which is actually the case with men), then the actions which objectively are recognised as necessary are subjectively contingent, and the determination of such a will according to objective laws is obligation, that is to say, the relation of the objective laws to a will that is not thoroughly good is conceived as the determination of the will of a rational being by principles of reason, but which the will from its nature does not of necessity follow.

The conception of an objective principle, in so far as it is obligatory for a will, is called a command (of reason); and the formula of the command is called an Imperative.

All imperatives are expressed by the word OUGHT [or SHALL], and thereby indicate the relation of an objective law of reason to a will, which from its subjective constitution is not necessarily determined by it (an obligation). They say that something would be good to do or to forbear, but they say it to a will which does not always do a thing because it is conceived to be good to do it. That is practically GOOD, however, which determines the will by means of the conceptions of reason, and consequently not from subjective causes, but objectively, that is on principles which are valid for every rational being as such. It is distinguished from the PLEASANT, as that which influences the will only by means of sensation from merely subjective causes, valid only for the sense of this or that one, and not as a principle of reason, which holds for every one. [Footnote 3: The dependence of the desires on sensations is called inclination, and this accordingly always indicates a WANT. The dependence of a contingently determinable will on principles of reason is called an INTEREST. This therefore is found only in the case of a dependent will, which does not always of itself conform to reason; in the Divine will we cannot conceive any interest. But the human will can also TAKE AN INTEREST in a thing without therefore acting FROM INTEREST. The former signifies the PRACTICAL interest in the action, the latter the PATHOLOGICAL in the object of the action. The former indicates only dependence of the will or principles of reason in themselves; the second, dependence on principles of reason for the sake of inclination, reason supplying only the practical rules how the requirement of the inclination may he satisfied. In the first case the action interests me; in the second the object of the action (because it is pleasant to me), We have seen in the first section that in an action done from duty we must look not to the interest in the object, but only to that in the action itself, and in its rational principle (viz. the law).]

A perfectly good will would therefore be equally subject to objective laws (viz. laws of good), but could not be conceived as OBLIGED thereby to act lawfully, because of itself from its subjective constitution it can only be determined by the conception of good. Therefore no imperatives hold for the Divine will, or in general for a HOLY will; OUGHT is here out of place, because the volition is already of itself necessarily in unison with the law. Therefore imperatives are only formulae to express the relation of objective laws of all volition to the subjective imperfection of the will of this or that rational being, e. g. the human will.

Now all IMPERATIVES command either HYPOTHETICALLY or CATEGORICALLY. The former represent the practical necessity of a possible action as means to something else that is willed (or at least which one might possibly will). The categorical imperative would be that which represented an action as necessary of itself without reference to another end, i. e., as objectively necessary.

Since every practical law represents a possible action as good, and on this account, for a subject who is practically determinable by reason, necessary, all imperatives are formulae determining an action which is necessary according to the principle of a will good in some respects. If now the action is good only as a means TO SOMETHING ELSE, then the imperative is HYPOTHETICAL; if it is conceived as good IN ITSELF and consequently as being necessarily the principle of a will which of itself conforms to reason, then it is CATEGORICAL.

Thus the imperative declares what action possible by me would be good, and presents the practical rule in relation to a will which does not forthwith perform an action simply because it is good, whether because the subject does not always know that it is good, or because, even if it know this, yet its maxims might be opposed to the objective principles of practical reason.

Accordingly the hypothetical imperative only says that the action is good for some purpose, POSSIBLE or ACTUAL. In the first case it is a Problematical, in the second an Assertorial practical principle. The categorical imperative which declares an action to be objectively necessary in itself without reference to any purpose, i. e., without any other end, is valid as an Apodictic (practical) principle.

Whatever is possible only by the power of some rational being may also be conceived as a possible purpose of some will; and therefore the principles of action as regards the means necessary to attain some possible purpose are in fact infinitely numerous. All sciences have a practical part, consisting of problems expressing that some end is possible for us, and of imperatives directing how it may be attained. These may, therefore, be called in general imperatives of Skill. Here there is no question whether the end is rational and good, but only what one must do in order to attain it. The precepts for the physician to make his patient thoroughly healthy, and for a poisoner to ensure certain death, are of equal value in this respect, that each serves to effect its purpose perfectly. Since in early youth it cannot be known what ends are likely to occur to us in the course of life, parents seek to have their children taught a great many things, and provide for their skill in the use of means for all sorts of arbitrary ends, of none of which can they determine whether it may not perhaps hereafter be an object to their pupil, but which it is at all events possible that he might aim at; and this anxiety is so great that they commonly neglect to form and correct their judgment on the value of the things which may be chosen as ends.

There is one end, however, which may be assumed to be actually such to all rational beings (so far as imperatives apply to them, viz. as dependent beings), and therefore, one purpose which they not merely MAY have, but which we may with certainty assume that they all actually HAVE by a natural necessity, and this is HAPPINESS. The hypothetical imperative which expresses the practical necessity of an action as means to the advancement of happiness is Assertorial. We are not to present it as necessary for an uncertain and merely possible purpose, but for a purpose which we may presuppose with certainty and a priori in every man, because it belongs to his being. Now skill in the choice of means to his own greatest well– being may be called prudence [The word prudence is taken in two senses; in the one it may bear the name of knowledge of the world, in the other that of private prudence. The former is a man's ability to influence others so as to use them for his own purposes. The latter is the sagacity to combine all these purposes for his own lasting benefit. This latter is properly that to which the value even of the former is reduced, and when a man is prudent in the former sense, but not in the latter, we might better say of him that he is clever and cunning, but, on the whole, imprudent. Compare on the difference between klug and gescheu here alluded to, Anthropologie, 45, ed. Schubert, p. no.] in the narrowest sense. And thus the imperative which refers to the choice of means to one's own happiness, i. e., the precept of prudence, is still always hypothetical; the action is not commanded absolutely, but only as means to another purpose.

Finally, there is an imperative which commands a certain conduct immediately, without having as its condition any other purpose to be attained by it. This imperative is Categorical. It concerns not the matter of the action, or its intended result, but its form and the principle of which it is itself a result, and what is essentially good in it consists in the mental disposition, let the consequence be what it may. This imperative may be called that of Morality.

There is a marked distinction also between the volitions on these three sorts of principles in the DISSIMILARITY of the obligation of the will. In order to mark this difference more clearly, I think they would be most suitably named in their order if we said they are either RULES of skill, or COUNSELS of prudence, or COMMANDS (LAWS) of morality. For it is LAW only that involves the conception of an UNCONDITIONAL and objective necessity, which is consequently universally valid; and commands are laws which must be obeyed, that is, must be followed, even in opposition to inclination. COUNSELS, indeed, involve necessity, but one which can only hold under a contingent subjective condition, viz. they depend on whether this or that man reckons this or that as part of his happiness; the categorical imperative, on the contrary, is not limited by any condition, and as being absolutely, although practically, necessary, may be quite properly called a command. We might also call the first kind of imperatives TECHNICAL (belonging to art), the second PRAGMATIC (to welfare), [It seems to me that the proper signification of the word pragmatic may be most accurately defined in this way. For sanctions [see Cr. of Pract. Reas., p. 271] are called pragmatic which flow properly, not from the law of the states as necessary enactments, but from precaution for the general welfare. A history is composed pragmatically when it teaches prudence, i. e. instructs the world how it can provide for its interests better, or at least as well as the men of former time.]; the third MORAL (belonging to free conduct generally, that is, to morals).

Now arises the question, how are all these imperatives possible? This question does not seek to know how we can conceive the accomplishment of the action which the imperative ordains, but merely how we can conceive the obligation of the will which the imperative expresses. No special explanation is needed to show how an imperative of skill is possible. Whoever wills the end, wills also (so far as reason decides his conduct) the means in his power which are indispensably necessary thereto. This proposition is, as regards the volition, analytical; for, in willing an object as my effect, there is already thought the causality of myself as an acting cause, that is to say, the use of the means; and the imperative educes from the conception of volition of an end the conception of actions necessary to this end. Synthetical propositions must no doubt be employed in denning the means to a proposed end; but they do not concern the principle, the act of the will, but the object and its realization. Ex. gr., that in order to bisect a line on an unerring principle I must draw from its extremities two intersecting arcs; this no doubt is taught by mathematics only in synthetical propositions; but if I know that it is only by this process that the intended operation can be performed, then to say that if I fully will the operation, I also will the action required for it, is an analytical proposition; for it is one and the same thing to conceive something as an effect which I can produce in a certain way, and to conceive myself as acting in this way.

If it were only equally easy to give a definite conception of happiness, the imperatives of prudence would correspond exactly with those of skill, and would likewise be analytical. For in this case as in that, it could be said, whoever wills the end, wills also (according to the dictate of reason necessarily) the indispensable means thereto which are in his power. But, unfortunately, the notion of happiness is so indefinite that although every man wishes to attain it, yet he never can say definitely and consistently what it is that he really wishes and wills. The reason of this is that all the elements which belong to the notion of happiness are altogether empirical, i. e. they must be borrowed from experience, and nevertheless the idea of happiness requires an absolute whole, a maximum of welfare in my present and all future circumstances. Now it is impossible that the most clear–sighted, and at the same time most powerful being (supposed finite), should frame to himself a definite conception of what he really wills in this. Does he will riches, how much anxiety, envy, and snares might he not thereby draw upon his shoulders? Does he will knowledge and discernment, perhaps it might prove to be only an eye so much the sharper to show him so much the more fearfully the evils that are now concealed from him, and that cannot be avoided, or to impose more wants on his desires, which already give him concern enough. Would he have long life, who guarantees to him that it would not be a long misery? would he at least have health? how often has uneasiness of the body restrained from excesses into which perfect health would have allowed one to fall? and so on. In short he is unable, on any principle, to determine with certainty what would make him truly happy; because to do so he would need to be omniscient. We cannot therefore act on any definite principles to secure happiness, but only on empirical counsels, ex. gr. of regimen, frugality, courtesy, reserve, which experience teaches do, on the average, most promote well- being. Hence it follows that the imperatives of prudence do not, strictly speaking, command at all, that is, they cannot present actions objectively as practically necessary; that they are rather to be regarded as counsels (consilia) than precepts (praecepta) of reason, that the problem to determine certainly and universally what action would promote the happiness of a rational being is completely insoluble, and consequently no imperative respecting it is possible which should, in the strict sense, command to do what makes happy; because happiness is not an ideal of reason but of imagination, resting solely on empirical grounds, and it is vain to expect that these should define an action by which one could attain the totality of a series of consequences which is really endless. This imperative of prudence would however be an analytical proposition if we assume that the means to happiness could be certainly assigned; for it is distinguished from the imperative of skill only by this, that in the latter the end is merely possible, in the former it is given; as however both only ordain the means to that which we suppose to be willed as an end, it follows that the imperative which ordains the willing of the means to him who wills the end is in both cases analytical. Thus there is no difficulty in regard to the possibility of an imperative of this kind either.

On the other hand the question, how the imperative of morality is possible, is undoubtedly one, the only one? demanding a solution, as this is not at all hypothetical, and the objective necessity which it presents cannot rest on any hypothesis, as is the case with the hypothetical imperatives. Only here we must never leave out of consideration that we cannot make out by any example, in other words empirically, whether there is such an imperative at all; but it is rather to be feared that all those which seem to be categorical may yet be at bottom hypothetical. For instance, when the precept is: Thou shalt not promise deceitfully; and it is assumed that the necessity of this is not a mere counsel to avoid some other evil, so that it should mean: thou shalt not make a lying promise, lest if it become known thou shouldst destroy thy credit, but that an action of this kind must be regarded as evil in itself, so that the imperative of the prohibition is categorical; then we cannot show with certainty in any example that the will was determined merely by the law, without any other spring of action, although it may appear to be so. For it is always possible that fear of disgrace, perhaps also obscure dread of other dangers, may have a secret influence on the will. Who can prove by experience the non−existence of a cause when all that experience tells us is that we do not perceive it? But in such a case the so−called moral imperative, which as such appears to be categorical and unconditional, would in reality be only a pragmatic precept, drawing our attention to our own interests, and merely teaching us to take these into consideration.

We shall therefore have to investigate a priori the possibility of a categorical imperative, as we have not in this case the advantage of its reality being given in experience, so that [the elucidation of] its possibility should be requisite only for its explanation, not for its establishment. In the mean−time it may be discerned beforehand that the categorical imperative alone has the purport of a practical law: all the rest may indeed be called principles of the will but not laws, since whatever is only necessary for the attainment of some arbitrary purpose may be considered as in itself contingent, and we can at any time be free from the precept if we give up the purpose: on the contrary, the unconditional command leaves the will no liberty to choose the opposite; consequently it alone carries with it that necessity which we require in a law.

Secondly, in the case of this categorical imperative or law of morality, the difficulty (of discerning its possibility) is a very profound one. It is an a priori synthetical practical proposition; [Footnote: I connect the act with the will without presupposing any condition resulting from any inclination, but d priori, and therefore necessarily (though only objectively, i. e. assuming the idea of a reason possessing full power over all subjective motives). This is accordingly a practical proposition which does not deduce the willing of an action by mere analysis from another already presupposed (for we have not such a perfect will), but connects it immediately with the conception of the will of a rational being, as something not contained in it.] and as there is so much difficulty in discerning the possibility of speculative propositions of this kind, it may readily be supposed that the difficulty will be no less with the practical.

In this problem we will first inquire whether the mere conception of a categorical imperative may not perhaps supply us also with the formula of it, containing the proposition which alone can be a categorical imperative; for even if we know the tenor of such absolute command, yet how it is possible will require further special and laborious study, which we postpone to the last section.

When I conceive a hypothetical imperative in general I do not know beforehand what it will contain until I am given the condition. But when I conceive a categorical imperative I know at once what it contains. For as the imperative contains besides the law only the necessity that the maxims [Footnote: A MAXIM is a subjective principle of action, and must be distinguished from the objective principle, namely, practical law. The former contains the practical rule set by reason according to the conditions of the subject (often its ignorance or its inclinations), so that it is the principle on which the subject acts; but the law is the objective principle valid for every rational being, and is the principle on which it ought to act that is an imperative.] shall conform to this law, while the law contains no conditions restricting it, there remains nothing but the general statement that the maxim of the action should conform to a universal law, and it is this conformity alone that the imperative properly represents as necessary. [Footnote: I have no doubt that "den" in the original before "Imperativ" is a misprint for "der," and have translated accordingly. Mr. Semple has done the same. The editions that I have seen agree in reading "den," and M. Barni so translates. With this reading, it is the conformity that presents the imperative as necessary.]

There is therefore but one categorical imperative, namely this: Act only on that maxim whereby thou canst at the same time will that it should become a universal law.

Now if all imperatives of duty can be deduced from this one imperative as from their principle, then, although it should remain undecided whether what is called duty is not merely a vain notion, yet at least we shall be able to show what we understand by it and what this notion means.

Since the universality of the law according to which effects are produced constiutes what is properly called nature in the most general sense (as to form), that is the existence of things so far as it is determined by general laws, the imperative of duty may be expressed thus: Act as if the maxim of thy action were to become by thy will a Universal Law of Nature.

We will now enumerate a few duties, adopting the usual division of them into duties to ourselves and to others, and into perfect and imperfect duties. [Footnote: It must be noted here that I reserve the division of duties for a future metaphysic of morals; so that I give it here only as an arbitrary one (in order to arrange my examples). For the rest, I understand by a perfect duty one that admits no exception in favour of inclination, and then I have not merely external, but also internal perfect duties. This is contrary to the use of the word adopted in the schools; but I do not intend to justify it here, as it is all one for my purpose whether it is admitted or not. [Perfect duties are usually understood to be those which can be enforced by external law; imperfect, those which cannot be enforced. They are also called respectively determinate and indeterminate, officia juris and officia virtutis.]]

I. A man reduced to despair by a series of misfortunes feels wearied of life, but is still so far in possession of his reason that he can ask himself whether it would not be contrary to his duty to himself to take his own life. Now he inquires whether the maxim of his action could become a universal law of nature. His maxim is: From self–love I adopt it as a principle to shorten my life when its longer duration is likely to bring more evil than satisfaction. It is asked then simply whether this principle founded on self–love can become a universal law of nature. Now we see at once that a system of nature of which it should be a law to destroy life by means of the very feeling whose special nature it is to impel to the improvement of life would contradict itself, and therefore could not exist as a system of nature; hence that maxim cannot possibly exist as a universal law of nature, and consequently would be wholly inconsistent with the supreme principle of all duty. [Footnote: On suicide cf. further Metaphysik der Sitten, p. 274.]

2. Another finds himself forced by necessity to borrow money. He knows that he will not be able to repay it, but sees also that nothing will be lent to him, unless he promises stoutly to repay it in a definite time. He desires to make this promise, but he has still so much conscience as to ask himself: Is it not unlawful and inconsistent with duty to get out of a difficulty in this way? Suppose, however, that he resolves to do so, then the maxim of his action would be expressed thus: When I think myself in want of money, I will borrow money and promise to repay it, although I know that I never can do so. Now this principle of self–love or of one's own advantage may perhaps be consistent with my whole future welfare; but the question now is, Is it right? I change then the suggestion of self–love into a universal law, and state the question thus: How would it be if my maxim were a universal law? Then I see at once that it could never hold as a universal law of nature, but would necessarily contradict itself. For supposing it to be a universal law that everyone when he thinks himself in a difficulty should be able to promise whatever he pleases, with the purpose of not keeping his promise, the promise itself would become impossible, as well as the end that one might have in view in it, since no one would consider that anything was promised to him, but would ridicule all such statements as vain pretences.

3. A third finds in himself a talent which with the help of some culture might make him a useful man in many respects. But he finds himself in comfortable circumstances, and prefers to indulge in pleasure rather than to take pains in enlarging and improving his happy natural capacities. He asks, however, whether his maxim of neglect of his natural gifts, besides agreeing with his inclination to indulgence, agrees also with what is called duty. He sees then that a system of nature could indeed subsist with such a universal law although men (like the South Sea islanders) should let their talents rust, and resolve to devote their lives merely to idleness, amusement, and propagation of their species—in a word, to enjoyment; but he cannot possibly WILL that this should be a universal law of nature, or be implanted in us as such by a natural instinct. For, as a rational being, he necessarily wills that his faculties be developed, since they serve him, and have been given him, for all sorts of

possible purposes.

4. A fourth, who is in prosperity, while he sees that others have to contend with great wretchedness and that he could help them, thinks: What concern is it of mine? Let everyone be as happy as heaven pleases, or as he can make himself; I will take nothing from him nor even envy him, only I do not wish to contribute anything to his welfare or to his assistance in distress! Now no doubt if such a mode of thinking were a universal law, the human race might very well subsist, and doubtless even better than in a state in which everyone talks of sympathy and good−will, or even takes care occasionally to put it into practice, but on the other side, also cheats when he can, betrays the rights of men, or otherwise violates them. But although it is possible that a universal law of nature might exist in accordance with that maxim, it is impossible to WILL that such a principle should have the universal validity of a law of nature. For a will which resolved this would contradict itself, inasmuch as many cases might occur in which one would have need of the love and sympathy of others, and in which, by such a law of nature, sprung from his own will, he would deprive himself of all hope of the aid he desires.

These are a few of the many actual duties, or at least what we regard as such, which obviously fall into two classes on the one principle that we have laid down. We must be ABLE TO WILL that a maxim of our action should be a universal law. This is the canon of the moral appreciation of the action generally. Some actions are of such a character that their maxim cannot without contradiction be even CONCEIVED as a universal law of nature, far from it being possible that we should WILL that it SHOULD be so. In others this intrinsic impossibility is not found, but still it is impossible to WILL THAT their maxim should be raised to the universality of a law of nature, since such a will would contradict itself. It is easily seen that the former violate strict or rigorous (inflexible) duty; the latter only laxer (meritorious) duty. Thus it has been completely shown by these examples how all duties depend as regards the nature of the obligation (not the object of the action) on the same principle.

If now we attend to ourselves on occasion of any transgression of duty, we shall find that we in fact do not will that our maxim should be a universal law, for that is impossible for us; on the contrary we will that the opposite should remain a universal law, only we assume the liberty of making an EXCEPTION in our own favour or (just for this time only) in favour of our inclination. Consequently if we considered all cases from one and the same point of view, namely, that of reason, we should find a contradiction in our own will, namely, that a certain principle should be objectively necessary as a universal law, and yet subjectively should not be universal, but admit of exceptions. As however we at one moment regard our action from the point of view of a will wholly conformed to reason, and then again look at the same action from the point of view of a will affected by inclination, there is not really any contradiction, but an antagonism of inclination to the precept of reason, whereby the universality of the principle is changed into a mere generality, so that the practical principle of reason shall meet the maxim half way. Now, although this cannot be justified in our own impartial judgment, yet it proves that we do really recognise the validity of the categorical imperative and (with all respect for it) only allow ourselves a few exceptions, which we think unimportant and forced from us.

We have thus established at least this much, that if duty is a conception which is to have any import and real legislative authority for our actions, it can only be expressed in categorical, and not at all in hypothetical imperatives. We have also, which is of great importance, exhibited clearly and definitely for every practical application the content of the categorical imperative, which must contain the principle of all duty if there is such a thing at all. We have not yet, however, advanced so far as to prove a priori that there actually is such an imperative, that there is a practical law which commands absolutely of itself, and without any other impulse, and that the following of this law is duty.

With the view of attaining to this it is of extreme importance to remember that we must not allow ourselves to think of deducing the reality of this principle from the particular attributes of human nature. For duty is to be a practical, unconditional necessity of action; it must therefore hold for all rational beings (to whom an imperative can apply at all) and for this reason only be also a law for all human wills. On the contrary, whatever is deduced from the particular natural characteristics of humanity, from certain feelings and propensions, [Footnote: Kant distinguishes "Hang (propensio)" from "Neigung (inclinatio)" as follows:—"Hang" is a predisposition to the desire of some enjoyment; in other words, it is the subjective possibility of excitement of a certain desire, which precedes the conception of its object. When the enjoyment has been experienced, it produces a "Neigung" (inclination) to it, which accordingly is defined "habitual sensible desire."—Anthropologie, 72, 79; Religion, p. 31.] nay even, if possible, from any particular tendency proper to human reason, and which need not necessarily hold for the will of every rational being; this may indeed supply us with a maxim, but not with a law; with a subjective principle on which we may have a propension and inclination to act, but not with an objective principle on which we should be enjoined to act, even though all our propensions, inclinations, and natural dispositions were opposed to it. In fact the sublimity and intrinsic dignity of the command in duty are so much the more evident, the less the subjective impulses favour it and the more they oppose it, without being able in the slightest degree to weaken the obligation of the law or to distinguish its validity.

Here then we see philosophy brought to a critical position, since it has to be firmly fixed, notwithstanding that it has nothing to support it either in heaven or earth. Here it must show its purity as absolute dictator of its own laws, not the herald of those which are whispered to it by an implanted sense or who knows what tutelary nature. Although these may be better than nothing, yet they can never afford principles dictated by reason, which must have their source wholly a priori and thence their commanding authority, expecting everything from the supremacy of the law and the due respect for it, nothing from inclination, or else condemning the man to self–contempt and inward abhorrence.

Thus every empirical element is not only quite incapable of being an aid to the principle of morality, but is even highly prejudicial to the purity of morals, for the proper and inestimable worth of an absolutely good will consists just in this, that the principle of action is free, from all influence of contingent grounds, which alone experience can furnish. We cannot too much or too often repeat our warning against this lax and even mean habit of thought which seeks for its principle amongst empirical motives and laws; for human reason in its weariness is glad to rest on this pillow, and in a dream of sweet illusions (in which, instead of Juno, it embraces a cloud) it substitutes for morality a bastard patched up from limbs of various derivation, which looks like anything one chooses to see in it; only not like virtue to one who has once beheld her in her true form. [Footnote: To behold virtue in her proper form is nothing else but to contemplate morality stripped of all admixture of sensible things and of every spurious ornament of reward or self– love. How much she then eclipses everything else that appears charming to the affections, every one may readily perceive with the least exertion of his reason, if it be not wholly spoiled for abstraction.]

The question then is this: Is it a necessary law for all rational beings that they should always judge of their actions by maxims of which they can themselves will that they should serve as universal laws? If it is so, then it must be connected (altogether a priori) with the very conception of the will of a rational being generally. But in order to discover this connexion we must, however reluctantly, take a step into metaphysic, although into a domain of it which is distinct from speculative philosophy, namely, the metaphysic of morals. In a practical philosophy, where it is not the reasons of what happens that we have to ascertain, but the laws of what ought to happen, even although it never does, i. e., objective practical laws, there it is not necessary to inquire into the reasons why anything pleases or displeases, how the pleasure of mere sensation differs from taste, and whether the latter is distinct from a general satisfaction of reason; on what the feeling of pleasure or pain rests, and how from it desires and inclinations arise, and from these again maxims by the co–operation of reason: for all this belongs to an empirical psychology, which would constitute the second part of physics, if we regard physics as the philosophy of nature, so far as it is based on empirical laws. But here we are concerned with objective practical laws, and consequently with the relation of the will to itself so far as it is determined by reason alone, in which case whatever has reference to anything empirical is necessarily excluded; since if reason of itself alone determines the conduct (and it is the possibility of this that we are now investigating), it must necessarily do so a priori.

The will is conceived as a faculty of determining oneself to action in accordance with the conception of certain laws. And such a faculty can be found only in rational beings. Now that which serves the will as the objective ground of its self–determination is the end, and if this is assigned by reason alone, it must hold for all rational beings. On the other hand, that which merely contains the ground of possibility of the action of which the effect is the end, this is called the means. The subjective ground of the desire is the spring, the objective ground of the volition is the motive; hence the distinction between subjective ends which rest on springs and objective ends which depend on motives valid for every rational being. Practical principles are formal when they abstract from all subjective ends, they are material when they assume these, and therefore particular springs of action. The ends which a rational being proposes to himself at pleasure as effects of his actions (material ends) are all only relative, for it is only their relation to the particular desires of the subject that gives them their worth, which therefore cannot furnish principles universal and necessary for all rational beings and for every volition, that is to say practical laws. Hence all these relative ends can give rise only to hypothetical imperatives.

Supposing, however, that there were something whose existence has in itself an absolute worth, something which, being an end in itself, could be a source of definite laws, then in this and this alone would He the source of a possible categorical imperative, i. e., a practical law.

Now I say: man and generally any rational being exists as an end in himself, not merely as a means to be arbitrarily used by this or that will, but in all his actions, whether they concern himself or other rational beings, must be always regarded at the same time as an end. All objects of the inclinations have only a conditional worth, for if the inclinations and the wants founded on them did not exist, then their object would be without value. But the inclinations themselves being sources of want, are so far from having an absolute worth for which they should be desired, that on the contrary it must be the universal wish of every rational being to be wholly free from them. Thus the worth of any object which is to be acquired by our action is always conditional. Beings whose existence depends not on our will but on nature's, have nevertheless, if they are irrational beings, only a relative value as means, and are therefore called things; rational beings, on the contrary, are called persons, because their very nature points them out as ends in themselves, that is as something which must not be used merely as means, and so far therefore restricts freedom of action (and is an object of respect). These, therefore, are not merely subjective ends whose existence has a worth for us as an effect of our action but objective ends, that is things whose existence is an end in itself: an end moreover for which no other can be substituted, which they should subserve merely as means, for otherwise nothing whatever would possess absolute worth; but if all worth were conditioned and therefore contingent, then there would be no supreme practical principle of reason whatever.

If then there is a supreme practical principle or, in respect of the human will, a categorical imperative, it must be one which, being drawn from the conception of that which is necessarily an end for every one because it is an end in itself, constitutes an objective principle of will, and can therefore serve as a universal practical law. The foundation of this principle is: rational nature exists as an end in itself. Man necessarily conceives his own existence as being so; so far then this is a subjective principle of human actions. But every other rational being regards its existence similarly, just on the same rational principle that holds for me: [Footnote: This proposition is here stated as a postulate. The grounds of it will be found in the concluding section.] so that it is at the same time an objective principle, from which as a supreme practical law all laws of the will must be capable of being deduced. Accordingly the practical imperative will be as follows: So act as to treat humanity, whether in thine own person or in that of any other, in every case as an end withal, never as means only. We will now inquire whether this can be practically carried out.

To abide by the previous examples:

Firstly, under the head of necessary duty to oneself: He who contemplates suicide should ask himself whether his action can be consistent with the idea of humanity as an end in itself. If he destroys himself in order to escape from painful circumstances, he uses a person merely as a mean to maintain a tolerable condition up to the end of life. But a man is not a thing, that is to say, something which can be used merely as means, but must in all his actions be always considered as an end in himself. I cannot, therefore, dispose in any way of a man in my own person so as to mutilate him, to damage or kill him. (It belongs to ethics proper to define this principle more precisely so as to avoid all misunderstanding, e. g., as to the amputation of the limbs in order to preserve myself; as to exposing my life to danger with a view to preserve it, This question is therefore omitted here.)

Secondly, as regards necessary duties, or those of strict obligation, towards others; he who is thinking of making a lying promise to others will see at once that he would be using another man merely as a mean, without the latter containing at the same time the end in himself. For he whom I propose by such a promise to use for my own purposes cannot possibly assent to my mode of acting towards him, and therefore cannot himself contain the end of this action. This violation of the principle of humanity in other men is more obvious if we take in examples of attacks on the freedom and property of others. For then it is clear that he who transgresses the rights of men, intends to use the person of others merely as means, without considering that as rational beings they ought always to be esteemed also as ends, that is, as beings who must be capable of containing in themselves the end of the very same action. [Footnote: Let it not be thought that the common: quod tibi non vis fieri, could serve here as the rule or principle. For it is only a deduction from the former, though with several limitations; it cannot be a universal law, for it does not contain the principle of duties to oneself, nor of the duties of benevolence to others (for many a one would gladly consent that others should not benefit him, provided only that he might be excused from showing benevolence to them), nor finally that of duties of strict obligation to one another, for on this principle the criminal might argue against the judge who punishes him, and so on.]

Thirdly, as regards contingent (meritorious) duties to oneself; it is not enough that the action does not violate humanity in our own person as an end in itself, it must also harmonise with it. Now there are in humanity capacities of greater perfection which belong to the end that nature has in view in regard to humanity in ourselves as the subject: to neglect these might perhaps be consistent with the maintenance of humanity as an end in itself, but not with the advancement of this end.

Fourthly, as regards meritorious duties towards others: the natural end which all men have in their own happiness. Now humanity might indeed subsist, although no one should contribute anything to the happiness of others, provided he did not intentionally withdraw anything from it; but after all, this would only harmonise negatively not positively with humanity as an end in itself, if everyone does not also endeavor, as far as in him lies, to forward the ends of others. For the ends of any subject which is an end in himself, ought as far as possible to be my ends also, if that conception is to have its full effect with me.

This principle, that humanity and generally every rational nature is an end in itself (which is the supreme limiting condition of every man's freedom of action), is not borrowed from experience, firstly, because it is universal, applying as it does to all rational beings whatever, and experience is not capable of determining anything about them; secondly, because it does not present humanity as an end to men (subjectively), that is as an object which men do of themselves actually adopt as an end; but as an objective end, which must as a law constitute the supreme limiting condition of all our subjective ends, let them be what we will; it must therefore spring from pure, reason. In fact the objective principle of all practical legislation lies (according to the first principle) in the rule and its form of universality which makes it capable of being a law (say, e. g., a law of nature); but the subjective principle is in the end; now by the second principle the subject of all ends is each rational being, inasmuch as it is an end in itself. Hence follows the third practical principle of the will, which is the ultimate condition of its harmony with the universal practical reason, viz.: the idea of the will of every rational being as a universally legislative will.

On this principle all maxims are rejected which are inconsistent with the will being itself universal legislator. Thus the will is not subject simply to the law, but so subject that it must be regarded as itself giving the law, and on this ground only, subject to the law (of which it can regard itself as the author).

In the previous imperatives, namely, that based on the conception of the conformity of actions to general laws, as in a physical system of nature, and that based on the universal prerogative of rational beings as ends in themselves—these imperatives just because they were conceived as categorical, excluded from any share in their authority all admixture of any interest as a spring of action; they were however only assumed to be categorical, because such an assumption was necessary to explain the conception of duty. But we could not prove independently that there are practical propositions which command categorically, nor can it be proved in this section; one thing however could be done, namely, to indicate in the imperative itself by some determinate expression, that in the case of volition from duty all interest is renounced, which is the specific criterion of categorical as distinguished from hypothetical imperatives. This is done in the present (third) formula of the principle, namely, in the idea of the will of every rational being as a universally legislating will.

For although a will which is subject to laws may be attached to this law by means of an interest, yet a will which is itself a supreme lawgiver so far as it is such cannot possibly depend on any interest, since a will so dependent would itself still need another law restricting the interest of its self-love by the condition that it should be valid as universal law.

Thus the principle that every human will is a will which in all its maxims gives universal laws [Footnote: I may be excused from adducing examples to elucidate this principle, as those which have already been used to elucidate the categorical imperative and its formula would all serve for the like purpose here.] provided it be otherwise justified, would be very well adapted to be the categorical imperative, in this respect, namely, that just because of the idea of universal legislation it is not based on any interest, and therefore it alone among all possible imperatives can be unconditional. Or still better, converting the proposition, if there is a categorical imperative (i.e. a law for the will of every rational being), it can only command that everything be done from maxims of one's will regarded as a will which could at the same time will that it should itself give universal laws, for in that case only the practical principle and the imperative which it obeys are unconditional, since they cannot be based on any interest.

Looking back now on all previous attempts to discover the principle of morality, we need not wonder why they all fail. It was seen that man was bound to laws by duty, but it was not observed that the laws to which he is subject are only those of his own giving, though at the same time they are universal, and that he is only bound to act in conformity with his own will; a will, however, which is designed by nature to give universal laws. For when one has conceived man only as subject to a law (no matter what), then this law required some interest, either by way of attraction or constraint, since it did not originate as a law from his own will, but this will was according to a law obliged by something else to act in a certain manner. Now by this necessary consequence all the labour spent in finding a supreme principle of duty was irrevocably lost. For men never elicited duty, but only a necessity of acting from a certain interest. Whether this interest was private or otherwise, in any case the imperative must be conditional, and could not by any means be capable of being a moral command. I will therefore call this the principle of Autonomy of the will, in contrast with every other which I accordingly reckon as Heteronomy? [Footnote: Cp. "Critical Examination of Practical Reason," p. 184.]

The conception of every rational being as one which must consider itself as giving in all the maxims of its will universal laws, so as to judge itself and its actions from this point of view—this conception leads to another which depends on it and is very fruitful, namely, that of a kingdom of ends.

By a kingdom I understand the union of different rational beings in a system by common laws. Now since it is by laws that ends are determined as regards their universal validity, hence, if we abstract from the personal differences of rational beings, and likewise from all the content of their private ends, we shall be able to conceive all ends combined in a systematic whole (including both rational beings as ends in themselves, and also the special ends which each may propose to himself), that is to say, we can conceive a kingdom of ends, which on the preceding principles is possible.

For all rational beings come under the law that each of them must treat itself and all others never merely as means, but in every case at the same time as ends in themselves. Hence results a systematic union of rational beings by common objective laws, i.e. a kingdom which may be called a kingdom of ends, since what these laws have in view is just the relation of these beings to one another as ends and means. It is certainly only an ideal.

A rational being belongs as a member to the kingdom of ends when, although giving universal laws in it, he is also himself subject to these laws. He belongs to it as sovereign when, while giving laws, he is not subject to the will of any other.

A rational being must always regard himself as giving laws either as member or as sovereign in a kingdom of ends which is rendered possible by the freedom of will. He cannot, however, maintain the latter position merely by the maxims of his will, but only in case he is a completely independent being without wants and with unrestricted power adequate to his will.

Morality consists then in the reference of all action to the legislation which alone can render a kingdom of ends possible. This legislation must be capable of existing in every rational being, and of emanating from his will, so that the principle of this will is, never to act on any maxim which could not without contradiction be also a universal law, and accordingly always so to act that the will could at the same time regard itself as giving in its maxims universal laws. If now the maxims of rational beings are not by their own nature coincident with this objective principle, then the necessity of acting on it is called practical necessitation, i. e., duty. Duty does not apply to the sovereign in the kingdom of ends, but it does to every member of it and to all in the same degree.

The practical necessity of acting on this principle, i. e., duty, does not rest at all on feelings, impulses, or inclinations, but solely on the relation of rational beings to one another, a relation in which the will of a rational being must always be regarded as legislative, since otherwise it could not be conceived as an end in itself. Reason then refers every maxim of the will, regarding it as legislating universally, to every other will and also to every action towards oneself; and this not on account of any other practical motive or any future advantage, but from the idea of the dignity of a rational being, obeying no law but that which he himself also gives.

In the kingdom of ends everything has either Value or Dignity. Whatever has a value can be replaced by something else which is equivalent; whatever, on the other hand, is above all value, and therefore admits of no equivalent, has a dignity.

Whatever has reference to the general inclinations and wants of mankind has a market value; whatever, without presupposing a want, corresponds to a certain taste, that is to a satisfaction in the mere purposeless play of our faculties, has a fancy value; but that which constitutes the condition under which alone anything can be an end in itself, this has not merely a relative worth, i. e., value, but an intrinsic worth, that is dignity.

Now morality is the condition under which alone a rational being can be an end in himself, since by this alone it is possible that he should be a legislating member in the kingdom of ends. Thus morality, and humanity as capable of it, is that which alone has dignity. Skill and diligence in labour have a market value; wit, lively imagination, and humour, have fancy value; on the other hand, fidelity to promises, benevolence from principle (not from instinct), have an intrinsic worth. Neither nature nor art contains anything which in default of these it could put in their place, for their worth consists not in the effects which spring from them, not in the use and advantage which they secure, but in the disposition of mind, that is, the maxims of the will which are ready to manifest themselves in such actions, even though they should not have the desired effect. These actions also need no recommendation from any subjective taste or sentiment, that they may be looked on with immediate favour and satisfaction: they need no immediate propension or feeling for them; they exhibit the will that performs them as an object of an immediate respect, and nothing but reason is required to IMPOSE them on the will; not to FLATTER it into them, which, in the case of duties, would be a contradiction. This estimation therefore shows that the worth of such a disposition is dignity, and places it infinitely above all value, with which it cannot for a moment be brought into comparison or competition without as it were violating its sanctity.

What then is it which justifies virtue or the morally good disposition, in making such lofty claims? It is nothing less than the privilege it secures to the rational being of participating in the giving of universal laws, by which it qualifies him to be a member of a possible kingdom of ends, a privilege to which he was already destined by his own nature as being an end in himself, and on that account legislating in the kingdom of ends; free as regards all laws of physical nature, and obeying those only which he himself gives, and by which his maxims can belong to a system of universal law, to which at the same time he submits himself. For nothing has any worth except what the law assigns it. Now the legislation itself which assigns the worth of everything, must for that very reason possess dignity, that is an unconditional incomparable worth, and the word RESPECT alone supplies a becoming expression for the esteem which a rational being must have for it. AUTONOMY then is the basis of the dignity of human and of every rational nature.

The three modes of presenting the principle of morality that have been adduced are at bottom only so many formulae of the very same law, and each of itself involves the other two. There is, however, a difference in them, but it is rather subjectively than objectively practical, intended namely to bring an idea of the reason nearer to intuition (by means of a certain analogy), and thereby nearer to feeling. All maxims, in fact, have—

1. A FORM, consisting in universality; and in this view the formula of the moral imperative is expressed thus, that the maxims must be so chosen as if they were to serve as universal laws of nature.

2. A MATTER [Footnote: The reading "Maxima," which is that both of Rosenkranz and Hartenstein, is obviously an error for "Materie."] namely, an end, and here the formula says that the rational being,

as it is an end by its own nature and therefore an end in itself, must in every maxim serve as the condition limiting all merely relative and arbitrary ends.

3. A COMPLETE CHARACTERISATION of all maxims by means of that formula, namely, that all maxims ought by their own legislation to harmonise with a possible kingdom of ends as with a kingdom of nature. [Footnote: Teleology considers nature as a kingdom of ends; Ethics regards a possible kingdom of ends as a kingdom of nature. In the first case, the kingdom of ends is a theoretical idea, adopted to explain what actually is. In the latter it is a practical idea, adopted to bring about that which is not yet, but which can be realised by our conduct, namely, if it conforms to this idea.] There is a progress here in the order of the categories of UNITY of the form of the will (its universality), PLURALITY of the matter (the objects, i. e. the ends), and TOTALITY of the system of these. In forming our moral JUDGMENT of actions it is better to proceed always on the strict method, and start from the general formula of the categorical imperative: ACT ACCORDING TO A MAXIM WHICH CAN AT THE SAME TIME MAKE ITSELF A UNIVERSAL LAW. If, however, we wish to gain an ENTRANCE for the moral law, it is very useful to bring one and the same action under the three specified conceptions, and thereby as far as possible to bring it nearer to intuition.

We can now end where we started at the beginning, namely, with the conception of a will unconditionally good. THAT WILL is ABSOLUTELY GOOD which cannot be evil, in other words, whose maxim, if made a universal law, could never contradict itself. This principle then is its supreme law: Act always on such a maxim as thou canst at the same time will to be a universal law; this is the sole condition under which a will can never contradict itself; and such an imperative is categorical. Since the validity of the will as a universal law for possible actions is analogous to the universal connexion of the existence of things by general laws, which is the formal notion of nature in general, the categorical imperative can also be expressed thus: ACT ON MAXIMS WHICH CAN AT THE SAME TIME HAVE FOR THEIR OBJECT THEMSELVES AS UNIVERSAL LAWS OF NATURE. Such then is the formula of an absolutely good will.

Rational nature is distinguished from the rest of nature by this, that it sets before itself an end. This end would be the matter of every good will. But since in the idea of a will that is absolutely good without being limited by any condition (of attaining this or that end) we must abstract wholly from every end TO BE EFFECTED (since this would make every will only relatively good), it follows that in this case the end must be conceived, not as an end to be effected, but as an INDEPENDENTLY existing end. Consequently it is conceived only negatively, i.e., as that which we must never act against, and which, therefore, must never be regarded merely as means, but must in every volition be esteemed as an end likewise. Now this end can be nothing but the subject of all possible ends, since this is also the subject of a possible absolutely good will; for such a will cannot without contradiction be postponed to any other object. The principle: So act in regard to every rational being (thyself and others), that he may always have place in thy maxim as an end in himself, is accordingly essentially identical with this other: Act upon a maxim which, at the same time, involves its own universal validity for every rational being. For that in using means for every end I should limit my maxim by the condition of its holding good as a law for every subject, this comes to the same thing as that the fundamental principle of all maxims of action must be that the subject of all ends, i. e., the rational being himself, be never employed merely as means, but as the supreme condition restricting the use of all means, that is in every case as an end likewise.

It follows incontestably that, to whatever laws any rational being may be subject, he being an end in himself must be able to regard himself as also legislating universally in respect of these same laws, since it is just this fitness of his maxims for universal legislation that distinguishes him as an end in himself; also it follows that this implies his dignity (prerogative) above all mere physical beings, that he must always take his maxims from the point of view which regards himself, and likewise every other rational being, as lawgiving beings (on which account they are called persons). In this way a world of rational beings (mundus intelligibilis) is possible as a kingdom of ends, and this by virtue of the legislation proper to all persons as members. Therefore every rational being must so act as if he were by his maxims in every case a legislating member in the universal kingdom of ends. The formal principle of these maxims is: So act as if thy maxim were to serve likewise as the universal law (of all rational beings). A kingdom of ends is thus only possible on the analogy of a kingdom of nature, the former however only by maxims, that is self–imposed rules, the latter only by the laws of efficient causes acting under necessitation from without. Nevertheless, although the system of nature is looked upon as a machine, yet so far as it has reference to rational beings as its ends, it is given on this account the name of a kingdom of nature. Now such a kingdom of ends would be actually realised by means of maxims conforming to the canon which the categorical imperative prescribes to all rational beings, IF THEY WERE UNIVERSALLY FOLLOWED. But although a rational being, even if he punctually follows this maxim himself, cannot reckon upon all others being therefore true to the same, nor expect that the kingdom of nature and its orderly arrangements shall be in harmony with him as a fitting member, so as to form a kingdom of ends to which he himself contributes, that is to say, that it shall favour his expectation of happiness, still that law: Act according to the maxims of a member of a merely possible kingdom of ends legislating in it universally, remains in its full force, inasmuch as it commands categorically. And it is just in this that the paradox lies; that the mere dignity of a man as a rational creature, without any other end or advantage to be attained thereby, in other words, respect for a mere idea, should yet serve as an inflexible precept of the will, and that it is precisely in this independence of the maxim on all such springs of action that its sublimity consists; and it is this that makes every rational subject worthy to be a legislative member in the kingdom of ends: for otherwise he would have to be conceived only as subject to the physical law of his wants. And although we should suppose the kingdom of nature and the kingdom of ends to be united under one sovereign, so that the latter kingdom thereby ceased to be a mere idea and acquired true reality, then it would no doubt gain the accession of a strong spring, but by no means any increase of its intrinsic worth. For this sole absolute lawgiver must, notwithstanding this, be always conceived as estimating the worth of rational beings only by their disinterested behaviour, as prescribed to themselves from that idea [the dignity of man] alone. The essence of things is not altered by their external relations, and that which abstracting from these, alone constitutes the absolute worth of man, is also that by which he must be judged, whoever the judge may be, and even by the Supreme Being. MORALITY then is the relation of actions to the autonomy of the will, that is, to the potential universal legislation by its maxims. An action that is consistent with the autonomy of the will is PERMITTED; one that does not agree therewith is FORBIDDEN. A will whose maxims necessarily coincide with the laws of autonomy is a HOLY will, good absolutely. The dependence of a will not absolutely good on the principle of autonomy (moral necessitation) is obligation. This then cannot be applied to a holy being. The objective necessity of actions from obligation is called DUTY.

From what has just been said, it is easy to see how it happens that although the conception of duty implies subjection to the law, we yet ascribe a certain DIGNITY and sublimity to the person who fulfills all his duties. There is not, indeed, any sublimity in him, so far as he is subject to the moral law; but inasmuch as in regard to that very law he is like–wise a legislator, and on that account alone subject to it, he has sublimity. We have also shown above that neither fear nor inclination, but simply respect for the law, is the spring which can give actions a moral worth. Our own will, so far as we suppose it to act only under the condition that its maxims are potentially universal laws, this ideal will which is possible to us is the proper object of respect, and the dignity of humanity consists just in this capacity of being universally legislative, though with the condition that it is itself subject to this same legislation.

The Autonomy of the Will as the Supreme Principle of Morality

Autonomy of the will is that property of it by which it is a law to itself (independently on any property of the objects of volition). The principle of autonomy then is: Always so to choose that the same volition shall comprehend the maxims of our choice as a universal law. We cannot prove that this practical rule is an imperative, i.e., that the will of every rational being is necessarily bound to it as a condition, by a mere analysis of the conceptions which occur in it, since it is a synthetical proposition; we must advance beyond the cognition of the objects to a critical examination of the subject, that is of the pure practical reason, for this synthetic proposition which commands apodictically must be capable of being cognised wholly a priori. This matter, however, does not belong to the present section. But that the principle of autonomy in question is the sole principle of morals can be readily shown by mere analysis of the conceptions of morality. For by this analysis we find that its principle must be a categorical imperative, and that what this commands is neither more nor less than this very autonomy.

Heteronomy of the Will as the Source of all spurious Principles of Morality

If the will seeks the law which is to determine it anywhere else than in the fitness of its maxims to be universal laws of its own dictation, consequently if it goes out of itself and seeks this law in the character of any of its objects, there always results HETERONOMY. The will in that case does not give itself the law, but it is given by the object through its relation to the will. This relation whether it rests on inclination or on conceptions of reason only admits of hypothetical imperatives: I ought to do something BECAUSE *I* WISH FOR SOMETHING ELSE. On the contrary, the moral, and therefore categorical, imperative says: I ought to do so and so, even though I should not wish for anything else. Ex. gr., the former says: I ought not to lie if I would retain my reputation; the latter says: I ought not to lie although it should not bring me the least discredit. The latter therefore must so far abstract from all objects that they shall have no INFLUENCE on the will, in order that practical reason (will) may not be restricted to administering an interest not belonging to it, but may simply show its own commanding authority as the supreme legislation. Thus, ex. gr., I ought to endeavour to promote the happiness of others, not as if its realization involved any concern of mine (whether by immediate inclination or by any satisfaction indirectly gained through reason), but simply because a maxim which excludes it cannot be comprehended as a universal law [Footnote: I read allgemeines instead of allgemeinem.] in one and the same volition.

Classification of all Principles of Morality which can be founded on the Conception of Heteronomy.

Here as elsewhere human reason in its pure use, so long as it was not critically examined, has first tried all possible wrong ways before it succeeded in finding the one true way.

All principles which can be taken from this point of view are either EMPIRICAL or RATIONAL. The FORMER, drawn from the principle of HAPPINESS, are built on physical or moral feelings; the LATTER, drawn from the principle of PERFECTION, are built either on the rational conception of perfection as a possible effect, or on that of an independent perfection (the will of God) as the determining cause of our will.

EMPIRICAL PRINCIPLES are wholly incapable of serving as a foundation for moral laws. For the universality with which these should hold for all rational beings without distinction, the unconditional practical necessity which is thereby imposed on them, is lost when their foundation is taken from the PARTICULAR CONSTITUTION OF HUMAN NATURE, or the accidental circumstances in which it is placed. The principle of PRIVATE HAPPINESS, however, is the most objectionable, not merely because it is false, and experience contradicts the supposition that prosperity is always proportioned to good conduct, nor yet merely because it contributes nothing to the establishment of morality—since it is quite a different thing to make a prosperous man and a good man, or to make one prudent and sharp- sighted for his own interests, and to make him virtuous—but because the springs it provides for morality are such as rather undermine it and destroy its sublimity, since they put the motives to virtue and to vice in the same class, and only teach us to make a better calculation, the specific difference between virtue and vice being entirely extinguished. On the other hand, as to moral feeling, this supposed special sense [Footnote: I class the principle of moral feeling under that of happiness, because every empirical interest promises to contribute to our well–being by the agreeableness that a thing affords, whether it be immediately and without a view to profit, or whether profit be regarded. We must likewise, with Hutcheson, class the principle of sympathy with the happiness of others under his assumed moral sense.] the appeal to it is indeed superficial when those who cannot THINK believe that FEELING will help them out, even in what concerns general laws: and besides, feelings which naturally differ infinitely in degree cannot furnish a uniform standard of good and evil, nor has anyone a right to form judgments for others by his own feelings: nevertheless this moral feeling is nearer to morality and its dignity in this respect, that it pays virtue the honour of ascribing to her IMMEDIATELY the satisfaction and esteem we have for her, and does not, as it were, tell her to her face that we are not attached to her by her beauty but by profit.

Amongst the RATIONAL principles of morality, the ontological conception of PERFECTION, notwithstanding its defects, is better than the theological conception which derives morality from a Divine absolutely perfect will. The former is, no doubt, empty and indefinite, and consequently useless for finding in the boundless field of possible reality the greatest amount suitable for us; moreover, in attempting to distinguish specifically the reality of which we are now speaking from every other, it inevitably tends to turn in a circle, and cannot avoid tacitly presupposing the morality which it is to explain; it is nevertheless preferable to the theological view, first, because we have no intuition of the Divine perfection, and can only deduce it from our own conceptions, the most important of which is that of morality, and our explanation would thus be involved in a gross circle; and, in the next place, if we avoid this, the only notion of the Divine will remaining to us is a conception made up of the attributes of desire of glory and dominion, combined with the awful conceptions of might and vengeance, and any system of morals erected on this foundation would be directly opposed to morality.

However, if I had to choose between the notion of the moral sense and that of perfection in general (two systems which at least do not weaken morality, although they are totally incapable of serving as its foundation), then I should decide for the latter, because it at least withdraws the decision of the question from the sensibility and brings it to the court of pure reason; and although even here it decides nothing, it at all events preserves the indefinite idea (of a will good in itself) free from corruption, until it shall be more precisely defined.

For the rest I think I may be excused here from a detailed refutation of all these doctrines; that would only be superfluous labour, since it is so easy, and is probably so well seen even by those whose office requires them to decide for one of these theories (because their hearers would not tolerate suspension of judgment). But what interests us more here is to know that the prime foundation of morality laid down by all these principles is nothing but heteronomy of the will, and for this reason they must necessarily miss their aim.

In every case where an object of the will has to be supposed in order that the rule may be prescribed which is to determine the will, there the rule is simply heteronomy; the imperative is conditional, namely, IF or BECAUSE one wishes for this object, one should act so and so: hence it can never command morally, that is categorically. Whether the object determines the will by means of inclination, as in the principle of private happiness, or by means of reason directed to objects of our possible volition generally, as in the principle of perfection, in either case the will never determines itself IMMEDIATELY by the conception of the action, but only by the influence which the foreseen effect of the action has on the will; I OUGHT TO DO SOMETHING, ON THIS ACCOUNT, BECAUSE I WISH FOR SOMETHING ELSE; and here there must be yet another law assumed in me as its subject, by which I necessarily will this other thing, and this law again requires an imperative to restrict this maxim. For the influence which the conception of an object within the reach of our faculties can exercise on the will of the subject in consequence of its natural properties, depends on the nature of the subject, either the sensibility (inclination and taste), or the understanding and reason, the employment of which is by the peculiar constitution of their nature attended with satisfaction. It follows that the law would be, properly speaking, given by nature, and as such, it must be known and proved by experience, and would consequently be contingent, and therefore incapable of being an apodictic practical rule, such as the moral rule must be. Not only so, but it is INEVITABLY ONLY HETERONOMY; the will does not give itself the law, but it is given by a foreign impulse by means of a particular natural constitution of the subject adapted to receive it. An absolutely good will, then, the principle of which must be a categorical imperative, will be indeterminate as regards all objects, and will contain merely the FORM OF VOLITION generally, and that as autonomy, that is to say, the capability of the maxims of every good will to make themselves a universal law, is itself the only law which the will of every rational being imposes on itself, without needing to assume any spring or interest as a foundation.

HOW SUCH A SYNTHETICAL PRACTICAL a priori PROPOSITION IS POSSIBLE and why it is necessary, is a problem whose solution does not lie within the bounds of the metaphysic of morals; and we have not here affirmed its truth, much less professed to have a proof of it in our power. We simply showed by the development of the universally received notion of morality that an autonomy of the will is inevitably connected with it, or rather is its foundation. Whoever then holds morality to be anything real, and not a chimerical idea without any truth, must likewise admit the principle of it that is here assigned. This section then, like the first, was merely analytical. Now to prove that morality is no creation of the brain, which it cannot be if the categorical imperative and with it the autonomy of the will is true, and as an a priori principle absolutely necessary, this supposes the POSSIBILITY OF A SYNTHETIC USE OF PURE PRACTICAL REASON, which however we cannot venture on without first giving a critical examination of this faculty of reason. In the concluding section we shall give the principle outlines of this critical examination as far as is sufficient for our purpose.

THIRD SECTION. TRANSITION FROM THE METAPHYSIC OF MORALS TO THE CRITIQUE OF PURE PRACTICAL REASOH

The Concept of Freedom is the Key that explains the Autonomy of the Will

The WILL is a kind of causality belonging to living beings in so far as they are rational, and FREEDOM would be this property of such causality that it can be efficient, independently on foreign causes DETERMINING it; just as PHYSICAL NECESSITY is the property that the causality of all irrational beings has of being determined to activity by the influence of foreign causes.

The preceding definition of freedom is NEGATIVE, and therefore unfruitful for the discovery of its essence; but it leads to a POSITIVE conception which is so much the more full and fruitful Since the conception of causality involves that of laws, according to which, by something that we call cause, something else, namely, the effect, must be produced [laid down]; [Footnote: (Gesetzt.–There is in the original a play on the etymology of Gesetz, which does not admit of reproduction in English. It must be confessed that without it the statement is not self–evident.)] hence, although freedom is not a property of the will depending on physical laws, yet it is not for that reason lawless; on the contrary it must be a causality acting according to immutable laws, but of a peculiar kind; otherwise a free will would be an absurdity. Physical necessity is a heteronomy of the efficient causes, for every effect is possible only according to this law, that something else determines the efficient cause to exert its causality. What else then can freedom of the will be but autonomy, that is the property of the will to be a law to itself? But the proposition: The will is in every action a law to itself, only expresses the principle, to act on no other maxim than that which can also have as an object itself as a universal law. Now this is precisely the formula of the categorical imperative and is the principle of morality, so that a free will and a will subject to moral laws are one and the same.

On the hypothesis then of freedom of the will, morality together with its principle follows from it by mere analysis of the conception. However the latter is still a synthetic proposition; viz., an absolutely good will is that whose maxim can always include itself regarded as a universal law; for this property of its maxim can never be discovered by analysing the conception of an absolutely good will. Now such synthetic propositions are only possible in this way: that the two cognitions are connected together by their union with a third in which they are both to be found. The POSITIVE concept of freedom furnishes this third cognition, which cannot, as with physical causes, be the nature of the sensible world (in the concept of which we find conjoined the concept of something in relation as cause to SOMETHING ELSE as effect). We cannot now at once show what this third is to which freedom points us, and of which we have an idea a priori, nor can we make intelligible how the concept of freedom is shown to be legitimate from principles of pure practical reason, and with it the possibility of a categorical imperative; but some further preparation is required.

Freedom must be presupposed as a Property of the Will of all Rational Beings

It is not enough to predicate freedom of our own will, from whatever reason, if we have not sufficient grounds for predicating the same of all rational beings. For as morality serves as a law for us only because we are RATIONAL BEINGS, it must also hold for all rational beings; and as it must be deduced simply from the property of freedom, it must be shown that freedom also is a property of all rational beings. It is not enough then to prove it from certain supposed experiences of human nature (which indeed is quite impossible, and it can only be shown a priori), but we must show that it belongs to the activity of all rational beings endowed with a will. Now I say every being that cannot act except UNDER THE IDEA OF FREEDOM is just for that reason in a practical point of view really free, that is to say, all laws which are inseparably connected with freedom have the same force for him as if his will had been shown to be free in itself by a proof theoretically conclusive. [Footnote: I adopt this method of assuming freedom merely AS AN IDEA which rational beings suppose in their actions, in order to avoid the necessity of proving it in its theoretical aspect also. The former is sufficient for my purpose; for even though the speculative proof should not be made out, yet a being that cannot act except with the idea of freedom is bound by the same laws that would oblige a being who was actually free. Thus we can escape here from the onus which presses on the theory. (Compare Butler's treatment of the question of liberty in his "Analogy," part I., ch. vi.)] Now I affirm that we must attribute to every rational being which has a will that it has also the idea of freedom and acts entirely under this idea. For in such a being we conceive a reason that is practical, that is, has causality in reference to its objects. Now we cannot possibly conceive a reason consciously receiving a bias from any other quarter with respect to its judgments, for then the subject would ascribe the determination of its judgment not to its own reason, but to an impulse. It must regard itself as the author of its principles independent on foreign influences. Consequently as practical reason or as the will of a rational being it must regard itself as free, that is to say, the will of such a being cannot be a will of its own except under the idea of freedom. This idea must therefore in a practical point of view be ascribed to every rational being.

Of the Interest attaching to the Ideas of Morality

We have finally reduced the definite conception of morality to the idea of freedom. This latter, however, we could not prove to be actually a property of ourselves or of human nature; only we saw that it must be presupposed if we would conceive a being as rational and conscious of its causality in respect of its actions, i. e., as endowed with a will; and so we find that on just the same grounds we must ascribe to every being endowed with reason and will this attribute of determining itself to action under the idea of its freedom.

Now it resulted also from the presupposition of this idea that we became aware of a law that the subjective principles of action, i.e., maxims, must always be so assumed that they can also hold as objective, that is, universal principles, and so serve as universal laws of our own dictation. But why then should I subject myself to this principle and that simply as a rational being, thus also subjecting to it all other beings endowed with reason? I will allow that no interest urges me to this, for that would not give a categorical imperative, but I must take an interest in it and discern how this comes to pass; for this "I ought" is properly an "I would," valid for every rational being, provided only that reason determined his actions without any hindrance. But for beings that are in addition affected as we are by springs of a different kind, namely, sensibility, and in whose case that is not always done which reason alone would do, for these that necessity is expressed only as an "ought," and the subjective necessity is different from the objective.

It seems then as if the moral law, that is, the principle of autonomy of the will, were properly speaking only presupposed in the idea of freedom, and as if we could not prove its reality and objective necessity independently. In that case we should still have gained something considerable by at least determining the true principle more exactly than had previously been done; but as regards its validity and the practical necessity of subjecting oneself to it, we should not have advanced a step. For if we were asked why the universal validity of our maxim as a law must be the condition restricting our actions, and on what we ground the worth which we assign to this manner of acting—a worth so great that there cannot be any higher interest; and if we were asked further how it happens that it is by this alone a man believes he feels his own personal worth, in comparison with which that of an agreeable or disagreeable condition is to be regarded as nothing, to these questions we could give no satisfactory answer.

We find indeed sometimes that we can take an interest [Footnote: "Interest" means a spring of the will, in so far as this spring is presented by Reason. See note, p. 391.] in a personal quality which does not involve any interest of external condition, provided this quality makes us capable of participating in the condition in case reason were to effect the allotment; that is to say, the mere being worthy of happiness can interest of itself even without the motive of participating in this happiness. This judgment, however, is in fact only the effect of the importance of the moral law which we before presupposed (when by the idea of freedom we detach ourselves from every empirical interest); but that we ought to detach ourselves from these interests, i. e., to consider ourselves as free in action and yet as subject to certain laws, so as to find a worth simply in our own person whiph can compensate us for the loss of everything that give worth to our condition; this we are not yet able to discern in this way, nor do we see how it is possible so to act—in other words, whence the moral law derives its obligation.

It must be freely admitted that there is a sort of circle here from which it seems impossible to escape. In the order of efficient causes we assume ourselves free, in order that in the order of ends we may conceive ourselves as subject to moral laws: and we afterwards conceive ourselves as subject to these laws, bjecause we have attributed to ourselves freedom of will: for freedom and self– legislation of will are both autonomy, and therefore are reciprocal conceptions, and for this very reason one must not be used to explain the other or give the reason of it, but at most only for logical purposes to reduce apparently different notions of the same object to one single concept (as we reduce different fractions of the same value to the lowest terms).

One resource retrains to us, namely, to inquire whether we do not occupy different points of view when by means of freedom we think ourselves as causes efficient a priori, and when we form our conception of ourselves from our actions as effects which we see before our eyes.

It is a remark which needs no subtle reflection to make, but which we may assume that even the commonest understanding can make, although it be after its fashion by an obscure discernment of judgment which it calls feeling, that all the "ideas" [Footnote: The common understanding being here spoken of, I use the word "idea" in its popular sense.] that comes to us involuntarily (as those of the senses) do not enable us to know objects otherwise than as they affect us; so that what they may be in themselves remains unknown to us, and consequently that as regards "ideas" of this kind even with the closest attention and clearness that the understanding can apply to them, we can by them only attain to the knowledge of appearances, never to that of things in themselves. As soon as this distinction has once been made (perhaps merely in consequence of the difference observed between the ideas given us from without, and in which we are passive, and those that we produce simply from ourselves, and in which we show our own activity), then it follows of itself that we must admit and assume behind the appearance something else that is not an appearance, namely, the things in themselves; although we must admit that as they can never be known to us except as they affect us, we can come no nearer to them, nor can we ever know what they are in themselves. This must furnish a distinction, however crude, between a world of sense and the world of understanding, of which the former may be different according to the difference of the sensuous impressions in—various observers, while the second which is its basis always remains the same. Even as to himself, a man cannot pretend to know what he is in himself from the knowledge he has by internal sensation. For as he does not as it were create himself, and does not come by the conception of himself a priori but empirically, it naturally follows that he can obtain his knowledge even of himself only by the inner sense, and consequently only through the appearances of his nature and the way in which his consciousness is affected. At the same time beyond these characteristics of his own subject, made up of mere appearances, he must necessarily suppose something else as their basis, namely, his ego, whatever its characteristics in itself may be. Thus in respect to mere perception and receptivity of sensations he must reckon himself as belonging to the world of sense, but in respect of whatever there may be of pure activity in him (that which reaches consciousness immediately and not through affecting the senses) he must reckon himself as belonging to the intellectual world, of which, however, he has no further knowledge. To such a conclusion the reflecting man must come with respect ito all the things which can be presented to him: it is probably to be met with even in persons of the commonest understanding, who, as is well known, are very much inclined to suppose behind the objects of the senses something else invisible and acting of itself. They spoil it, however, by presently sensualizing this invisible again; that is to say, wanting to make it an object of intuition, so that they do not become a whit the wiser.

Now man really finds in himself a faculty by which he distinguishes himself from everything else, even from himself as affected by objects, and that is Reason. This being pure spontaneity is even elevated above the understanding. For although the latter is a spontaneity and does not, like sense, merely contain intuitions that arise when we are affected by things (and are therefore passive), yet it cannot produce from its activity any other conceptions than those which merely serve to bring the intuitions of sense under rulesf and thereby to unite them in one consciousness, and without this use of the sensibility it could not think at all; whereas, on the contrary, Reason shows so pure a spontaneity in the case of what I call Ideas [Ideal Conceptions] that it thereby far transcends everything that the sensibility can give it, and exhibits its most important function in distinguishing the world of sense from that of understanding, and thereby prescribing the limits of the understanding itself.

For this reason a rational being must regard himself qua intelligence (not from the side of his lower faculties) as belonging not to the world of sense, but to that of understanding; hence he has two points of view from which he can regard himself, and recognise laws of the exercise of his faculties, and consequently of all his actions: first, so far as he belongs to the world of sense, he finds himself subject to laws of nature (heteronomy); secondly, as belonging to the intelligible world, under laws which being independent on nature have their foundation not in experience but in reason alone.

As a rational being, and consequently belonging to the intelligible world, man can never conceive the causality of his own will otherwise than on condition of the idea of freedom. for independence on the determining causes of the sensible world (an independence which Reason must always ascribe to itself) is freedom. Now the idea of freedom is inseparably connected with the conception of autonomy, and this again with the universal principle of morality which is ideally the foundation of all actions of rational beings, just as the law of nature is of all phenomena.

Now the suspicion is removed which we raised above, that there was a latent circle involved in our reasoning from freedom to autonomy, and from this to the moral law, viz.: that we laid down the idea of freedom because of the moral law only that we might afterwards in turn infer the latter from freedom and that consequently we could assign no reason at all for this law, but could only [present] [Footnote: The verb is wanting in the original.] it as a petitio principii which well disposed minds would gladly concede to us, but which we could never put forward as a provable proposition. For now we see that when we conceive ourselves as free we transfer ourselves into the—world of understanding as members of it, and recognise the autonomy of the will with its consequence, morality; whereas, if we conceive ourselves as under obligation we consider ourselves as belonging to the world of sense, and at the same time to the world of understanding.

How is a Categorical Imperative Possible?

Every rational being reckons himself qua intelligence as belonging to the world of understanding, and it is simply as an efficient cause belonging to that world that he calls his causality a will. On the other side he is also conscious of himself as a part of the world of sense in which his actions which are mere appearances [phenomena] of that causality are displayed; we cannot, however, discern how they are possible from this causality which we do not know; but instead of that, these actions as belonging to the sensible world must be viewed as determined by other phenomena, namely,—desires and inclinations. If therefore I were only a member of the world of understanding, then all my actions would perfectly conform to the principle of autonomy of the pure will; if I were only a part of the world of sense they would necessarily be assumed to conform wholly to the natural law of desires and inclinations, in other words, to the heteronomy of nature. (The former would rest on morality as the supreme principle, the latter on happiness.), Since, however, the world of understanding contains the foundation of the world of sense, and consequently of its laws alsof and accordingly gives the law to my will (which belongs wholly to the world of understanding) directly, and must be conceived as doing so, it follows that, although on the one side I must regard myself as a being belonging to the world of sense, yet on the other side I must recognise myself as subject as an intelligence to the law of the world of understanding, i. e., to reason, which contains this law in the idea of freedom, and therefore as subject to the autonomy of the will: consequently I must regard the laws of the world of understanding as imperatives for me, and the actions which conform to them as duties.

And thus what makes categorical imperatives possible is this, that the idea of freedom makes me a member of an intelligible world, in consequence of which if I were nothing else all my actions would always conform to the autonomy of the will; but as I at the same time intuite myself as a member of the world of sense, they ought so to conform, and this categorical "ought" implies a synthetic a priori proposition, inasmuch as besides my will as affected by sensible desires there is added further the idea of the same will but as belonging to the world of the understanding, pure and practical of itself, which contains the supreme condition according to Reason of the former will; precisely as to the intuitions of sense there are added concepts of the understanding which of themselves signify nothing but regular form in general, and in this way synthetic a priori propositions become possible, on which all knowledge of physical nature rests.

The practical use of common human reason confirms this reasoning. There is no one, not even the most consummate villain, provided only that he is otherwise accustomed to the use of reason, who, when we set before him examples of tionesty of purposea of steadfastness in following good maxims, of sympathy and general benevolence (even combined with great sacrifices of advantages and comfort), does not wish that he might also possess these qualities. Only on account of his inclinations and impulses he cannot attain this in himself, but at the same time he wishes to be free from such inclinations which are burdensome to himself. He proves by this that he transfers himself in thought with a will free from the impulses of—the sensibility into an order of things wholly different from that of his desires in the field of the sensibility; since he cannot expect to obtain by that wish any gratification of his desires, nor any position which would satisfy any of his actual or supposable inclinations (for this would destroy the pre−eminence of the very idea which wrests that wish from him): he can only expect a greater intrinsic worth of his own person. This better person, however, he imagines himself to be when he transfers himself to the point of view of a member of the world of the understanding, to which he is involuntarily forced by the idea of freedom, i. e., of independence on determining causes of the world of sense; and from this point of view he is conscious of a good will, which by his own confession constitutes the law for the bad will that he possesses as a member of the world of sense−a law whose authority he recognises while transgressing it. What he morally "ought" is then what he necessarily "would" as a member of the world of the understanding, and is conceived by him as an "ought" only inasmuch as he likewise considers himself as a member of the world of sense.

On the Extreme Limits of all Practical Philosophy

All men attribute to themselves freedom of will. Hence come all judgments upon actions as being such as ought to have been done, although they have not been done. However, this freedom is not a conception of experience, nor can it be so, since it still remains, even though experience shows the contrary of what on supposition of freedom are conceived as its necessary consequences. On the other side it is equally necessary that everything that takes place should be fixedly determined according to laws of nature. This necessity of nature is likewise tot an empirical conception, just for this reason, that it involves the motion of necessity and consequently of a priori cognition. But this conception of a system of nature is confirmed by experience, and it must even be inevitably presupposed if experience itself is to be possible, that is, a connected knowledge of the objects of sense resting on general laws. Therefore freedom is only an Idea [Ideal Conception] of Reason, and its objective reality in itself is doubtful, while nature is a concept of the understanding which proves, and must necessarily prove, its reality in examples of experience.

There arises from this a dialectic of Reason, since the freedom attributed to the will appears to contradict the necessity of nature, and placed between these two ways Reason for speculative purposes finds the road of physical necessity much more beaten and more appropriate than that of freedom; yet for practical purposes the narrow footpath of freedom is the only one on which it is possible to make use of reason in our conduct; hence it is just as impossible for the subtlest philosophy as for the commonest reason of men to argue away freedom. Philosophy must then assume that no real contradiction will be found between freedom and physical necessity of the same human actions, for it cannot give up the conception of nature any more than that of freedom.

Nevertheless, even though we should never be able to comprehend how freedom is possible, we must at least remove this apparent contradiction in a convincing manner. For if the thought of freedom contradicts either itself or nature, which is equally necessary, it must in competition with physical necessity be entirely given up.

It would, however, be impossible to escape this contradiction if the thinking subject, which seems to itself free, conceived itself in the same sense or in the very same relation when it calls itself free as when in respect of the same action it assumes itself to be subject to the law of nature. Hence it is an indispensable problem of speculative philosophy to show that its illusion respecting the contradiction rests on this, that we think of man in a different sense and relation when we call him free, and when we regard him as subject to the laws of nature as being part and parcel of nature. It must, therefore, show that not only can both these very well co– exist, but that both must be thought as necessarily united in the same subject, since otherwise no reason could be given why we should burden reason with an idea which, though it may possibly without contradiction be reconciled with another that is sufficiently established, yet entangles us in a perplexity which sorely embarrasses Reason in its theoretic employment. This duty, however, belongs only to speculative philosophy, in order that it may clear the way for practical philosophy. The philosopher then has no option whether he will remove the apparent contradiction or leave it untouched; for in fhe latter case the theory respecting this would be bonum vacans into the possession of which the fatalist would have a right to enter, and chase all morality out of its supposed domain as occupying it without title.

We cannot, however, as yet say that we are touching the bounds of practical philosophy. For the settlement of that controversy does not belong to it; it only demands from speculative reason $hat it should put an end to the discord in which it entangles itself in theoretical questions, so that practical reason may have rest and security from external attacks which might make the ground debatable on which it desires to build.

The claims to freedom of will made even by common reason are founded on the consciousness and the admitted supposition that reason is independent on merely subjectively determined causes which together Constitute what belongs to sensation only, and which consequently come under the general designation of sensibility. Man considering himself in this way as an intelligence, places himself thereby in a different order of things and in a relation to determining grounds of a wholly different kind when on the one hand he thinks of himself as an intelligence endowed with a will, and consequently with causality, and when on the other he perceives himself as a phenomenon in the world of sense (as he really is also), and affirms that his causality is subject to external determination according to laws of nature. [Footnote: The punctuation of the original gives the following sense: "Submits his causality, as regards its external determination, to laws of nature." have ventured to make what appears to be a necessary correction, by simply removing a comma.] Now he soon becomes aware that both can hold good, nay, must hold good at the same time. For there is not the smallest contradiction in saying that a thing in appearance (belonging to the world of sense) is subject to certain laws, on which the very same as a thing or being in itself is independent; and that he must conceive and think of himself in this twofold way, rests as to the first on the consciousness of himself as an object affected through the senses, and as to the second on the consciousness of himself as an intelligence, i. e., as independent on sensible impressions in the employment of his reason (in other words as belonging to the world of understanding).

Hence it comes to pass that man claims the possession of a will which takes no account of anything that comes under the head of desires and inclinations, and on the contrary conceives actions as possible to him, nay, even as necessary, which can only be done by disregarding all desires and sensible inclinations. The causality of such actions [Footnote: M. Barni translates as if he read desselben instead of derselben, "the causality of this will." So also Mr. Semple.] lies in him as an intelligence and in the laws of effects and actions [which depend] on the principles of an intelligible world, of which indeed he knows nothing more than that in it pure reason alone independent on sensibility gives the law; moreover since it is only in that world, as an intelligence, that he is his proper self (being as man only the appearance of himself) those laws apply to him directly and categorically, so that the incitements of inclinations and appetites (in other words the whole nature of the world of sense) cannot impair the laws of his volition as an intelligence. Nay, he does not even hold himself responsible for the former or ascribe them to his proper self, i. e., his will: he only ascribes to his will any indulgence which he might yield them if he allowed them to influence his maxims to the prejudice of the rational laws of the will.

When practical Reason thinks itself into a world of understanding it does not thereby transcend its own limits, as it would if it tried to enter it by intuition or sensation. The former is only a negative thought in respect of the world of sense, which does not give any laws to reason in determining the will, and is positive only in this single point that this freedom as a negative characteristic is at the same time conjoined with a (positive) faculty and even with a causality of reason, which we designate a will, namely, a faculty of so acting that the principle of the actions shall conform to the essential character of a rational motive, i. e., the condition that the maxim have universal validity as a law. But were it to borrow an object of will, that is, a motive, from the world of understanding, then it would overstep its bounds and pretend to be acquainted with something of which it knows nothing. The conception of a world of the understanding is then only a point of view which Reason finds itself compelled to take outside the appearances in order to conceive itself as practical, which would not be possible if the influences of the sensibility had a determining power on man, but which is necessary unless he is to be denied the consciousness of himself as an intelligence, and consequently as a rational cause, energizing by reason, that is, operating freely. This thought certainly involves the idea of an order and a system of laws different from that of the mechanism of nature which belongs to the sensible world, and it makes the conception of an intelligible world necessary (that is to say, the whole system of rational beings as things in themselves). But it does not in the least authorize us to think of it further than as to its formal condition only, that is, the universality of the maxims of the will as laws, and consequently the autonomy of the latter, which alone is consistent with its freedom; whereas, on the contrary, all laws that refer to a definite object give heteronomy, which only belongs to laws of nature, and can only apply to the sensible world.

But Reason would overstep all its bounds if it undertook to explain how pure reason can be practical, which would be exactly the same problem as to explain how freedom is possible.

For we can explain nothing but that which we can reduce to laws, the object of which can be given in some possible experience. But freedom is a mere Idea [Ideal Conception], the objective reality of which can in no wise be shown according to laws of nature, and consequently not in any possible experience; and for this reason it can never be comprehended or understood, because we cannot support it by any sort of example or analogy. It holds good only as a necessary hypothesis of reason in a being that believes itself conscious of a will, that is, of a faculty distinct from mere desire (namely, a faculty of determining itself to action as an intelligence), in other words, by laws of reason independently on natural instincts. Now where determination according to laws of nature ceases, there all explanation ceases also, and nothing remains but defence, i. e. the removal of the objections of those who pretend to have seen deeper into the nature of things, and thereupon boldly declare freedom impossible. We can only point out to them that the supposed contradiction that they have discovered in it arises only from this, that in order to be able to apply the law of nature to human actions, they must necessarily consider man as an appearance: then when we demand of them that they should also think of him qua intelligence as a thing in itself, they still persist in considering him in this respect also as an appearance. In this view it would no doubt be a contradiction to suppose the causality of the same subject (that is, his will) to be withdrawn from all the natural laws of the sensible world. But this contradiction disappears, if they would only bethink themselves and admit, as is reasonable, that behind the appearances there must also lie at their root (although hidden) the things in themselves, and that we cannot expect the laws of these to be the same as those that govern their appearances.

The subjective impossibility of explaining the freedom of the will is identical with the impossibility of discovering and explaining an interest [Footnote: Interest is that by which reason becomes practical, i. e., a cause determining the will. Hence we say of rational beings only that they take an interest in a thing; irrational beings only feel sensual appetites. Reason takes a direct interest in action then only when the universal validity of its maxims is alone sufficient to determine the will. Such an interest alone is pure. But if it can determine the will only by means of another object of desire or on the suggestion of a particular feeling of the subject, then Reason takes only an indirect interest in the action, and as Reason by itself without experience cannot discover either objects of the will or a Special feeling actuating it, this latter interest would only be empirical, and not a pure rational interest. The logical interest of Reason (namely, to extend its insight) is never direct, but presupposes purposes for which reason is employed.] which man can take in the moral law. Nevertheless he does actually take an interest in it, the basis of which in us we call the moral feeling, which some have falsely assigned as the standard of our moral judgment, whereas it must rather be viewed as the subjective effect that the law exercises on the will, the objective principle of which is furnished by Reason alone.

In order indeed that a rational being who is also affected through the senses should will what Reason alone directs such beings that they ought to will, it is no doubt requisite that reason should have a power to infuse a feeling of pleasure or satisfaction in the fulfilment of duty, that is to say, that it should have a causality by which it determines the sensibility according to its own principles. But it is quite impossible to discern, i. e., to make it intelligible a priori, how a mere thought, which itself contains nothing sensible, can itself produce a sensation of pleasure or pain; for this is a particular kind of causality of which as of every other causality we can determine nothing whatever a priori, we must only consult experience about it. But as this cannot supply us with any relation of cause and effect except between two objects of experience, whereas in this case, although indeed the effect produced lies within experience, yet the cause is supposed to be pure reason acting through mere ideas which offer no object to experience, it follows that for us men it is quite impossible to explain how and why the universality of the maxim as a law, that is, morality, interests. This only is certain, that it is not because it interests us that it has validity for us (for that would be heteronomy and dependence of practical reason on sensibility, namely, on a feeling as its principle, in which case it could never give moral laws), but that it interests us because it is valid for us as men, inasmuch as it had its source in our will as intelligences, in other words in our proper self, and what belongs to mere appearance is necessarily subordinated by reason to the nature of the thing in itself.

The question then: How a categorical imperative is possible can be answered to this extent that we can assign the only hypothesis on which it is possible, namely, the idea of freedom; and we can also discern the necessity of this hypothesis, and this is sufficient for the practical exercise of reason, that is, for the conviction of the validity of this imperative, and hence of the moral law; but how this hypothesis itself is possible can never be discerned by any human reason. On the hypothesis, however, that the will of an intelligence is free, its autonomy, as the essential formal condition of its determination, is a necessary consequence. Moreover, this freedom of will is not merely quite possible as a hypothesis (not involving any contradiction to the principle of physical necessity in the connexion of the phenomena of the sensible world) as speculative philosophy can show: but further, a rational being who is conscious of a causality [Footnote: Reading "einer" for "seiner."] through reason, that is to say, of a will (distinct from desires), must of necessity make it practically, that is, in idea, the condition of all his voluntary actions. But to explain how pure reason can be of itself practical without the aid of any spring of action that could be derived from any other source, i. e. how the mere principle of the universal validity of all its maxims as laws (which would certainly be the form of a pure practical reason) can of itself supply a spring, without any matter (object) of the will in which one could antecedently take any interest; and how it can produce an interest which would be called purely moral; or in other words, how pure reason can be practical—to explain this is beyond the power of human reason, and all the labour and pains of seeking an explanation of it are lost.

It is just the same as if I sought to find out how freedom itself is possible as the causality of a will. For then I quit the ground of philosophical explanation, and I have no other to go upon. I might indeed revel in the world of intelligences which still remains to me, but although I have an idea of it which is well founded, yet I have not the least knowledge of it, nor can I ever attain to such knowledge with all the efforts of my natural faculty of reason. It signifies only a something that remains over when I have eliminated everything belonging to the world of sense from the actuating principles of my will, serving merely to keep in bounds the principle of motives taken from the field of sensibility; fixing its limits and showing that it does not contain all in all within itself, but that there is more beyond it; but this something more I know no further. Of pure reason which frames this ideal, there remains after the abstraction of all matter, i. e., knowledge of objects, nothing but the form, namely, the practical law of the universality of the maxims, and in conformity with this the conception of reason in reference to a pure world of understanding as a possible efficient cause, that is a cause determining the will. There must here be a total absence of springs; unless this idea of an intelligible world is itself the spring, or that in which reason primarily takes an interest; but to make this intelligible is precisely the problem that we cannot solve.

Here now is the extreme limit of all moral inquiry, and it is of great importance to determine it even on this account, in order that reason may not on the one hand, to the prejudice of morals, seek about in the world of sense for the supreme motive and an interest comprehensible but empirical; and on the other hand, that it may not impotently flap its wings without being able to move in the (for it) empty space of transcendent concepts which we call the intelligible world, and so lose itself amidst chimeras. For the rest, the idea of a pure world of understanding as a system of all intelligences, and to which we ourselves as rational beings belong (although we are likewise on the other side members of the sensible world), this remains always a useful and legitimate idea for the purposes of rational belief, although all knowledge stops at its threshold, useful, namely, to produce in us a lively interest in the moral law by means of the noble ideal of a universal kingdom of ends in themselves (rational beings), to which we can belong as members then only when we carefully conduct ourselves according to the maxims of freedom as if they were laws of nature.

Concluding Remark

The speculative employment of reason with respect to nature leads to the absolute necessity of some supreme cause of the world: the practical employment of reason with a view to freedom leads also to absolute necessity, but only of the laws of the actions of a rational being as such. Now it is an essential principle of reason, however employed, to push its knowledge to a consciousness of its necessity (without which it would not be rational knowledge). It is however an equally essential restriction of the same reason that it can neither discern the necessity of what is or what happens, nor of what ought to happen, unless a condition is supposed on which it is or happens or ought to happen. In this way, however, by the constant inquiry for the condition, the satisfaction of reason is only further and further postponed. Hence it unceasingly seeks the unconditionally necessary, and finds itself forced to assume it, although without any means of making it comprehensible to itself, happy enough if only it can discover a conception which agrees with this assumption. It is therefore no fault in our deduction of the supreme principle of morality, but an objection that should be made to human reason in general, that it cannot enable us to conceive the absolute necessity of an unconditional practical law (such as the categorical imperative must be). It cannot be blamed for refusing to explain this necessity by a condition, that is to say, by means of some interest assumed as a basis, since the law would then cease to be a moral law, i. e. a supreme law of freedom. And thus while we do not comprehend the practical unconditional necessity of the moral imperative, we yet comprehend its incomprehensibility, and this is all that can be fairly demanded of a philosophy which strives to carry its principles up to the very limit of human reason.

BYRON AND GOETHE

BY GIUSEPPE MAZZINI

INTRODUCTORY NOTE

Giuseppe Mazzini, the great political idealist of the Italian struggle for independence, was born at Genoa, June 22, 1805. His faith in democracy and his enthusiasm for a free Italy he inherited from his parents; and while still a student in the University of Genoa he gathered round him a circle of youths who shared his dreams. At the age of twenty–two he joined the secret society of the Carbonari, and was sent on a mission to Tuscany, where he was entrapped and arrested. On his release, he set about the formation, among the Italian exiles in Marseilles, of the Society of Young Italy, which had for its aim the establishment of a free and united Italian republic. His activities led to a decree for his banishment from France, but he succeeded in outwitting the spies of the Government and going on with his work. The conspiracy for a national rising planned by Young Italy was discovered, many of the leaders were executed, and Mazsini himself condemned to death.

Almost at once, however, he resumed operations, working this time from Geneva; but another abortive expedition led to his expulsion from Switzerland. He found refuge, but at first hardly a livelihood, in London, where he continued his propaganda by means of his pen. He went back to Italy when the revolution of 1848 broke out, and fought fiercely but in vain against the French, when they besieged Rome and ended the Roman Republic in 1849.

Defeated and broken, he returned to England, where he remained till called to Italy by the insurrection of 1857. He worked with Garibaldi for some time; but the kingdom established under Victor Emmanuel by Cavour and Garibaldi was far from the ideal Italy for which Mazsini had striven. The last years of his life were spent mainly in London, but at the end he returned to Italy, where he died on March 10,1872. Hardly has any age seen a political martyr of a purer or nobler type.

Massini's essay on Byron and Goethe is more than literary criticism, for it exhibits that philosophical quality which gives so remarkable a unity to the writings of Massini, whether literary, social, or political.

BYRON AND GOETHE

I stood one day in a Swiss village at the foot of the Jura, and watched the coming of the storm. Heavy black clouds, their edges purpled by the setting sun, were rapidly covering the loveliest sky in Europe, save that of Italy. Thunder growled in the distance, and gusts of biting wind were driving huge drops of rain over the thirsty plain. Looking upwards, I beheld a large Alpine falcon, now rising, now sinking, as he floated bravely in the very midst of the storm and I could almost fancy that he strove to battle with it. At every fresh peal of thunder, the noble bird bounded higher aloft, as if in answering defiance. I followed him with my eyes for a long time, until he disappeared in the east. On the ground, about fifty paces beneath me, stood a stork; perfectly tranquil and impassive in the midst of the warring elements. Twice or thrice she turned her head towards the quarter from whence the wind came, with an indescribable air of half indifferent curiosity; but at length she drew up one of her long sinewy legs, hid her head beneath her wing, and calmly composed herself to sleep.

I thought of Byron and Goethe; of the stormy sky that overhung both; of the tempest–tossed existence, the lifelong struggle, of the one, and the calm of the other; and of the two mighty sources of poetry exhausted and closed by them.

Byron and Goethe—the two names that predominate, and, come what may, ever will predominate, over our every recollection of the fifty years that have passed away. They rule; the master–minds, I might almost say the tyrants, of a whole period of poetry; brilliant, yet sad; glorious in youth and daring, yet cankered by the worm in the bud, despair. They are the two representative poets of two great schools; and around them we are compelled to group all the lesser minds which contributed to render the era illustrious. The qualities which adorn and distinguish their works are to be found, although more thinly scattered, in other poets their contemporaries; still theirs are the names that involuntarily rise to our lips whenever we seek to characterize the tendencies of the age in which they lived. Their genius pursued different, even opposite routes; and yet very rarely do our thoughts turn to either without evoking the image of the other, as a sort of necessary complement to the first. The eyes of Europe were fixed upon the pair, as the spectators gaze on two mighty wrestlers in the same arena; and they, like noble and generous adversaries, admired, praised, and held out the hand to each other. Many poets have followed in their footsteps; none have been so popular. Others have found judges and critics who have appreciated them calmly and impartially; not so they: for them there have been only enthusiasts or enemies, wreaths or stones; and when they vanished into the vast night that envelops and transforms alike men and things—silence reigned around their tombs. Little by little, poetry had passed away from our world, and it seemed as if their last sigh had extinguished the sacred flame.

A reaction has now commenced; good, in so far as it reveals a desire for and promise of new life; evil, in so far as it betrays narrow views, a tendency to injustice towards departed genius, and the absence of any fixed rule or principle to guide our appreciation of the past. Human judgment, like Luther's drunken peasant, when saved from falling on one side, too often topples over on the other. The reaction against Goethe, in his own country especially, which was courageously and justly begun by Menzel during his lifetime, has been carried to exaggeration since his death. Certain social opinions, to which I myself belong, but which, although founded on a sacred principle, should not be allowed to interfere with the impartiality of our judgment, have weighed heavily in the balance; and many young, ardent, and enthusiastic minds of our day have reiterated with Bonne that Goethe is the worst of despots; the cancer of the German body.

The English reaction against Byron—I do not speak of that mixture of cant and stupidity which denies the poet his place in Westminster Abbey, but of literary reaction—has shown itself still more unreasoning. I have met with adorers of Shelley who denied the poetic genius of Byron; others who seriously compared his poems with those of Sir Walter Scott. One very much overrated critic writes that "Byron makes man after his own image, and woman after his own heart; the one is a capricious tyrant, the other a yielding slave." The first forgot the verses in which their favorite hailed

"The pilgrim of eternity, whose fame

Over his living head like Heaven is bent;"
[Footnote: Adonais.]

the second, that after the appearance of "The Giaour" and "Childe Harold," Sir Walter Scott renounced writing poetry. [Footnote: Lockhart.] The last forgot that while he was quietly writing criticisms, Byron was dying for new–born liberty in Greece. All judged, too many in each country still judge, the two poets, Byron and Goethe, after an absolute type of the beautiful, the true, or the false, which they had formed in their own minds; without regard to the state of social relations as they were or are; without any true conception of the destiny or mission of poetry, or of the law by which it, and every other artistic manifestation of human life, is governed.

There is no absolute type on earth: the absolute exists in the Divine Idea alone; the gradual comprehension of which man is destined to attain; although its complete realization is impossible on earth; earthly life being but one stage of the eternal evolution of life, manifested in thought and action; strengthened by all the achievements of the past, and advancing from age to age towards a less imperfect expression of that idea. Our earthly life is one phase of the eternal aspiration of the soul towards progress, which is our law ascending in increasing power and purity from the finite towards the infinite; from the real towards the Ideal; from that which is, towards that which is to come. In the immense storehouse of the past evolutions of life constituted by universal tradition, and in the prophetic instinct brooding in the depths of the human soul, does poetry seek inspiration. It changes with the times, for it is their expression; it is transformed with society, for— consciously or unconsciously—it sings the lay of Humanity; although, according to the individual bias or circumstances of the singer, it assumes the hues of the present, or of the future in course of elaboration, and foreseen by the inspiration of genius. It sings now a dirge and now a cradle song; it initiates or sums up.

Byron and Goethe summed up. Was it a defect in them? No; it was the law of the times, and yet society at the present day, twenty years after they have ceased to sing, assumes to condemn them for having been born too soon. Happy indeed are the poets whom God raises up at the commencement of an era, under the rays of the rising sun. A series of generations will lovingly repeat their verses, and attribute to them the new life which they did but foresee in the germ.

Byron and Goethe summed up. This is at once the philosophical explanation of their works, and the secret of their popularity. The spirit of an entire epoch of the European world became incarnate in them ere its decease, even as—in the political sphere—the spirit of Greece and Rome became incarnate before death in Caesar and Alexander. They were the poetic expression of that principle, of which England was the economic, France the political, and Germany the philosophic expression: the last formula, effort, and result of a society founded on the principle of individuality. That epoch, the mission of which had been, first through the labors of Greek philosophy, and afterwards through Christianity, to rehabilitate, emancipate, and develop individual man—appears to have concentrated in them, in Fichte, in Adam Smith, and in the French school des drolls de l'homme, its whole energy and power, in order fully to represent and express all that it had achieved for mankind. It was much; but it was not the whole; and therefore it was doomed to pass away. The epoch of individuality was deemed near the goal; when low immense horizons were revealed; vast unknown lands in whose untrodden forests the principle of individuality was an insufficient guide. By the long and painful labors of that epoch the human unknown quantity had been disengaged from the various quantities of different nature by which it had been surrounded; but only to be left weak, isolated, and recoiling in terror from the solitude in which it stood. The political schools of the epoch had proclaimed the sole basis of civil organization to be the right to liberty and equality (liberty for all), but they had encountered social anarchy by the way. The philosophy of the epoch had asserted the sovereignty of the human Ego, and had ended in the mere adoration of fact, in Hegelian immobility. The Economy of the epoch imagined it had organized free competition, while it had but organized the oppression of the weak by the strong; of labor by capital; of poverty by wealth. The Poetry of the epoch had represented individuality in its every phase; had translated in sentiment what science had theoretically demonstrated; and it had encountered the void. But as society at last discovered that the destinies of the race were not contained in a mere problem of liberty, but rather in the harmonization of liberty with association—so did poetry discover that the life it had hitherto drawn from individuality alone was doomed to perish for want of aliment; and that its future existence depended on enlarging and transforming its sphere. Both society and poetry uttered a cry of despair: the death–agony of a form of society produced the agitation we have seen constantly increasing in Europe since 1815: the death–agony of a form of poetry evoked Byron and Goethe. I believe this point of view to be the only one that can lead us to a useful and impartial appreciation of these two great spirits.

There are two forms of individuality; the expressions of its internal and external, or—as the Germans would say—of its subjective and objective life. Byron was the poet of the first, Goethe of the last. In Byron the Ego is revealed in all its pride of power, freedom, and desire, in the uncontrolled plenitude of all its faculties; inhaling existence at every pore, eager to seize "the life of life." The world around him neither rules nor tempers him. The Byronian Ego aspires to rule it; but solely for dominion's sake, to exercise upon it the Titanic force of his will. Accurately speaking, he cannot be said to derive from it either color, tone, or image; for it is he who colors; he who sings; he whose image is everywhere reflected and reproduced. His poetry emanates from his own soul; to be thence diffused upon things external; he holds his state in the centre of the universe, and from thence projects the light radiating from the depths of his own mind; as scorching and intense as the concentrated solar ray. Hence that terrible unity which only the superficial reader could mistake for monotony.

Byron appears at the close of one epoch, and before the dawn of the other; in the midst of a community based upon an aristocracy which has outlived the vigor of its prime; surrounded by a Europe containing nothing grand, unless it be Napoleon on one side and Pitt on the other, genius degraded to minister to egotism; intellect bound to the service of the past. No seer exists to foretell the future: belief is extinct; there is only its pretence: prayer is no more; there is only a movement of the lips at a fixed day or hour, for the sake of the family, or what is called the people; love is no more; desire has taken its place; the holy warfare of ideas is abandoned; the conflict is that of interests. The worship of great thoughts has passed away. That which is, raises the tattered banner of some corpse–like traditions; that which would be, hoists only the standard of physical wants, of material appetites: around him are ruins, beyond him the desert; the horizon is a blank. A long cry of suffering and indignation bursts from the heart of Byron: he is answered by anathemas. He departs; he hurries through Europe in search of an ideal to adore; he traverses it distracted, palpitating, like Mazeppa on the wild horse; borne onwards by a fierce desire; the wolves of envy and calumny follow in pursuit. He visits Greece; he visits Italy; if anywhere a lingering spark of the sacred fire, a ray of divine poetry, is preserved, it must be there. Nothing. A glorious past, a degraded present; none of life's

227

poetry; no movement, save that of the sufferer turning on his couch to relieve his pain. Byron, from the solitude of his exile, turns his eyes again towards England; he sings. What does he sing? What springs from the mysterious and unique conception which rules, one would say in spite of himself, over all that escapes him in his sleepless vigil? The funeral hymn, the death–song, the epitaph of the aristocratic idea; we discovered it, we Continentalists; not his own countrymen. He takes his types from amongst those privileged by strength, beauty, and individual power. They are grand, poetical, heroic, but solitary; they hold no communion with the world around them, unless it be to rule, over it; they defy alike the good and evil principle; they "will bend to neither." In life and in death "they stand upon their strength;" they resist every power, for their own is all their, own; it was purchased by

"Superior science—penance—daring–
And length of watching–strength of mind—and skill
In knowledge of our fathers."

Each of them is the personification, slightly modified, of a single type, a single idea—the individual; free, but nothing more than free; such as the epoch now closing has made him; Faust, but without the compact which submits him to the enemy; for the heroes of Byron make no such compact. Cain kneels not to Arimanes; and Manfred, about to die, exclaims:

"The mind, which is immortal, makes itself
Requital for its good and evil thoughts–
Is its own origin of ill, and end–
And its own place and time, its innate sense,
When stripped of this mortality, derives
No color from the fleeting things without,
But is absorbed in sufferance or in joy;
Born from the knowledge of its own desert."

They have no kindred: they live from their own life only they repulse humanity, and regard the crowd with disdain. Each of them says: "I have faith in myself"; never, "I have faith in ourselves." They all aspire to power or to happiness. The one and the other alike escape them; for they bear within them, untold, unacknowledged even to themselves, the presentiment of a life that mere liberty can never give them. Free they are; iron souls in iron frames, they climb the Alps of the physical world as well as the Alps of thought; still is their visage stamped with a gloomy and ineffaceable sadness; still is their soul–whether, as in Cain and Manfred, it plunge into the abyss of the infinite, "intoxicated with eternity," or scour the vast plain and boundless ocean with the Corsair and Giaour—haunted by a secret and sleepless dread. It seems as if they were doomed to drag the broken links of the chain they have burst asunder, riveted to their feet. Not only in the petty society against which they rebel does their soul feel fettered and restrained; but even in the world of the spirit. Neither is it to the enmity of society that they succumb; but under the assaults of this nameless anguish; under the corroding action of potent faculties "inferior still to their desires and their conceptions"; under the deception that comes from within. What can they do with the liberty so painfully won? On whom, on what, expend the exuberant vitality within them? They are alone; this is the secret of their wretchedness and impotence. They "thirst for good"—Cain has said it for them all—but cannot achieve it; for they have no mission, no belief, no comprehension even of the world around them. They have never realized the conception of Humanity in the multitudes that have preceded, surround, and will follow after them; never thought on their own place between the past and future; on the continuity of labor that unites all the generations into one whole; on the common end and aim, only to be realized by the common effort; on the spiritual post–sepulchral life even on earth of the individual, through the thoughts he transmits to his fellows; and, it may be— when he lives devoted and dies. in faith—through the guardian agency he is allowed to exercise over the loved ones left on earth.

Gifted with a liberty they know not how to use; with a power and energy they know not how to apply; with a life whose purpose and aim they comprehend not; they drag through their useless and convulsed existence. Byron destroys them one after the other, as if he were the executioner of a sentence decreed in heaven. They fall unwept, like a withered leaf into the stream of time.

> "Nor earth nor sky shall yield a single tear,
> Nor cloud shall gather more, nor leaf shall fall,
> Nor gale breathe forth one sigh for thee, for all."

They die, as they have lived, alone; and a popular malediction hovers round their solitary tombs.

This, for those who can read with the soul's eyes, is what Byron sings; or rather what humanity sings through him. The emptiness of the life and death of solitary individuality has never been so powerfully and efficaciously summed up as in the pages of Byron. The crowd do not comprehend him: they listen; fascinated for an instant; then repent, and avenge their momentary transport by calumniating and insulting the poet. His intuition of the death of a form of society they call wounded self–love; his sorrow for all is misinterpreted as cowardly egotism. They credit not the traces of profound suffering revealed by his lineaments; they credit not the presentiment of a new life which from time to time escapes his trembling lips; they believe not in the despairing embrace in which he grasps the material universe—stars, lakes, alps, and sea—and identifies himself with it, and through it with God, of whom—to him at least—it is a symbol. They do, however, take careful count of some unhappy moments, in which, wearied out by the emptiness of life, he has raised—with remorse I am sure—the cup of ignoble pleasures to his lips, believing he might find forgetfulness there. How many times have not his accusers drained this cup, without redeeming the sin by a single virtue; without—I will not say bearing—but without having even the capacity of appreciating the burden which weighed on Byron! And did he not himself dash into fragments the ignoble cup, so soon as he beheld something worthy the devotion of his life?

Goethe—individuality in its objective life—having, like Byron, a sense of the falsehood and evil of the world round him–followed exactly the opposite path. After having—he, too, in his youth— uttered a cry of anguish in his Werther; after having laid bare the problem of the epoch in all its terrific nudity, in Faust; he thought he had done enough, and refused to occupy himself with its solution. It is possible that the impulse of rebellion against social wrong and evil which burst forth for an instant in Werther may long have held his soul in secret travail; but that he despaired of the task of reforming it as beyond his powers. He himself remarked in his later years, when commenting on the exclamation made by a Frenchman on first seeing him: "That is the face of a man who has suffered much": that he should rather have said: "That is the face of a man who has struggled energetically;" but of this there remains no trace in his works. Whilst Byron writhed and suffered under the sense of the wrong and evil around him, he attained the calm—I cannot say of victory—but of indifference. In Byron the man always ruled, and even at times, overcame the artist: the man was completely lost in the artist in Goethe. In him there was no subjective life; no unity springing either from heart or head. Goethe is an intelligence that receives, elaborates, and reproduces the poetry affluent to him from all external objects: from all points of the circumference; to him as centre. He dwells aloft alone; a mighty watcher in the midst of creation. His curious scrutiny investigates, with equal penetration and equal interest, the depths of the ocean and the calyx of the floweret. Whether he studies the rose exhaling its Eastern perfume to the sky, or the ocean casting its countless wrecks upon the shore, the brow of the poet remains equally calm: to him they are but two forms of the beautiful; two subjects for art.

Goethe has been called a pantheist. I know not in what sense critics apply this vague and often ill–understood word to him. There is a materialistic pantheism and a spiritual pantheism; the pantheism of Spinoza and that of Giordano Bruno; of St. Paul; and of many others— —all different. But there is no poetic pantheism possible, save on the condition of embracing the whole world of phenomena in one unique conception: of feeling and comprehending the life of the universe in its divine unity. There is nothing of this in Goethe. There is pantheism in some parts of Wordsworth; in the third canto of "Childe Harold," and in much of Shelley; but there is none in the most admirable compositions of Goethe; wherein life, though admirably comprehended and reproduced in each of its successive manifestations, is never understood as a whole. Goethe is the poet of details, not of unity; of analysis, not of synthesis. None so able to investigate details; to set off and embellish minute and apparently trifling points; none throw so beautiful a light on separate parts; but the connecting link escapes him. His works resemble a magnificent encyclopaedia, unclassified. He has felt everything but he has never felt the whole. Happy in detecting a ray of the beautiful upon the humblest blade of grass gemmed with dew; happy in seizing the poetic elements of an incident the most prosaic in appearance—he was incapable of tracing all to a common source, and recomposing the grand ascending scale in which, to quote a beautiful expression of Herder's "every creature is a numerator of the grand denominator, Nature." How, indeed, should he comprehend these things, he who had no place in his works or in his poet's heart for humanity, by the light of which conception only can the true worth of sublunary things be determined? "Religion and politics," [Footnote: Goethe and his Contemporaries.] said he, "are a troubled element for art. I have always kept myself aloof from them as much as possible." Questions of life and death for the millions were agitated around him; Germany re–echoed to the war songs of Korner; Fichte, at the close of one of his lectures, seized his musket, and joined the volunteers who were hastening (alas! what have not the Kings made of that magnificent outburst of nationality!) to fight the battles of their fatherland. The ancient soil of Germany thrilled beneath their tread; he, an artist, looked on unmoved; his heart knew no responsive throb to the emotion that shook his country; his genius, utterly passive, drew apart from the current that swept away entire races. He witnessed the French Revolution in all its terrible grandeur, and saw the old world crumble beneath its strokes; and while all the best and purest spirits of Germany, who had mistaken the death–agony of the old world for the birth–throes of a new, were wringing their hands at the spectacle of dissolution, he saw in it only the subject of a farce. He beheld the glory and the fall of Napoleon; he witnessed the reaction of down–trodden nationalities—sublime prologue of the grand epopee of the peoples destined sooner or later to be unfolded— —and remained a cold spectator. He had neither learned to esteem men, to better them, nor even to suffer with them. If we except the beautiful type of Berlichingen, a poetic inspiration of his youth, man, as the creature of thought and action; the artificer of the future, so nobly sketched by Schiller in his dramas, has no representative in his works. He has carried something—of this nonchalance even into the manner in which his heroes conceive love. Goethe's altar is spread with the choicest flowers, the most exquisite perfumes, the first-fruits of nature; but the Priest is wanting. In his work of second creation—for it cannot be denied that such it was—he has gone through the vast circle of living and visible things; but stopped short before the seventh day. God withdrew from him before that time; and the creatures the poet has evoked wander within the circle, dumb and prayerless; awaiting until the man shall come to give them a name, and appoint them to a destination.

No, Goethe is not the poet of Pantheism; he is a polytheist in his method as an artist; the pagan poet of modern times. His world is, above all things, the world of forms: a multiplied Olympus. The Mosaic heaven and the Christian are veiled to him. Like the pagans, he parcels out Nature into fragments, and makes of each a divinity; like them, he worships the sensuous rather than the ideal; he looks, touches, and listens far more than he feels. And what care and labor are bestowed upon the plastic portion of his art! what importance is given—I will not say to the objects themselves—but to the external representation of objects! Has he not somewhere said that "the beautiful is the result of happy position?"[Footnote: In the Kunst und Alterthum, I think.]

Under this definition is concealed an entire system of poetic materialism, substituted for the worship of the ideal; involving a whole series of consequences, the logical result of which was to lead Goethe to indifference, that moral suicide of some of the noblest energies of genius. The absolute concentration of every faculty of observation on each of the objects to be represented, without relation to the ensemble; the entire avoidance of every influence likely to modify the view taken of that object, became in his hands one of the most effective means of art. The poet, in his eyes, was neither the rushing stream a hundred times broken on its course, that it may carry fertility to the surrounding country; nor the brilliant flame, consuming itself in the light it sheds around while ascending to heaven; but rather the placid lake, reflecting alike the tranquil landscape and the thunder-cloud; its own surface the while unruffled even by the lightest breeze. A serene and passive calm with the absolute clearness and distinctness of successive impressions, in each of which he was for the time wholly absorbed, are the peculiar characteristics of Goethe. "I allow the objects I desire to comprehend, to act tranquilly upon me," said he; "I then observe the impression I have received from them, and I endeavor to render it faithfully." Goethe has here portrayed his every feature to perfection. He was in life such as Madame Von Arnim proposed to represent him after death; a venerable old man, with a serene, almost radiant countenance; clothed in an antique robe, holding a lyre resting on his knees, and listening to the harmonies drawn from it either by the hand of a genius, or the breath of the winds. The last chords wafted his soul to the East; to the land of inactive contemplation. It was time: Europe had become too agitated for him.

Such were Byron and Goethe in their general characteristics; both great poets; very different, and yet, complete as is the contrast between them, and widely apart as are the paths they pursue, arriving at the same point. Life and death, character and poetry, everything is unlike in the two, and yet the one is the complement of the other. Both are the children of fatality—for it is especially at the close of epochs that the providential law which directs the generations assumes towards individuals the semblance of fatality—and compelled by it unconsciously to work out a great mission. Goethe contemplates the world in parts, and delivers the impressions they make upon him, one by one, as occasion presents them. Byron looks upon the world from a single comprehensive point of view; from the height of which he modifies in his own soul the impressions produced by external objects, as they pass before him. Goethe successively absorbs his own individuality in each of the objects he reproduces. Byron stamps every object he portrays with his own individuality. To Goethe, nature is the symphony; to Byron it is the prelude. She furnishes to the one the entire subject; to the other the occasion only of his verse. The one executes her harmonies; the other composes on the theme she has suggested. Goethe better exgresses lives; Byron life. The one is most vast; the other more deep. The first searches everywhere for the beautiful, and loves, above all things, harmony and repose; the other seeks the sublime, and adores action and force. Characters, such as Coriolanus or Luther, disturbed Goethe. I know not if, in his numerous pieces of criticism, he has ever spoken of Dante; but assuredly he must have shared the antipathy felt for him by Sir Walter Scott; and although he would undoubtedly have sufficiently respected his genius to admit him into his Pantheon, yet he would certainly have drawn a veil between his mental eye and the grand but sombre figure of the exiled seer, who dreamed of the future empire of the world for his country, and of the world's harmonious development under her guidance. Byron loved and drew inspiration from Dante. He also loved Washington and Franklin, and followed, with all the sympathies of a soul athirst for action, the meteor–like career of the greatest genius of action our age has produced, Napoleon; feeling indignant— perhaps mistakenly—that he did not die in the struggle.

When travelling in that second fatherland of all poetic souls— Italy—the poets still pursued divergent routes; the one experienced sensations; the other emotions; the one occupied himself especially with nature; the other with the greatness dead, the living wrongs, the human memories. [Footnote: The contrast between the two poets is nowhere more strikingly displayed than by the manner in which they were affected by the sight of Rome. In Goethe's Elegies and in his Travels in Italy we find the impressions of the artist only. He did not understand Rome. The eternal synthesis that, from the heights of the Capitol and St. Peter, is gradually unfolded in ever–widening circles, embracing first a nation and then Europe, as it will ultimately embrace humanity, remained unrevealed to him; he saw only the inner circle of paganism; the least prolific, as well as least indigenous. One might fancy that he caught a glimpse of it for an instant, when he wrote: "History is read here far otherwise than in any other spot in the universe; elsewhere we read it from without to within; here one seems to read it from within to without; "but if so, he soon lost sight of it again, and became absorbed in external nature." Whether we halt or advance, we discover a landscape ever renewing itself in a thousand fashions. We have palaces and ruins; gardens and solitudes: the horizon lengthens in the distance, or suddenly contracts; huts and stables, columns and triumphal arches, all lie pell–mell, and often so close that we might find room for all on the same sheet of paper."

At Rome Byron forgot passions, sorrows, his own individuality, all, in the presence of a great idea; witness this utterance of a soul born for devotedhess:—

"O Rome! my country! city of the soul!
  The orphans of the heart must turn to thee,
  Lone mother of dead empires! and control
  In their shut breasts their petty misery."

When at last he came to a recollection of himself and his position, it was with a hope for the world (stanza 98) and a pardon for his enemies. From the fourth canto of Childe Harold, the daughter of Byron might learn more of the true spirit of her father than from all the reports she may have heard, and all the many volumes that have been written upon him.]

And yet, notwithstanding all the contrasts, which I have only hinted at, but which might be far more elaborately displayed by extracts from their works; they arrived—Goethe, the poet of individuality in its objective life—at the egotism of indifference; Byron—the poet of individuality an its subjective life—at the egotism (I say it with regret, but it, too, is egotism) of despair: a double sentence upon the epoch which it was their mission to represent and to close!

Both of them—I am not speaking of their purely literary merits, incontestable and universally acknowledged—the one by the spirit of resistance that breathes through all his creations; the other by the spirit of sceptical irony that pervades his works, and by the independent sovereignty attributed to art over all social relations— —greatly aided the cause of intellectual emancipation, and awakened in men's minds the sentiment of liberty. Both of them—the one, directly, by the implacable war he waged against the vices and absurdities of the privileged classes, and indirectly, by investing his heroes with all the most brilliant qualities of the despot, and then dashing them to pieces as if in anger;—the other, by the poetic rehabilitation of forms the most modest, and objects the most insignificant, as well as by the importance attributed to details— combated aristocratic prejudices, and developed in men's minds the sentiment of equality. And having by their artistic excellence exhausted both forms of the poetry of individuality, they have completed the cycle cf its poets; thereby reducing all followers in the same sphere to the subaltern position of imitators, and creating the necessity of a new order of poetry; teaching us to recognize a want where before we felt only a desire. Together they have laid an era in the tomb; covering it with a pall that none may lift; and, as if to proclaim its death to the young generation, the poetry of Goethe has written its history, while that of Byron has graven its epitaph.

And now farewell to Goethe; farewell to Byron! farewell to the sorrows that crush but sanctify not—to the poetic flame that illumines but warms not—to the ironical philosophy that dissects without reconstructing—to all poetry which, in an age where there is so much to do, teaches us inactive contemplation; or which, in a world where there is so much need of devotedness, would instil despair. Farewell to all types of power without an aim; to all personifications of the solitary individuality which seeks an aim to find it not, and knows not how to apply the life stirring within it; to all egotistic joys and griefs:

"Bastards of the soul;
O'erweening slips of idleness: weeds—no more–
Self–springing here and there from the rank soil;
O'erflowings of the lust of that same mind
Whose proper issue and determinate end,
When wedded to the love of things divine,
Is peace, complacency, and happiness."

Farewell, a long farewell to the past! The dawn of the future is announced to such as can read its signs, and we owe ourselves wholly to it.

The duality of the Middle Ages, after having struggled for centuries under the banners of emperor and pope; after having left its trace and borne its fruit in every branch of intellectual development; has reascended to heaven—its mission accomplished—in the twin flames of poesy called Goethe and Byron. Two hitherto distinct formulae of life became incarnate in these two men. Byron is isolated man, representing only the internal aspect of life; Goethe isolated man, representing only the external.

Higher than these two incomplete existences; at the point of intersection between the two aspirations towards a heaven they were unable to reach, will be revealed the poetry of the future; of humanity; potent in new harmony, unity, and life.

But because, in our own day, we are beginning, though vaguely, to foresee this new social poetry, which will soothe the suffering soul by teaching it to rise towards God through humanity; because we now stand on the threshold of a new epoch, which, but for them, we should not have reached; shall we decry those who were unable to do more for us than cast their giant forms into the gulf that held us all doubting and dismayed on the other side? From the earliest times has genius been made the scapegoat of the generations. Society has never lacked men who have contented themselves with reproaching the Chattertons of their day with not being patterns of self−devotion, instead of physical or moral suicides; without ever asking themselves whether they had, during their lifetime, endeavored to place aught within the reach of such but doubt and destitution. I feel the necessity of protesting earnestly against the reaction set on foot by certain thinkers against the mighty−souled, which serves as a cloak for the cavilling spirit of mediocrity. There is something hard, repulsive, and ungrateful in the destructive instinct which so often forgets what has been done by the great men who preceded us, to demand of them merely an account of what more might have been done. Is the pillow of scepticism so soft to genius as to justify the conclusion that it is from egotism only that at times it rests its fevered brow thereon? Are we so free from the evil reflected in their verse as to have a right to condemn their memory? That evil was not introduced into the world by them. They saw it, felt it, respired it; it was around, about, on every side of them, and they were its greatest victims. How could they avoid reproducing it in their works? It is not by deposing Goethe or Byron that we shall destroy either sceptical or anarchical indifference amongst us. It is by becoming believers and organizers ourselves. If we are such, we need fear nothing. As is the public, so will be the poet. If we revere enthusiasm, the fatherland, and humanity; if our hearts are pure, and our souls steadfast and patient, the genius inspired to interpret our aspirations, and bear to heaven our ideas and our sufferings, will not be wanting. Let these statues stand. The noble monuments of feudal times create no desire to return to the days of selfdom.

But I shall be told, there are imitators. I know it too well; but what lasting influence can be exerted on social life by those who have no real life of their own? They will but flutter in the void, so long as void there be. On the day when the living shall arise to take the place of the dead, they will vanish like ghosts at cock− crow. Shall we never be sufficiently firm in our own faith to dare to show fitting reverence for the grand typical figures of an anterior age? It would be idle to speak of social art at all, or of the comprehension of humanity, if we could not raise altars to the new gods, without overthrowing the old. Those only should dare to utter the sacred name of progress, whose souls possess intelligence enough to comprehend the past, and whose hearts possess sufficient poetic religion to reverence its greatness. The temple of the true believer is not the chapel of a sect; it is a vast Pantheon, in which the glorious images of Goethe and Byron will hold their honored place, long after Goetheism and Byronism shall have ceased to be.

When, purified alike from imitation and distrust, men learn to pay righteous reverence to the mighty fallen, I know not whether Goethe will obtain more of their admiration as an artist, but I am certain that Byron will inspire them with more love, both as man and poet—a love increased even by the fact of the great injustice hitherto shown to him. While Goethe held himself aloof from us, and from the height of his Olympian calm seemed to smile with disdain at our desires, our struggles, and our sufferings—Byron wandered through the world, sad, gloomy, and unquiet; wounded, and bearing the arrow in the wound. Solitary and unfortunate in his infancy; unfortunate in his first love, and still more terribly so in his ill–advised marriage; attacked and calumniated both in his acts and intentions without inquiry or defence; harassed by pecuniary difficulties; forced to quit his country, home, and child; friendless—we have seen it too clearly since his death—pursued even on the Continent by a thousand absurd and infamous falsehoods, and by the cold malignity of a world that twisted even his sorrows into a crime; he yet, in the midst of inevitable reaction, preserved his love for his sister and his Ada; his compassion for misfortune; his fidelity to the affections of his childhood and youth, from Lord Clare to his old servant Murray, and his nurse Mary Gray. He was generous with his money to all whom he could help or serve, from his literary friends down to the wretched libeller Ashe. Though impelled by the temper of his genius, by the period in which he lived, and by that fatality of his mission to which I have alluded, towards a poetic individualism, the inevitable incompleteness of which I have endeavored to explain, he by no means set it up as a standard. That he presaged the future with the prevision of genius is proved by his definition of poetry in his journal—a definition hitherto misunderstood, but yet the best I know: "Poetry is the feeling of a former world and of a future." Poet as he was, he preferred activity for good, to all that his art could do. Surrounded by slaves and their oppressors; a traveller in countries where even remembrance seemed extinct; never did he desert the cause of the peoples; never was he false to human sympathies. A witness of the progress of the Restoration, and the triumph of the principles of the Holy Alliance, he never swerved from his courageous opposition; he preserved and publicly proclaimed his faith in the rights of the peoples and in the final

[Footnote:
Yet, Freedom! yet, thy banner torn, but flying,
  Streams, like the thunder–storm, against the wind:
Thy trumpet voice, though broken now and dying,
  The loudest still the tempest leaves behind.
  The tree hath lost its blossomes, and the rind,
Chopped by the axe, looks rough and little worth,
  But the sap lasts—and still the seed we find
Sown deep, even in the bosom of the North,
So shall a better spring less bitter fruit bring forth."]

triumph of liberty. The following passage from his journal is the very abstract of the law governing the efforts of the true party of progress at the present day: "Onwards! it is now the time to act; and what signifies self, if a single spark of that which would be worthy of the past [Footnote: Written in Italy.] can be bequeathed unquenchably to the future? It is not one man, nor a million, but the SPIRIT of liberty which must be spread. The waves which dash on the shore are, one by one, broken; but yet the OCEAN conquers nevertheless. It overwhelms the armada; it wears the rock; and if the Neptunians are to be believed, it has not only destroyed but made a world." At Naples, in the Romagna, wherever he saw a spark of noble life stirring, he was ready for any exertion; or danger, to blow it into a flame. He stigmatized baseness, hypocrisy, and injustice, whencesoever they sprang.

Thus lived Byron, ceaselessly tempest-tossed between the ills of the present and his yearnings after the future; often unequal; sometimes sceptical; but always suffering—often most so when he seemed to laugh;

[Footnote:
"And if I laugh at any mortal thing,
  'Tis that I may not weep."]
  and always loving, even
    when he seemed to curse.

Never did "the eternal spirit of the chainless mind" make a brighter apparition amongst us. He seems at times a transformation of that immortal Prometheus, of whom he has written so nobly; whose cry of agony, yet of futurity, sounded above the cradle of the European world; and whose grand and mysterious form, transfigured by time, reappears from age to age, between the entombment of one epoch and the accession of another; to wail forth the lament of genius, tortured by the presentment of things it will not see realized in its time. Byron, too, had the "firm will" and the "deep sense;" he, too, made of his "death a victory." When he heard the cry of nationality and liberty burst forth in the land he had loved and sung in early youth, he broke his harp and set forth. While the CHRISTIAN Powers were protocolizing or worse—while the CHRISTIAN nations were doling forth the alms of a few piles of ball in aid of the CROSS struggling with the Crescent; he, the poet, and pretended sceptic, hastened to throw his fortune, his genius, and his life at the feet of the first people that had arisen in the name of the nationality and liberty he loved.

I know no more beautiful symbol of the future destiny and mission of art than the death of Byron in Greece. The holy alliance of poetry with the cause of the peoples; the union—still so rare—of thought and action—which alone completes the human Word, and is destined to emancipate the world; the grand solidarity of all nations in the conquest of the rights ordained by God for all his children, and in the accomplishment of that mission for which alone such rights exist—all that is now the religion and the hope of the party of progress throughout Europe, is gloriously typified in this image, which we, barbarians that we are, have already forgotten.

The day will come when democracy will remember all that it owes to Byron. England, too, will, I hope, one day remember the mission—so entirely English, yet hitherto overlooked by her—which Byron fulfilled on the Continent; the European role given by him to English literature, and the appreciation and sympathy for England which he awakened amongst us.

Before he came, all that was known of English literature was the French translation of Shakespeare, and the anathema hurled by Voltaire against the "intoxicated barbarian." It is since Byron that we Continentalists have learned to study Shakespeare and other English writers. From him dates the sympathy of all the true-hearted amongst us for this land of liberty, whose true vocation he so worthily represented among the oppressed. He led the genius of Britain on a pilgrimage throughout all Europe.

England will one day feel how ill it is—not for Byron but for herself—that the foreigner who lands upon her shores should search in vain in that temple which should be her national Pantheon, for the poet beloved and admired by all the nations of Europe, and for whose death Greece and Italy wept as it had been that of the noblest of their own sons.

In these few pages—unfortunately very hasty—my aim has been, not so much to criticise either Goethe or Byron, for which both time and space are wanting, as to suggest, and if possible lead, English criticism upon a broader, more impartial, and more useful path than the one generally followed. Certain travellers of the eleventh century relate that they saw at Teneriffe a prodigiously lofty tree, which, from its immense extent of foliage, collected all the vapors of the atmosphere; to discharge them, when its branches were shaken, in a shower of pure and refreshing water. Genius is like this tree, and the mission of criticism should be to shake the branches. At the present day it more resembles a savage striving to hew down the noble tree to the roots.

CPSIA information can be obtained at www.ICGtesting.com
Printed in the USA
BVOW052334130613

323308BV00004B/208/A